Pulling Newspapers Apart

Pulling Newspapers Apart: Analysing Print Journalism explores contemporary UK national and local newspapers at a significant and pivotal moment in their development when some pundits are busily, if mistakenly, announcing their demise.

The book offers a detailed examination of features which previous studies have tended to neglect, such as **editorial formats** (News, op-ed pages, readers' letters, cartoons, obituaries, advice columns, features and opinion columns), **aspects of newspaper design** (page layout, photographs, supplements, online editions, headlines, the emergence of the compact and Berliner editions), **newspaper contents** (sport, sex and page 3, royalty, crime, moral panics and politics) as well as the content of newspapers which is not generated by in-house journalists (advertising, TV listings, horoscopes, agency copy and public relations materials).

Edited by Bob Franklin, Professor of Journalism Studies at the Cardiff School of Journalism, Media and Cultural Studies, individual chapters are written in an authoritative but accessible style by distinguished academics and journalists including Nicholas Brett, Nicholas Campion, Peter Cole, Ros Coward, Chas Critcher, Aeron Davis, John Ellis, Jim Hall, Jackie Harrison, Tim Holmes, Nicholas Jones, Eamonn McCabe, Brian McNair, Paul Manning, Peter Meech, Sarah Niblock, Angela Phillips, Eamonn Rafferty, John Richardson, Karen Ross, Colin Seymour-Ure, Nigel Starck, John Sugden, Mark Tattersall, Alan Tomlinson, Karin Wahl-Jorgensen and Claire Wardle.

This innovative and accessibly written collection provides journalism and media students with an invaluable study of newspapers in the digital age.

Bob Franklin is Professor of Journalism Studies at Cardiff University. He is the Editor of *Journalism Studies* and *Journalism Practice*. Previous publications include *Local Journalism and Local Media* (2006), *Television Policy: The MacTaggart Lectures* (2005), *Packaging Politics* (2004) and *Newszak and News Media* among many others.

Dr James Thomas (1971–2007)

On the day that this book was posted to the publisher, news about the death of Dr James Thomas began to reach his many students, colleagues and friends at Cardiff University and around the world. James was a brilliant young historian of journalism studies; a field in which there are too few. He was a scholar of considerable achievement but even greater potential, an inspirational teacher and a warm and generous colleague. He valued his roots in the Rhondda Valleys which helped to shape the radical voice which informed much of his published work. This book is dedicated to his memory. I shall miss very much not hearing his good humoured, gently prodding but forensic criticisms of our efforts to analyse recent developments in the UK press across the following pages.

Pulling Newspapers Apart

Analysing Print Journalism

Edited by Bob Franklin

 Routledge
Taylor & Francis Group

LONDON AND NEW YORK

First published 2008
by Routledge
2 Park Square, Milton Park, Abingdon, Oxon OX14 4RN

Simultaneously published in the USA and Canada
by Routledge
270 Madison Ave, New York, NY 10016

Transferred to Digital Printing 2009

Routledge is an imprint of the Taylor & Francis Group, an informa business

Editorial Selection and Material © 2008 Bob Franklin
Chapters © 2008 The Contributors

Typeset in Goudy Old Style and Gill Sans by Saxon Graphics Ltd, Derby
Printed and bound in Great Britain by TJI Digital, Padstow, Cornwall

British Library Cataloguing in Publication Data
A catalogue record for this book is available from the British Library

Library of Congress Cataloging in Publication Data
Pulling newspapers apart : analysing print journalism / edited by
Bob Franklin.
p. cm.
Includes index.
1. Journalism—Great Britain. 2. British newspapers—History—20th century.
3. Newspaper layout and typography—Great Britain. I. Franklin, Bob, 1949–
PN5119P85 2008
072'.0904—dc22
2007036727

ISBN 10: 0–415–42555–7 (hbk)
ISBN 10: 0–415–42556–5 (pbk)
ISBN 10: 0–203–63070–X (ebk)

ISBN 13: 978–0–415–42555–1 (hbk)
ISBN 13: 978–0–415–42556–8 (pbk)
ISBN 13: 978–0–203–63070–9 (ebk)

Contents

List of Contributors

Nicholas Brett is Deputy Managing Director of BBC Magazines. He worked his way to his current position through local and national newspapers and then through magazines, starting as a reporter and ending up as Editor of *Radio Times* before moving into management. The British Society of Magazine Editors recently honoured him with the Mark Boxer Award for Lifetime Achievement. This is the highest accolade in British magazine publishing, decided by his peers in the industry. He has recently been appointed Chair of the Periodicals Training Council, the industry's training and development body.

Nicholas Campion read History at Queens' College, Cambridge, and London University, and is Senior Lecturer in Archaeology and Anthropology at the University of Wales, Lampeter, where he is Head of the Centre for the Study of Cosmology in Culture, and Course Director of the MA in Cultural Astronomy and Astrology. He was formerly Senior Lecturer in History at Bath Spa University, where he taught courses on the history of astrology, the occult and magic, as well as contemporary New Age and pagan beliefs. He has an insider's knowledge of media astrology, having written the *Daily Mail*'s horoscope column from 1986 to 1992.

Peter Cole is Professor and Head of the Department of Journalism Studies at the University of Sheffield. Before joining the academy Cole worked as a national newspaper journalist. He was a Reporter, lobby correspondent, News Editor and Deputy Editor on the *Guardian*. He was founder Editor of the *Sunday Correspondent*, Editor of the 'News Review' section of the *Sunday Times*, Londoner's Diary Editor on the *Evening Standard* and reporter, diary writer and New York correspondent on the *London Evening News*. He is on the board of the National Council for the Training of Journalists and the Society of Editors. He chairs the Society's training committee, where he has been responsible for reports on training and newsroom diversity. He wrote a weekly column on media affairs for the *Independent on Sunday* from 2004 to 2007.

Rosalind Coward is Professor of Journalism at Roehampton University. Before this, she worked for many years as a freelance journalist. Her career in journalism includes feature writing for many national newspapers and magazines, including the *Evening Standard*, the *Daily Mail*, *New Statesman*, *Cosmopolitan* and *She* magazine. Her main journalism has been for the *Observer* and the *Guardian* and, along with feature writing, she has written regular columns for both papers. She has also been a columnist for the *Ecologist* magazine. She is the author of several books including *Language and Materialism* (with John Ellis), *Female Desire* and *Diana: The Authorised Portrait*. She has most recently written *Mandela: The Authorised Portrait*. Her research interests include royalty and the media, celebrity culture and journalism and the environment. She is on the board of Greenpeace UK and patron of Transport 2000.

Chas Critcher is Emeritus Professor of Communications at Sheffield Hallam University and Visiting Professor in Media and Communications at Swansea University. He originally co-authored *Policing The Crisis* (Macmillan, 1979), a study of social reaction to mugging. His most recent publications include for the Open University Press *Moral Panics and the Media* (2003) and an edited collection *Critical Readings in Moral Panics and the Media* (2006). His current research interests include a range of perceived threats to children, from the mass media to mass inoculation.

Aeron Davis is a Senior Lecturer and Director of the MA in Political Communications in the Department of Media and Communications, Goldsmiths College. His research interests include: public relations, politics and political communications; promotional culture, media sociology and news production; markets and economic sociology/cultural economy. He has conducted research on communications at Westminster, the London Stock Exchange, among the major political parties and across the trades unions movement. He has published on each of these topics in journals and edited collections and is the author of *Public Relations Democracy* (2002) and the *Mediation of Power* (2007). He is currently researching the influence of media on decision making in politics and is also working on a book on the rise of promotional culture for Polity Press.

John Ellis is Professor of Media Arts at Royal Holloway University of London. He is the author of *TV FAQ* (2007), *Seeing Things* (2000) and *Visible Fictions* (1982) and has written for journals including *Screen* and *Media Culture and Society*. Between 1982 and 1999 he ran the independent TV production company Large Door making series about cinema, food and other cultural issues. He still watches too much TV.

Bob Franklin is Professor of Journalism Studies in the Cardiff School of Journalism, Media and Cultural Studies. He is the Editor of *Journalism Studies and Journalism Practice*, as well as co-editor of Sage's new series entitled 'Journalism Studies: Key Texts'. Recent book-length publications include *Local Journalism and Local Media: Making the Local News* (2006), *Television Policy: The MacTaggart Lectures* (2005), *Key Concepts in Journalism Studies* (2005) and *Packaging Politics: Political Communication in Britain's Media Democracy* (2004).

Jim Hall teaches and writes about online journalism at University College, Falmouth, where he is the course leader of BA (Hons) Journalism. He is the author of *Online*

Journalism: A Critical Primer and speaks and writes extensively on the subject. He has been Visiting Professor in Online Journalism at Concordia Audentes University in Estonia and teaches the online newspaper elements at the annual Diena School in Riga, Latvia. He is currently working on the second edition of *Online Journalism.*

Jackie Harrison is Professor of Public Communication in the Department of Journalism Studies at the University of Sheffield. She is currently researching the 'Architecture of News'. This examines the news, its constituent features and modes of representations, its cultures of production and how it deals with issues of truth and truthfulness, spatial stories and multiple histories and user-generated content. She is the author of *News* (Routledge, 2006).

Tim Holmes is Course Co-ordinator of the Postgraduate Diploma in Magazine Journalism at Cardiff University. He started his career in journalism in 1978 as a staff writer on a motorcycle magazine and ended up as a partner in a magazine publishing house. He began teaching at Cardiff in 1995. Since then he has championed magazine journalism as a distinctive form, has initiated magazine modules at undergraduate and masters level and is happy to be supervising an increasing number of dissertations in the field. Recent publications include guest editing a special issue of *Journalism Studies* (2007) on Magazine Journalism.

Nicholas Jones was a BBC political and industrial correspondent for 30 years. He began his career as a journalist on *The News*, Portsmouth in 1960 and continues to write and lecture on the relationship between politicians and the news media. His books include *Strikes and the Media* (1986), *Soundbites and Spin Doctors* (1995), *Sultans of Spin* (1999), *Control Freaks* (2002) and *Trading Information* (2006).

Eamonn McCabe was Picture Editor of the *Guardian* from 1988 until 2001. He won many awards for his photography and was named Picture Editor of the Year a record six times. He has published several books on photography and appears regularly on radio and television talking about photography.

Brian McNair is Professor of Journalism and Communication at the University of Strathclyde. He is the author of several books on journalism, including *An Introduction to Political Communication* (4th edition, Routledge, 2007), *News and Journalism In the UK* (4th edition, Routledge, 2003) and *The Sociology of Journalism* (Arnold, 1998). He is a regular contributor to the UK press, and has written columns and essays on a variety of topics for *Scotland On Sunday*, the *Sunday Herald*, the *Evening Times*, the *Guardian* and other newspapers.

Paul Manning is Head of the School of Media and Film at the University of Winchester. His research interests and publications have focused upon the politics of news sources and news organisations, the symbolic representation of drug and substance misuse, and the relationship between crime and media.

Peter Meech is a member of the Stirling Media Research Institute and Senior Lecturer in the Department of Film and Media Studies, University of Stirling.

Sarah Niblock is Reader in Journalism at Brunel University. She has worked in journalism for nearly 20 years as a regional and national news reporter, and wrote features for *Cosmopolitan* and *Company* for a number of years. Sarah is the author of several books including *Inside Journalism* (1996) and *News Production: Theory and Practice* (2006, co-authored with David Machin). She has published papers in leading journals including *Journalism Practice*, *Journalism* and *British Journalism Review*. She has written chapters in *Story: The Heart of the Matter* (2007), *Print Journalism: A Critical Introduction* (2005), *Reading Sex and the City* (2004) and *Feminist Visual Culture* (2000). A further book, on journalism ethics as portrayed in cinema since the dawn of film, is in production.

Angela Phillips is Senior Lecturer at Goldsmiths College, University of London. She has been a journalist for over 30 years, starting in the alternative press of the 1970s and moving on to work for national newspapers, magazines, television and radio. She worked for several years as a photojournalist before moving into print, and she now teaches feature writing and journalism studies. She is interested in critical journalism research from a practitioner point of view and has recently written a book: *Good Writing for Journalists* (Sage, 2006), which attempts to bring together critical theory with critical practice.

Eamonn Rafferty is Sub-editor on the *Financial Times*.

John E. Richardson is Lecturer in the Department of Social Sciences, Loughborough University, and co-editor for the online peer-reviewed journal *Studies in Language and Capitalism* (www.languageandcapitalism.info/). His research interests include racism in journalism, readers' letters, (critical) discourse analysis and argumentation, with recent publications including the book *Analysing Newspapers* (Palgrave, 2007) and the co-edited book *Muslims and News Media* (I.B. Tauris, 2006).

Karen Ross is Professor of Media and Public Communication at the University of Liverpool. She teaches and researches on political communication, and gender and media. Recent books include: *Rethinking Media Education: Critical Pedagogy and Identity Politics* (2007, co-edited with Anita Nowak and Sue Abel); *Women and Media: A Critical Introduction* (with Carolyn Byerly); *Gender and Newsroom Practice* (2004, co-edited with Marjan de Bruin).

Colin Seymour-Ure is Emeritus Professor of Government at the University of Kent. His work on political communication and mass media includes studies of cartoons in General Elections; Prime Ministers and cartoons; and a biography of the great twentieth-century cartoonist David Low. He was for many years chairman of Kent University's unique cartoon archive, now the British Cartoon Archive.

Nigel Starck (of the University of South Australia) has been described by the *Guardian* as 'the acknowledged world expert on the obituarist's craft'. His collection offers an unrivalled private archive of obituary publishing over 400 years; he contributes obituaries to the British and Australian press; and he teaches university students how to write them. His doctoral thesis, *Writes of Passage* (Flinders University), is a comparative study of newspaper obituary practice in Australia,

Britain and the United States. Dr Starck's book on the obituary, *Life After Death* (2006), supplies a definitive history of journalism's dying art. For recreation, he walks the surf beaches near his home in Adelaide – thinking about obituaries.

John Sugden is Professor of Sociology of Sport at the University of Brighton's Chelsea School. He has researched and written extensively about sport and society and is best known for his works on boxing, sport in divided societies, and the political economy of global sports. John is co-founder and Director of Football for Peace, a sport-based coexistence project in the Middle East, and is Editor of the *International Review for the Sociology of Sport*.

Mark Tattersall is a sub-editor on the Press Association's page-ready sports unit. He previously taught journalism on Cardiff University's postgraduate diploma in newspaper journalism, specialising in production and sports journalism. He has also worked as a sports reporter, sports editor, production editor and deputy editor on weekly, evening and regional morning newspapers in England and Wales.

Alan Tomlinson is Professor of Leisure Studies at the University of Brighton, where he is area leader for Sport and Leisure Cultures and Head of Chelsea School Research Division. He has published extensively on sport, leisure and popular culture: his articles have appeared in *Media, Culture & Society*, *Journalism Practice*, *American Behavioural Scientist*, and *Tourism Cultures and Communication*, as well as leading journals and edited research monographs in sport and leisure studies. From 2000 to 2003 he edited the *International Review for the Sociology of Sport*. His book *Sport and Leisure Cultures* was published by the University of Minnesota Press in 2005, and his edited text *The Sport Studies Reader* was published by Routledge in 2007. Tomlinson's writings have also appeared in *Der Tagesspiegel*, *When Saturday Comes*, *Financial Times* and *New Statesman*.

Karin Wahl-Jorgensen is Senior Lecturer in the Cardiff School of Journalism, Media and Cultural Studies. She is the author of two books: *Journalists and the Public* (Hampton Press, 2007) and *Citizens or Consumers?* (Open University Press, 2005; co-authored with Justin Lewis and Sanna Inthorn). She is editor of *Mediated Citizenship* (Routledge, 2007), and the *Handbook of Journalism Studies* (with Thomas Hanitzsch), due out in 2008. Her work on journalism, democracy and citizenship has also appeared in more than 20 different journals.

Claire Wardle is Lecturer at the Cardiff School of Journalism, Media and Cultural Studies. Her research interests focus on press coverage of law and order in the UK and the US, and the representation of social and political issues in primetime television. Her research has been published in *Journalism Studies*, *Journalism* and the *European Journal of Communication*.

Newspapers: trends and developments

Bob Franklin

Times of 'change, challenge and churn'

On 11 June 2007, the *Guardian* published its 50,000th edition. To commemorate the occasion, the newspaper reproduced 50 'memorable' front pages from its archives including the very first issue of the paper published on 5 May 1821. There are striking differences in almost every aspect of the contents and design of that first issue and the newspaper published some 186 years later into which it had been inserted as a supplement.

The changing face of newspapers: telling stories in different ways

Perhaps the most obvious difference is the absence of any news on the front page. Instead, 42 small adverts and public announcements filled the six vertical columns spread across the page. Adverts offered a range of goods and services including parasols and umbrellas manufactured by John Dryden, 'Mr Eagland's improved trusses for ruptures', alongside places for cabin and steerage passengers aboard the *George Washington* about to set sail for Baltimore. The most prominent advertisement had been placed by a reader who had rescued a 'black Newfoundland bitch', which was to be sold to 'defray expenses' if the owner didn't claim her in two weeks. The *Guardian* acknowledges that 'our news values have changed a bit since then' and that 'it is unlikely we would lead the paper now with an ad for a lost dog'.

Other aspects of the layout and design of that launch issue seem anachronistic. There are no headlines, no lead story, no variation in the size of font to signal the news salience of stories and only a modest masthead compared to the modern and expansive 'flannel panel' which incorporates and previews stories published inside the paper and accounts for almost half the space above the fold. There are no photographs, much less colour photographs, while the only graphics to enliven the unrelentingly dull layout of this early front page are the curious and rather crude drawings of Mr Dryden's parasols, Mr Eagland's trusses and a poorly reproduced version of the Royal Crest above an advert for John Watts – 'Draper, Silk maker, Lace-man and Glover' – who claimed the 'Patronage of the Royal Family' (*Guardian* 5 May 1821). The comparison with the design features of the *Guardian* front page on 12 September 2001 is stark. A full-page colour photograph of a hijacked plane crashing into the Twin Towers in New York created an unforgettable image, accompanied by a chilling headline in large and dramatic font, which announced 'A Declaration of War'; no text accompanied the photograph. Picture Editor Eamonn McCabe claimed editor Alan Rusbridger wanted the photojournalists 'to tell the story of 9/ll' (see McCabe, chapter 16, this volume). In 2005, radical design changes at the *Guardian* shifted the shape and size of the paper from broadsheet to Berliner, revised almost every aspect of its page layout and created greater space and opportunities for journalists and photojournalists to tell stories (Cole, chapter 15).

The modern newspaper is also bigger, with substantial increases in pagination reflecting, in part, the emergence of Saturday supplements pioneered by the *Financial Times* in the mid-1980s (Brett and Holmes, chapter 17). The facsimile of the 1821 launch issue, for example, was included in the *Guardian*'s Saturday edition, which, alongside the main newspaper, included six supplements focused on work, family, sport, money, travel and the book review, along with the *Weekend* colour supplement and the entertainments listing/TV guide (Ellis, chapter 22). But the contemporary newspaper is incalculably larger than its predecessor of even a decade ago because all UK newspapers have developed an online presence which offers readers an almost endless supply of news and comment, archives and databases. Newspapers, moreover, have long since extended their interactivity beyond readers' letters with invitations to post comment online, which constructs a continuously expansive discussion and debate that makes the task of reading a modern newspaper somewhat akin to painting the Forth Bridge (Hall, chapter 19; Wahl-Jorgensen, chapter 4).

Finally, the readership of newspapers has changed since the early nineteenth century. John Edward Taylor published 1,000 copies of the launch issue of the *Guardian* targeted at 'the class of readers to whom ... advertisements are generally addressed' (Rusbridger 2007, p.1). Some things it seems never change; advertising remains a major source of revenue for all newspapers (Meech, chapter 21). But *Guardian* readers are more widely spread than ever. The *Manchester Guardian* began life as a provincial paper addressing a local, at best regional, audience, but today the *Guardian Unlimited* is read by 16 million readers ('unique users') every month with almost one-third of them in America and has become the most widely read UK newspaper website, attracting nearly 147 million page impressions in March 2007 (ABC April 2007 in Kiss and Brook 2007, p.9; Rusbridger 2007, p.2). But hard copy sales, like those for other UK newspapers, are in long-term decline. In June 2007 the *Guardian* sold 363,562 copies (ABC July 2007), 20 years earlier the circulation figure averaged 487,000 copies daily: a loss of 25.4 per cent circulation, with associated revenue losses from cover price and advertising sales (Franklin 1997, p.89).

An endangered species?

This sustained decline in circulation, sales and readers for print editions of newspapers, coupled with the more recent challenge to advertising revenues posed by the internet, has prompted pundits to speculate about the fortunes of the UK press. Some predictions are bleak, if not dire. A special issue of the *Economist* devoted to the 'Future of Newspapers' described them as an 'endangered species'. Sounding the death knell for contemporary newspapers, the *Economist* claimed, 'the business of selling words to readers and selling readers to advertisers, which has sustained their role in society, is falling apart' (*Economist* 24 August 2006a). In similar vein, American academic Philip Meyer in *The Vanishing Newspaper* extrapolated current trends in daily newspaper reading habits since 1970 to conclude, with enviable if dubious precision, that the last reader will disappear 'late in the first quarter of 2043' (Meyer 2004, p.16). Other observers offer even gloomier prognoses. Bill Gates recently claimed that, 'the number of people who buy or subscribe to the newspaper and read it, has started an inexorable decline'. Gates identifies 2012 as newsprint's final deadline (*Seattle Times* 9 May 2007); *Financial Times* journalist John Lloyd concurs – at least so far as paid-for dailies are concerned (Barkham 2006, p.14).

But Meyer and others spoil a good argument by overstating it. Rusbridger's alliterative characterisation of current times as 'a moment of change, challenge and churn' seems more appropriate (Rusbridger 2005). Precocious valedictories for newspapers articulate a peculiarly western preoccupation which ignores the expansion of newspaper titles and circulations in many parts of the globe. More locally, they fail to acknowledge the highly variegated character of the UK newspaper market and the disparate fortunes of distinctive market sectors.

While the decline in newspapers' circulations is undoubtedly significant, the suggestion here is that newspapers are not about to 'vanish' or disappear. Newspapers *are* changing and adapting their contents, style and design in response to the challenges they confront in the increasingly competitive and fragmented market for readers and advertisers posed by other newspapers, but additionally by the new media platforms of the internet and mobile telephony, which deliver news, blogs, text alerts, news updates, podcasts and user-generated content (UGC) to 'readers' at a greater pace, in more accessible formats and when readers demand them. This is not to offer a complacent 'business as usual' argument, but to suggest that adapting to increased competition, often driven by new technology, is historically what has triggered change in the newspaper industry; accommodating to a shifting business, political and technological environment is what newspapers have always done. On occasion, the pace of adaptation has been too slow, if not ill judged. This was precisely the inspiration and key message of Rupert Murdoch's public *mea culpa* to the American Society of Editors in April 2005, in which the previously 'internet sceptic' proprietor announced (Pilling 2006, p.110):

I come before you today with the best of my intentions. My subject is one near and dear to all of us: the role of newspapers in this digital age. Scarcely a day goes by without some claim that the new technologies are fast writing newsprint's obituary. Yet as an industry, most of us have been remarkably, unaccountably complacent. Certainly, I didn't do as much as I should have after all the excitement of the late 1990s. I suspect many of you did the same, quietly hoping that this thing called the digital revolution would just limp away. Well it hasn't… it won't… and it's a reality we had better get used to – and fast.

(Rupert Murdoch cited in Nguyen 2008)

True to his word, Murdoch immediately established 'online expansion' as News Corporation's top priority, ring-fenced A\$1.3 billion for acquiring internet businesses, and promptly purchased Intermix (A\$770 million), which incorporated the social networking site Myspace.com, and the sports content site Scout.com for A\$60 million (Nguyen 2008). But significantly, during July 2007, Murdoch's very public preoccupations seemed curiously old-fashioned: he fervently engaged in protracted, but eventually successful, negotiations to win control of one of the world's most respected print newspaper brands, albeit with an extensive online presence – the *Wall Street Journal* (*Guardian* 2 August 2007, p.27).

What connects Murdoch's seemingly disparate ambitions here is the important understanding that what constitutes a newspaper has long since expanded beyond the confines of the printed paper edition which, in the context of the ready availability of online news and news updates delivered via the internet and mobile telephones, has become an increasingly modest element in this multimedia mix. Consequently, the question, 'What is a newspaper?' is attracting diverse and shifting responses. For distinguished journalist Peter Preston, newspapers remain essentially newsgathering and reporting organisations which identify an audience and then use journalistic skills and experience to 'hit that niche market'. On this account, Google News does not constitute a newspaper since it has eschewed any pretence of newsgathering, preferring simply to sub existing news trawled from global newspapers (Preston 2006).

But increasingly the news may be gathered, edited and reported by amateurs as much as professionals, and consumers as much as producers (Deuze, Bruns and Neuberger 2007, pp.322–38), or in Rosen's delightful phrase 'the people formally known as the audience' (Rosen 2006). The contribution of UGC and 'citizen journalism' to mainstream news organisations was exemplified on 7 July 2005, when the BBC received approximately 22,000 emails and text messages, 300 photos (50 within an hour) and several videos of the London Bombings; while the Corporation began receiving 'user-generated content' (UGC) within 13 minutes of the Buncefield oil refinery explosion, 5,000 images by lunchtime and 10,000 by the end of the day (Bivens 2008; Allan 2006, pp.143–52). Consequently, a second question, 'What is a journalist?', is also generating more complex, but contested, responses. As Singer observes, 'while all journalists still publish information not all publishers of information are journalists' (Singer 2006, p.3).

There is a third significant question. It raises issues concerning what might be termed the public service or civic and democratic functions of newspapers, which *Guardian* Editor Alan Rusbridger has addressed. In this 'crowded media hyper-market', he asks, 'What is a newspaper for?' and 'What task should it set itself?' 'For generations there has been a quiet understanding', he claims, about the three key tasks he attributes to them. Newspapers are there,

> [1] primarily to tell society about itself, to act as a pollinator of information. To be a conduit between subjects and rulers, citizens and legislators, legislators and citizens, citizens and citizens ... Of course, [2] newspapers sought to entertain as well. [3] And they were also there to challenge power – to hold it to account. And in this country, as elsewhere, there has been for 200 years or more a tradition of robust, unfettered comment ... But – in the story we told to others in our attempts to win our freedom of speech, not to mention additional privileges and protection – there was at its heart the civic value of news telling.
>
> (Rusbridger 2005)

These shifting, as well as constant, elements in the understanding of what constitutes a newspaper signal continuity rather than any rupture with the past, and they will inform the discussion and analysis here. This introduction offers an overview of recent trends and developments in UK newspapers and assesses the evidence that informs the occasionally gloomy speculations about newspapers in the UK. The argument which unravels suggests that a business strategy designed to maintain profitability by minimising costs by reducing numbers of journalists, necessarily creates a growing reliance on public relations materials and agency copy to fill the expansive news hole. Such a strategy also reduces journalists to *processors* rather than *originators* of news – as in the case of Google News mentioned above – and thereby reduces newspapers' claims to that title by diminishing their newsgathering activities. The introduction is in three sections. The first looks at newspapers as businesses, examining recent changes in the number of published titles, circulations, advertising revenues and profitability. The second explores newspapers' shifting editorial priorities alongside changes in journalists' working practices reflecting a growing prominence for public relations and news agency copy in newspapers' editorial pages. A final section examines newspapers' business strategies for winning revenues from their online editions, as well as management strategies to reskill journalists for working in the contemporary, multimedia and online journalism age.

Newspapers as businesses: readers, revenues and profitability

The vanishing newspaper?

Globally the number of newspapers is on the up! Daily paid titles expanded by an average of 17 per cent from 9,533 titles in 2002 to 11,142 in 2006, exceeding the

11,000 barrier for the first time. The picture differs across regions, with variable growth rates for daily papers in Asia (33.1%), Africa (16.7%), South America (12.6%), Europe (5.6%) and Australia (1.4%), as well as the decline in newspapers recorded in North America (0.8%). In some settings the growth of titles and readerships has been striking. In India, for example, the 330 daily titles with 2.5 million readers in the early 1950s mushroomed to an estimated 5,638 titles and 59.1 million readers in 2001 (Bhaskar 2005, p.19). Wasserman's study of the new South African tabloid, the *Daily Sun*, similarly, underscores the high demand for additional titles. The black majority, which constitutes the paper's readership, is too poor to afford the cover price but buys the paper in a lively second- and even third-hand market for avidly read but discarded copies. Other new South African papers such as the *Kaapse Sun*, the *Cape Sun* and the *Daily Voice* claim similarly expansive copy sales and advertising revenues (Wasserman 2007).

The global circulation of paid daily newspapers is also expanding by 2 per cent (to 510 million copies) in 2005–6 and by 8.7 per cent across the previous five years. During the same period free daily newspaper circulations tripled from 13,795 million to 40,802 million in 2006. In all regions the relatively new free daily newspapers are piling on circulation with growth figures for 2005–6 increasing by as much as 77 per cent in South America, 65 per cent in Europe but only 18.4 per cent in Asia. Market share is uneven, however, with Europe claiming 66 per cent of the free daily market by circulation, while Australasia manages only 1 per cent (WAN 2007).

By contrast, the number of published titles in the UK market seems to have been relatively stable. There are currently 11 national daily papers if the *Daily Record*, the sister paper of the *Daily Mirror*, which only publishes in Scotland, is included. The Audit Bureau of Circulation (ABC) places them in three broad categories reflecting their circulation, the extent and style of their editorial contents and, before the arrival of the compact editions, the size of the newspapers. The *Daily Mirror*, the *Daily Record*, the *Daily Star* and the *Sun* constitute the 'national morning popular' papers or 'red tops'; the *Daily Express* and the *Daily Mail* are the 'national morning mid-market papers'; while the 'national morning quality' titles include the *Daily Telegraph*, the *Financial Times*, the *Guardian*, the *Independent* and *The Times*. The Sunday newspaper market is similarly differentiated into 'national Sunday popular' (the *Daily Star Sunday*, *News of the World*, *Sunday Mirror*, *Sunday Sport* and the *People*), the 'national Sunday mid-market' (*Mail on Sunday* and *Sunday Express*) and the 'national Sunday quality' (*Independent on Sunday*, the *Observer*, the *Sunday Telegraph* and the *Sunday Times*).

The sense of stasis in the UK market since the Second World War, however, is more apparent than real and is generated by the launch of a number of new, sometimes short-lived, newspapers being 'balanced' by the closure or merger of existing titles. The merger of the *News Chronicle* (1960) and the *Daily Sketch* (1971) with the *Daily Mail*, as well as the closure of *Today* in 1995, offset the emergence of the tabloid *Daily Star* (1979) and quality *Independent* (1986), for example, to create an illusion of overall calm in the newspaper market. Similar comings and goings characterise the Sunday market. The *Sunday Business*, launched in April 1996, ceased publication a decade later by which time the *Star on Sunday* had launched (2002).

The period between 1986 and 2000, following News International's move of its major titles to Wapping, east London, was dubbed the age of 'the Fleet Street revolution'; in the provinces the revolution was spearheaded by Thatcherite folk hero Eddie Shah (Goodhart and Wintour 1986, p.xi). It was marked by a flurry of launches and closures of titles reflecting a new optimism and 'revolutionary fervour' among journalists and proprietors, triggered by buoyant advertising revenues and the substantially reduced labour and production costs delivered by a new 'direct input' printing technology. *Today* (1986), the *Independent* (1986), the *Sport* (1986), the *Sunday Sport* (1986), the *London Daily News* (1987), the *News on Sunday* (1987), the *Post* (1988), the *Correspondent* (1989), the *Independent on Sunday* (1990) and the *European* (1990) were launched across an unprecedented five-year period of publishing innovation. But the 'revolution' was short-lived, with some titles closing promptly (the *London Daily News* survived only five months; *News on Sunday* only eight months), while others like *Today* struggled through to 1995. Others still fight for survival. The *Independent* and the *Independent on Sunday* have joined Tony O'Reilly's Independent Newspaper group, appointed a succession of editors and spearheaded the innovative shift to compact, but such changes have failed to revive the business fortunes of the papers: circulation and advertising revenues continue to decline after an initial fillip from the move to compact.

In the local market the decline of titles is more pronounced, although the shifting composition of the different elements of the local and provincial press generates a complexity which confounds simple characterisation by the term 'decline'. The 108 paid daily and 1,306 weekly titles published in 1948 had crashed to 94 daily and 526 weekly papers by 2005: a 56 per cent reduction in titles. But the loss of paid weekly titles has stabilised and been complemented by the emergence of free weekly papers during the 1970s. These papers (disdained by journalists as 'freesheets') enjoyed remarkable growth from 325 titles in 1980 to a peak of 882 six years later; currently 637 titles are published (Franklin 2006, pp.4 and 153). Additionally, since 1999, Associated Newspapers has published an expansive portfolio of (currently ten) daily free *Metro* titles, which have captured wide readerships and advertising revenues and for some commentators offer a possible business model for the national press (Addis 2006; Berry 2005, p.55). In London, Associated's free *London Lite* and Murdoch's *London Paper* vie for distribution supremacy and advertising revenues. The local newspaper market also delivers 12 paid and nine free Sunday newspapers (Franklin 2006, p.4).

Vanishing readers?

It is the decline in circulations which prompts the greatest concern and speculation about the UK newspaper market. Circulation trends, however, may be misrepresented if the diverse fortunes of different sectors of a fragmented, as well as highly competitive, market are not acknowledged. While the overall trend for readerships and circulation is broadly downwards, for example, the national 'quality' dailies are not merely 'holding the line' but enjoying circulation growth of 27.5 per cent (2.598 million in 2007) on 1965 ABC figures, with *The Times*, the *Financial Times* and the *Guardian* all recording expansive circulations across 40 years; and this without the arrival of the *Independent* in 1986! (see Table 1). By contrast only the *Daily Mail* in the popular and mid-market tabloid sector has demonstrated growth; overall this category is 31 per cent (8.838 million copies) down on 1965 figures. Some titles are losing readers rapidly. Between May 2006 and 2007, the circulation of the *Daily Express* declined by a substantial 9.4 per cent, while the *Sun* (−3.4%) and *Mirror* (−5%) suffered considerable losses in readership (ABC June 2007).

In the Sunday market it is also the 'red tops' which are haemorrhaging readers. The Sunday 'qualities' lost only 8 per cent of sales across the four decades analysed, helped by the arrival of the *Independent on Sunday* in 1990. Across the same period, the Sunday popular and mid-market papers suffered a 58 per cent fall from their 1965 circulation despite the launch of the *Mail on Sunday* and the *Daily Star on Sunday* (see Table 2). The losses continue and it is difficult to imagine that papers like the *Sunday Express* and *Sunday People* can continue to lose 8 per cent and 13 per cent of readership respectively year on year (May 2006–May 2007, ABC) and remain financially viable.

In summary, aggregate circulations for national daily and Sunday titles declined from 38,420,000 in 1965 to 32,619,000 in 1985 but then crashed to 22,747,000 in

Table 1 *UK daily newspaper circulations 1965, 1985 and 2007*

Newspaper title	Circulations (in 1,000s)		
	1965	1985	2007
Daily Mirror	4,957	3,252	1,554
Daily Record	—	—	404[a]
Sun	1,361	4,065	3,043
Daily Star	—	1,435[b]	778
Daily Express	3,981	1,875	765
Daily Mail	2,425	1,828	2,294
Total popular/mid-market	**12,724**	**12,455**	**8,838**
Daily Telegraph	1,352	1,221	894
The Times	258	480	636[c]
Guardian	276	487	371
Independent	—	—	245[d]
Financial Times	152	229	452
Total quality	**2,038**	**2,417**	**2,598**
TOTAL all papers	**14,762**	**14,872**	**11,436**

Notes
a   The *Daily Record*, the 'Scottish Mirror' is now recorded separately by ABC.
b   Launched 1979.
c   Sales of *The Times* rose sharply following the 'price war' launched by Rupert Murdoch in July 1993 which reduced cover price of the paper to 10 pence.
d   Launched 1986.

Table 2 *UK Sunday newspaper circulations 1965, 1985 and 2007*

Newspaper title	Circulations (in 1,000s)		
	1965	1985	2007
News of the World	6,175	4,787	3,270
Sunday Mirror	5,022	3,211	1,377
Sunday People	5,509	3,090	729
Daily Star on Sunday	—	—	381[a]
Sunday Express	4,187	2,405	744
Mail on Sunday	—	1,605[b]	2,274
Total popular/mid-market	**20,893**	**15,098**	**8,775**
Sunday Times	1,275	1,258	1,221
Observer	829	746	451
Sunday Telegraph	662	690	655
Independent on Sunday	—	—	209[c]
Total quality	**2,766**	**2,694**	**2,536**
TOTAL all papers	**23,659**	**17,792**	**11,311**

Notes
a Launched September 2002.
b Launched May 1982.
c Launched January 1990.

2007: a loss of 15.8 million copy sales representing 41 per cent of the market with losses accruing at an accelerating rate.

In local markets, the city-based daily evening, but especially morning, titles have suffered dramatic losses, with papers like the *Birmingham Evening Mail* losing 54 per cent of readership across the decade 1995–2005 (see Table 3); for all but one of the cited titles the rate of decline accelerated during the second period (i.e. between 2000 and 2005). The 526 paid weekly and 637 free weekly papers enjoyed relative stability across the last decade with the paid papers showing signs of some modest circulation growth (Franklin 2006, pp.4–5).

The *Metro* free titles enjoy continued success, with aggregate distribution figures for the ten titles which are given away each day in Birmingham, Glasgow, Cardiff and other major cities hitting 1.9 millions, which Associated claim makes the *Metro* the fourth largest newspaper in the UK (Meeke 2005),[1] although the title only moved into profit in 2006 (Franklin 2006, pp.155–60). In London, Associated's *London Lite* claims a daily distribution of 400,614 copies, while its rival, *London Paper*, claims 491,387; both are subject to allegations of 'dumping' copies into rubbish bins and Westminster Council argues that News International and Associated Newspapers should contribute to the £500,000 daily costs for collecting and recycling the three tons of discarded newspapers (Bilton 2007, p.11). But the success of the free newspapers does little to militate against the overall downwards trends in readership.

Reduced revenues from copy sales is one consequence of these 'vanishing' readers and falling circulations. But newspapers also confront a more competitive

Table 3 *Circulation of selected evening and morning titles 1995, 2000 and 2005*

Newspaper title	Circulation		
Evening	*1995*	*2000*	*2005*
Belfast Telegraph	136,714	114,961	96,299 (−29.6%)[a]
Birmingham Evening Mail	201,476	136,743	93,339 (−53.7%)
Glasgow Evening Times	138,987	106,839	92,088 (−33.7%)
Newcastle Evening Chronicle	120,604	107,346	91,703 (−23.9%)
Leicester Mercury	118,594	111,652	82,232 (−30.66%)
Yorkshire Evening Post	106,794	100,794	68,767 (−35.6%)
Sheffield Star	100,971	84,327	62,850 (−37.8%)
Morning			
Aberdeen Press and Journal	108,963	101,642	86,942 (−20.2%)
Northern Echo	77,425	66,032	55,979 (−27.7%)
Yorkshire Post	79,094	76,424	50,541 (−36.1%)
Western Mail	64,602	55,273	42,981 (−33.5%)
Newcastle Journal	57,677	50,295	38,187 (−33.8%)
Ulster Newsletter	33,233	33,435	26,270 (−21.0%)
Birmingham Post	28,054	20,922	14,256 (−49.2%)

Source: ABC and VFD data from the Newspaper Society website www.newspapersoc.org.uk/default.aspx?page=g accessed 7 November 2007.

Note: [a] Bracketed figures in the 2005 column represent percentage circulation declines for the period 1995 to 2005.

market for advertising revenues as online predators, such as the classified websites craigslist and eBay, increasingly colonise valuable revenues, challenging newspapers' other key revenue stream. To remain profitable, newspaper companies can try to increase revenues, although efforts to maintain circulation via bulk sales, free DVDs and CDs have not proved effective recruiting sergeants for readers, although they may have served to limit the growing army of deserters. Alternatively newspapers can seek to control expenditure by reducing journalism staff and minimising salary costs.

Vanishing journalists?

In late 2006 the *Press Gazette*, the industry's weekly paper, posed a simple question above its front page lead, 'How many journalists do you need to run a national newspaper?' The answer: '16 (If your name is Richard Desmond)'. Below the headline, the article discussed the proprietor's recently announced plans to cut 55 journalists' jobs across two of his titles (the *Daily Express* and the *Sunday Express*) leaving just 16 full-time journalists producing the Sunday paper. In the late 1980s, the *Sunday Express* employed between 70 and 80 journalists (Ponsford 2006, p.1).

In recent years, despite the undoubted expansion of online editions, most newspaper groups have barely increased their journalism staffs; some have reduced them. In March 2007, the *Independent* announced '40 voluntary redundancies' as part of a new cost-cutting strategy which will 'result in the departure of some of the paper's most experienced journalists' (Silver 2007, p.5). On occasion, job losses have been a direct consequence of new technology. The *Financial Times*, for example, cut 51 journalism posts in July 2006 when it merged its online and print operations (Barriaux 2006, p.28). Meanwhile the Barclays made 'swingeing job cuts' of more than 90 journalists at their newly acquired *Telegraph* titles in 2005 in an effort to recover some of their £655 million purchase cost while also making monies available for investment in a new multimedia newsroom (Greenslade 2005, pp.2–4).

Establishing the numbers of working journalists in the UK has typically more closely resembled soothsaying than social science. In his classic study of *Journalists At Work*, Tunstall suggests there were 20,375 UK journalists in 1969 (Tunstall 1971, p.13), while a 'guesstimate' extrapolating from membership of journalists' trades unions and professional associations in 1995, arrives at the figure of 39,692 journalists (Franklin 1997, pp.51–3). A more optimistic calculus identifies between 60,000 and 70,000 journalists in the UK working across the various media platforms on staff and freelance contracts, with a further 20,000 journalists anticipated by 2010 (Journalism Training Forum 2002, pp.17–18).

A recent study, which analysed trends in staffing at major UK newspaper groups across the two decades between 1985 and 2004, concludes that 'throughout the 1990s, the total number of employees in these groups remained at a fairly stable average of 1000 employees per group with average editorial employees also being fairly constant at around 500 employees per group' (Lewis *et al.* 2006, p.7).[2] In 1985 the average number of editorial staff for each group was 786, falling to a low of 427 in 1987 following News International's move to Wapping, but rising again through the 1990s to an average 741 editorial staff in 2005 – a figure very close to the number of journalists employed 20 years earlier. There are of course considerable differences between newspaper groups. At Express Newspapers Ltd, journalist numbers reduced from 968 to 532 between 1996 and 2004, with a sharp increase in job losses following Richard Desmond's purchase of the titles. But at the *Guardian* the total number of employees (editorial and other staffs) effectively doubled from 725 to 1,429 between 1991 to 2000; at the *Financial Times* there was a similarly marked growth in overall staff from 795 to 1,131 between 1985 and 2004 (ibid., pp.7–8).

But significantly, while employment levels for journalists have remained relatively stable or increased only slightly, journalists' workloads have increased markedly. The same research study identified 'a very substantial increase in the overall size of … national daily newspapers' with the average number of pages devoted to news and other editorial effectively tripling from 'a 14.6 page average in 1985 to 41 pages by 2006' (ibid., pp.10–11). Alongside this expansion in newspapers' main sections has been a similar growth in the number and size of supplements as well as the development of online editions and other services. The study concludes that journalists' productivity has increased significantly across the period, signalling a 'relative decline' in staffing compared with the 1980s up to the mid-1990s. The substantial role for public relations professionals and newspapers' extensive use of agency copy to fill this expansive news hole while employing fewer journalists is discussed below.

In the local and regional press, job cuts and the non-replacement of staff, intended to deliver cuts and improve profitability, are similarly commonplace. At Trinity Mirror, which is the UK's largest provincial newspaper publisher, with 232 titles in its portfolio, numbers of journalists and other production workers in post have reduced by almost 20 per cent (19.2%) from 6,898 to 5,575 between 2000 and 2005 (Williams and Franklin 2007, p.20). At the Johnston Press Group's prestigious *Yorkshire Post*, the Chief Sub-editor analysed staffing changes since he began working at the paper in 1977. 'Two features sub-editors producing 25 pages a week', he claims, have been replaced by seven subs, but they were required 'to produce 180 pages ... Bottom lines have become more vivid', he observes, 'It was a different era then' (Martinson 2005, p.18). In a recent survey-based study, distributed among NUJ members at a Trinity Mirror chapel, 94 per cent of respondents (48 from 51) suggested that the number of editorial staff in their newsroom had declined in recent years.[3] Respondents (84%) also claimed that their workloads had increased, with 62 per cent suggesting their workload was 'considerably higher' than a decade ago. An NUJ official interviewed for the study argued, 'over the last ten years, we've probably lost about a quarter of the reporting staff ... obviously that has had an impact on our ability to produce the newspaper. Now we are really cut right to the bone with no spare capacity at all' (Williams and Franklin 2007, p.34).

Low wages combine with job cuts to deliver minimum production costs for newspapers. In the provincial press wages are low across the career range: from trainee to senior journalist. Half of British journalists earn less than the national average wage of £26,161; 50 per cent of journalists working in the regional press earn less than £20,000 a year (Greenslade 2004, p.9). Pay is especially low for new entrants, who will typically be graduates and may have completed one year of postgraduate training in journalism. Salaries vary between different newspaper groups, reflecting the local character of pay settlements: at Trinity Mirror Wales (renamed Media Wales in November 2007) the entry salary is £11,113; at the *Yorkshire Post* it is £16,440. Journalists' salaries compare poorly with average graduate entry level pay of £20,300, prompting the General Secretary of the NUJ to claim that local journalists are leaving the industry, because 'they can earn more money serving behind a bar than in journalism' (Dear 2006, p.8; Williams and Franklin 2007, pp.15 and 32–7).

Nationally, salaries for journalists are modest; some celebrity journalists, but mainly columnists, command significant incomes. Again, some variation is evident for journalists working in different locations and on distinctive media platforms, but the average salary is low at £22,500 per annum, with 10 per cent earning less than £12,000, 34 per cent less than £20,000, while 18 per cent earn more than £40,000; only 8 per cent receive more than £50,000 per annum (Journalism Training Forum 2002, pp.55–6). Women journalists' salaries are on average £5,000 less than those of their male counterparts, although the women are typically younger than the men and this may offer a partial explanation for the lower salary (Journalism Training Forum 2002, p.57).

Establishing this strict control over labour costs has been crucial to sustaining newspapers' profitability, but equally significant has been newspapers' success in maintaining their share of advertising revenues, despite the challenge offered by expansive online advertising sites (Newspaper Society 2005).

Vanishing profits?

Globally, advertising revenues for newspapers are expanding. In 2006, newspapers captured 29.4 per cent of a global advertising market estimated to be worth $425 billion; when the share of magazines (12.9%) is included, the total market share for prints is 42.3 per cent; and this is in the context of 4 per cent year on year advertising growth in 2006 with a five-year growth of 15.6 per cent. By contrast the internet captured 5.7 per cent of the market (WAN 8 February 2007 accessed 22 May 2007).

In the UK, both local and national newspapers enjoy profitable returns on their investment. For some national titles and most local newspaper groups, profits have been exceptionally high compared to other industries (Franklin 2006, pp.7–9; Lewis et al. 2006, pp.8–9). Typical rates of return for local newspaper groups have varied between 25 per cent and 30 per cent, although Johnston Press profits have approached 35 per cent (Dear 2006, p.8; Franklin 2006, p.8), while Media Wales achieved quite remarkable pre-tax profits of 38.2 per cent (£20.999 million) in 2005 on a turnover of £54.596 million; this compared very favourably to the 10.7 per cent (£3.916 million) profits on a turnover of £36.681 million in 1996 (Williams and Franklin 2007, p.29). Advertising is the crucial element in this profitability and constitutes an average 80 per cent of local newspapers' revenues (Mintel 2005). Additionally, advertising income has remained high for the regional and provincial press at £3.132 billion in 2004/5, with local (20%) and national (13%) newspapers taking 33 per cent of total UK advertising revenues, followed by television (26%), magazines (12%), radio (4%), the internet (4%) and cinema (1%) (Newspaper Society 2005).

Trinity Mirror, the largest provincial newspaper group, which also owns national titles like the *Daily Mirror*, *Sunday Mirror* and the *Daily Record*, has recorded growing profitability across the last decade because of its ability to sustain advertising revenues (apart from slight dips in 2002 and 2005), while maintaining sales income by offsetting declining circulations with regular increases in copy price (see Table 4).

While national newspaper groups have not generally enjoyed the high levels of profitability of their local counterparts, they have managed to secure healthy profits and high turnovers across the last 20 years (Lewis et al. 2006, pp.8–9). Between 1985 and 2004, average profit returns for the nine newspaper groups in one study were 7.8 per cent. Although figures for profitability vary between lows

Table 4 *Trinity Mirror revenues 1999–2005*

Year	Advertising (£000s)	Copy sales (£000s)	Other (£000s)	Total (£000s)
2005	611,700	396,400	113,900	1,122,000
2004	644,400	395,400	101,900	1,141,700
2003	620,600	376,000	98,500	1,095,100
2002	618,200	373,300	100,700	1,092,200
2001	634,100	393,700	103,300	1,131,100
2000	574,800	396,800	106,700	1,078,300
1999	332,000	173,600	90,200	595,800

Source: Williams and Franklin 2007, p.22.

of 0.2 per cent in 1986 and highs of 15.5 per cent in 1988, there is a striking consistency of recorded profits with average levels of 7.5 per cent between 1985 and 1994 and 8.1 per cent between 1995 and 2004. The latest figures available for 2004 reveal an average 9.4 per cent profits (pre-tax £30,354,333) on a turnover of £324,175,784 (ibid., p.9). Some groups fare better than others. The Guardian Media Group, for example, enjoyed a 47 per cent rise in pre-tax profits from £66.4 million to £97.7 million during the year ending April 2007, reflecting a 2 per cent increase in turnover to £716.1 million in what was judged to be a 'difficult and challenging' year (Allen 2007, p.27).

'Newszak': newspapers' changing editorial priorities and newsgathering and reporting practices

Newspaper groups' strategies to sustain profitability in an increasingly competitive and corporatised market with declining circulations, has obliged them to minimise their salary costs by cutting back on editorial and other staffs. This in turn has a crucial impact on the newsgathering and reporting processes of newspapers and triggers shifts in the range, quality and independence of their editorial contents. Intensified competition and the increasingly frenzied search for the elusive, if not 'vanishing' reader, has triggered a shift in journalists' editorial priorities prompting a move 'downmarket'. This strategic 'move downmarket' is curious since the discussion of newspaper circulations above illustrates that it is precisely the 'national morning popular' titles (the daily and Sunday tabloids) which are losing circulation most readily, while the 'national morning qualities' (the old broadsheets now compacts) are markedly more successful in retaining their readerships.

The neologism 'newszak', originally coined by journalist Malcolm Muggeridge, has been used previously to capture and describe these changes in newspapers' editorial formats (Franklin 1997). So what is newszak and why has it emerged? The argument concerning newszak suggests that across the last two decades newspapers have increasingly tended:

To retreat from investigative journalism and hard news to the preferred territory of 'softer' or 'lighter' stories ... Entertainment has superseded the provision of information; human interest has supplanted the public interest;
measured judgement has succumbed to sensationalism; the trivial has
triumphed over the weighty; the intimate relationships of celebrities from
soap operas, the world of sport or the royal family are judged more 'newsworthy' than the reporting of significant issues and events of international consequence. Traditional news values have been undermined by new values;
'infotainment' is rampant ... Journalists are more concerned to report stories
which interest the public rather than stories which are in the public interest
... Newszak understands news as a product designed and 'processed' for a
particular market and delivered in increasingly homogenous snippets which
make only modest demands on the audience.

(Franklin 1997, pp.4–5)

Four particular features of this general trend symbolise newspapers' shifting priorities. First, newspapers seem less concerned to report news, especially foreign news,
parliamentary and political news and investigative stories (Sampson 1996; see
Harrison, chapter 1; Jones, chapter 14). Foreign news now focuses almost wholly
on wars, famines and natural disasters such as tsunamis, earthquakes and volca-
noes (Wilby 2005, p.9).

Second, news has been replaced by views with 'celebrity' columnists command-
ing premium salaries above reporters and enjoying higher editorial priority; the
'commentariat' are in the ascendancy (White and Hobshawm 2007, pp.283–92).
Independent Editor Simon Kelner has unashamedly dubbed his newspaper a
'viewspaper'. The job of the growing army of columnists, such as David
Aaronovitch, Julie Burchill, Nick Cohen, Richard Littlejohn, Simon Jenkins and
Polly Toynbee, is to generate a 'fit-to-burst' mailbag of letters and comments
posted online; they trade in opinions, while reporters inform by presenting the
facts (see McNair, chapter 8).

Third, quality papers now report stories, typically focused on celebrities, which
previously they disdained as merely 'fit for the tabloids'. The Beckhams offer not
simply news value, but also good value: 'two for the price of one'. Consequently,
the compacts featured reports of David Beckham's move to an American football
team, with his recently reconstituted 'Spice Girl' wife Victoria, alongside the
traditional red top coverage and pictures on 13 July 2007.

Finally, the emergence of newszak is also reflected in changes in format and
style as well as content, with the old broadsheets as likely as the red tops to use
'tabloid-style banner headlines, alliterative and punny headlines, large print, less
text, shorter words, bigger pictures, colour pictures and more of them' (Franklin
1997, p.7; see Tattersall, chapter 18 and Rafferty, chapter 20). The radical shift of
broadsheet newspapers to compact formats pioneered by the *Independent*, followed
by *The Times*, with the *Guardian* preferring the Berliner style, has blurred further
the differences in design and page layout between the tabloids and broadsheets,

although the debate continues concerning whether a move to tabloid format necessarily implies a move to tabloid content (see Rusbridger 2005 and Cole, chapter 15).

Media academics (Sampson 1996), as well as distinguished journalists (Marr 2004) and broadcasters (Cronkite 1997), have noted and criticised these trends in newspapers' editorial contents and design. McNair prefers the phrase 'bonk journalism' (McNair 1994, p.145) to characterise them, while Marr dismisses this new journalistic mood as 'bite sized McNugget journalism which is small, tasty, brightly coloured and easy to ingest' (cited in Franklin 1997, p.5). But many editors and academic observers demurred. Advocates of the 'dumbing down debate', they suggested, were ignoring the 'economic realities facing British newspapers', especially the drive to increase circulation, as well as the increase in pagination which allowed 'infinitely more comprehensive coverage of domestic news'. In reality the debate derived its inspiration from nothing more worthy than good old-fashioned 'snobbery', although even the most ardent defenders of this shift in news values and design conceded that 'the proliferation of columnists was undeniable' (Greenslade 2003, pp.627–9).

The usual suspects were rounded up and paraded as perpetrators of this move towards newszak. First, the increasingly competitive markets in which newspapers operate, which generate pressures to move 'downmarket' and offer what is increasingly described as 'market driven journalism' or 'bottom line journalism' (McManus 1994). Second, the absence of statutory press regulation permits newspaper prurience, and routine press incursions into the privacy of individuals, especially celebrities and members of the royal family, despite the best efforts of the Press Complaints Commission, which operates a voluntary code of practice (Frost 2004, p.102; Pinker 2006, pp.115–26). Third, technological developments in both print and broadcast media have facilitated the cuts in journalist numbers, noted above, prompting the growth of freelance working within the journalism profession, while empowering proprietors with greater influence over editorial concerns.

Finally, but crucially, the growth of both public and private sector public relations, combined with the relatively declining numbers of journalists, encourages an increasing media reliance on PR 'subsidies' (Gandy 1982), as well as the 'outsourcing' of journalism, reflecting a similar dependency on pre-packaged editorial copy from news agencies such as the Press Association (Davis 2002; Hamer 2000; see also Davis, chapter 25 and Manning, chapter 24). The rest of this section considers the growing influence of public relations professionals and agency services in the newsmaking process. The argument here is that news is increasingly generated and shaped outside of formal media organisations and newsrooms by a growing army of what have been termed 'journalism literate PR professionals' and this has significant implications for journalists' newsgathering and reporting activities, as well as the changing content and character of news (Franklin 1997, ch.1).

Who's leading the tango? Newspapers, public relations and news agencies

In a classic statement of the relationship between journalists and their sources of information, Herb Gans employed a dance metaphor suggesting a degree of cooperation between them. 'It takes two to tango', Gans suggested, but 'sources usually lead' (Gans 1979). More recent studies of this relationship suggest that who 'leads', and becomes the dominant partner in the relationship, varies at different stages in the news cycle (Reich 2006, pp.497–514). Others characterise this as a 'love–hate relationship' (White and Hobsbawm 2007, pp.284–5) which brings journalists and sources into conflict, but in day-to-day terms demands 'mutal reciprocity' and more cooperative ways of working, which enable both groups to achieve their professional objectives (Blumler and Gurevitch 1995). Deuze goes further, suggesting that the 'distinct professional identities' or 'boundaries' between journalists and PR professionals are 'vanishing' (Deuze 2007, p.141). Journalists have objected to this formulation since it suggests an unduly dominant role for sources but also offends journalism's professional culture, which stresses editorial autonomy and independence; 'getting too close' to sources is judged highly dangerous.

But the belief that public relations is influential in shaping news and editorial contents in newspapers has become increasingly commonplace among academics (Davis 2002; Maloney 2006), journalists (Marr 2004) and public relations professionals (Hobsbawm 2005; Hobsbawm and White 2007). *Financial Times* journalist John Lloyd makes this dependence explicit:

> The normal journalistic approach to PRs – i.e. dogs and lampposts – is grossly self serving from the point of view of journalists. It glosses over, ignores or even denies the fact that much of current journalism both broadcast and press is public relations in the sense that stories, ideas, features and interviews are either suggested, or in the extreme actually written by public relations people. Until that becomes open and debated between PR people and journalists, we will continue to have this artificially wide gulf where journalists pose as fearless seekers of truth and PRs are slimy creatures trying to put one over on us. It is not remotely like that.
>
> (*Guardian* 10 April 2006, p.3)

More than a decade ago, the Editor of *PR Week* made the following claims about the extent of public relations materials in national newspapers:

> A considered estimate would put this at 50 per cent in a broadsheet newspaper in every section apart from sport. In the local press and the mid market and national tabloids the figure would undoubtedly be higher. Music and fashion journalists and PRs work hand in hand in the editorial process. It is often a game of bluff and brinkmanship, but the relationship is utterly

interdependent. PRs provide fodder, but the clever high-powered ones do a lot of journalists' thinking for them.

(cited in the *Guardian* 13 May 1996, p.10)

Journalists promptly dismissed such claims by the public relations profession as self-serving gossip, unsupported by independent evidence. Similar suggestions concerning newspapers' growing reliance on news agencies, as the most cost-effective surrogate for employing in-house journalists, are long-standing. At its 1968 centenary celebration, the Press Association (PA) Chair W. D. Barnetson claimed 'the plain and challenging fact is that we [PA] are now the prime artery of news on this island' (*The Link* 1968, vol.26). This reliance on PA copy was confirmed by the Chair of the *Yorkshire Post* group, who acknowledged that 'most of our newspapers contain so much news wired from the PA that it would look monotonous if every message from its giant building ... had a Press Association byline' (Linton, *Yorkshire Post* 13 March 1968). Forty years on, the claims for the role of news agencies continue with hyperbolic suggestions that 'by default, PA has become the UK's monopoly reporter' (Aspinall 2005, p.2). Even journalist Martin Wainwright concedes the PA has become 'the new heart of British journalism' (2005, p.25).

The findings of a recent study of national quality newspapers' uses of agency copy and PR materials, based on a substantive analysis of 2,207 items of domestic news coverage in the *Guardian*, the *Independent*, *The Times*, the *Telegraph* and the mid-market *Daily Mail* sampled across two periods in 2005, generated unequivocal evidence to support these claims (Lewis *et al.* 2006).[4] Researchers analysed each item of domestic news coverage to establish, identify and quantify the precise extent of any element of public relations source materials or agency copy in the published item. This was achieved by comparing newspaper stories with copy from agency wire services and by internet searches for press releases for comparison with published newspaper text. This involved painstaking research since newspaper stories rarely acknowledged PR and wire sources. It also delivered necessarily conservative estimates since published items were coded as containing agency copy and PR materials only when conclusive evidence deriving from direct textual comparison of a press release with a published story could be established; strong suspicion that a particular story was based on a press release or agency copy was discarded. After such sustained speculation, it was important to establish evidence of newspapers' reliance on these sources of news that would 'stand up in court'.

The great majority of the 2,207 newspaper stories analysed comprised 1,564 (71%) main page articles of variable length, and 561 (25.5%) shorter news in brief items (Nibs), which typically form a strip across the top or a column down the side of an editorial page; the remainder were 'picture only' stories (0.5%) or opinion pieces (3%) which had strayed into the news sections from the op-ed pages (see Wahl-Jorgensen, chapter 4). These news items focused on eight key subject areas. The most popular was 'crime' (20%), with items exploring individual crimes rather than criminal policy or trends (see Wardle, chapter 11). Crime enjoyed greater coverage than the cluster category of 'domestic issues' (15%) which included the NHS, education, the environment and immigration. Other editorial foci included 'politics' (15%), 'business/consumer' news (12% – a high figure given that business sections were not coded), 'health/natural world' (10%), 'entertainment and sport' (10%), 'accidents/disasters' (5%), 'defence/foreign policy' (2%) and 'other' (11%) (Lewis et al. 2006, pp.13–14).

The great majority of articles were attributed to a bylined reporter (72%) with only 1 per cent of stories attributed to the PA or another wire service, as well as a small proportion (2%) to a less specific identity such as an 'independent reporter'; approximately a quarter (24.5%) carried no byline but these were typically the shorter nibs. By identifying journalists in this way newspapers created an impression that articles reflected the assiduous efforts of diligent in-house reporters. But when news coverage was analysed, findings revealed that 30 per cent of published items were wholly dependent on agency copy with a further 19 per cent strongly derivative from agency materials. In a further 13 per cent of stories agency copy was evident along with information from other sources, while 8 per cent of items used 'mainly other information', and in a further 5 per cent the wire service reported the story but the copy was not used in the newspaper report; in 25 per cent of stories there was no evidence of dependence on agency copy. In summary, approximately half (49%) of news stories published in the quality press and analysed for this study were wholly or mainly dependent on materials produced and distributed by wire services with a further fifth (21%) of stories containing some element of agency copy (ibid., p.15).

Newspapers make little acknowledgement of this reliance on agency copy even when it is published more or less verbatim. On 24 March 2006, for example, the Daily Mail attributed its front page story about the health risks of eating oily fish ('Why oily fish might not be so good for your health after all') to a Daily Mail reporter, even though it directly replicates quotations and factual materials from Press Association and Mercury news wire stories (ibid., pp.35–8). Wainwright's claim that the PA is the 'new heart' of British journalism seems confirmed; 47 per cent of published stories in the study sample replicated PA materials to some extent, with an equivalent figure of 17 per cent for the Mercury regional news service.

Journalists' editorial reliance on PR materials is similarly striking with almost a fifth (19%) of the analysed stories deriving wholly (10%) or mainly (9%) from PR sources. A further quarter (22%) were either a mix of PR with other materials (11%) or mainly other information (11%), while 13 per cent of stories appeared to contain PR materials which could not be identified, and 46 per cent contained no evidence of PR sources. Again, stories which offered near verbatim replication of source materials were found. The Times report, 'George Cross For Iraq War Hero' on 24 March 2006, which carried Michael Evans' byline, for example, reproduces almost exactly a Ministry of Defence press release (ibid., p.17).

This journalistic reliance on public relations is not necessarily a negative outcome of changing newsgathering routines, of course, since public relations professionals may generate highly newsworthy stories and may, in this way, increase the plurality of sources of news from which journalists and editors can select for publication. But examination of the origins of PR materials suggests otherwise. The corporate sector dominates with 38 per cent of PR materials referenced in press coverage deriving from the 'business/corporate' world. Other contributors to press reports via public relations activity include 'public bodies' (the police, NHS, universities – 23%), 'government and politicians' (21%), NGO/charities (11%) and 'professional associations' (5%). The voice of the ordinary citizen, however, remains almost mute; the opinions of ordinary men and women informed only 2% of stories (ibid., pp.21–3). One consequence of journalists' increased reliance on public relations subsidies is that corporate and governmental voices enjoy extensive and unrepresentative access into the public debating chamber which the press provides.

When the reliance of the quality press on both public relations and agency copy is examined, only 12 per cent of published stories are without content sourced from outside the newsroom; 60 per cent of published stories rely wholly or mainly on external news sources (see Table 5). *The Times* (68%) is the most reliant on sources of news (all or mainly) from outside the newsroom; the *Guardian* (53%) displays the most editorial independence; while the *Telegraph*, *Mail* and *Independent* display a proximate parity of reliance on these news sources.

There is, moreover, a mutually reinforcing effect between PR materials and agency copy in shaping newspapers' editorial reports. Journalists use PR materials directly, but PR text is also encoded in the agency copy which journalists use so routinely in news production. Indeed 47 per cent of press stories which were based 'wholly' around PR materials closely replicated agency copy, suggesting the existence of what might be termed a 'news ladder' or a 'multi-staged news agenda' in which PR materials initially generate agency stories which in turn promote coverage in newspapers.

Interviews conducted with journalists confirm these high levels of reliance on public relations subsidies and editorial copy from wire sources; significantly, they also suggest it is increasing – and as a result of journalists' growing workload. An editor at *The Times* argued, 'We are churning stories today not writing them. Almost everything is recycled from another source … It wouldn't be possible to

Table 5 *Newspaper stories with content derived from PR/wires*

Sources of editorial content	%
All from PR/wires/other media	38
Mainly from PR/wires/other media	22
Mix of PR/Wires/other media with other information	13
Mainly other information	7
All other information	12
Unclear	8

Source: Lewis *et al.* 2006, p.25.

write so many stories otherwise'; while an editor at another national paper claimed, 'We've always been reliant on wire copy, but we use it a hell of a lot more these days ... it's quite common for us to cut and paste a story off PA, renose it a bit to mask where it has come from, then put it out there as our own' (cited in ibid., pp.48–53).

The role of public relations and agency copy in shaping news agendas in the local press has long been acknowledged (Franklin 2004, ch.5; Harrison 2006; O'Connor and O'Neill 2007). An early study of local government public relations' influence on local press contents in the county of Northumberland concluded that 96 per cent of press releases generated stories in local newspapers. Significantly, most releases triggered stories in three or four papers. Editing of the press releases, or the inclusion of any additional information, was rare (Franklin 1986, pp.25–33). In a later national study of local government public relations, 82 per cent of responding press officers confirmed that 'more than three-quarters of press releases' generated stories in the local press (Franklin 1988, p.81).

Local papers' willingness to accept these public relations 'subsidies', as well as the extent of rewriting of news releases, related directly to journalistic resources. At daily papers with a specialist municipal correspondent, press releases were extensively edited, while at the weeklies with leaner editorial resources, press releases were typically reproduced verbatim or edited by removing complete paragraphs or changing their order; in free papers, editing of releases was non-existent (Franklin 1986). Newspapers' variable journalism staffs create a hierarchy of dependence on PR subsidies with 42 per cent of press officers identifying free papers as 'most likely to use a press release', compared to 30 per cent for paid weeklies, 22 per cent evening and 5 per cent for daily newspapers (Franklin 1988, p.82). The value of the PR subsidy is substantial. A local government press officer calculated an illustrative exemplar: 'I estimate at Westminster', he suggested, that 'we spend at least 30% of our time, equivalent to one and a half press officers costing £50,000 on servicing the local media ... Many of the requests from local papers are ... pleas for letters and press releases to fill the gaps in pages. In this sense media officers are simply filling the gaps in the newsroom staff' (cited in Harrison 2006, p.188).

Local papers' reliance on copy from wire services is similarly considerable with an equivalent 'subsidy' effect on the costs of news production. The PA's special evening newspaper service PACE (PA Choice for Evenings) supplies camera-ready pages with text and statistical information for most regional newspapers. Costs reflect whether the content required is shared with other customers or 'bespoke' – i.e. uniquely requested by a particular customer. Hamer (2000) offers an example of the savings available (based on year 2000 costs) to newspapers using this service. *Sport First*'s Sunday edition, for example, uses 15 pages of statistics (11 at £75 and 4 bespoke at £150) and 14 pages of editorial (headlines, stories and match reports at £100) from the PA across the UK football season. Additionally, it buys horse racing information for around £400 each week. The cost of generating this editorial copy across the 40-week season is approximately

£133,000; a 30 per cent profit means cost to the customer of £172,900. But the costs of generating this copy in-house are approximately £400,000 given *Sport First*'s London location and higher labour, rental and equipment costs: a saving of approximately £220,000 (55%) (Hamer 2000, p.16).

Journalists readily acknowledge the time and resource constraints that increasingly oblige them to use the cost-effective, pre-packaged news subsidies which public relations and agency copy offer. More than 90 per cent of respondents to a survey of local journalists claimed that their use of public relations materials had increased across the last decade; 80 per cent suggested their use of PR materials had similarly increased (Williams and Franklin 2007, p.39). A journalist acknowledged in interview that 'if a story crops up on PA that had a local tie in that would be a bonus, but if you could make it a page lead without involving a reporter then you'd do that on the news desk. You'd just rehash the PA' (Williams and Franklin 2007, p.40).

This reliance on public relations, moreover, has radically changed the processes of journalistic validation and verification of stories. These days, journalists rarely leave the office; journalism has become a desk-based job. There is little time or opportunity to check stories, to be sure that the claims they make 'stand up'. Journalists believe the victim of these revised news production practices is the integrity and independence of the resulting journalism. 'I think it's inevitable that the quality of the news has suffered', a journalist confided. 'Sometimes we're in a state of desperation just to fill the paper and that means the quality can't possibly be the same as it would be if we spent the time doing the job and developing stories.' A fellow journalist acknowledged that, 'if we are getting more copy for free from PR, and we are, this raises lots of questions about journalistic independence and integrity' (cited in Williams and Franklin 2007, pp.39–40).

In summary, the current business strategy of national and local newspaper groups, which stresses cutting costs via reduced staffing while increasing pagination and supplements to attract more readers and advertisers, requires fewer journalists with reduced resources to produce bigger newspapers and more supplements, in both print and online editions. To 'square the circle' and fill the increasingly gaping news hole requires that journalists accept news subsidies from public relations professionals and substitute agency copy for their own independent journalistic enquiries. This process imposes changes on journalists' working practices, revises editorial priorities and reduces markedly both the independence and integrity of journalism. Contemporary newspapers and journalists bear little resemblance to what Francis Williams described in his classic study of the press, as the 'dangerous estate' (Williams 1957). Newspaper groups are increasingly seeking a solution to what they judge to be a 'crisis of profitability' which, in truth, is more a 'crisis of journalistic integrity', by producing online editions of their newspapers.

Moving newspapers online: problems and prospects

The internet has become a major source of news for people globally. In the US, across the decade ending in 2002, from a baseline of almost zero, 3,112 online newspapers, 3,900 online magazines and a total of 13,536 news sites of all types have been established (Nguyen 2008). In the UK, online media have experienced similarly rapid growth. All national newspapers now enjoy a web presence following the *Telegraph*'s lead in 1994, and there are 800 regional newspaper websites (Newspaper Society 2006). Significantly, four of the largest provincial newspaper groups (Trinity Mirror, Northcliffe, Newsquest and Guardian Media) have established Fish4 – a searchable database of regional advertising designed to offset the challenge posed by classified sites such as craigslist and online auction site eBay (Williams and Franklin 2007, p.14). This expansion of online news services has coincided with the continued and, in some sectors, accelerating decline of printed newspapers, prompting some observers to identify online growth as a key factor exacerbating the decline of printed newspapers. The motive behind newspaper groups' decisions to move online was, of course, precisely the opposite: namely to support and buttress print editions by attracting new readers, advertisers and revenues.

Online editions of newspapers have won both advocates and detractors (Thelen 2003; Kaplan 2003). *Guardian* Editor Alan Rusbridger, for example, presenting prizes to the winners of student media awards in 2006, cautioned about the need to acquire the skills necessary to work across multiple media platforms. 'It has dawned on reporters', he argued,

> that the years when they worked with just a notebook and pencil are over and that they now have to work in at lest five media, keyboard, sound, stills and moving pictures, podcasts and hyperlinks ... your generation are probably comfortable with all those media and won't find it shocking to work across them.
>
> (cited in Keating 2006, p.6)

The *Guardian* has spearheaded online developments since the launch of *Guardian Unlimited* in 1999, which has subsequently become the largest and most widely read website of any UK newspaper (Kiss and Brook 2007, p.9). The paper also crossed a journalistic Rubicon with the announcement that from 13 June 2006, the *Guardian* would publish stories first to the web, ending the primacy of the printed newspaper and initiating a new phase in UK journalism (Fletcher 2006, p.7). The move online requires the constant updating of stories, expert analysis of breaking news and triggers the collapse of the deadlines which previously structured print journalists' working days. A favourite adage of journalists, 'file by three and home for tea', has become an anachronism (ibid.). Other editors express doubts about online journalism.

Simon Kelner, editor of the *Independent*, remains sceptical about the commercial value of online editions. He is 'willing to be called a flat earther' (Thomas 2006) but claims 'there is absolutely no model for a newspaper website to make money', but 'what it can do is hit the value and currency of the printed product'. Kelner is fundamentally opposed to the *Guardian*'s web first policy, suggesting that 'if you have an exclusive story at five o'clock to go in the following day's newspaper, the idea that you would put it on the website for nothing strikes me as complete madness' (ibid.).

The opposing views of these two senior newspaper editors reflect the uncertainty that has characterised the expansion of online news services, which has typically been uneven, developing episodically, rather than having any more stable unilinear progression. Nguyen claims there are two distinct periods in the development of online news services. The first spans the decade from the early 1990s until the bursting of the 'dot.com bubble' early in the new millennium; the second dates from Murdoch's Pauline conversion to the 'digital revolution' articulated in his 2005 speech to the American Society of Newspaper Editors (ASNE). Both phases are informed and shaped by a 'defensive innovation culture' among traditional media and are based on the 'fear of becoming irrelevant in the Internet age'. The approach of traditional newspaper groups has been essentially defensive, seeking to engage only minimally with the new online media but sufficiently to protect their investment and sustain the old media world.[5] Consequently many of the unique features of online news 'such as multimedia and interactivity' have only recently been developed, while 'shovelware' (reformatted copy from the print edition), which minimises production costs, 'is very popular among all types of traditional commercial news organisations online' (Nguyen 2008).

But post 2005, the internet has established its credentials as a mainstream news medium, online advertising has expanded markedly and Murdoch's endorsement of online news services has been catalytic in promoting substantial investment and expansion in online news (Nguyen 2008). The remainder of this section explores two aspects of the development of online news media. First we examine UK newspapers' recent (post 2002) willingness to charge for certain elements of their online services; second we analyse journalists' responses to the strategy of a major local and regional newspaper publisher for introducing multiple platform working.

A business strategy for online news: virtual readers and virtual customers

Independent Editor Simon Kelner's claim that there is 'absolutely no model for a newspaper website to make money' ignores much recent and relevant research (Dalzotto 2007; Bleyen and Van Hove 2007), although the suggestion that 'most online newspapers have yet to find a business strategy with which they are completely comfortable' is probably fair comment (Herbert and Thurman 2007, p.210). The majority of online news sites remain unprofitable (Nguyen 2008) and constitute 'a financial drain on the newspapers that support them' (Crosbie 2004). When newspaper groups declare online editions 'profitable', moreover, this may simply mean that current revenues exceed costs, although this calculus may not include the need to repay start-up investment, or the fact that online editions 'don't pay many of their expenses' and enjoy free copy from print editions (shovelware), with established newspapers paying many of their overhead costs (Crosbie 2004).

Newspaper groups have identified three potential revenue streams for their online products and have constructed a 'one-off' or 'bespoke', rather than 'standardised', business model which draws to varying degrees on each income source: subscription, advertising and 'ad hoc sales'. The focus here is on ad hoc sales since this best exemplifies the emerging business model and illustrates the expansive and wide range of online revenues.

Generating online revenues via subscription has proved controversial and problematic. The business model for newspapers simply does not translate to online news. The fundamental difficulty is that, unlike newspapers which charge cover prices, generating revenues from charges for online news content is unlikely to succeed when this same news is widely available for free on myriad other news sites at the click of a mouse. Worse, the opportunity cost of each newly won online reader is a lost reader for the print edition: the problem of 'cannibalisation'. Such a shift is economically damaging since '(1) the company no longer receives revenues [i.e. cover price] directly from the user; and (2) the value of that user in terms of advertising is still considerably lower online' (Herbert and Thurman 2007, p.211). In terms of a reader's value, the rate of exchange favours print to the extent that 'newspapers need between 20–100 readers online to make up for losing just one print reader'; this is a 'daunting multiple' (*Economist* 2006a).

In America, *USA Today* and the *Philadelphia Inquirer* quickly dropped their subscription fees and shifted their search for revenue to advertising. The *Wall Street Journal Online* provides an exception. The paper's success in generating online subscription revenues is attributed to a globally successful brand name serving a niche market for business news. But by 2005, the Newspaper Association of America identified only 44 from 1,500 online newspapers charging a subscription fee (Mensing and Rejfek 2005, p.3). In May 2002, *The Times Online* became the pioneer UK newspaper website to charge for access to content, imposing an annual subscription fee of £39.99 for overseas users. Shortly after, the *Financial Times* introduced an annual charge of £75 and a premium fee of £195 (now £200) for which subscribers enjoyed access to business databases as well as specialised business news, but subscriptions triggered a substantial exodus of the sites' unique users, with numbers plummeting from 604,000 in May 2002 to 463,000 in a single month (hAnluain 2004).

Advertising is crucial to newspapers' website profitability and typically accounts for at least 80 per cent of revenues (ibid.); by contrast subscription fees constituted a mere 10 per cent average in US online revenues (Mensing and Rejfek 2005; Table 1, this chapter). But while UK online advertising is growing rapidly, with estimates suggesting a 41 per cent year on year growth in 2006 to a record expenditure of £2.016 billion (Internet Advertising Bureau 2007), this constitutes only 11.4 per cent of UK market share. Globally, online advertising wins only 5.7 per cent of total advertising expenditure (WAN 2007) even though some online sites practise 'upselling' and oblige those who buy print classified adverts to also buy online (Crosbie 2004).

There is a significant tension, moreover, between advertising and charging for content. Subscription and other content charges reduce access to the site and thereby advertising revenues; the maxim runs 'too many fees and readers flee … and advertising flees along with them' (hAnluain 2004). The experience at the *FT* proved salutary. Similarly when *The Times Online* removed subscription charges for overseas readers, it experienced a huge increase in traffic (Herbert and Thurman 2007, p.212). Consequently, a successful business strategy for online newspapers must strike a careful, judicious and profitable balance between advertising and revenues raised from charging for different types of content.

Recent studies (Herbert and Thurman 2007; hAnluain 2004) identify the wide-ranging contents for which UK newspapers currently charge (see Table 6).

Only *FT.com* charges for news content. It can generate revenue in this way because, like *WSJ.com*, the website produces specialist, authoritative and in-depth news about business and finance which is not available to would-be readers of more general news sites. Three newspaper sites – *Independent.co.uk*, *DailyMail.co.uk* and *FT.Com* – charge readers for access to columnists. The *Independent* has introduced charges for four 'portfolios' of content – news and sport, comment and analysis, the crossword and, perhaps surprisingly, their Middle East correspondent Robert Fisk. Uniquely popular with readers, subscription to the Fisk portfolio costs $50 annually (hAnluain 2004). Five newspapers charge for access to archives and prices are high: £1 for each article downloaded from *The Times Online*, for example, exceeds the price of the printed edition. Access to the archive at the *Scotsman.com* allows digital searches of facsimiles of

Table 6 *Charges for content in selected UK national and regional online newspapers*

Title	News	Columnists	Archive	Digital edition	Email Alerts	Mobile services	Games
DailyExpress.co.uk	—	—	—	Yes	—	—	—
DailyMail.co.uk	—	All	—	Yes	—	—	—
DailyStar.co.uk	—	—	—	Yes	—	—	—
FT.com	Some	Some	Some	Subscriber only	Subscriber only	Paid	—
Guardian Unlimited	—	—	—	Yes	Some paid	—	Some paid
Independent.co.uk	—	All	All	—	—	—	—
Mirror.co.uk	—	—	—	—	—	—	—
Scotsman.com	—	—	Paid digital archive	Yes	—	—	Subscriber only
Telegraph.co.uk	—	—	—	Yes	—	Mixed free/paid	Paid
The Sun.co.uk	—	—	All	—	—	—	—
ThisisLondon.co.uk	—	—	—	Yes	—	—	—
The Times Online	—	—	All	Yes	Mixed free/paid	Mixed free/paid	Paid

Source: Compilation of Tables 1, 2 and 3 in Herbert and Thurman 2007, pp.215–20.

the paper's editions between 1817 and 1950 but costs £7.95 for one day (Herbert and Thurman 2007, pp.217–19). All but three of the selected online sites produce an electronic version of the printed newspaper, identical in terms of content, design and layout. These editions are cheap to produce, piggyback on the print edition, raise only modest revenues, but risk cannibalisation. Most papers offer free email alerts although *Guardian Unlimited* offers them as part of 'the Wrap', a daily news summary that costs £2 each month (Herbert and Thurman 2007, p.220). The rationale informing the offer of free email alerts is the ambition to increase site traffic and hence advertising. Online charges for services to mobile telephony signal a potential rather than actual market, but one in which customers are accommodated to paying. Services currently tend to target PDA users, who are typically more affluent, willing to pay and can be sold as a target group to advertisers. *The Times Online* charges for its crossword even though it generates only modest income, while other papers (from *Mirror.co.uk* to *FT.com*) prefer to offer readers crosswords and sudoku for free – again the ambition is to increase site traffic and increase advertising revenues. Finally, all online sites use the newspaper's valued brand to associate themselves with a range of goods and services from bingo, dating, music downloads, travel and cars to jobs, property and wine clubs. These services provide a growing income source for the sites ('20–30% or more each year' at *Guardian Unlimited*, for example) and also attract traffic (ibid., pp.221–2).

Herbert and Thurman conclude that all online papers are now charging for some elements of their services but typically they 'charge for what is unique to them … this unique content may vary between newspapers – the *Independent*'s star columnists, *The Times*'s crossword, the *Financial Times*'s business news and analysis – but the principle remains the same. As it is not available elsewhere newspapers feel able to charge for it' (ibid., p.223). Consequently, no papers are charging for general interest news since this is universally available. Moreover, newspapers believe that offering content for free makes business sense since this maximises traffic, enhances prospects for advertising and encourages the sale of commercial services online, which are the most rapidly expansive income stream. This is broadly the *Guardian Unlimited* model, which has proved highly influential (hAnluain 2004).

Local and regional newspapers confront similar challenges and opportunities in seeking to move online, remain profitable and sustain high quality journalism. Journalists' responses to company initiatives in one regional setting form the focus of the next section, although each of the four companies (Trinity Mirror, Newsquest, Johnston and Northcliffe) which dominate the local and regional press industry by their ownership of titles and control of circulations (Williams and Franklin 2007),[6] are investing in equipping newsrooms for the move online.

From journalists to 'cross-platform content providers': moving online in the regional setting

A circular distributed to journalists and editorial production workers at the Western Mail and Echo newsroom (Media Wales), part of the UK's largest regional newspaper group Trinity Mirror, set out the broad ambitions for the company's proposed transition to online working. 'To survive and thrive' the company needs:

> to respond swiftly to the emerging trends, both commercially and in terms of the journalism we produce. From the editorial viewpoint, that means rein-venting ourselves as a multimedia content provider ... by turning our print newsrooms into genuine multimedia hubs with our journalists producing content for a range of media. Our traditional media will continue to be vitally important, but video reports for publication on our websites, radio style podcasts and content directed at mobile phone users will become increasingly important elements in the content mix.
>
> (Western Mail and Echo 17 November 2006)

Journalists' responses to the proposed strategy have been mixed[7] reflecting, at least in part, recollections of the costly failure of an earlier attempt to move to multiple platform working in 2000, which prompted redundancies, severe finan-cial losses and a short-term cap of £10 million per annum for developing online projects (Hagerty 2001, p.27; Williams and Franklin 2007, pp.45–9). A recent study found that while journalists supported the company's new online strategy in principle, they opposed it in practice, or certain of its outcomes. Consequently, 86 per cent of journalists believed the future of journalism lies in multiple platform working which seeks creative and profitable synergies between print and online news services. Moreover, when asked if they were interested in undertaking train-ing to equip them with new skills in producing video journalism for news websites, respondents split almost evenly with 49 per cent saying 'yes' and 51 per cent saying 'no'. Journalists also believed there were benefits to be derived from such training including the acquisition of new skills (58%), enhancing their employa-bility (55%), increasing their potential for varied work (43%) and increasing their prospects for promotion (42%) (ibid., p.77).

Journalists, however, also expressed critical reservations about the feasibility of the strategy focusing their concerns on the availability of sufficient resources to implement the move online, the implications for journalists' existing and potentially increased workloads, the quality of the online news products, the adequacy of the training available to develop the new skills required for producing high quality video clips, as well as doubts about the prospects for additional remuneration.

Concerns about adequate resourcing of the online strategy were widespread, with 96 per cent of journalists suggesting that more appointments were necessary to meet the additional demands of working online; 88 per cent of journalists argued that these new posts would not be created. A local NUJ representative offered 'no principled objection to any of these developments' but entertained a 'very serious concern ... that nothing will be properly resourced' and that the move to multimedia, including journalists producing video clips for posting on the news site, will be achieved 'at the expense of the core products of this company which are its newspapers' (ibid., p.69).

Journalists were also worried about the implications for workloads: 84 per cent believed their workload had increased since they began working as a journalist, with 62 per cent suggesting it had increased 'considerably' (ibid. p.35); 84 per cent claimed they were already 'too busy' (ibid., p.77). Plans to remove journalists from the current leanly staffed newsrooms, and retrain them to work on video news-making, suggested those remaining would carry a heavier workload. 'It's not that they don't want to do it', a journalist confided, 'It's that they can't do it. They're just gonna say I've got 20 million other things to do, there aren't enough hours in the day' (ibid., p.72).

Journalists expressed twofold concerns about possible impacts on the quality of news. Moving journalists to work online would diminish the quality of the print editions, they argued, but additionally journalists were highly critical of the quality of some of the video materials they had seen posted on the company website, as well as the news sites of rival companies such as Johnston Press. Without considerable investment in training and equipment, the video news on the company site would compare poorly with the BBC Wales website, which, as a national broadcaster, offers 'very high quality content' because it has 'a load of people working on the website to produce its stories. People interested in getting up-to-the-minute news just tap into that ... and it's very well resourced' (ibid., p.73). Local journalists producing video for online also lack the time and skills necessary to produce sufficient materials to deadline, it was suggested, and resort to 'news subsidies' by 'lifting' pre-packed video clips from public relations and other sources. A journalist at Johnston's *Lancashire Evening Post* digital newsroom claimed 'quite a bit of CCTV and police stuff goes up if it's relevant and local'; while a journalist at a Newcastle newsroom confirmed that 'one thing that's becoming more popular on the website is using footage from ... *You Tube*... which you can just take and use on the site for free without any copyright implications. If you go to *You Tube* and type in Newcastle and come up with a fight that happened last week, you can just stick it straight on the website for nothing. Its quick and it doesn't take any effort' (ibid., p.84).

A further concern was that the company would not provide adequate training to equip print journalists for the move to online video working. NUJ National Official Jenny Lennox suggested journalists 'only get a few weeks training' but 'what can you learn about video journalism and editing video in that time' (ibid., p.97). Discussions with a number of journalism academics, who had been approached by the company to run a training programme, suggested Lennox's estimate was overly optimistic; the company's preference was to fund programmes of a week's duration. One journalism academic claimed, 'some of the training is happening at Howden ... the PA now organise their own training there and local papers can send their journalists down. It's very small scale, quick turnaround, very cheap indeed' (ibid., p.98).

Finally, journalists stressed that any additional workload and training should be rewarded with additional pay; 84 per cent of journalists cited the lack of additional pay as a disincentive to training for video work. 'It is necessary to use the internet to accompany print editions ... to survive in the future', a journalist acknowledged, 'but journalists, who are very underpaid already, should be given financial rewards for extra training and more staff should be employed, otherwise the future of journalism as a career is bleak' (ibid., p.76).

In summary, the move online for local and regional newspapers in particular settings has experienced opposition and criticism from journalists. While they support the move online in principle and consider it to be an essential development of printed newspapers' accommodation to changing technology and markets for news, they express concerns about the potentially damaging consequences of the move online for their workloads and pay, as well as broader concerns such as the impact on their daily newsgathering and reporting practices and the quality of news. Unless it is fully resourced with substantive capital investment in technology and staffing, the move online risks merely replicating the worst aspects of existing local journalism and newsmaking, with journalists increasingly obliged to rely on pre-packaged news subsidies to fill an ever growing news hole created by newspaper groups' demands for more stories with relatively fewer and less well-paid journalists. The need for local newspapers to move to multiple platform working to secure the future of these highly valued, long-standing archivists and chroniclers of local communities is evident, but it will require an investment in journalism as well as technology. An academic specialising in new media and convergence claimed:

> There's not a contradiction, between investing in journalism and investing in the web. I think they should put money into journalism but that journalists should not be platform specific. I think there should be better journalism and you do need to pay journalists more, but that doesn't mean that all they do is put out a newspaper. I think companies should pay journalists more money and pay them to learn to tell stories in a way that's going to reach more people.
>
> (ibid., p.106)

The book in outline

It is a pivotal moment in the history of newspapers. Some observers believe newspapers confront significant changes which challenge their very existence. But newspapers are not a dying breed, although they are metamorphosing under pressures of technological developments and operating in increasingly competitive markets for readers and revenues. Newspapers are experiencing fundamental changes to their formats and contents, their economic organisation and finance, the newsgathering and reporting practices of the journalists who deliver the news, as well as the technology employed to produce and distribute them. The simple understanding of a newspaper as 'news' printed on 'paper' offers a less credible and comprehensive account than a decade ago; it is already a contested concept in a multimedia environment. A key ambition of *Pulling Newspapers Apart* is therefore to take a series of still shots, to capture this moment of 'change, challenge and churn' in newspapers' history and to examine and analyse their editorial and design features towards the end of the first decade of the new millennium. But still images offer an illusion unless they are understood as part of a larger moving picture. Consequently, a second purpose for each chapter is to explore trends and developments, to provide a recent history of the particular editorial format or content which forms the focus for the chapter.

Consequently, *Pulling Newspapers Apart* explores the broad distinction between 'form' and 'content' in the context of UK national and local newspapers by offering detailed analysis of editorial formats (editorials, features, columns, and readers' letters), aspects of newspaper design (page layout, headlines, the emergence of the compact and Berliner editions), newspaper contents (sport, crime and politics), as well as the content of newspapers which is not generated by in-house journalists (advertising, agency copy and public relations materials). Individual chapters explore a particular constituent of newspapers' editorial content or design, focusing on those elements which previous texts have tended to neglect or to offer only marginal consideration. These include discussions of advice columns, cartoons, headlines, horoscopes, moral panics, obituaries, online editions, op-ed pages, photojournalism, royalty, sex and page3, supplements and television listings. Chapters are written by distinguished journalists and academics specialising in journalism and news media, but in an accessible if authoritative style. In brief, *Pulling Newspapers Apart* provides readers with an engaging, novel but comprehensive account of local and national newspapers alongside analysis of recent trends and developments in UK print journalism.

The most significant of these developments, the changing market for news and developments in media technology, which have proliferated platforms for the production and dissemination of news journalism, prompt reconsideration of fundamental questions for the analysis and practice of newspaper journalism such as: What is a Newspaper? Who is a Journalist? and What is a newspaper for? Readers will find a good deal of argument and evidence in *Pulling Newspapers Apart* to help them shape and assess their responses to these questions.

Notes

1   The nature of the *Metro* series of newspapers is uncertain. Associated Press identifies and brands the paper as a national title, while the Newspaper Society, which is the lobby organisation representing the interests of the local and regional press, recognises only the constituent titles (*Glasgow Metro*, *Yorkshire Metro*, etc.) and includes them in Society listings of regional titles.

2   The study was based on data derived from the annual accounts of companies registered with Companies House for 1985–2004 for the following newspaper groups: Express Newspapers Ltd (the *Daily Express*, the *Sunday Express*, the *Daily Star*, the *Daily Star Sunday*); The Financial Times Ltd (the *Financial Times*); MGN Ltd (*Daily Mirror*, and *Sunday Mirror*); News Group Newspapers Ltd (the *Sun* and *News of the World*); the Telegraph Group Ltd (the *Daily Telegraph*, the *Sunday Telegraph* and the *Weekly Telegraph*); Guardian Newspapers Ltd (*Guardian* and the *Observer*); Times Newspapers

Ltd (*The Times* and the *Sunday Times, TLS, THES, TES*); Associated Newspapers Ltd (the *Daily Mail*, the *Mail on Sunday*, the *Evening Standard*, the *Metro* and the *Ireland on Sunday*).

3   Survey questionnaires were distributed to 130 members of the Western Mail and Echo chapel and 51 replies (39.2%) were received and analysed for the study.

4   The study analysed domestic news coverage in a sample of two comprehensive single weeks (one in late March and a second in late April 2005) in the four quality UK newspapers – the *Guardian*, the *Independent*, *The Times* and the *Telegraph*, as well as the mid-market *Daily Mail*. BBC and ITV evening news programmes as well as Radio 4's *Today* programme and *The World at One* were also analysed. A total of 2,609 items of news coverage were analysed.

5   Even the most ardent enthusiasts of online journalism betray their essentially defensive ambitions for multiple platform working. Dan Bradley, Vice President of News, Media and General Broadcast Group, for example, titles his essay in support of online media 'Convergence: A survival strategy for local media' (*Journalism Studies* 2003, vol. 4 no. 4, p.518).

6   Johnston Press bought Archant Scotland in April 2007. The four largest of the 87 existing local newspaper groups now own 912 (70%) of the 1,303 local press titles. The largest 20 groups own 96.5% of the market by circulation (Newspaper Society 2007 www.newspapersoc.org.uk/default.aspx?page+g. Accessed 6 August 2007).

7   A study of the implementation of Trinity Mirror's (Media Wales since November 2007) 2006 online strategy involved distributing questionnaires to 130 members of the Western Mail and Echo NUJ chapel, interviewing local journalists, academics and trades unionists, as well as studying company records. Fifty-one (40%) of journalists responded to the survey and percentages are based on these responses (Williams and Franklin 2007).

References

Addis, R. (2006) 'Newspaper Free-For-All' *Media Guardian* 11 September, p.1.

Allan, S. (2006) *Online News* Maidenhead: Open University Press.

Allen, K. (2007) 'Guardian Media Group Seek Acquisitions as Profits rise by 47%' *Guardian* 2 August, p.27.

Aspinall, C. (2005) 'The News Monopoly' *Free Press* No. 144 January/February 2005, p.2.

Audit Bureau of Circulation (ABC) June (2007) www.ABC.org.uk/cgi-bin/nov/abc. Accessed 7 November 2007.

Audit Bureau of Circulation (ABC) July (2007) www.ABC.org.uk/cgi-bin/nov/abc. Accessed 7 November 2007.

Barkham, P. (2006) 'Giving It All Away' *Guardian* G2 22 September, pp.12–16.

Barriaux, M. (2006) 'FT To Shed 51 Journalists in Merger of Print and Website' *Guardian* 12 July, p.28.

Berry, D. (2005) 'News Shouldn't Be A Free Ride' *British Journalism Review* vol. 16 no. 2, pp.55–9.

Bhaskar, B. R. P. (2005) 'Flourishing Papers, Floundering Craft: The Press and the Law' in Rajan, N. (Ed.) *Practising Journalism* New Delhi: Sage of India, pp.19–36.

Bilton, J. (2007) 'Freesheet Fiasco Compromises the Press's Image' *Media Guardian* 21 May, p.11.

Bivens, R. (2008) 'The Internet, Mobile Phones And Blogging: How New Media are Transforming Traditional Journalism' *Journalism Practice* vol. 2 no. 1.

Bleyen, V. A. and Van Hove, L. (2007) 'To Bundle or Not To Bundle? How Western European Newspapers Price their Online Content'. Unpublished paper presented to the 'Future of Newspapers' conference, Cardiff School of Journalism, Media and Cultural Studies, Cardiff University 12–13 September.

Blumler, J. G. and Gurevitch, M. (1995) *The Crisis in Public Communication* London: Routledge.

Bradley, D. (2003) 'Convergence: A Survival Strategy for Local Media' *Journalism Studies* vol. 4 no. 4 pp.518–22.

Cronkite, W. (1997) 'More Bad News' *Guardian* 27 January, p.2.

Crosbie, V. (2004) 'What Newspapers and their Websites Must Do To Survive' *Online Journalism Review* 4 March www.ojr.org/ojr/business/1078349998.php. Accessed 10 January 2007.

Dalzotto, C. (2007) 'New Business Models for Newspaper Publishing Companies'. Unpublished paper presented to the 'Future of Newspapers' conference, Cardiff School of Journalism, Media and Cultural Studies, Cardiff University 12–13 September.

Davis, A. (2002) *Public Relations Democracy: Public Relations, Politics and the Mass Media in Britain* London: Routledge.

Dear, J. (2006) 'Put People Before Profits' *Guardian* 2 January, p.8.

Deuze, M. (2007) *Mediawork* Cambridge: Polity Press.

Deuze, M., Bruns, A. and Neuberger, C. (2007) 'Preparing for an Age of Participatory News' in *Journalism Practice* vol. 1 no. 3, pp.322–38.

Economist (2006a) 'Who Killed The Newspaper?' 24 August www.economist.com/opinion/cfm?story_id=7830218. Accessed 10 January 2007.

Economist (2006b) 'More Media, Less News' 24 August www.economist.co/opinion/printer-friendly.cfrm?story_id+7827135. Accessed 10 January 2007.

Fletcher, K. (2006) 'The Web Trail' *Media Guardian* 12 June, p.7.

Franklin, B. (1986) 'Public Relations, the Local Press and the Coverage of Local Government' *Local Government Studies*, pp.25–33.

Franklin, B. (1988) *Public Relations Activities In Local Government* London: Charles Knight Ltd.

Franklin, B. (1997) *Newszak and News Media* London: Arnold.

Franklin, B. (2004) *Packaging Politics: Political Communications in Britain's Media Democracy* London: Arnold.

Franklin, B. (2006) (Ed.) *Local Journalism and Local Media: Making the Local News* London: Routledge.

Frost, C. (2004) 'The Press Complaints Commission: A Study of Ten Years of Adjudications on Press Complaints' *Journalism Studies*, vol. 5 no. 1 pp.101–14.

Gans, H. (1979) *Deciding What's News* London: Constable.

Goodhart, G. and Wintour, P. (1986) *Eddie Shah and the Newspaper Revolution* London: Coronet Books.

Greenslade, R. (2003) *Press Gang: How Newspapers Make Profits from Propaganda* Basingstoke: Macmillan.

Greenslade, R. (2004) 'The Great Pay Divide' *Guardian* 6 December, p.9.

Greenslade, R. (2005) 'Murdoch Versus Murdoch' *Media Guardian* 7 February, pp.2–4.

Hagerty, B. (2001) 'Amiable Ulsterman at Trinity Mirror' *British Journalism Review* vol. 12, pp.15–28.

Hamer, M. (2000) 'The Press Association At Work.' Unpublished MA Thesis, Liverpool John Moores University, Liverpool.

hAnluain, D. O. (2004) 'Free Content Becoming Thing of the Past for UK's Online Newspaper Sites' *Online Journalism Review* 13 February http:www.209.200.80.136/ojr/business/1067472919.php. Accessed 10 January 2007.

Harrison, S. (2006) 'Local Government Public Relations and the Local Press' in Franklin, B. (Ed.) *Local Journalism and Local Media: Making the Local News* London: Routledge, pp.175–88.

Herbert, J. and Thurman, N. (2007) 'Paid Content Strategies for News Websites: An Empirical Study of British Newspapers' Online Business Strategies' *Journalism Practice* vol. 1 no. 2, pp.208–26.

Hobsbawm, J. (2005) *Where The Truth Lies: Trust and Morality in PR and Journalism* London: Atlantic Books.

Internet Advertising Bureau (2007) 'Online Advertising Spend' http://www.iabuk.net/en/1/iabadspend2006.mxs. Accessed 10 January 2007.

Journalism Training Forum (2002) *Journalists at Work: Their Views on Training, Recruitment and Conditions* London: NTO/Skillset.

Kaplan, J. (2003) 'Convergence: Not a Panacea' *Journalism Studies* vol. 4 no. 4, pp.515–18.

Keating, M. (2006) 'Young, Gifted and Hacks' *Media Guardian* 13 November, p.6.

Kiss, J. and Brook, S. (2007) 'Another Month, Another Painful Fall' *Media Guardian* 11 June, p.9.

Lewis, J., Williams, A., Franklin, B., Thomas, J. and Mosdell, N. (2006) *The Quality and Independence of British Journalism* Cardiff University, Cardiff.

McManus, J. (1994) *Market Driven Journalism* London and New York: Sage.

McNair, B. (1994) *News and Journalism in the UK* London: Routledge.

Maloney, K. (2006) *Rethinking Public Relations* London: Routledge.

Marr, A. (2004) *My Trade: A Short History of British Journalism* Basingstoke: Macmillan.

Martinson, J. (2005) 'Yorkshire Post Survives the Wringer' *Guardian* 14 June, p.18.

Meeke, K. (2005) 'The Short Listing of Metro as the National Newspaper of the Year Has Been Controversial' *Press Gazette* 4 March http://www.pressgazette.co.uk/article/030305. Accessed 10 January 2007.

Mensing, D. and Rejfek, J. (2005) 'Prospects For Profit: The (Un) Evolving Business Model for Online News' Paper presented to the 6th International Symposium on Online Journalism, Austin, Texas, 9 April.

Meyer, P. (2004) *The Vanishing Newspaper: Saving Journalism in the Information Age* Columbia and London: University of Missouri Press.

Mintel (2005) *Regional Newspapers* London: The Newspaper Society.

Newspaper Society (2005) www.newspapersoc.org.uk/default.asp?page=10. Accessed 10 January 2007.

Newspaper Society (2006) www.newspapersoc.org.uk/default.aspx?page=1227. Accessed 10 January 2007.

Nguyen, A. (2008) 'Facing "The Fabulous Monster": The Traditional Media's Fear-driven Innovation Culture in the Development of Online News' *Journalism Studies* vol. 9 no. 1.

O'Connor, C. and O'Neill, D. (2007) 'The Passive Journalist: How Sources Dominate Local News'. Unpublished paper presented to the 'Future of Newspapers' conference, Cardiff School of Journalism, Media and Cultural Studies, Cardiff University 12–13 September.

Pilling, R. (2006) 'Local Journalists and the Local Press: Waking up to Change' in Franklin, B. (Ed.) *Local Journalism and Local Media: Making the Local News* London: Routledge, pp.104–14.

Pinker, R. (2006) 'Regulating the Local Press' in Franklin, B. (Ed.) *Local Journalism and Local Media: Making the Local News* London: Routledge, pp.115–26.

Ponsford, D. (2006) 'Q: How Many Journalists Do You Need To Run A National Newspaper?' *Press Gazette* 17 November, p.1.

Preston, P. (2006) 'The Future of Newspapers'. Lecture in the Reporters and Reported Series, delivered at Cardiff School of Journalism, Media and Cultural Studies, Cardiff University, 10 November.

Reich, Z. (2006) 'The Process Model of News Initiative: Sources Lead First, Journalists Thereafter' *Journalism Studies* vol. 7 no. 4, pp.497–514.

Rosen, J. (2006) 'PressThink weblog' 27 June http://journalism.nyu.edu/pubzone/weblogs/pressthink/2006/06/27/ppl_frmr.html. Accessed 10 January 2007.

Rusbridger, A. (2005) 'What Are Newspapers For?' The Inaugural Hugo Young Lecture, University of Sheffield, 9 March.

Rusbridger, A. (2007) 'Napoleon To Iraq, and Still Going Strong' *Guardian* 11 June, pp.1–2.

Sampson, A. (1996) 'The Crisis at the Heart of Our Media' *British Journalism Review* vol. 7 no. 3, pp.42–56.

Silver, J. (2007) 'No One Listens to Podcasts: An Interview with Simon Kelner' *Media Guardian* 19 March, p.5.

Singer, J. (2006) 'The Socially Responsible Existentialist: A Normative Emphasis for Journalists in a New Media Environment' *Journalism Studies* vol. 7 no. 1, pp.2–18.

Thelen, G. (2003) 'For Convergence' *Journalism Studies* vol. 4 no. 4, pp.513–15.

Thomas, L. (2006) '"Website Must Come Second" says Independent's Kelner' *Press Gazette* 20 July www.pressgazette.co.uk/article/200706/independent_website_second. Accessed 10 January 2007.

Tunstall, J. (1971) *Journalists At Work* London: Constable.

Wainwright, M. (2005) 'The New Heart Of British Journalism' *Guardian* 20 September, p.25.

Wasserman, H. (2007) 'Attack of the Killer Newspapers! The "Tabloid Revolution" and the Future of Newspapers in South Africa'. Unpublished paper presented to the 'Future of Newspapers' conference, Cardiff School of Journalism, Media and Cultural Studies, Cardiff University 12–13 September.

White, J. and Hobsbawm, J. (2007) 'Public Relations and Journalism: The Unquiet Relationship – A View from the United Kingdom' *Journalism Practice* vol. 1 no. 2, pp.283–92.

Wilby, P. (2005) 'Foreign News A Distant Memory' *Media Guardian* 25 July, p.9.

Williams, A. and Franklin, B. (2007) *Turning Around The Tanker: Implementing Trinity Mirror's Online Strategy* Cardiff University, Cardiff.

Williams, F. (1957) *Dangerous Estate: The Anatomy of Newspapers* London: Longmans, Green and Co.

World Association of Newspapers (2007) 'Newspaper Circulation Rises Worldwide' 8 May www.wan-press.org/print.php3?id_article=14032ÿ§. Accessed 22 May 2007.

Part I

Editorial formats

Chapter 1

News

Jackie Harrison

Introduction

Communicating the news through newspapers has faced constant challenges. From the early seventeenth century to today (in the UK) these challenges have ranged across widespread illiteracy, poor transport and communication networks, active oppression and censorship, burdensome tax regimes, technological constraints and innovations, the concentration of ownership, commercialisation, government meddling, competition from other media and most recently declining circulations and advertising revenues associated with changing news consumption habits. Equally newspapers have, throughout this period, constantly changed their understanding of what is judged to be newsworthy and adopted different ways of telling people the news. Today there coexist different news forms which utilise modes of expression that range from the formal to the vernacular, the serious to the irreverent, the conservative to the progressive and the neutral to the partisan (with some too tendentious to allow easy definition). All of which are pursued in the name of anticipating a newspaper's readers' needs and interests. To be blunt, the category of 'news' in the UK press constantly evades a concise single definition of what it is and what form it takes.

Pulling newspaper news apart

To begin with the obvious, reporting the news for a newspaper has always necessitated the commercial management of time with issues of design and space. The former in terms of deadlines and of being 'ahead' of a competitor, the latter in terms of the particular layout and 'look and feel' of the newspaper. While the former is a concern for the latest, or at least a distinctive version of a news event, the latter reflects the fact that newspaper news coexists with other forms of content: photos, graphics, features, television guides, motoring information, columns, fashion pages, lifestyle articles, cartoons, crosswords, sport and so on and must sit aside advertisements. All of which combine to ensure that today's newspapers are anything but papers solely about news. To accommodate this variety of content newspapers are divided into different editorial formats or 'books'. Newspaper news is one type of editorial format, which can and does take different forms.

Usually newspapers and their associated form of news are described using a conventional taxonomy which operates according to four different types: (1) newspapers, which are variously referred to as positioned upmarket, also known as broadsheet or qualities (this now includes compacts and Berliner midi-sizes); (2) those which are positioned as middle market also known as popular or black tops; (3) those which are positioned downmarket also known as tabloid or red tops; and (4) those which position themselves as alternative to the mainstream (Atton 2002) and typically refer to themselves as radical, underground or, under special circumstances, samizdat.[1] Unfortunately these four types are each subject to different interpretations, to hybridisation (for example, 'broadloid') and to disagreements over what is being described and what exactly is being referred to; they are not the best guide to newspaper news forms. I suggest a different taxonomy consisting of three generic newspaper news forms: discursive, descriptive and tendentious.

Importantly, a discursive newspaper form is not *exclusively* the preserve of upmarket newspapers, a descriptive form of middle market newspapers and a tendentious form of downmarket newspapers or alternative newspapers. I do not offer arguments that slavishly stereotype each newspaper, or type of newspaper, with only one news form. Rather these terms are used to describe news forms per se. In short, all newspapers can and do regularly change their news forms according to the news events they are covering. This flexible way of telling the news across all newspapers can appear (especially to those concerned with news journalism standards) as a narrowing of some of the traditional differences between newspapers, a point that overlooks the fact that newspapers have retained their own distinctive approach and identity.

Three forms of newspaper news: discursive, descriptive and tendentious

News events are rarely straightforward; they are usually ambiguous and reflect different histories and competing spatial stories and are reported from a particular perspective. Perspective is a way of interpreting the news based upon the claim (made by all newspapers) to both represent and speak for their readers whose worldview they have adopted or try to anticipate. It is in accordance with this worldview that the news is subsequently presented.

With regard to news in the UK there are two dominant versions of the readers' worldview adopted by newspapers. First, a Burkean kind of perspective, which consists of a traditionalist worldview, is inherently conservative and claims 'common sense' as its principal virtue. Second, a Lockean kind of perspective, which consists of a worldview based on a belief in contractual politics and civic mindedness, combined with a sense of activism and protest. It is in accordance to either one of these worldviews that newspapers, to borrow a phrase from Hayek, judge their readers' concern for issues of 'law, legislation and liberty' in the context of a particular news event (Hayek 1973–9). This is not a simple right/left distinction, as recent political history shows, but is essentially how newspapers judge a particular news event and its subsequent relevance to its readers' interests. Because of the diversity of the UK press no one news event is reported exclusively or independently according to one worldview.

The discursive form of news

Consider the following:

> We are not there to bat for one side or the other, but to report on the situation on the ground as we find it. But it makes no sense to report events in isolation from one another, so we strive to place stories within a narrative thread, to provide context to events.

> I also owe (almost everything) to those committed journalists, commentators and others who have done so much to bridge the gap between my desk and the world I have tried to present in these pages. Part of my purpose has been to try to work out what it is possible to know about 'there' from 'here.' These essays are not frontline reports; I can't claim the privilege of presence. But then few of us can: so how are we to make sense of events that take place around the world in which we are like it or not, involved and implicated? Part of the answer is to do with critical reading but that in turn, is impossible without critical reporting and writing

The two quotes – the former from Harriet Sherwood (2006, p.14) at the time of writing the *Guardian*'s Foreign Editor, the latter from the social and human geographer Derek Gregory (2004, p.xvii, but also see Fred Inglis 2002, p.3) – span what I mean by a discursive form of news reporting: critical narrative. This is a form of news that is often said (incorrectly) to be exclusively the preserve of those newspapers described as upmarket, broadsheet or qualities. Essentially for this form, news stories are serious, well researched or sourced, offer analysis and commentary, use experts and are written by specialists. They are independent of 'official versions of events' often seeking to expose the limited character of 'official accounts' and follow what I have described elsewhere (Harrison 2007) as the logic of question and answer, in which the complex and ambiguous nature of a news event and the way it is officially reported can be addressed, understood and challenged. With this remit discursive news reports are often concerned with a critical relationship to political authority. It is also this form of news, referring to the continuing contemporary use of the phrase 'Fourth Estate' and which originally Carlyle (1901, p.152), following Burke, found so admirable.

Discursive news tends to describe itself as covering a hard news agenda that includes as its staple national and international political and economic affairs. It is historically grounded in a tradition of such coverage since *The Times*, originally called *The Daily Universal Register*, was established in 1788. Also it is a news form which is comfortable with intellectual or technical issues and is written for a readership perceived to be capable of understanding and following an argument. A readership therefore assumed to be intelligent and educated, people who do not require that everything be explained to them. The language is of equals talking to equals. And the claim (and some would argue the true value of this news form) is that this type of news serves the public interest, helps sustain civil society and its independence from government, and supports the public sphere of democratic debate. It is the home of news written by journalist intellectuals which, to borrow an idea from Bourdieu (1998, p.74), but not his analysis, exists between 'academic esotericism and journalism "exotericism"', or in the more readily understandable phrase of C. W. Mills, journalists who possess a 'sociological imagination' (1970, p.21), or more mundanely of scholarly hacks (adapted from Hastings 2004).

The descriptive form of news

The descriptive form of news is in one instance neutral and in another reflects and displays support for one of the two worldviews outlined above: to take them in order.

The neutral descriptive news form is expressed by C. P. Scott's (1921) dictum, 'Comment is free, but facts are sacred',[2] a view that only makes sense alongside the requirement to be able to obtain the facts and then in a clear and intelligible way report them. Thus according to the descriptive and neutral form of news, the most complex events are expressed in terms of a deliberate reductionism, of complexity to simplicity, achieved by a process of paring down a news event to its core or essential facts. With the neutral descriptive news form news journalism seeks to be reporting without comment or opinion. In this way news journalism achieves one of its most valuable functions, to simply describe events as they are and not as one would like them to be or approve of. In this it is the opposite of tendentious news (see below) and is profoundly antithetical to propaganda. The neutral descriptive news form is usually short, derived as it is from a bulletin style of expression. Sometimes it is referred to as news in brief (nibs), one paragraph long, or it consists of no more than a few paragraphs. At its best, neutral descriptive news is instructive. In essence, short, neutral descriptive news bulletins of events are used when the reader is perceived as requiring no more than a minimum report or accurate summary, or when an event is deemed less important than others. Newspapers use neutral descriptive news of the shorter kind to a lesser or greater extent. See, for example, the 'World Bulletin' in the *Daily Telegraph* and the 'Briefing' or 'World News Digest' in the *Financial Times*.

Occasionally the neutral descriptive news form is long, and is written in an accessible, direct and basically informative way. It may use verbatim quotes, a section from a report or public document, or a transcript (for example, the *Sun*'s 'Friendly Fire' Transcript of the cockpit video 6 February 2007). In its longer version it often relies on supporting the detail provided and compiled with graphics and photographs. For example, the front page of the *Independent* on 6 February 2007 provided a detailed graphic showing the amount and different types of deaths suffered in the Iraq War over 31 days. Accurate description is central to all that this form of news claims to achieve, since the guiding motif is that the facts must speak for themselves and that once we are in possession of these facts we are equipped to know what is going on and, if motivated to do so, then find out about the situation they describe. Often this further detail is supplied within the newspaper itself.

This does not mean that the descriptive news form (especially in its longer version) is always neutral. Letting the facts speak for themselves also produces news reports which are evaluative and judgemental. As noted above, newspapers in the UK claim to represent and speak for their readers in accordance with either a Burkean or Lockean perspective. The former is depicted as belonging to middle England: England's quiet and silent majority, or in the words of G. K. Chesterton (1874–1936), *The Secret People*, 'But we are the people of England; and we have not spoken yet'.[3] The latter is depicted as consisting of a progressively conscientious, motivated and urban citizenry capable of various forms of political and social activism. It is via these different perspectives that newspapers select and choose the facts, which combine to form a descriptive news report. For example, on the 2 February 2007 *The Times* ran a story in which the readers are told that, 'Adultery in the Archers is a scandal too far as 200,000 listeners switch off'. The story is backed up with plenty of facts and figures supplied by RAJAR (Radio Joint Audience Research Ltd) and reflects a traditionalism and moral propriety that any conservative would approve of. On the same day the *Independent*'s front page provides a detailed graphic on the types and number of deaths in Iraq in January, from which the reader is directed to longer news reports full of facts and figures, the call to protest at the Iraq War is palpable. Both stories are factual, descriptive and accurate and yet both ensure that the particular worldview of their readers is reaffirmed. This is not dishonestly or surreptitiously undertaken; rather it is the employment of a perspective, which is judged to be one that serves the readers' real and genuine interests and needs.

Unfortunately the use of perspective in the name of readers' worldviews and their interests can easily become attenuated (or distorted) into a tendentious news form, which while making the claim to serve the interests of the public, is in fact more interested in advocacy, sensationalism and entertainment.

The tendentious form of news

The movement away from the descriptive forms of news is most clearly manifest when news becomes the direct advocacy of a specific cause (to be distinguished from the consistent interpretation of news from a certain perspective and subsequent worldview), or offers to explain events in terms solely of the personal, so-called human interest stories. These promote the view that to show people as they are in their personal lives is to reveal the true motives or causes for events being as they are.

Tendentious news based upon the direct advocacy of a specific cause adopts a campaigning and universalistic style – it is aimed at persuading everyone. Thus, the *Daily Express* ran a campaign entitled 'New Inheritance Tax Crusade' (2 February 2007, pp.1 and 9). A crusading style is one that at one time or another is taken up by almost all newspapers. When a newspaper campaigns it is obvious: the cause is clearly and stridently announced, the paper seeks to actively elicit support, devotes prominent positions in the paper to its advocacy and opts for a didactic tone. Campaigns in newspapers have a long history and can range from the high minded and well intentioned, to the sentimental and mawkish, and the genuinely unpleasant. Campaigns can have mixed effects. The campaign by the *News of the World* since 2000 for a law, popularly referred to as 'Sarah's Law', to allow public access to the Sex Offenders Register, also resulted in hundreds of residents taking to the streets of an estate in Portsmouth to protest against suspected paedophiles living in the area. The 'Naming and Shaming' campaign was discontinued as the public began to act as vigilantes and attack innocent people.

Tendentious news based upon human interest stories marks the point where, for some, news today concentrates on the extremes of human behaviour and experience (Conboy 2006). As such the tendentious form of news is becoming more and more sensational, wrapped in entertainment values, or just ridiculously trivial and is increasingly defined through prurience, salaciousness, voyeurism and celebrity. It adopts an overtly sensational style and is usually associated (though not exclusively) with those newspapers which are positioned downmarket and are known as tabloid or red tops. When a newspaper deals in human interest stories in a tendentious way it often relies on 'emotive language, the bizarre, the lewd, sex, suppression fees, cheque book journalism, gossip, police news, marriage and divorce, royal news, celebrities, political bias and any form of prurience which can be included under the general heading of human interest' (Conboy 2006, p.12) and one could also add, unlawful attempts at phone tapping, entrapment and 'stings'. News in the form of human interest stories requires of the reader nothing more than a response of moral approval or moral disapproval. This successful commercial formula has led to charges of increasing trivialisation and 'tabloidisation', and a way of speaking to the reader as someone who should be engaged solely at the emotive level. The end result is called 'junk food news' (i.e. of no value whatsoever). The fact that this form of tendentious news is a commercial success has ensured its continued promotion and any talk of 'drinking at the last chance saloon'[4] now seems risible.

Charges against the tendentious news form per se are not new. Writing in 1939 R. G. Collingwood argued that Victorian news values, which consisted of 'full and accurate information about matters of public concern', were corrupted by the *Daily Mail*, 'the first English newspaper for which the word "news" lost its old meaning of facts which a reader ought to know if he was to vote intelligently' (1939, p.155).

Newspapers, news forms and convergence

Today's newspapers are no longer just that, they are now often referred to as platforms horizontally integrated into other platforms. The current mantra (or fiat) of newspaper management is convergence and 'smart publishing'. Both, it is said, create efficiencies and value in the gathering, management and distribution of newspaper news. Consequently the current emphasis is that once a news story has been gathered it will be given the widest possible distribution across other platforms. It is a newspaper management strategy for survival and is grounded in the fact that the 'media' are increasingly converging (little is stand alone) and the term media is now so extended as to include:

> the globalized, the regional, the national, the local, the personal media; the broadcast and interactive media; the audio and audio visual and the printed media; the electronic and the mechanical, the digital and the analogue media; the big screen and the small screen media; the dominant and alternative media; the fixed and the mobile, the convergent and the stand alone media.
>
> (Silverstone 2007, p.5)

It is from this new and constantly evolving media environment that the persistent demand for the further and further integration of newspaper news and other content, to acquire a multi-platform presence, is made. Old separations we are confidently told are now redundant.

Unless newspapers become horizontally integrated, other news outlets remain competitors. In the gathering, management and distribution of news any stand-alone newspaper now faces increased competition from expanding national and local radio news, 24-hour television news, ultra local television news, news services on mobile telephones, internet news sites, electronic billboards, free newspapers, citizen journalists, bloggers and podcasters, and as if that were not enough, online editions of their own paper editions. The result of this is that revenue sources (such as classified ads) are increasingly migrating to the internet, with the result that many newspapers are cutting back on staff and their own internal newsgathering capacity. So what of the future for news in newspapers? The current view is that newspapers must train or employ multi-skilled news journalists who can produce stories that fit the requirements of different platforms. Needless to say there are two schools of thought: one, this is the end of newspaper news as we have known it; the other, this is the salvation of news across all platforms including newspapers.

To illustrate this debate I shall take the example of the *Manchester Evening News*, a regional newspaper, now part of MEN Media. MEN Media describe themselves as horizontally integrated and this integration is served by a central core of news journalists who are adept at writing for print and for the electronic media. They occupy a 'news hub' which houses staff writing for their television channel, Channel M, their online team, a print news desk and a chief sub-editor, while a core decision-making team sits in the centre. The 'news hub' is shaped like a doughnut and is nothing like the layout of a traditional newsroom. To rationalise the use of shared resources and address the problem of their duplication, MEN Media adopted protocols for sharing archives, information and attendance at an event. At the same time they challenged the ingrained tendency among print journalists to protect exclusives. Now greater consideration is given to where, when and how to break a news story.

A news story, which might have been a front page exclusive for the *Manchester Evening News*, may well be broken at 9pm on Channel M and the MEN Media website, thereby ensuring that competitors cannot run with the late story before the *Manchester Evening News* prints it the following day. Each platform carries different aspects of the story to ensure cross-promotion and retain reader/viewer interest. In this way the three platforms (television, web and newspaper) seek to reinforce each other. However, the 'media neutral reporting pool' still has a natural skew towards writing for print, and currently when news journalists face a deadline they become increasingly single skilled.

The expectation is twofold: first, news journalists will be able to deal with all media and be truly multi-skilled, and second, fewer and better news reporters will be recruited. It is too early to tell if this type of newspaper-led convergence will be the salvation of newspapers. Certainly newspaper news is changing, but then as I said in the introduction, its history is one of adapting to technological, economic and social change.

Conclusion

The editorial format for newspaper news can assume one of three forms: discursive, descriptive and tendentious. And, as noted above, these three forms of newspaper are to varying degrees found in all our newspapers (sometimes in the same edition). These news forms do not provide us with a strict correspondence to the traditional taxonomy of newspapers. As such they are the news forms of today's UK newspapers as they compete for readers and revenues.

As for the future, it seems as if newspaper newsgathering, management and distribution will continue to converge, increasingly so, as competition for readers and revenues intensifies. But, as I have said before (Harrison 2007), news journalism reporting is also dominated by the practical considerations of conforming to rigid limits. This is so for no other reason than news journalism is always a practical activity governed by the limitations imposed upon itself by its own platform for expression. The question now is if these platforms for expression continue to converge what will be the impact on the current newspaper-centred news forms? For better or worse will we have more scope for discursive news? Will there be a greater use of short form descriptive news bulletins? Or will the ascendancy of tendentious human interest news stories continue? Whatever the answers may prove to be, one thing I remain convinced of is the survival of newspapers and therefore of all three news forms therein.

Notes

1 A borrowed term used to describe an alternative publication. The original samizdat consisted of the secret copying and distribution of censored material during the Communist regime of Russia.
2 I should say only partially expressed, since in the same essay in the *Manchester Guardian* centenary edition May 1921, he also recognised the role of editorial comments as fairness and went on to recommend good newspaper business practices. Nonetheless, the dictum stands as a leitmotif for the descriptive form of newspaper news.
3 These words have become persistently quoted expressions of English identity and used to support a wide variety of positions, mainly associated with protecting English rural values and a nostalgic version of English identity.
4 The phrase was used by David Mellor, the Secretary of State for National Heritage 9 April–24 September 1992, following calls by MPs for curbs to be placed on the activities of certain elements of the press.

References

Atton, C. (2002) *Alternative Media* London: Sage.
Bourdieu, P. (1998) *On Television and Journalism* London: Pluto Press.
Carlyle, T. (1901) *On Heroes and Hero Worship* London: Chapman and Hall.
Chesterton, G. K. (1927) 'The Secret People' in *The Collected Poems of G. K. Chesterton* London: Cecil Palmer, pp.157–60.
Collingwood, R. G. (1939) *An Autobiography* London: Oxford University Press.
Conboy, M. (2006) *Tabloid Britain* London: Routledge.
Gregory, D. (2004) *The Colonial Present* Oxford: Blackwell Publishing.
Gripsrud, J. (2000) 'Tabloidization, Popular Journalism and Democracy' in Sparks, C. and Tulloch, J. (Eds) *Tabloid Tales: Global Debates Over Media Standards* Lanham, MD: Rowman and Littlefield Publishers Inc, pp.285–300.
Harrison, J. (2006) *News* London: Routledge.
Harrison, J. (2007) 'Critical Foundations and Directions for the Teaching of News Journalism' *Journalism Practice* vol. 1 no. 2, pp.175–99.
Hastings, M. (2004) 'Hacks and Scholars: Allies of a Kind' in Cannadine, D. (Ed.) *History and the Media* Basingstoke: Palgrave Macmillan, pp.103–17.
Hayek, F. A. (1973, 1976 and 1979) *Law, Legislation and Liberty* 3 vols London: Routledge and Kegan Paul.
Inglis, F. (2002) *People's Witness* New Haven and London: Yale University Press.
Mills, C. W. (1970) *The Sociological Imagination* Harmondsworth: Penguin.
Scott, C. P. (1921) *Manchester Guardian Centenary Edition*, May.
Sherwood, H. (2006) 'News Coverage' in *Living Our Values: Social, Ethical and Environmental Audit* London: The Guardian Media Group.
Silverstone, R. (2007) *Media and Morality: On the Rise of the Mediapolis* Cambridge: Polity Press.

Chapter 2

Features

Sarah Niblock

What are features for? At first glance, that seems a trite question as features have been an integral part of newspapers for 250 years. Without the need of a hard news 'hook', features take the reader behind the headlines; they can amuse, infuriate, stimulate and inform. They offer a contrast in tone and length to the news coverage at the front of the newspaper, allowing the reader space to reflect on issues of import and whimsy, and to engage in opinion as they are confronted by a wide range of voices. As such, they tend to be written with a great deal more stylistic freedom and in a variety of different formats to news, with its inverted pyramid model of informational hierarchies. Their purpose seems obvious, which is why almost all analyses of features have centred upon the 'how-tos' of journalism practice, coaching students on the various methods of intro/outro construction, peaks and troughs and in-depth interviewing.

But does that normative view of the function of newspaper features sufficiently explain the role that features play in contemporary newspapers? Far from being buried in the centre pages of newspapers, features permeate the whole edition from as early as page 3, once the preserve of pithy news coverage. Today, readers are as likely to be confronted by a feature on British pagan relics (the *Guardian* Monday 5 February 2007) on turning over the first page as they are the latest dispute over health service reforms. Whereas the feature content of newspapers might have been less than 10 per cent in the 1750s, now it can be argued that some papers' feature content stretches to 70 per cent. Richard Wallace, Editor of the UK's third best-selling national daily newspaper, the *Daily Mirror*, recently announced that his strategy is to make the paper more like a magazine with predominantly feature coverage. He said: 'It's no secret that I have taken the *Mirror* down a more magazine-style road, and skew a degree of content to the 35-plus working woman' (Wallace 2007). In order to understand the rationale and effect of these changes, we need to analyse the *function* of the newspaper feature rather than its form.

Some of the recent developments in features, evident across all market sectors, include:

- new themes and categories of features, such as the shift from women's pages to lifestyle (Harp 2006), that reflect the increasingly consumer- and advertiser-driven approach to content;

- the 'featurisation' of news, whereby writers use feature-style techniques to cover 'hard' news stories;
- emerging techniques of feature writing, which embrace 'new journalism' approaches of immersionism and foregrounding emotion over facts.

These developments are not so easily explained by a view of features that focuses upon the format alone. The choice of content and presentational format is inter-linked with a range of contextual factors that ensure the feature plays an integral part in the commercial viability of the newspaper product. Joseph C. Manzella (2002) has shown how 'the lineage of contemporary cultures of writing includes the English essayists, the muckrakers and the new journalism of the 1960s ... often (they) were concerned with the details of everyday life and with the exposition of socio-cultural issues' (Manzella 2002, p.34).

But while their antecedents were working somewhat in contradiction with journalism norms and conventions, contemporary feature writers are very much part of the machinery of the newspaper operation. Jane Taylor (2005, pp.118–19) identifies the tensions between the feature writer's perceived freedom to adopt a more literary and subjective form of writing set against the precisely defined parameters of market-driven journalism business:

> Each has a precisely defined readership determined, to a very large extent, by advertisers seeking likely buyers for their goods and services. For any features section, it is the delivery of readers to lucrative advertisers that keeps the publication afloat, which is where genre identification (in the sense of leading writers to an understanding of the nature of their market and so helping deliver readers to advertisers) comes in.
>
> (ibid.)

Classifying features by format or function?

Features are not a recent phenomenon – British newspapers have been carrying some form of feature since the eighteenth century in the form of literary or political essays, letters to the editor and verse (Ferdinand 1997, p.135). While these essays were few and far between, they illuminated and opined upon such activities as cock throwing, and campaigned for foundling hospitals to stem the tide in infanticide. In 1740, for instance, the *Salisbury Journal*, based in the county of Wiltshire and the south-west of England, averaged about 70 per cent news and 26 per cent advertising, while the remaining 4 per cent was divided between essays and verse. By the end of the century, however, non-news and advertising had grown (ibid., p.163). In the twenty-first century, the term 'Newspaper features' encompasses not only the extended articles but also horoscopes, crosswords, reviews, critics and TV. However, this chapter will focus on analysing key trends in what we conventionally understand as a feature article.

Newspapers today aim to inform and entertain their readers with features that put news into perspective and create a three-dimensional standpoint. In other words, they bring characters to life and provide a wider range of voices and perspectives than might be possible within the structures of the hard news pages. But they also capture the inconsequential quirks and trends, characters and pleasures, that captivate us, without necessarily being based upon a so-called 'news hook'.

Features have been classified in many ways, but here are some common forms:

- the profile interview
- the news backgrounder
- the self-help guide
- historical/nostalgia article
- the how-to piece
- the exposé
- humorous article
- general interest piece
- the eyewitness account.

In addition to the feature article, other feature sections include:

- comment, sometimes known as op-ed (opinion and editorial)
- reviews
- entertainment
- Specialist sections.

While it may be tempting to categorise, there are many slippages between these formats as editors seek to embrace new communities of readers. Taylor (2005, p.23) helpfully describes genres, or 'functional fields', of journalism that provide a more thematic and stylistic overview:

- information-based journalism
- opinion-making journalism
- entertainment journalism
- literary journalism.

Within each of these fields, a range of formats and topics occur. An eyewitness account can be a news backgrounder, as, for example, in the case of the *Daily Mirror* rail worker piece where a reporter went undercover (12 December 2000, pp.1, 4–5), or humorous, such as in the example of a feature questioning the appeal of high fashion in the *Daily Telegraph* (Coulson 2007). It is perhaps the purpose of the feature that is more significant than the format, as it enables us to think of the connections between target reader and content selection and packaging.

Technological and organisational change: impacts on features

The newspaper industry has undergone significant change driven by technological developments and shifting patterns of ownership which, in turn, impact upon features' content. The dynamic process and practices of feature production are reflected in staffing arrangements, syndication of features locally and globally, the growth in newspaper supplements and the drive for new formats to maintain reader and, in turn, advertiser interest.

Multi-tasking editorial staff

The structure of newspaper editorial departments now requires journalists to multi-task, so that it is rare to find a journalist dedicated solely to feature writing. Even within specialist sections of newspapers, such as motoring, gardening and homes, there will be a mixture of news and feature content. At one time, features staff bore very different professional identities to their news counterparts, often working different hours and to different deadlines. With the exception of the smallest local papers, news and features were almost always separate entities, physically demarcated from one another both in the newspaper itself and in the layout of the newsroom. Now, in the contemporary context of media convergence, multi-skilling and a challenging economic environment, the barriers between the formats and styles of news and features – and their respective practitioners – are shifting. The net result is that features often have to be written at quieter times to fit around the pressures of news deadlines. One journalist, who works for a regional daily newspaper, said:

> Unless we have a massive story requiring instant backgrounders, features will be written well in advance of when they are actually needed and often kept on hold for weekend editions or holiday periods, when the paper is being produced with few journalists on duty. This means that the majority of features we write are not time-sensitive.
>
> (name withheld, interviewed 4 January 2007)

This suggests that one of the functions of newspaper features is to ensure steady copy flow, which means the format and content is for the most part flexible enough to be published at any time that suits the production calendar.

Syndication

The numbers of staff writing for titles has fallen as newspapers have come under new ownership, which means less available time for feature writing. Features can be expensive to write if they involve travel or time on the part of the journalist. Newspapers have responded to this through sharing content, particularly in the health, travel and lifestyle sections of local and regional newspapers. Archant,

Trinity Mirror and Newsquest are among the companies which have some shared feature content across their titles. This means that some feature content and its writing style must be sufficiently generic to fit in several titles. Furthermore, newspaper companies have syndication departments aimed at selling their own content to other publishers. For instance, Archant, the sixth largest regional chain, has a syndication department to sell its stories to the nationals. The national and international market for features is also growing. In response, NI Syndication, which is part of News International Limited, publishers of *The Times*, *Sun*, *Sunday Times* and *News of the World*, is the business-to-business division working with organisations who wish to license or re-use content from News International's newspapers and archives. It seems that a further function of features is that they can be produced and reproduced efficiently, thus keeping editorial budgets manageable. In this way, the commercial function of features means inevitably less local content. Sharing feature content therefore makes good economic sense, but at the expense of in-depth local reporting.

Technology and pagination

As well as changing working practices, developments in production technology have enabled newspapers to expand their pagination and to insert a raft of supplements. In the mid-1980s the Wapping Revolution, as it became known, heralded a new era for the industry. Within a few years the other titles had moved out of Fleet Street, many of them to greenfield sites in London's Docklands. The benefits of lower production costs were largely reflected in the extension of editorial services and bigger newspapers. 'It became fashionable to complain about the size of the *Sunday Times* with its many sections' (Heren, cited in Griffiths 1992, p.61). It is often cited that the feature content, especially of the Sunday papers, is a major weapon in the battle for readerships. Following the abolition of newsprint rationing in 1958, newspapers were free to revolutionise their format and content in order to attract new readers. The *Sunday Times Colour Section* was the first major development in this direction when it launched in 1962, with the *Observer* following suit two years later. Similarly the fortunes of the tabloid press have worked in tandem with the development of television, so that a significant quantity of their daily and weekly feature content is about celebrities, soap stars and premiership footballers. Thus a further inherent function of features is to reinforce the intertextuality (Kristeva 1980, p.69) brought about by cross-ownership of the media. News Corps, for example, is a giant among media conglomerates, accused over promoting its film and television products such as Fox TV, through its newspapers.

Competition

Competition brought by new technology means that papers are veering away from breaking news and steering towards feature-led approaches. In the United States, three recent studies – by the Project for Excellence in Journalism in 2004, the Pew

Research Center in 2005, and The Media Center (at the American Press Institute) in 2005 – signal a 'long-term decline in news consumption' (Pew Research Center 2005, p.44). A survey among American 18- to 34-year-olds conducted in May 2004 shows that, with the exception of web portals, the vast majority of them rarely, if ever, turn to the news in any medium (Brown 2005).

While the speed of new technology may have placed greater strictures upon some news journalists, for others, especially in the print sector, it has offered a way to break free. Newspapers and magazines are turning their attentions back to what they do best – in-depth narratives based on days, weeks, even months of meticulous first-hand reporting. In effect, print journalism is responding to readers who might get their first news snap from electronic media, but who ultimately still like to read. James E. Murphy has identified three specific characteristics of immersion journalism, a term coined in the US but increasingly in evidence in the UK press. First, there is the use of adverbs, adjectives and dialogue to transport the reader to the scene. Secondly, the reporter recognises and imparts their subjectivity as opposed to impartial detachment. They interpret events as they see them rather than trying to write as if they were but a faceless conduit. Thirdly, there is immersion, the act of being absorbed experientially in the story (Murphy 1974).

Recent prominent examples of immersion reporting might include the descriptive and emotive eyewitness narrative accounts of conflict, such as the journalism of the *Independent*'s correspondent Robert Fisk. With increasing numbers of newspapers publishing on the web first, the move towards extended feature-style reporting may ensure the articles have a 'cut-out-and-keep' permanence that makes readers want to acquire them in their printed form. Harold Evans, under whose legendary editorship *The Times* broke the thalidomide scandal in the 1960s using extended feature-style reporting, commented that '"news" is defined too episodically and too topically' (Evans 1986, p.91). Rather, journalism needs to find ways to write about processes, not just events. Current interest in immersion journalism may be an attempt to revitalise values from a distant journalistic past, expressing those values in innovative reporting. Thus the reporter becomes an interpreter of life rather than the messenger.

Whereas national newspapers can deliver features to carefully demarcated consumer groups, selecting topics and modes of presentation that cohere with the lifestyle and consumption patterns of their target reader, local and regional newspapers face a significant challenge in needing to reflect a far broader demographic.

Local features, global economics

It is perhaps in the realm of local and regional newspapers that the shifts in feature form and function have become most apparent. The remit of the local newspaper's features has traditionally been to reflect and celebrate the breadth and depth of its community, a notion that does not sit easily with the drive for consumer/lifestyle-targeted content. A useful benchmark for the comparative analysis of local and regional newspaper features is Ian Jackson's (1971) book,

The Provincial Press and the Community. Jackson's study, under the auspices of the newly opened Centre for Contemporary Cultural Studies at the University of Birmingham, occurred at a time when evening newspapers in the cities of Birmingham, Leeds, Leicester, Manchester and Nottingham were being closed down or merged in a general rationalisation of the few remaining competitive situations. Jackson's study aimed to analyse the function of local newspapers, but also to examine their social and historical context and thus the values and attitudes that informed it.

In 1966, the year of Jackson's sample of local papers, the feature content of the weekly press usually consisted of the community diary, special features for women and children, extracts from past issues of the newspaper, summaries of church, youth club and Women's Institute activities, an entertainment guide, and columns for the gardener and/or motorist. These features, some of which were also provided by evening newspapers, helped to foster a feeling of local togetherness in trade, and of common domestic or leisure interests. Jackson pointed out that the 1947 Royal Commission was not quite doing justice to the weekly press when describing its content as 'almost entirely advertisements and local news' (1947 Royal Commission, p.239)

Jackson identified three key functions of the local newspaper feature:

1   Reflector: 'the reflector function characterises features about local history; these may serve to sharpen a reader's sense of his [sic] community's particularity' (Jackson 1971, p.180).
2   Booster: 'For an individual to become the subject of a provincial newspaper "booster" feature, the achievement of success or the display of notable enterprise are, in the majority of cases, necessary conditions. Most individual "booster" features concern various types of local hero: the successful sportsman, the defeater of adverse circumstances, or the champion of some local cause' (ibid., p.182).
3   Watchdog and pump primer: 'the function of watchdog ... is also fulfilled through feature articles. These occur intermittently as and when suitable subjects suggest themselves ... First, they should interest a sizeable body of readers, and second, they should preferably not risk alienating the good will of important advertisers or opinion leaders' (ibid., p.188).

In surveying a small selection of local and regional newspapers published 40 years after Jackson's sample was analysed, the marked distinction is not so much between weekly and daily titles, rather between papers serving towns and cities as opposed to more rural communities. In the papers catering for readers based in urban areas, features are much less local and much more oriented towards consumer interests. Simultaneously, in the papers serving a more rural market, there is often more of an attempt to create a community-centred feel to feature coverage. For example, the *Eastern Daily Press*, covering Norfolk, has been running an ongoing feature campaign to preserve local traders from the threat of out-of-town developers, which serves as a 'watchdog/pump-priming' function. Though, as Jackson argues, this type of coverage is also important for preserving a steady advertising base from local businesses. However, a feature entitled 'Fakenham is our kind of town' (by Kieron Pim, 23 January 2007), which hits back at claims that it was 'the most boring place on earth', challenges consumerist values, putting community bonds above the pursuit of cheaper prices. Having delved into the town's colourful history and heritage and celebrated its lively present, it ends with the remark that it 'is far from boring, and is actually rather exciting'.

In a similar way, the *Halifax Evening Courier* strives to celebrate local heroes in a 'booster' feature about two local football players, reunited 65 years after they played in the non-league village team. The introduction compares their importance more favourably than the premiership, thus emphasising the significance of the local over the global:

> As football stories go this is not one that will reverberate round the hallowed soccer palaces of Old Trafford or Stamford Bridge. No, this is far more important. This is about two teenage lads and their football team that played at a local rec and changed in a nearby washhouse.
>
> (Hanson 2007)

The paper contains a series of other booster features, such as interviews with the new Chief Constable and the new District Rotary Governor, which further embed the paper in the community it serves.

Jackson's study highlighted how the locally rooted feature, carrying the functions of reflector, booster, and watchdog and pump primer are fulfilled, which in turn can sharpen the reader's awareness of the community's particularity – whether reflected in the reader's sense of its past development, its current strength and limitations or its future role and character. Weekly and daily papers centred on metropolitan areas contain fewer of these types of story. The *Belfast Telegraph*, which on its marketing website says that more than half its readers are in the ABC1 social category, centres its feature coverage on travel, health and beauty, food and drink, and motoring. In this way it is typical of a number of metropolitan regional titles surveyed: local London weeklies, for example, are similar. The Belfast title's feature pages on Monday, 5 January 2007 foregrounded international talking points rather than local debates, such as 'The cult of the "granny mother"' and the prevalence of religious leaders on mainstream radio. Across the sector, it is evident that local and regional newspapers are organising their feature content into categories that mirror those of the nationals. Features that may be local in terms of their subjects closely mimic lifestyle features in the national press. The *Argus*, based in Brighton, does have a number of local-based features, especially within its 'Life and Health' category, which are not time sensitive. For instance, 'Not Too Late for the Queen of Jazz' (29 January 2007) about an 83-year-old female phenomenon. There is also a feature about a woman who was only able to conceive after cutting wheat and dairy from her diet (26 June 2006). Either would sit well in a mid-market national, where the emotions and the experiences of the individual take priority over a sense of community. These concerns tally with Jackson's closing assertion:

> The functions of reflecting and evaluating local life constitute the principal justifications for the existence of provincial newspapers. Community-rooted features are an important means of fulfilling these functions … For this reason, the steady growth – during the 1960s – of London agencies that ply the provincial Press with non-local feature material must be seen as an unhealthy development that needs checking.
>
> (Jackson 1971, p.191)

Futurologist Richard Scase told senior journalists and editors at the 2005 Society of Editors conference that instead of using demographics, such as age and gender, to define readerships, they should now be targeting 'purchasing clusters' defined by leisure activities (cited in Tryhorn 2005). The prevalence of targeting in journalism is now very evident, and it seems this trend will continue (Machin and Niblock 2006).

Concluding thoughts

The newspaper sector is experiencing marked transformation in its feature coverage. Recent trends, such as the growth in first-person reporting and the move to lifestyle-based rather than issue-based journalism, have been in evidence across local, regional and national titles. Each of these trends, it can be shown, is directly linked to the drive by newspaper publishers to market their products against a backdrop of increasingly fierce competition and declining advertising revenues. This is particularly so in the regional and local sectors where more than three-quarters of revenue may come from advertising.

Whereas news can to some extent fulfil the targeting function, through such means as choice of angle and vocabulary, it is the areas of feature articles that best lend themselves to playing a key role in the marketing function. This situation is a cause for considerable concern if we believe newspaper journalism should play an important role in reflecting the lives of communities of readers. Feature writing geared towards serving the needs of several titles simultaneously, and which is produced at minimal cost, allows little if any opportunity for journalists to interrogate local issues or celebrate their community and its various facets. There is still strong community-focused feature writing in some titles; whether or not it is under threat by the concerns of the commercial nature of newspapers remains to be seen. However, competition from new technology may herald a resurgence in quality feature writing, as titles reflect upon the distinctiveness of their medium and its special relationship with readers.

References

Belfast Telegraph (2007) http://www.belfast telegraph.co.uk/services/media-kit/print-media-kit/circulation. Accessed 1 February 2007.

Brown, M. 'Abandoning the News'. *Carnegie Reporter* 3(2), spring 2005. http://www.carnegie.org/reporter/10/news/index.html. Accessed 1 February 2007.

Coulson, C. (2007) 'Who Wears These Clothes?' in the *Daily Telegraph*, Wednesday, 14 February 2007.

Daily Mirror, Tuesday 12 December 2000, pp. 1, 4–5.

Evans, H. (1986) *Good Times Bad Times* London: Coronet.

Ferdinand, C.Y. (1997) *Benjamin Collins and the Provincial Newspaper Trade in the Eighteenth Century* Oxford: Clarendon Press.

Hanson, D. (2007) 'Champions Reunited' in *Halifax Evening Courier* http://www.halifaxtoday.co.uk/ViewArticle.aspx?ArticleID+2013647&SectionID=1880. Accessed 29 January 2007.

Harp, D. (2006) 'Newspapers' Transition from Women's to Style Pages: What Were They Thinking?' *Journalism* vol 7, pp.197–216.

Heren, L. in Griffiths, D. (Ed.) (1992) *The Encyclopaedia of the British Press 1422–1992* Basingstoke: Macmillan Press.

Jackson, I. (1971) *The Provincial Press and the Community* Manchester: Manchester University Press.

Kristeva, J. (1980) *Desire in Language: A Semiotic Approach to Literature and Art* New York: Columbia University Press.

Machin, D. and Niblock, S. (2006) *News Production: Theory and Practice* London: Routledge.

Manzella, J. (2002) *The Struggle to Revitalize American Newspapers* Lewiston, NY: The Edwin Mellen Press.

Murphy, J. (1974) 'The New Journalism: A Critical Perspective'. Paper presented to the Association for Education in Journalism, San Diego.

Pew Research Center (2005) *Trends 2005*, p.44, http://pewresearch.org/trends. Accessed 1 February 2007.

Ross, W. D. (1949) *Report of the Royal Commission on the Press 1947–49* London: HMSO Cmd 7700.

Royal Commission on the Press (1947–9) *Royal Commission on the Press 1947–1949: Report* London: HMSO.

Taylor, J. (2005) 'What Makes a Good Feature? The Different Genres' in Keeble, R. (Ed.) *Print Journalism: An Introduction* London: Routledge.

Tryhorn, C. (2005) 'Play Down Bad News, Local Newspapers Warned' *Guardian* Monday, 17 October http://media.guardian.co.uk/presspublishing/story/0,,1594155,00.html. Accessed 1 February 2007.

Wallace, R. (2007) http://www.editorsweblog.org/print_newspapers/2007/02/uk_daily_mirrors_magazine_style.php. Accessed 13 February 2007.

Chapter 3

Readers' letters

John Richardson

Introduction

> For every letter, there are 100 readers. The letter writers say 'did you see my letter in the paper today?' They do their own personal marketing on behalf of the newspaper. It allows each day's paper to go wider than yesterday's. So letters to the editor improve circulation.
>
> (Managing Editor of San Francisco Bay newspaper chain, quoted in Wahl-Jorgensen 2001, p.310)

Letters to the editor play an important role in the marketing and circulation success of a newspaper (Mayes 2001). As well as encouraging the kind of reader-initiated marketing described above, letters to the editor help to communicate a newspaper's brand identity through representing the quotidian preoccupations of its readership. Further, since readers 'place a high priority on interactivity in their relationships with the traditional newspaper press' (Bromley 1998, p.147), various readership surveys 'have found that newspaper letters sections are popular with readers, with readership rates of at least 50 per cent' (Gregory and Hutchins 2004, p.189). In sum, the letters pages have great importance for newspaper and reader alike, since they 'enable both the press and the readership to keep an ear to the ground and listen in to some of the leading themes of local conversation' (Jackson 1971, p.174).

This chapter discusses 'letters to the editor' and introduces some of the principal ways that academics and journalists have examined this editorial format. The next section discusses the editorial selection of letters, followed by studies of letter writers and, finally, the analysis of the contents of letters. The discussion draws on a sample of the letters pages of three British newspapers – the *Sun*, *The Times* and the Nottingham *Evening Post* – over a four-week period (Monday, 13 November– Saturday, 9 December 2006).

'Getting in': studying selection

Ian Mayes (2001), the Readers' Editor for the *Guardian*, describes the letters page as 'among the more important parts of the paper' and 'the paper's principal forum of reader opinion'. On any normal day, the *Guardian* receives around 300 letters competing for a place in this forum, a figure that can increase considerably in times of political controversy – it doubled during the first week of the 2003 invasion of Iraq, for example (Mayes 2003). Such an observation begs a number of questions, not least the criteria that newspapers like the *Guardian* use to distinguish between the letters thought good enough to be included and those to be spiked. Wahl-Jorgensen (2002) has suggested four criteria of 'newsworthiness' which letters editors use in selecting or rejecting readers' letters. These selection criteria, which are 'shaped in part by concern for the public interest and in part by the need for newspapers to succeed in the market, play a central role in helping letters' editors to decide which contributions from readers have a legitimate place in the newspaper's column' (Wahl-Jorgensen 2002, p.73).

First, Wahl-Jorgensen suggests the rule of relevance, which favours topics that 'have earned a legitimate place in the public debate by virtue of newsworthy events or actions by institutions or other sources of authority' (2002, p.73). While letter writers do not necessarily follow a newspaper's *angle* on these reported events or actions, their letters are nevertheless coupled to this coverage, meaning that 'regular citizens' attempts at introducing their own topics to the agenda will almost invariably fail' (ibid.). The red top tabloids appear to interpret this 'rule' in a particularly stringent way. Bromley (1998, p.158) shows fewer than 25 per cent of letters in the *Sun* and just over one-third in the *Mirror* commented upon the newspapers' reporting of an event and 'neither paper published a letter of criticism of its own performance or even its editorial views'. What is relevant to a tabloid editor, it seems, are letters compatible with their narrow news agenda.

Second, Wahl-Jorgensen proposes the rule of entertainment. Calling some letters 'entertaining' may seem a little misplaced, but given that all newspapers try to 'turn on readers by offering more sparkly, entertaining op-ed pages and letters sections' (2002, p.74), they all employ this selection criteria. On occasion, this preference for punchy copy favours combative and overly disputatious correspondence, which endangers 'the pursuit of shared understanding and empathy' (ibid., p.75). On this point Pasternack (1983, p.311) reveals that 'some newspapers still do not verify letters and many allow harsher language in their open forums than they would elsewhere in the publication', frequently leading to litigation. Contrary to the misconception that letters enjoy a special status, 'a person who believes he has been defamed in a letter to the editor may sue the letter writer, the newspaper, or both' (Pasternack 1983, p.313). Indeed, of the 72 American regional newspapers he surveyed, 12 per cent had been sued for libel based on a letter to the editor in the last decade (ibid., p.314), demonstrating the prevalence of malicious correspondence in these publications.

Third, the rule of brevity favours succinct letters over lengthy deliberation. Wahl-Jorgensen (2002, p.75) shows that this 'bite-size debate approach expresses the desire to hear the opinions of as many persons as possible'. Indeed Wober

(2004, p.51) shows that 'The Times slowly but steadily increased the number of letters published' from an average of nine per day 1953–5 to 16 per day 2003–4. Given that the space dedicated to letters was not increased, what this must logically mean is that the length of the average letter has dropped by 44 per cent since 1953–5. Finally, Wahl-Jorgensen (2002, p.76) suggests the rule of authority, which letters page editors use to select 'culturally specific forms of competence for participation'. All included letters are at the very least competently written: all are grammatically correct, make a relevant point and are 'well versed in hegemonic standards of expression' (Bohle 1991, cited in Wahl-Jorgensen 2002, p.77). In keeping with the other selection criteria, different newspapers have different understandings of what personal authority actually means: tabloid letter writers tend to argue from personal experience, while many 'broadsheet' authors draw credibility from more institutional forms of authority. These different understandings have a profound impact on the kinds of letters that are chosen for inclusion, and the ways that arguments are supported through a claim to authority.

This picture is further complicated when we acknowledge the potential for individuals and groups endowed with sufficient social or linguistic capital (Bourdieu 1991) to orchestrate letters campaigns. Certain powerful groups are aware of the editorial practices used to select letters for publication, and they construct their correspondence accordingly (Richardson and Franklin 2004). For instance, on 14 October 2003, the Daily Mirror and the Daily Mail reported that 'US Army spin doctors' (propagandists by any other name) had ghostwritten letters sent to local US newspapers that claimed to be from infantry soldiers. The Mirror wrote: 'Dozens of letters were sent to newspapers across the US but now it has emerged that the soldiers were given the wording and many did not sign them' ('Iraqi letters of mass deception', 14 October 2003). The letters were largely identical, containing a number of arguments supportive of the occupation. A key sentence of the falsified letters claimed: 'American forces have brought life in the war-torn country back to normal for the local population, with new electricity, water and sewage plants installed' ('Storm over fake letters from US soldiers in Iraq', Daily Mail 14 October 2003).

As Gregory and Hutchins (2004, p.194) point out, a prerequisite for the letters page of a local newspaper is the 'localism or proximity' of the copy and 'a belief in the right of local people to speak in their forum'. In other words, for a local newspaper, a relevant and authoritative voice is a local voice. The US Army recognised and capitalised on this editorial preference. They identified the newspapers distributed in the hometowns of the soldiers of the Second Battalion 503rd Airborne Infantry Regiment, and sent them a letter detailing the Army's rosy version of the Iraq occupation. The intention of this was clear: to steer public (mis)understanding of the invasion, at a time when 'a growing number of Americans question the war and the wisdom of a drawn-out occupation of Iraq' (Daily Mail 14 October 2003).

The 'Green-Ink Gang'? Studying authors

> Many of those who dispatch letters for publication to newspapers are not
> entirely sane, and this seemed especially true of our correspondents. The
> *Telegraph* postbag was dominated by readers complaining about falling stan-
> dards or service / lack of respect among the young / criminal justice / the
> presumptuous ambition of black men to govern themselves, or a combination
> of these issues [...] Today [...] I am amazed that so many veterans of the
> Crimea, together with their prejudices, survive to dominate the columns.
>
> (Hastings 2002, p.53)

There are two main ways in which the authors of letters to the editor may be
studied. First, the published letters themselves may be examined, focusing specifically on how authors reveal social categories (including status, occupation and/or
institutional affiliation) in the ways that they sign their correspondence. Using
this method, 'Tunstall [1977, p.221] calculated that in the mid-1970s the letters
appearing in newspapers were written by less than 1 per cent of the population,
and came predominantly from white, middle-class men' (cited in Bromley 1998,
p.150). More specifically, Wober (2004, p.53) argues that the letters page of *The
Times* is dominated by members of the social elites – in other words, MPs, professors, officers of associations (e.g. the Christian Socialists Movement, Dorset
Natural History and Archaeological Society) and 'people in organisations which
speak for and try to keep order'. He shows the percentage of letters from 'elite
writers' stayed relatively static, rising only marginally to 36.9 per cent in 2003–4
from 34.9 per cent in 1953–5.

There are clear problems, of course, with using printed *letters* to draw a conclusion about the typical characteristics of letter *writers*, given that the letters included
for publication may not accurately represent the total submitted. Nevertheless,
studying the ascribed authorship of printed letters can still tell us a great deal about
the newspaper and the relationship it shares with its readers. Looking to my sample
of letters pages, for example, there are clearly differences between the kinds of letter
writers selected by these different papers (see Table 3.1).

As Table 3.1 shows, the majority of letters were signed by named individuals
without reference to their job, status or membership of any special interest groups:
a remarkable 98.6 per cent of letters printed in the *Sun* were from such authors,
reflecting the valorisation of the 'ordinary' *Sun*-reader throughout the paper's
editorial content. In contrast, 71.6 per cent of letters in *The Times* were signed by
'ordinary readers', meaning the remainder (28.4%) were from elite individuals
and groups. This percentage of elite signatories is down significantly on Wober's
data (2004), which may be due to chance fluctuations in news agenda or may
indicate a more significant shift in either readership or editorial policy.

A more accurate picture of the kind of people writing letters may be gained
through examining the letters actually received by a newspaper prior to their
selection and publication. Access to such letters is often difficult, but can be

Table 3.1 *Author signature and newspaper*

Author signature	Evening Post		Sun		The Times		Total	
	Count	Col %	Count	Col %	Count	Col %	Count	Col %
Individual	194	77.0	412	98.6	290	71.6	896	83.3
Representative of association	33	13.1	1	0.2	27	6.7	61	5.7
Local/national government	20	7.9	1	0.2	22	5.4	43	4.0
Education	—	—	—	—	24	5.9	24	2.2
Religious	3	1.2	—	—	8	2.0	11	1.0
Peers	—	—	—	—	7	1.7	7	0.7
Business/corporate	1	0.4	2	0.5	4	1.0	7	0.7
Elite	1	0.4	—	—	7	1.7	8	0.7
Armed forces	—	—	2	0.5	5	1.2	7	0.7
Legal	—	—	—	—	8	2.0	8	0.7
Other media	—	—	—	—	3	0.7	3	0.3
Total	252	100	418	100	405	100	1,075	100

achieved through conducting a newsroom ethnography or by using archive source materials. Nord (1995, p.66), for example, conducted research drawing on 'a manuscript collection of letters sent by readers to James Keeley, editor of the *Chicago Tribune* and *Chicago Herald* in the early 20th century'. Known as the James Keeley Papers, the collection, held by the Chicago Historical Society, 'consists of six folders of manuscript material, including family letters, office memos, a magazine article typescript, a gallery proof of a speech, and letters from readers. The letters from readers – between 200 and 300 – form the bulk of the collection' (ibid., p.89). Examining this archive, Nord was able to piece together three motivations for letter writers, distinguished by the audience to whom the reader was writing:

> Published letters to the editor almost always were intended for the public, for other readers. Some of the manuscript letters in the Keeley collection fall into that category. Most of the letters, however, were addressed to the editor as editor. Their purpose was to speak directly to the person in charge of the paper. Still other letters were quite introspective, almost reflexive – as if the readers were speaking to themselves.
>
> (ibid., p.71)

Most published letter writers appear to be motivated by a number of predictable reasons for writing letters to the editor, including 'expressing personal views to the public', 'informing' or 'influencing public opinion' (see Singletary and Cowling 1979). However, Nord's research reminds us that newspapers perform a number of functions in addition to learning and information. For the letter writers in the Keeley Collection – who write letters never intended for publication – the newspaper and its editor appear to represent a valuable social contact.

Studying contents

Over the four-week sample (Monday, 13 November–Saturday, 9 December 2006), a total of 1,075 letters to the editor were printed (*Evening Post*, 252; the *Sun*, 418; *The Times*, 405). The *Sun* does not print letters in its Saturday edition, meaning that across the sample (20 papers), they included an average of 20.9 letters per page. *The Times* printed an average of 16.9 letters per page (24 papers); while the *Evening Post* printed an average of only 5.25 letters per page (24 papers), due to their letters page being a double-page spread. These recorded items were all coded for eight variables (including date, authorship, theme, genre and argument) and the data analysed using SPSS.[1] The top ten themes featuring in readers' letters pages are listed in Table 3.2.

First, it is interesting to note how well the letters pages reflect the wider editorial content of the newspaper. I would suggest that most people would have little difficulty in picking out which of the three columns summarises a tabloid newspaper, given the high priority the *Sun* gives to crime/law and order, celebrity and the putative threat posed by immigration (combined, these themes represent 46 per cent of all *Sun* letters). Second, Table 3.2 shows the comparative thematic diversity of letters printed in the *Evening Post* and especially *The Times*. The ten most frequent themes in these two newspapers constituted only around two-thirds of

Table 3.2 *Theme of printed letters to the editor*

Evening Post		Sun		The Times	
Environment	9.1% (n=23)	Crime/law & order	23.0% (n=96)	Crime/law & order	10.6% (n=43)
Regional policy/amenities	9.1% (n=23)	Celebrity	13.4% (n=56)	Health/NHS	9.1% (n=37)
Europe	8.3% (n=21)	'Race'/immigration	9.6% (n=40)	Defence/war/terrorism	7.9% (n=32)
Transport/congestion	7.9% (n=20)	Health/NHS	8.4% (n=35)	The arts/entertainment	5.7% (n=23)
Health/NHS	7.1% (n=18)	Taxation	6.9% (n=29)	Education	5.7% (n=23)
The arts/entertainment	6.3% (n=16)	The arts/entertainment	5.5% (n=23)	Shopping/consumption	5.7% (n=23)
Crime/law & order	6.0% (n=15)	Industry/employment	5.5% (n=23)	Party politics	5.4% (n=22)
Charity	5.2% (n=13)	Sport	4.3% (n=18)	Sport	5.2% (n=21)
Pensions/expenditure	4.8% (n=12)	Welfare/social services	2.9% (n=12)	Foreign affairs	4.7% (n=19)
'State of the nation'	4.4% (n=11)	Regional policy/amenities	2.4% (n=10)	Transport/congestion	4.7% (n=19)
Others	31.7% (n=80)		18.2% (n=76)		35.3% (n=143)

total printed letters, making for a much wider variation of themes than those included in the *Sun*.

When coding the genre of the letters, I considered a letter argumentative if (1) 'it expressed a certain positive or negative position with respect to a proposition' (van Eemeren and Grootendorst 2004, p.3) and (2) this expression occurs in a context of disagreement.

While each of the letters pages contains letters that do not advance arguments – with jokes being popular for letters in *The Times* and 'Thank yous' popular in the *Evening Post* – it is interesting to note that the percentage of argumentative letters is almost equal across all three newspapers. The data in Table 3.3 support a claim made elsewhere that letters to the editor should be viewed primarily as an argumentative discourse genre, 'designed to convince readers of the acceptability of a point of view and to provoke them into an immediate or future course of action' (Atkin and Richardson 2007, p.2).

Following from this, the letter writers' use of argument schemes – that is, the manner in which these writers use arguments to support their own standpoints and/or attack those of others – was also coded. There are three rhetorical argument schemes arguers use to support their standpoints: symptomatic argument (arguing from example); comparative argument (analogy); and causal arguments (see Atkin and Richardson 2007; van Eemeren, Grootendorst and Snoeck Henkemans 2002). Successful rhetorical argumentation is always tailored to the audience, and so it is interesting to see how reasoning differs between the three sampled newspapers. Aristotle observed: 'men [sic] learn with less effort from

Table 3.3 *Genre of the printed letters*

Genre of letter	Evening Post		Sun		The Times		Total	
	Count	Col %	Count	Col %	Count	Col %	Count	Col %
Argument	196	77.8	330	78.9	319	78.8	845	78.6
Anecdote/observation	29	11.5	46	11.0	40	9.9	115	10.7
Joke	1	0.4	22	5.3	42	10.4	65	6.0
Request	8	3.2	5	1.2	1	0.2	14	1.3
Thank you	17	6.7	15	3.6	3	0.7	35	3.3
Apology	1	0.4	—	—	—	—	1	0.1
Total	252	100	418	100	405	100	1,075	100

Table 3.4 *Use of argument schemes in letters*

Argument scheme	Evening Post		Sun		The Times		Total	
	Count	Col %	Count	Col %	Count	Col %	Count	Col %
Symptomatic	143	56.7	256	61.2	188	46.4	587	54.6
Comparative	10	4.0	50	12.0	49	12.1	109	10.1
Causal	43	17.1	24	5.7	82	20.2	149	13.9
N/A	56	22.2	88	21.1	86	21.2	230	21.4
Total	252	100	418	100	405	100	1,075	100

examples for they learn individual facts' (*Problemata*, cited in Grimaldi 1972, p.95). Therefore, symptomatic argumentation 'is more appropriate for the ordinary person' than other forms of reasoning, 'since it permits more ready comprehension and understanding' (ibid.).

As expected, letters in the *Sun* argued from example more frequently than those in the other two newspapers. In keeping with the findings of Jackson (1971, p.154), the letters pages in the *Evening Post* were far more similar in approach to those of *The Times* than the *Sun*, in which letters were printed 'as principally a form of 'entertainment' (Tunstall 1977, p.209). Arguments from causation are more difficult to support convincingly than those from example or analogy, which provides one explanation why we see so few of them in the *Sun*, whose letters are significantly shorter than those in the other two papers.

It is not sufficient, of course, simply to code an argument as 'symptomatic' or 'analogous' without explaining how these arguments were structured and how their standpoints were supported. Symptomatic arguments are based on relations of typicality, symptoms or concomitance. A symptomatic relation can be indicated in an argument by a wide variety of terms, including: '... *is characteristic of* ...'; '... *is typical of* ...'; '... *illustrates* ...'; '... *is evidence of* ...'; and '... *a prime example of* ...' (see Snoeck Henkemans 2002, p.188). Often in such arguments, an individual example is used to illustrate a wider pattern or trend – an argument that can fail due to an insufficient supporting premise and hasty generalisation. Take this letter, on the subject of 'Muslim terrorism' printed in the *Sun* (15 November 2006):

> Every time we encounter terrorists and suicide bombers in this country they seem to be Islamic. The head of MI5 tells us there are at least 200 cells plotting terror attacks and her agents are tracking 1,600 fanatics, who are Islamic. When the BNP's Nick Griffin says that Islam is a wicked faith, who can honestly say he is wrong?

Here we can assume (from the rhetorical question) that the letter's standpoint is: 'the BNP's Nick Griffin is not wrong when he says that Islam is a wicked faith'. The argument fails due to both an insufficient supporting premise and overgeneralisation. Claiming '*Islam* is a wicked faith' on the basis of premises claiming *certain* Muslims are 'terrorists and suicide bombers' (even assuming the cited data are accurate) is a crude overgeneralisation of the type frequently seen in prejudiced argumentation. More precisely, it is a fallacy of composition, in which the characteristics of a part (some Muslims) are transferred to the whole ('Islam').

Second, an argument may be supported by a comparative relation, or analogy. In such cases, a letter writer defends a standpoint by showing that what is stated in the *argument* is similar to that which is stated in the *standpoint* 'and that on the grounds of this resemblance the standpoint should be accepted' (van Eemeren, Grootendorst and Snoeck Henkemans 2002, p.99). Comparative arguments can be indicated in a letter by terms such as: '... *equally* ...', '... *any more than* ...', '... *the same as* ...', '... *just like* ...', as well as by using more implicit allusions or evocations. Take this example from *The Times* (15 November 2006) on the subject of compensation paid to drug addicts in UK prisons:

> Sir, How can the Government justify the payment by the Home Office of compensation to convicted criminals with drug habits for withholding access to drugs in prison and the refusal by the Department of Health to pay proper compensation and adequately provide for the 370 surviving haemophiliacs out of 1,250 in total who were infected in the 1980s with HIV and hepatitis C by NHS-administered contaminated blood products? The latter were entirely innocent but condemned to the probability of an early death and the daily intake of large doses of toxic drugs just to stay alive.

Here, the implicit standpoint is something on the lines of: 'the Government were wrong to deny proper compensation to these innocent haemophiliacs when they paid it out to convicted (therefore guilty) criminals'. A key concept for this letter is the idea of '*proper* compensation', which implies these victims of contaminated blood *have* been given compensation, but the author views this as unsatisfactory. However, it was not in the government's power to set the level of compensation to the victims of contaminated blood, nor was it their *choice* to pay compensation to the convicts – indeed they made a concerted attempt to avoid doing exactly that. It was only when six claimants sued that the government decided they should settle out of court.[2] Therefore, while there is arguably a resemblance between the standpoint (haemophiliac claim for compensation) and the argument (convicted drug addicts' claim for compensation), blaming the government for this injustice is misplaced.

Third, some letters use causal arguments, in which something (or someone) is presented as the cause of that which is stated in the standpoint. Such arguments can take a positive or a negative form – that is, the letter writer may defend a causal connection or may be attacking it. But regardless of whether a standpoint is defended or attacked, causal relation is indicated by terms that refer to consequences or outcomes, such as: '… *leads to* …', '… *makes* …', '… *gives rise to* …', and many others. In the following letter (*Evening Post* 5 December 2006) a causal connection is drawn between immigration and infectious disease:

> Your front page article 'HIV trebles in five years' stated that one of the main causes was infected immigrants. Why aren't we like Australia and America which insist on health checks before allowing admittance, and not admitting anyone with diseases. TB was virtually eliminated in this country and has increased due to immigration. They then get free treatment on the NHS which is already struggling to cope with the health problems of the indigenous population.

The gist of this argument – that immigration brings disease – is as old as immigration itself (see Bivins n.d.) and has been a lasting preoccupation of racist letters to the editor since at least the *Windrush* (Richardson and Franklin 2004). The letter above demonstrates the fallacious mono-causality typical of racist and ethnicist argumentation. Simply put: the appearance of black and brown faces is presented as the sole determinant of a host of social ills. In fact, the 'foreign origin' of TB infection is false. Recent studies, for instance, carried out by the Public Health Laboratory Service, show that the vast majority of infected people 'contracted the disease after they arrived in Britain when they were forced to live in poor housing with insufficient funds to have a proper diet' (Kundnani 2003). A clear determinant is therefore poverty, 'especially when the poor are socially and medically segregated from those whose deaths might be considered more important' (Farmer 1996, p.263).

Conclusion

Letters published in newspapers suggest a great deal about the paper and its readers. As Bromley (1998, p.149) has put it, the 'ecology of correspondence between readers and newspapers is relatively complex [...] incorporating several overlapping contours – public and private – in terms of at least both the subject matter and the nature of the correspondence'. Most obviously letters are written by readers, drawing on their cultural and linguistic resources and reflecting their ideas, stories, jokes and arguments. Given that they are usually written in response to previous editorial contents and selected for inclusion by the letters editor, they also say something about a newspaper's news values. Once selected, they are often placed alongside letters that offer different standpoints, in ways that also reveal the editorial or political position of the paper. This chapter has shown that the vast majority of letters to the editor are argumentative, designed to convince an audience of the acceptability of a point of view and to provoke them into an immediate or future course of action. As such, it is important to examine in detail the ways that standpoints are supported by rhetorical argument schemes.

Notes

1   In addition to the sampled letters, each letters page contained other forms of correspondence. These letters were beyond the remit of this chapter, but it is still interesting to comment briefly on them. In this sample, the Nottingham *Evening Post* published up to four poems written by readers, covering subjects as diverse as racehorses, the milkman and fruit jam. While it is tempting to laugh at such parochial foci, we should remember this popular column serves to represent the views and interests of a section of the paper's readership. The *Sun*, like other red top tabloids, prints mobile phone text messages alongside letters from its readers (and see Billig *et al.* 2006 for an analysis of racist text messages including in the *Daily Star* during the build-up to the 2005 UK General Election). Although these offer an extremely interesting insight into the preoccupations of the '*Sun*-reader', their extreme brevity (readers are limited to a maximum 160 *characters*) would have skewed and distorted the sample. Finally, everyday *The Times* uses the bottom of its letters page to invite its readers to 'Join the debate

with *Times* readers worldwide' on their online debate page. Although the trail is accompanied by brief comments from readers, its function is more in keeping with advertising rather than editorial content.

2 See 'Payments for prisoner "cold turkey"', http://news.bbc.co.uk/1/hi/uk/6142416.stm. Accessed 17 January 2007.

References

Atkin, A. and Richardson, J. E. (2007) 'Arguing about Muslims: (Un)Reasonable Argumentation in Letters to the Editor' *Text and Talk* vol. 27 no. 1.

Bivins, R. (n.d.) 'A Question of Control: Diversity, Disease, and Post-colonial Medicine in Britain, http://www.brighton.ac.uk/cappe/presentations/BivinsBodyPol.pdf. Accessed 12 January 2006.

Bourdieu, P. (1991) *Language and Symbolic Power*, Ed. J. B. Thompson, Trans. G. Raymond London: Polity Press.

Bromley, M. (1998) '"Watching the Watchdogs?" The Role of Readers' Letters in Calling the Press to Account' in Bromley, M. and Stephenson, H. (Eds) *Sex, Lies and Democracy* London: Longman, pp.147–62.

Eemeren, F. H. van and Grootendorst, R. (2004) A *Systematic Theory of Argumentation* Cambridge: Cambridge University Press.

Eemeren, F. H. van, Grootendorst, R. and Snoeck Henkemans, F. (2002) *Argumentation Analysis, Evaluation, Presentation* Mahwah, NJ: Lawrence Erlbaum.

Farmer, P. (1996) 'Social Inequalities and Emerging Infectious Diseases' *Emerging Infectious Diseases* vol. 2 no. 4, pp.259–69.

Gregory, L. and Hutchins, B. (2004) 'Everyday Editorial Practices and the Public Sphere: Analyzing the Letters to the Editor Page of a Regional Newspaper', *Media International Australia incorporating Culture and Policy* vol. 112, pp.186–200.

Grey, D. L. and Brown, T. R. (1970) 'Letters to the Editor: Hazy Reflections of Public Opinion' *Journalism Quarterly* vol. 47 pp.450–6.

Grimaldi, M. A. (1972) 'Studies in the Philosophy of Aristotle's Rhetoric' in Enos, R. L. and Agnew, L. P. (Eds) (1998) *Landmark Essays on Aristotelian Rhetoric* Mahwah, NJ: Erlbaum, pp.15–160.

Hastings, M. (2002) *Editor: An Inside Story of Newspapers* London: Macmillan.

Jackson, I. (1971) *The Provincial Press and the Community* Manchester: Manchester University Press.

Kundnani, A. (2003) 'The Hate Industry", http://www.irr.org.uk/2003/march/ak000003.html. Accessed 12 January 2006.

Mayes, I. (2001) 'Sincerely Yours. The Readers' Editor On… the Value, and the Hazards, of the Letters Page' *Guardian* 23 June 2001.

Mayes, I. (2003) 'Readers Between the Lines' *Guardian* 22 March 2003.

Nord, D. P. (1995) 'Reading the Newspaper: Strategies and Politics of Reader Response, Chicago, 1912–1917' *Journal of Communication* vol. 45 no. 3, pp.66–93.

Pasternack, S. (1983) 'Editors and the Risk of Libel in Letters' *Journalism Quarterly*, vol. 60 no. 2, pp.311–15, 328.

Richardson, J. E. and Franklin, B. (2003) '"Dear Editor": Race, Readers' Letters and the Local Press' *Political Quarterly* vol. 74 no. 2, pp.184–92.

Richardson J. E. and Franklin, B. (2004) 'Letters of Intent: Election Campaigning and Orchestrated Public Debate in Local Newspapers' Letters to the Editor' *Political Communication* vol. 21 no. 4, pp.459–78.

Singletary, M. W. and Cowling, M. (1979) 'Letters to the Editor of the Non-daily Press' *Journalism Quarterly* vol. 56 no. 1, pp.165–8.

Snoeck Henkemans, F. (2002) 'Clues for Reconstructing Symptomatic Argumentation' in F. H. van Eemeren (Ed.) *Advances in Pragma-Dialectics* Amsterdam: Sic Sat, pp.197–214.

Tunstall, J. (1977) 'Letters to the Editor' Royal Commission on the Press, *Studies on the Press* Working Paper No. 3 London: HMSO, pp.203–48.

Wahl-Jorgensen, K. (2001) 'Letters to the Editor as a Forum for Public Deliberation: Modes of Publicity and Democratic Debate' *Critical Studies in Mass Communications* vol. 18 no. 3, pp.303–20.

Wahl-Jorgensen, K. (2002) 'Understanding the Conditions for Public Discourse: Four Rules for Selecting Letters to the Editor' *Journalism Studies* vol. 3 no. 1, pp.69–81.

Wober, J. M. (2004) 'Top People Write to *The Times*' *British Journalism Review* vol. 15 no. 2, pp.49–54.

Chapter 4

Op-ed pages

Karin Wahl-Jorgensen

The editorial and op-ed (opposite-editorial) pages are central to a newspaper's identity. They are the only place in the paper where journalists are authorised to express opinion, often guided by the political leanings of the newspaper (Wahl-Jorgensen 2004, p.59). It is in editorials that newspapers speak both for and to their audience, creating a distinctive voice for the newspaper that is otherwise buried under the conventions of objective journalism (Fowler 1991, p.209). To Santo 'the most precise barometer of a newspaper's position on political and social questions is assumed to reside on the editorial page – the heart, soul, and conscience of the newspaper' (1994, p.94). Opinion journalism of this sort allows media the 'power to set the dominant political agenda, as elaborated over weeks, months and years ... In this capacity the institutions of the press take the lead in establishing the dominant interpretative frameworks within which ongoing political events are made sense of' (McNair 2000, p.30). Through the features of opinion journalism, including editorials, columns and letters to the editor, newspapers can contribute to shaping and articulating public opinion.

This chapter takes a closer look at the news format of the editorial and op-ed pages, as a distinctive genre of journalistic writing. I look at the history of opinion journalism and then examine in more detail the form it takes in British newspapers today. Although opinion journalism is valued by all papers, it also takes a variety of forms that depend crucially on whether the publication is tabloid or 'quality', national or local. Nevertheless, one of the most glaring conceptual problems in examining this format in the British context is that the expression of judgements and opinions is frequently not limited to the op-ed and editorial pages, but increasingly pervades every section of the newspaper.

A brief history of opinion journalism

The history of opinion journalism is closely tied to the history of the press itself. The first newspapers were focused on information provision over opinion and interpretation. Barnhurst and Nerone's observation about early American colonial newspapers that they 'were short, stale, dull, unintelligible and unprofitable' (2001, p.32) applies equally well to early British commercial publications. The

Daily Courant – the first regularly published English-language newspaper – began publication on 11 March 1702 and 'purported to give no comments or conjectures' (Hart 1970, p.86). Nevertheless, printers quickly found that a more opinionated and interactive style of journalism won over readers. When Thomas Fleet took over the *Boston Weekly Rehearsal* in the 1730s, he 'solicited opinion writers by inviting "all Gentlemen of Leisure and Capacity ... to write anything of a political nature, that tends to enlighten and serve the Publick, to communicate their productions, provided they are not overlong"' (ibid., p.111). The solicitation of argumentative letters from the public became integral to the appeal of early newspapers. As a fairly typical example, the *Hartford Connecticut Courant* featured two opinion pieces, in the form of letters addressed to the editor, Mr Green, on its 9 March 1767 front page (Barnhurst and Nerone 2001, p.38). As such, even the earliest newspapers contained many of the key ingredients of today's op-ed and editorial pages, often encompassing styles of today's editorials, columns and letters to the editor.

Over time, this information-oriented, commercial early press was transformed into a partisan journalism of opinion. In Britain, this shift occurred after the imposition of the Stamp Duty in 1712, while the US press changed its modus operandi towards the end of the eighteenth century (Schudson 2001). The partisan press was born of commercial necessity, but was also centrally shaped by a recognition of the political power of opinion writing. As Park wrote about partisan papers, the

> opinion that had formerly found expression in a broadside was now expressed in the form of editorial leading articles. The editorial writer, who had inherited the mantle of the pamphleteer, now assumed the role of a tribune of the people ... when we read in the political literature ... references to 'the power of the press' it is the editor and the editorial rather than the reporter and the news of which these writers are thinking.
>
> (1923, p.281)

Jean Chalaby has expressed his reluctance to characterise the partisan press as a legitimate form of journalism. For him, the publications of this time were compiled by 'publicists' whose 'discursive production was determined by their political conviction' (1998, pp.9–10). Instead, he argues that journalism, as a 'fact-centred' practice which relies on 'clusters of discursive norms' emerged around the turn of the twentieth century, alongside the professionalisation of journalism. As such, Chalaby sees the separation of 'information' and 'opinion' as central to the professional identity of the journalist. Schudson argues that the rise to prominence of the penny press in the US at the turn of the twentieth century 'led to the triumph of "news" over the editorial and "facts" over opinion, a change which was shaped by the expansion of democracy and the market, and which would lead, in time, to the journalist's uneasy allegiance to objectivity' (1978, p.14). By the time a professionalised press was making such distinctions, opinions – whether in the form of signed or unsigned editorials, or letters to the editor –

began to be separated off from information, both in the self-understanding of jour-nalists and in the physical layouts of newspapers.

A peek at examples available from the British Library Online Newspaper Archive hints at these shifts. Among other things, this resource gives access to issues of the *Daily News* (a predecessor of the *Daily Mail*) from 1851, 1856, 1886, 1900 and 1918. Up to and including 1900, the *Daily News* did not separate news from opinion. Instead, opinionated dispatches about the Boer War appeared next to notices of shippings of the Royal Mail Steam Packet Company and the results of the German Emperor's Cup yachting competition. By 1918, however, a newspa-per form had emerged which closely resembles today's styles. This includes head-lines of varying sizes, indicating a hierarchy of newsworthiness, an 'inverted pyramid' structure of information within articles, and an organisation of content according to subject matter, with dedicated sections for news about the war, sports and culture, among other topics.

Alongside these markers of professionalised journalism came a clear sense that public opinion is articulated through newspaper discussions, and that this discus-sion takes place in a dedicated space within a publication otherwise focused on disseminating information. For example, on 2 December 1918, page 4 of the *Daily News* was devoted to editorials and letters about key issues in the forthcoming election. This included an editorial which opened with the observation that the 'past fortnight has seen a marked change in the temper of the electorate, of which those sensitive indications of the trend of public opinion, Lord Northcliffe's news-papers, have given a faithful reflection' (*Daily News* 2 December 1918). The page also featured thoughts on electoral apathy among ex-servicemen from a Chris Massie, who argued that 'as a private soldier with three years active service in France, I can speak for my comrades with all the confidence of inside knowledge'. He wrote that soldiers 'are apathetic about voting because they have lost both faith and interest in the old parties' (ibid., p.4).

A closer look at opinion journalism

If we examine today's British newspapers more closely, it appears that most of them – whether they are quality, mid-market or tabloid, national, regional or local – value, and mark out as distinctive, forms of opinion journalism. Examining all the major national newspapers, along with a regional and a local Welsh paper on one day – 21 March 2007 – gives a flavour of some key similarities and differences between formats for opinion journalism.

All the papers have in common the commitment to designated spaces for opinion expression. However, the traditional designation of editorial and op-ed pages does not translate straightforwardly to the British context: most of the quality newspa-pers devote between three and five pages to opinionated journalism including edito-rials, columns and letters to the editor. These appear in sections marked out with headings such as 'Comment and Analysis' (*Financial Times*), 'Comment and Debate' (*Guardian*), and 'Editorial & Opinion' (*Independent*). The layout of these sections is visually less imposing and more text-heavy than the remainder of the newspaper, with small headlines and few photographs. Typically, the only photographs on the opinion pages in quality papers are black-and-white thumbnail images of columnists. In addition, the opinion pages also usually feature editorial cartoons – on 21 March 2007, several of these depicted then Chancellor Gordon Brown, about to announce his annual budget. Overall, the layout style of the opinion pages, which appears to be conventional and shared across publications, means that the debate pages strike a sombre and serious tone.

The style of opinion writing, and the mode of address that results from it, can vary within and between publications. As McNair puts it:

> Sometimes [editorials] are presented as the 'voice of the reader', and directed at policy-makers. Alternatively, they may be constructed as the calm, authoritative voice of the editor, viewing the political scene from a detached distance. In both cases, the editorial is intended as a political intervention, and often read as such by a government or a party.
>
> (1995, p.13)

To McNair, it is in part on the basis of this type of journalism that media can be seen to intervene in the political process – when they endorse particular candidates or policies, media become political actors in their own right. Of course, the editorials are designed not merely to influence governments or parties, but also the newspapers' readers, who are presumed to draw on the information contained in the editorials for their political knowledge and judgements.

The quality papers publish three editorials each day. The first two editorials focus on issues high on the news agenda. For example, the *Daily Telegraph* led with a complaint about 'the hoops through which new applicants [for a British passport] will have to jump', concluding that 'this is simply the most sinister example of Labour's insatiable appetite to control – and a testimony to the failure of Parliament to protect individual freedom and liberty' (*Daily Telegraph* 21 March 2007, p.25). By contrast, the *Independent*'s top editorial celebrates the fiftieth anniversary of the European Union as a 'potent symbol of peace and unity' (*Independent* 21 March 2007, p.40). The third editorial is conventionally a rather different creature: if the first two focus on heavy-duty political issues, the third tends to be shorter, and muses on a topic that is either humorous or a 'soft news' item, frequently focused on a particular individual. For example, *The Times*' third editorial on 21 March 2007 was a plea for a musical devoted to Margaret Thatcher:

> The pitch: Iron Lady tapdances all over Billy Elliott and his miserable striking miner dad … Outline: Curtain up reveals Mrs T amid giant heaps of stinking black binliners looming out of semi-darkness. It's 1979. Grimy union activists in Doc Martens pull at her twinset and pearls while chanting the *Internationale*.
>
> (*The Times* 21 March 2007, p.16)

The tone of this editorial is both more humorous and informal than the remainder of the editorials, signalling the exceptionalism of the third editorial. At the same time, the conservative politics of *The Times* shines through in the veneration of Margaret Thatcher. Such a pattern can be seen across the quality newspapers. In *The Times*, the third editorial celebrated the ninetieth birthday of Dame Vera Lynn, who boosted the troops' morale in the Second World War (ibid., p.25), while the *Guardian* sang the praises of Michael Foot, whose biography had just been released, arguing that few 'literary politicians have risen so high' (*Guardian* 21 March 2007, p.38).

While it is difficult to determine when and why this 'third editorial' convention was established, it is clearly a feature across the quality newspapers. It indicates that even within the heavyweight journalism of the opinion pages, there is space for 'light relief'. The overall feel of the quality papers' opinion pages, nevertheless, remains that of a serious conversation with an informed insider.

Tabloid newspapers, on the other hand, defy any easy distinctions between opinion and information-oriented journalism. The partisan nature of journalism in Britain, which is particularly evident in the popular press (Tunstall 1996) means that far from being relegated to the designated sections of the paper, opinions and judgements pervade every single page. Thus, the *Sun*'s front page exhibits a typical disregard for the discursive conventions of objective reporting when it exclaims that 'SOHAM liar Maxine Carr has confessed she STILL loves child killer Ian Huntley' (Parker, 21 March 2007, p.1), while another front page story bemoans 'a busybody council [that] is to hide cameras in **BAKED BEAN** tins – to spy on residents who put rubbish out on the wrong day' (Wheeler, 21 March 2007, p.1). The *Daily Mirror* leads with a story about 'Mrs Evil: Foster Mum's horrific torture of 3 children' (Smith, 21 March 2007, p.1). This language, typical of the style of tabloids, is informal and emotive and often relies on slang, alliteration and puns (see Conboy 2006). Tabloid editorials draw on similarly colourful language, as when the *Daily Star* approvingly cites Lord Turnbull's comparison of Gordon Brown with Joseph Stalin, suggesting that Brown is 'a dangerous egomaniac who should not be let anywhere near No 10. The Labour Party MUST find someone else to succeed Mr Blair' (*Daily Star* 21 March 2007, p.6).

Another convention which blurs the line between information and opinion in tabloids is the separation of editorials, columns and letters: these appear on pages that are often far apart in the newspaper, with high profile members of the 'commentariat' scattered throughout the newspaper. For example, the *Sun*'s editorials, editorial cartoon and a commentary on why the word 'McJob' should be removed from the dictionary, appear on page 6. However, regular columnists appear elsewhere – David Blunkett's column on Westminster politics, for example, is on page 26. Meanwhile, the *Sun*'s letters section, appearing under the heading 'Dear Sun: The page where you tell Britain what you think', is at the top of page 35. Similarly, the mid-market *Daily Express* splits up its editorial and commentary (on page 12), from its letters (on page 32). The tabloid practice of severing the various forms of opinion journalism – conventionally bound up together in quality newspa-

pers – hints at the different roles of editorials, columns and letters in these two journalism cultures. In particular, the debate on the opinion pages of quality newspapers
– whether it comes in the forms of editorials, columns or letters – is dominated by
elite voices. Here, letters from MPs, think tank directors, and celebrities feed into
the construction of an insider public opinion that also characterises editorials and
columns. By contrast, in tabloids, letters tend to be contributed by readers who are
rarely identified by their title or expertise, but only by name and location. The
tabloid separation of letters from other forms of opinion journalism constructs the
letters section as a service for readers who want their voices to be heard by others,
separate from the elite formation of public opinion.

Overall, it appears that even if opinion pages are a key site for the formation of
public opinion, it is often – particularly in the context of national newspapers – an
elite opinion (see also Day and Golan 2005; Page 1996; Wahl-Jorgensen 2004).
As Day and Golan (2005) found in their study of op-ed page debates, the *New
York Times*'s pages only allowed for very limited diversity of sources, relying mostly
on government officials, experts and journalists. Benjamin Page aptly describes
the orientation of editorial page debate as follows:

> Because airtime and print space are expensive, and because citizens want
> only the most concise and vivid messages, most of those who speak in or
> through the media are professional communicators, highly skilled at produc-
> ing political discourse and paid to do so. These professional communicators
> include reporters, writers, commentators and television pundits, as well as
> public officials and selected experts from academia or think tanks.
>
> (1996, p.6)

By contrast, local and regional opinion journalism offers more of a space for 'ordinary people' to voice their concerns. Most British local newspapers feature
opinion journalism in some form (cf. Wahl-Jorgensen 2005, 2007). Indeed, editors
of local papers view their editorials as important sites for influencing opinion in
their communities (e.g. Hynds 1984; Hynds and Martin 1979). Local papers tend
to take particular pride in their letters section, and often print almost all letters
they receive. For example, the *South Wales Echo* has two pages of editorials,
columns and letters, and these pages are dominated by letters from community
members. The paper features two brief (150- to 200-word) editorials encapsulat-
ing the newspaper's opinion. In addition, the *Echo*'s op-ed page also includes
other features designed to highlight community voices – on the day studied, it
featured five vox pops with local people on Gordon Brown's performance as
Chancellor. These are accompanied by the results of an online readers' poll on the
same topic.

If local newspapers seek to produce a 'journalism of consensus', editorials represent a challenge: the genre of editorial writing is tied to criticism and controversy,
and local newspaper editors have been compelled to develop strategies to avoid
giving offence while being seen to express opinion (Wahl-Jorgensen 2005). One

such strategy is to compose 'good news' editorials on non-controversial topics, highlighting the achievement of local individuals and communities. As Neveu (2002) has argued, the particular strength of opinion journalism in local newspapers is that it articulates a unique local public opinion, and often one that is sympathetic to positive developments within the papers' communities. This is certainly the case for the *Western Mail*'s editorial, which draws on discourses of Welsh national pride to call attention to the plight of the Welsh valleys, suggesting that they 'have contributed a lot to Wales, and it's good to see they are getting back on their feet after years of decline. But more action is needed from all levels of government if this is to be more than a temporary blip' (*Western Mail* 21 March 2007, p.16).

Making sense of British opinion journalism

Paolo Mancini has recently argued that compared to North American and British journalistic practices, continental European journalism has developed to embrace a much more interpretive and argumentative style, characterised by the fact that 'comment, interpretation and the evaluation of what has taken place are privileged rather than a simple description of the events' (2005, p.86). He therefore argues that the line separating news from opinion and interpretation has always been less than strictly demarcated in continental European countries. What has become apparent from the present exploration of British opinion journalism is that even if journalism scholars have typically assumed a distinction between news and opinion, and have written about opinion journalism in isolation from other types of content, this distinction has always been challenged by the partisan nature of journalism in Britain. The ideal of objectivity, which continues to hold sway in North American practices of journalism, has certainly shaped British newspaper journalism, insofar as it is predicated on fact-centred discursive practices, such as the principles of fairness, accuracy and balance (Chalaby 1998). Yet for tabloids in particular, it may be more useful to view editorials, columns and letters as embodying a distinctive mode of address rather than as a privileged site within the newspaper for the expression of opinion.

The future of opinion journalism

All these observations, however, may soon be due for revision. As online journalism and platform convergence are challenging conventional journalistic forms, this is particularly true for opinion journalism. Certainly, the websites for key UK newspapers treat opinion journalism very differently from their paper versions: they often visually foreground interactive options that give readers the opportunity to participate in online discussion, respond to newspaper content or vote in online polls, and they tend to downplay more conventional forms of opinion journalism.

A further complication is the rise of blogging: though it was originally viewed as a transformative 'citizen journalism', empowering ordinary people to express political opinions (Lasica 2003), it was also readily appropriated by mainstream news organisations, signalling a new and more interactive epistemology of journalism (Matheson 2004). The wholesale entrance of mainstream British newspapers into the blogosphere has transformed opinion journalism online, taking advantage of the medium's interactive possibilities. The *Sun*, for example, hosts readers' blogs in addition to those composed by journalists employed by the newspaper. Readers' blogs are advertised as follows: 'With a **MY Sun** blog, you can get your own voice heard on the web. You can talk about whatever you like, and get feedback from other users.' Newspapers including the *Guardian*, the *Daily Mail*, the *Daily Telegraph* and the *Daily Mirror* employ professional journalists to blog on their websites. Some of these blogs combine opinion writing with more conventional journalistic reporting. The tone of these blogs varies, from formal journalistic style which signals that the piece has, in fact, been recycled from the print edition, to opinionated rants and informal diary entries. This highlights a greater diversity of discursive strategies in a context divorced from the conventions of editorial and op-ed pages. As such, it appears to further challenge the separation of news and opinion, and along with it any remnants of the ideal of objectivity.

Blogging – whether by journalists, other elites or simply articulate 'regular folks' – is increasingly seen as an alternative to the public opinion formation of columns, letters and editorials. As newspapers are scrambling to adapt to the age of convergence, the styles and genres of opinion journalism may be among those most profoundly affected.

References

Barnhurst, K. G. and Nerone, J. (2001) *The Form of News: A History* New York: Guilford Press.

Chalaby, J. (1998) *The Invention of Journalism* London: Palgrave Macmillan.

Conboy, M. (2006) *Tabloid Britain: Constructing a Community Through Language* London: Routledge.

Day, A. G. and Golan, G. (2005) 'Source and Content Diversity in Op-ed Pages: Assessing Editorial Strategies in *The New York Times* and the *Washington Post*' *Journalism Studies* vol. 6 no. 1, pp.61–71.

Fowler, R. (1991) *Language in the News* London: Routledge.

Hart, J. A. (1970) *The Developing Views on the News Editorial Syndrome 1500–1800* Carbondale, IL: Southern Illinois University Press.

Hynds, E. C. (1984) 'Editorials, Opinion Pages Still Have Vital Roles at Most Newspapers' *Journalism Quarterly* vol. 61, pp.634–9.

Hynds, E. C. and Martin, C. H. (1979) 'How Non-daily Editors Describe Status and Function of Editorial Pages' *Journalism Quarterly* vol. 56, pp.318–23.

Lasica, J. D. (2003) 'Blogs and Journalism Need Each Other' *Nieman Reports* Fall, pp.70–4.

McNair, B. (1995) *Introduction to Political Communication* London: Routledge.

McNair, B. (2000) *Journalism and Democracy: An Evaluation of the Political Public Sphere* London: Routledge.

Mancini, P. (2005) 'Is There a European Model of Journalism?' in De Burgh, H. (Ed.) *Making Journalists: Diverse Models, Global Issues* London: Routledge.

Matheson, D. (2004) 'Weblogs and the Epistemology of News: Some Trends in Online Journalism' *New Media & Society* vol. 6 no. 4, pp.443–68.

Neveu, E. (2002) 'The Local Press and Farmers' Protests in Brittany: Proximity and Distance in the Local Newspaper Coverage of a Social Movement' *Journalism Studies* vol. 3 no. 1, pp.53–67.

Page, B. (1996) *Who Deliberates? Mass Media in Modern Democracy* Chicago: Chicago University Press.

Park, R. E. (1923) 'The Natural History of the Newspaper' *The American Journal of Sociology* vol. 29 no. 3, pp.273–89.

Santo, A. (1994) '"In Our Opinion ..." Editorial Page Views of Clinton's First Year' *Media Studies Journal* vol. 8 no. 2, pp.97–106.

Schudson, M. (1978). *Discovering the News* New York: Basic Books.

Schudson, M. (2001) 'The Objectivity Norm in American Journalism' *Journalism* vol. 2 no. 2, pp.149–70.

Tunstall, J. (1996) *Newspaper Power: The New National Press in Britain* Oxford: Clarendon Press.

Wahl-Jorgensen, K. (2004) 'Playground of the Pundits or Voice of the People? Comparing British and Danish Opinion Pages' *Journalism Studies* vol 5 no. 1, pp.59–70.

Wahl-Jorgensen, K. (2005) 'The Market vs. the Right to Communicate: The Anti-political Local Press in Britain and the Journalism of Consensus' *Javnost/The Public* vol. 12 no. 3, pp.79–94.

Wahl-Jorgensen, K. (2007) *Journalists and the Public: Newsroom Culture, Letters to the Editor, and Democracy* Creskill, NJ: Hampton Press.

Chapter 5

Cartoons

Colin Seymour-Ure

People often put cartoon anthologies in the lavatory, and collectors tend to hang originals there. This is a perverse tribute to their entertainment value and – more subtly – to their power to cut down to size the public figures they depict, for lavatories are a reminder of our common humanity.

But why are cartoons in newspapers anyway? They are graphic in a primarily verbal medium. They exaggerate and distort in a type of publication which values accuracy. They assert opinions, generally critical and often emotionally, alongside editorials using reasoned argument. For humorous or 'gag' cartoons – strips and single-frame drawings that may just be illustrated jokes – the answer to this puzzle lies in the forerunners of the popular press. The first full-time staff cartoonist on a mass-circulation daily paper, W. K. Haselden (1872–1953), was hired by the future Lord Northcliffe in 1904 specifically to help relaunch a popular illustrated paper, the *Daily Mirror*. He was a great success and stayed until 1940.

Much of Haselden's work went beyond gags: it was light social observation and was thus at the 'editorial' end of the cartoon spectrum. The word 'editorial' is the key to the presence, and the prominence, of political cartoons in the press. These complement the editorial role of interpretation and comment. They are editorials in pictures. The first staff cartoonist on any daily paper, the evocatively named Sir Francis Carruthers Gould ('FCG'; 1844–1925), was knighted by a grateful Liberal Party in 1906 precisely because of his effectiveness as a Liberal propagandist.

Having got a foothold in the new press developing at the start of the twentieth century, both editorial and gag cartoons flourished. By the 1920s, the metropolitan papers were flooding the country; the provincial press was reduced to a rump. This development stretched the idea of a newspaper. Just as readers of the popular papers learned to expect gossip, racing tips and, later, nudes on page 3, so they expected cartoonists.

Moreover readers expected a favourite cartoonist. Haselden was by no means alone in staying with one paper for a long time. In the 1930s to 1950s Lord Beaverbrook courted the cartoonists on his *Daily Express*, *Sunday Express* and London *Evening Standard*. The likes of David Low and George Strube had trophy status and trophy salaries. So did the sport cartoonist Tom Webster on the rival

Daily Mail. Table 5.1 shows how this longevity has continued. The five listed cartoonists drawing in 2007 averaged more than 33 years on one paper.

One reason for long service is that cartoonists start young. But familiarity is surely another. Newspapers are a paradoxical combination of the predictable and the unexpected. They help to order the world beyond the breakfast table. Among the certainties of idiom, style and news values are those of layout and format. These are a kind of reassurance about the paper's personality. A principal editorial page, with a leading article set within a box or beneath a special masthead, is found daily in a familiar place. On this page, or nearby, will be the editorial cartoon, also often in a standard shape and size. Size and location, as with post-codes and menu items, are signs of status. If a cartoonist is diminished or moved around, readers may wonder if the editor has stopped taking him (it is still almost always a him) seriously. Gag cartoons and strips, many of which are syndicated and so less 'personal', lack the connection with news and can be tucked away.

A further, crucial reason for readers to know their cartoonist well concerns how cartoons work. The cartoonist necessarily lays on readers the task of working out what he means. He has few words to help him, beyond a caption, perhaps a little text within the frame, and a few labels dotted around. The scope for misunderstanding is therefore wide. The reader, first of all, must be aware of the people, events or ideas which are the subject of the drawing. Cartoons are nearly always

Table 5.1 *Selected editorial cartoonists: length of service*

Cartoonist[a]	Paper	No. of years	Dates	Age on leaving
FCG (F. Carruthers Gould)	*Pall Mall Gazette/ Westminster Gazette*	27	1887–1914	70
W. Haselden	*Daily Mirror*	36	1904–40	68
G. Strube	*Daily Express*	30	1918–48	56
D. Low	*Evening Standard*	22	1927–49	58
L. Illingworth	*Daily Mail*	30	1939–69	67
C. Giles	*Daily/Sunday Express*	46	1943–89	73
M. Cummings	*Daily/Sunday Express*	47	1949–96	77
Trog (W. Fawkes)	*Observer*	31	1965–96	72
Jak (R. Jackson)	*Evening Standard*	31	1966–97	70
N. Garland[b]	*Daily Telegraph*	41	1966–	—
G. Scarfe	*Sunday Times*	39	1968–	—
Mac (S. McMurtry)	*Daily Mail*	36	1971–	—
S. Franklin	*Sun*	24	1974–98	68
P. Brookes	*The Times*	25	1982–	—
S. Bell	*Guardian*	25	1982–	—

Source: Various, but especially The British Cartoon Archive (University of Kent) and Mark Bryant, *Dictionary of Twentieth-century British Cartoonists and Caricaturists*, London: Ashgate, 2000.

Notes: [a] This is not an inclusive list. Since the emphasis is on service at a particular paper, cartoonists who moved or worked freelance may be excluded despite very long careers – e.g. C. Griffin, M. Heath, W. Caldwell.
[b] Garland worked for the *Independent* from 1986–1991.

reactive: they cannot easily anticipate the news. But once a cartoonist gets away from the headlines, at least some of his readers risk losing all or part of his point purely through imperfect knowledge of the subject. This must be especially true for the diverse readership of the mass-circulation tabloids.

Next the reader has to work out the cartoonist's interpretation of the subject ('the latest fighting in Iraq escalates the crisis'); his evaluation ('it has become a civil war'); and his opinion ('American policy is outrageous'). Sometimes, moreover, the reader may wonder if the cartoonist is expressing his own opinion, or indicating what he believes to be the opinion of persons represented or alluded to in the drawing. This last possibility provides the cartoonist with one of his possibly disingenuous defences against criticism. 'You may think I believe that', he can say, 'but it's not what I personally believe at all.'

The problems of understanding a cartoon as the artist intended arise overwhelmingly because cartoons work principally by comparison and imagery: this party leader is a pygmy; that election is a one-horse race. They rely on nuance, double meanings, allusions, puns, irony. Often, certainly not always, they use humour: of contrast, recognition, paradox or bewilderment. They use well-understood stylistic devices. Big means strong, small weak; fat/rich, thin/poor. If they can get a good likeness, they may use caricature, tweaking features in order to suggest particular characteristics, even if the person depicted is intended as the symbol of an attitude or policy, say, rather than as culpable personally for it.

Cartoonists rely too on a range of images which has remained strikingly consistent over at least the last hundred years. Politicians are shown in everyday occupations, or are clothed as historical figures, or linked to topical events. They become animals, as in Peter Brookes' colourful weekly 'Nature Notes' in The Times and in Steve Bell's grotesque image of President George W. Bush as a simian midget in the Guardian. In another variant, Nick Garland (Daily Telegraph), for instance, has often found ingenious contemporary comparisons in literature, painting, sculpture, mythology and folklore. National symbols – the British lion, Britannia, even John Bull – still make occasional appearances. Often the image may come simply from everyday speech ('he's a dead duck') or from our stock of common knowledge – what everyone knows everyone knows.

Readers learn these conventions as part of growing up – and they are illustrated in the two cartoons in Figures 5.1 and 5.2. But knowing the cartoonist's visual language, as with the spoken word, does not guarantee it will be correctly applied. Irony, for instance, is notoriously open to misinterpretation. A classic example in the 1950s was a play on the character 'Superman' by Vicky (Viktor Weisz; London Evening Standard), the most admired cartoonist of his day. Vicky, a Labour supporter, teased the Conservative Prime Minister, Harold Macmillan, as a posturing 'Supermac'. The spoof rebounded, for the name stuck – but without the irony. The Conservatives were delighted (Seymour-Ure 2003, pp.261–3).

It seems improbable that cartoons are often understood to mean the exact opposite of what was intended. But incomplete understanding must be commonplace. Nick Garland's literary comparisons, for example, include the schoolboy cast of Richmal Crompton's 'Just William' books. Are these still on the shelves even of many *Daily Telegraph* readers? For those who cannot respond with the chortle of recognition, the point must be blunted.

A different kind of difficulty is where the point is grasped correctly but the reader hugely overreacts. The very advantage of wordlessness is that cartoon images can say the unsayable. One reason Peter Brookes likes animal images, for instance, is that he can show animal politicians doing things (including the indecent) which he could not possibly make human politicians do. But the cartoonist is absolutely in the hands of the reader, when a judgement is made about how

Figure 5.1
Steve Bell, no caption, *Guardian*, 2 June 2006 (copyright Steve Bell). Reprinted with permission.

Steve Bell puts the reader to work. Bell's version of President George W. Bush, more than five years in office, is instantly recognisable. It bears little resemblance to the man, so what are we to make of it? The limbs are ape-like, but the horizontal ears, the mouth like a hooter and the eyes jammed together can signify whatever you like – idiocy? Incapacity for complex speech? Bell does not need to tell us the scene is Iraq. He needs labels, however, to make his specific point about the contrast between Bush's war-like behaviour and his claim to green credentials. The soldier – passive and, with hidden eyes, anonymous – bears a 'fairtrade weapon'. The shroud is 'toxin free', the evil-looking dog is 'carbon neutral'. The only explicit reference to carnage is the human leg. Its ridiculous appearance means it is not upsetting and also that it provides the only piece of humour in the drawing. What would Bell like us to feel – and what does he feel himself? Anger? Contempt? Or a simple appreciation of irony?

TORY STRIKER'S REMARKABLE RECOVERY

Figure 5.2
Nicholas Garland, 'Tory Striker's Remarkable Recovery', *Daily Telegraph*, 7 June 2006 (copyright Nicholas Garland and Daily Telegraph Group Ltd). Reprinted with permission.
The traditional imagery of politics as a game. The topical reference is to the Football World Cup of 2006 and the injury which nearly kept England's Wayne Rooney from playing. Garland draws the Conservative leader, David Cameron, poised and in command of the opinion polls – perhaps, before too long, to enjoy success at the real polls. Blair and Brown, meanwhile, clumsily tumble over each other (or are they actually fighting?). Garland does not make clear how far he thinks the pair are personally the cause of Labour's decline and how far he is using them as symbols of it. Either way, their disarray and Cameron's poise make a sharp contrast.

strongly a cartoon is to be felt. Cartoons have the potential to cause offence: a joke may be taken as an insult; a pinprick as a stab.

This combustibility makes cartoonists something of a risk, from the viewpoint of an editor. It is understandable that, especially in the mass-circulation papers, they do not stray far from the tastes of their readers and that they are subject to closer editorial supervision than on the upmarket papers. As long ago as 1929 David Low, the most famous cartoonist of the mid-twentieth century, grumbled that mass-circulation cartoonists had to please everybody, which meant generalising points until they practically disappeared altogether. On these papers cartoonists typically produce four or five 'roughs', from which their editor will choose the one to be worked up into the final cartoon. As the *Daily Mail*'s 'Mac' (Stan McMurtry) explained, this is seen not as censorship but as a normal exercise of editorial and, ultimately, proprietorial right (British Cartoon Archive 2007).

Cartoonists on the former broadsheets, comparing themselves with columnists or feature writers, prize their independence of thought. Problems about publication are more likely to be about execution than ideas. For example, Nick Garland had a cartoon turned down in 1980, showing Mrs Thatcher with her underpants round her ankles (the 'Iron Lady' caught in a vulnerable moment). The editor thought the image inappropriate for *Daily Telegraph* readers. The *Spectator* published it instead (1 November 1980). Steve Bell had to negotiate with a *Guardian* editor about an acceptable number of turds splatted around a lavatory on which crouched his simian George W. Bush (4 April 2003). They agreed on six. He had started with nine (Bell 2005).

If individual cartoonists, regardless of paper, did not develop a broad sympathy with their readers, they surely would not survive. The most effective and best loved succeed, on the evidence of readers, in capturing the essence of events, issues and personalities. They develop tabs of identity which make their characters instantly recognisable: Hitler's forelock and moustache, Churchill's V sign, Thatcher's hair, Major's lip, Blair's ears and teeth. These can go beyond personal features. For *Guardian* readers Bell made day after day of inventive fun with the image of John Major wearing cellular underpants outside his trousers. Eventually they left his trousers altogether, serving ineptly (which was the point) as tea-strainer, carrier bag and far more (Bell 1999, esp. pp.110–44).

That example epitomises the combination of familiarity and freshness which makes a cartoonist (and a daily paper in general) attractive. Cartoonists create characters, families, entire parallel universes, for their fans to share. This is true not just for editorial cartoons. It is the point of strips (whether serial or not) and of those pocket cartoons which depend on stock characters or types – such as 'Matt' (Matthew Pritchett) in the *Daily Telegraph*. It is crucial, too, to editorial cartoonists providing social not political comment. Much of the success of Giles during his 46 years with the *Express* titles involved the activities of his large family of characters, whom *Express* readers took to their hearts. The key personality was Grandma – arguably the embodiment of Giles' own feelings.

Editorial cartoonists prominent in the national press in the mid-2000s are listed in Table 5.2. Their work is tracked only for the month of June 2006, so it cannot be assumed to be entirely typical. Papers generally run at least two regulars, and a few also use stand-ins. The list shows emphatically what a middle-aged and elderly bunch they are. Two are under 30 and the remainder over 40, with an average age of 52.

The images these artists used are summarised in Tables 5.3 and 5.4. Table 5.3 sorts them into the categories alluded to earlier. These are self-explanatory, except perhaps for the difference between 'common cultural references' and 'everyday images'. The former refers to matters of common knowledge (pubs, cowboys, the White Cliffs of Dover); while the latter are figures of speech (carrots and sticks, snail's pace, shooting yourself in the foot). The table also separates out those which can be described as childhood images: images not *of* childhood but learned

Table 5.2 *Selected cartoonists: national daily and Sunday newspapers, June 2006*

Newspaper	Cartoonists: editorial/**pocket**	Age	Number of cartoons	Circulation (000s)
Daily Express	P.Thomas	45	21	803
Daily Mail	'Mac' (S. McMurtry)	70	12	2,358
	K. Mahood	76	19	
Daily Mirror	N. Kerber & ? Black	44/?	21	1,608
	C. Griffin	59	2	
	M. Rowson	46	3	
Daily Telegraph	N. Garland	71	14	900
	'JAS' (J. Sillivan)	?	9	
	M. Daley	61	1	
	'Matt' (M. Pritchett)	40	19	
Guardian	S. Bell	54	12	376
	M. Rowson	46	5	
	A. Davey	?	2	
	D. Parkins	64	1	
Independent	D. Brown	47	23	254
	T. Sanders	47	6	
Sun	W. Caldwell	58	13	3,145
	C. Griffin	59	8	
	T. Johnston	52	5	
The Times	P. Brookes	48	15	662
	M. Morland	26	9	
	N. Bennett	64	7	
	J. Pugh	43	22	
Independent on Sunday	P. Schrank	53	3 (?)	219
Mail on Sunday	M. Heath	70	3 (?)	2,319
Observer	C. Riddell	43	3 (?)	455
	R. Thompson	44	2 (?)	
Sunday Express	'Scott' (S. Clissold)	27	4	797
Sunday Telegraph	J. Springs	43	4	797
	'Matt' (M. Pritchett)	40	3	
Sunday Times	G. Scarfe	69	4	1,301

Source: The British Cartoon Archive (University of Kent). List of cartoons may be incomplete.
Note: Excludes papers without regular political and social cartoons. Excludes strips.

in childhood. There is a column, too, which shows that, even during a single month, particular images crop up in more than one cartoon.

A selection of specific images from some of the categories is set out in Table 5.4. The obvious comment is that overwhelmingly they are *clichés*. (The cartoonist's challenge is to find fresh ways of using them.) Their great advantage is that they can be instantly understood – especially, perhaps, those familiar since childhood. These last in particular underline how far cartoons draw on the reader's imaginative experience. They take us straight into fantasy worlds, where we immediately start thinking in the cartoonist's terms. But even the mundane images may be more familiar in the imagination than through direct experience. How many people have actually seen a cowboy, had their fortune told by a gypsy, been to a knacker's yard, fingered a hangman's noose, or taken part in an identity parade?

Table 5.3 *Cartoon images: national daily and Sunday newspapers, June 2006*

Category	Total Different Images	Total Childhood Images	Total Cartoons	Total Childhood Cartoons)
Common cultural references	38	(22)	50	(29)
Everyday images	23	(8)	24	(8)
Literature, theatre, visual arts, film, etc.	18	(10)	21	(12)
Occupations	9	(8)	13	(11)
Animal	9	(8)	9	(8)
Topical references	8	(1)	13	(5)
Inanimate objects	6	(4)	13	(9)
Sports and games	6	(5)	12	(11)
Historical	5	(2)	5	(2)
TOTAL	122	(68)	160	(95)

Source: The British Cartoon Archive (University of Kent).

Note: Only editorial cartoons included. The list may not be complete. A small proportion of images (e.g. 'Footballer') are included in more than one category. For definition of 'Childhood Images', see text.

Table 5.4 *Cartoon images: examples, national daily and Sunday newspapers, June 2006*

Common cultural references	Everyday images	Literature, theatre, visual arts, etc.
Scales of justice	Throw the book at someone	Hay Wain (Constable)
St George and the Dragon	Burning your bridges	Venus (Botticelli)
British Grenadiers	Miracle cure	Moby Dick
Hot air balloon	Hitting the bullseye	Noddy and Big Ears
Hoodies	Saving her blushes	Wizard of Oz
Heart transplant	Blank sheet	Big Brother (TV)
Occupations	*Animals*	*Inanimate Objects*
Postman	Ass	Rocket warhead
Caretaker	Gnu	Egg
Racing driver	Elephant	Football
Toreador	Bulldog	Balloon
Sports and games	*Historical*	*Topical References*
'Monopoly'	Napoleon	'Blairforce One' (PM's jet)
Relay race	Nelson ('England expects')	Rooftop hunger strike
Ascot	First World War trenches	Ming vase restored
Croquet	Karl Marx	Football World Cup

Source: The British Cartoon Archive (University of Kent).

Note: Examples taken from the list in Table 5.3.

This analysis has emphasised continuity, tradition and familiarity in the purpose and methods of newspaper cartoons. But newspapers are changing. How may cartoons be affected?

Papers have been changing shape and size. Until 1970 there were generally two tabloids among about ten national dailies. By 2007 tabloid was the normal format, with the *Guardian* an intermediate 'Berliner' size and only the *Daily Telegraph* hanging on as a broadsheet (excluding here the broadsheet *Financial Times*, which has no cartoonist). Papers have become unprecedentedly thick. Fifty years ago most had eight or ten pages. Thirty years ago the broadsheets had about 26 and the tabloids 30. By the 2000s, the *Daily Mail* could have around 100, the red top tabloids 60 to 80 and the 'quality' papers 30 to 50 in their main sections.

More papers have split into self-contained sections, with their own editorials and cartoonists – some very popular, such as the *Guardian*'s Harry Venning, whose 'Clare in the Community' (about a social worker) became a Radio 4 comedy series. As to readership, changes in popularity have blurred the simple distinction between mass-circulation tabloids with predominantly working-class readers and low-circulation broadsheets read mainly by the middle classes. The former have shrunk and the latter have grown, while mostly abandoning the broadsheet format, both in proportion and in number of titles. The *Daily Mail*, first of the middle-class papers to go tabloid, dominates the middle market, but with a circulation similar to the old working-class tabloids.

Aided by changes in technology, there is far more flexibility in the design of papers than when the current senior cartoonists started work: more air in the paper; much more variety in graphics, artwork, photography and computer-generated design. Amidst all this, the old certainties of the cartoon can get lost. The arrival of colour in the 1990s, for instance, worried some cartoonists. They thought theirs was a black-and-white art; besides, working in colour took longer. Still not all of them work in colour, or not all the time – Paul Thomas (*Daily Express*) and Nick Garland among them. Others, including Bell, and Brookes, who started his 'Nature Notes' in response to the introduction of colour, have used it to great effect.

Although tabloid format still accommodates a principal editorial page ('The Voice of the *Daily Mirror*'), there is literally less space for an editorial cartoon. The *Daily Mirror* and the *Sun*, which remain essentially working-class papers, frequently shrink their editorial cartoons and/or put them beside columnists. The shrinkage can look strange, if the drawing was done for a larger format. Caricatures too lose much of their impact if shrunk. Often the *Daily Mirror*'s only editorial cartoon, a social more than political comment, is by Kerber and Black, who draw specifically for a column width. Regularly, too, the *Sun* publishes political pocket cartoons by Tom Johnston.

Kerber and Black, prolific freelancers, shade the editorial cartoon towards a gag. A further development reducing the distinctiveness of the traditional editorial cartoon is the increased and widespread use of illustrators. Their purpose is to illuminate an article without providing a comment of their own. But the line is fine – particularly if the drawing is a caricature, and particularly too in the more nuanced pages of the upmarket papers. The *Financial Times*, for instance, seems happy with illustrators instead of cartoonists. The artist 'JAS' (James Sillivan) may not be alone in drawing illustrations for one paper (*Guardian*) and cartoons for another (*Daily Telegraph*).

The new diversity allows variety of format. Martin Rowson, for instance, is one of the principal editorial cartoonists of the *Guardian*. But for the *Independent on Sunday* he also draws a cartoon and rhyming commentary on 'the Abuses of Literacy', and a multi-frame review called 'The Week Digested'. In addition he does occasional editorial cartoons for the *Daily Mirror*. Steve Bell, similarly, continues the political strip, 'If', which was commissioned by the *Guardian* in 1981. Although certainly a form of 'editorial' comment, such a strip would not sit comfortably on a leader page. Nor would the *Daily Telegraph*'s 'Alex' strip about City of London financiers, although some of its social comment resonates more widely. 'Alex' lives in the business section, while 'If' is in the *Guardian*'s tabloid section – together with the cult American strip 'Doonesbury'. 'Doonesbury' exemplifies the ambiguity of the format. Widely syndicated in the United States, some 900 papers in the 1990s published it with their comics section, 300 among the 'op-ed' pages (*Guardian* 25 October 1995).

The near-universal adoption of the tabloid format has obscured the most striking change in editorial cartoons. This was their decline in the mass-circulation press and their being embraced by the formerly broadsheet 'quality' papers. Until the *Guardian* became a fully national paper in the 1960s and the *Independent* was founded in 1986, *The Times* and *Daily Telegraph* were the only two 'quality' dailies anyway. Neither had a cartoonist. The *Daily Telegraph* appointed Garland in 1966. *The Times* started with Kenneth Mahood in the same year but did not find quite the right voice until Peter Brookes joined in 1982. In contrast the fluctuating group of mass-circulation middle market papers, dominated by the *Daily Express* and *Daily Mail*, each boasted a stable of cartoonists until about the last quarter of the twentieth century. The *Daily Express* had prominent social and political cartoons, a front page 'editorial' pocket cartoon by Osbert Lancaster – originator of the *genre* in Britain – a sporting strip ('The Gambols') and a general sporting cartoonist. The *Daily Mail*'s range was similar, including the highly original serial strip of social comment by Wally Fawkes ('Trog') centred on a mythical furry animal, 'Flook'. The two tabloids of the post-Second World War era, the *Daily Mirror* and the much smaller *Daily Sketch*, also had cartoonists.

By the 1980s the market, loosely speaking, had polarised, with the advance of the 'quality' broadsheets and the tabloid *Sun*, and the decline of the middle-market papers. For cartoonists, having their natural home on a 'quality' paper has had several implications. One is a shorter reach. 'Mac', on the *Daily Mail*, reaches more readers than the cartoonists of all the quality papers added together. In the heyday of mass circulation, Mac's reach – or more – was normal. Secondly, the 'quality' papers spray their sections and pages with named columnists. (*The Times* website listed 29 in early 2007.) These have strongly individual tones. The result muffles the traditional single editorial voice of a newspaper – the sound of 'The Thunderer' in the Victorian pomp of *The Times*, and the obvious arrangement in the days of anonymous journalism. Now the editorial 'we' has fanned out and opinions throng the leader pages. The editorial cartoonist waves a drawing in a crowd of people shouting.

This decline of the single editorial voice is probably linked to the decline of party orthodoxy in the British press. Even during general elections in the last 20 years, many papers have failed to endorse a party or – famously in 1997 – they have changed sides. Such equivocation must make it easier for 'quality' paper cartoonists to plough their own furrow. Similarly, a loose editorial rein may help Bell and Rowson indulge their scatological imagery of turds and feculence at the *Guardian*, rediscovering the uninhibited methods of eighteenth-century forebears like Gillray. It is easier, too, for cartoonists such as Rowson and Griffin to moonlight between one paper and another. Indeed Griffin appeared in both the *Sun* and the *Daily Mirror* on the same day (2 June) during the period represented in Tables 5.2 to 5.4.

Cartoons are very closely linked to their home culture because of the ways in which they work. Styles differ, too, because of varying graphic traditions. The structure of the press is also important. Countries with a predominantly regional press, which is the norm outside small states, cannot stray far from the parish pump. Many cartoons in the United States, for instance, notwithstanding syndication, are parochial.

Such considerations apart, there are good grounds for arguing that the conventions of cartooning include much that is international. When a row broke out in 2005 about cartoons published in Denmark depicting the Prophet Mohammed, the cartoons were readily comprehensible far and wide. The row was caused by his depiction of Mohammed at all: what varied were the reactions, not the comprehension. Danish Embassies were attacked in Syria and Beirut. Danish exports to the Middle East dropped by 15 per cent. At least 139 people were killed in demonstrations in various countries (Hiley 2006).

That row escalated partly via the internet, a technology which is putting newspapers into ferment. The future inclination of readers, the boundaries of a paper's web version and the right relation to the newsprint copy – all are in the melting pot. Web versions can make a paper even less of a 'news' paper than did the growth of radio and TV. So far cartoonists seem to be benefiting from the trend for papers to use their web versions to promote the print version and also to extend its contents. *Guardian Unlimited* is the most developed example. There is a certain self-consciousness about the site, for it is promoting not so much a masthead as a whole brand. Such self-promotion risks confusing the news with the newspaper (or the story with how we got the story). But for cartoonists it is a boon. Links take you to pictures of the principal cartoonists (Bell, Rowson – even Austin, who is now dead), as well as to their cartoons. Other links bring up a history of the 'If' strip and its characters; cartoonists from the *Education* and *Society* supplements and the *Weekend* magazine; and a 'cartoon shop', offering cartoon T-shirts and downloadable greetings cards by Rowson.

Other papers follow similar but currently less ambitious lines. *The Times* invites readers of its newsprint version to 'see a gallery of recent cartoons by Peter Brookes' on its website. On the *Daily Telegraph* site copies of some 350 of 'Matt's' back catalogue of cartoons are available for purchase. The work of his fellow cartoonists is retrievable too. The *Daily Mail* site carries an archive of 'Mac's' cartoons back to 2004, with signed copies promised for early in 2007.

All that illustrates some simple truths: that cartoons, as comment, are less ephemeral than news; that they may look good on the wall (not only in the smallest room); and that readers may become curious about the artists. These are reasons to be cheerful. Cartoonists do not have the prominence they enjoyed in the mass-circulation press during most of the twentieth century. But even if the worst miserablists are correct and electronic newspapers supersede the printed form, we can surely hope that cartoons will continue as a part of them.

References

Bell, S. (1999) *Bell's Eye* London: Methuen.
Bell, S. (2005) Talk at the British Library, 18 October.
British Cartoon Archive, University of Kent (2007) Biographical note on Stan McMurtry ('Mac') www.kent.ac.uk. Accessed 7 November 2007.
Hiley, N. (2006) 'Detached Irony Doesn't Always Travel that Well', *Times Higher Education Supplement* 24 February.
Seymour-Ure, C. (2003) *Prime Ministers and the Media* London: Blackwell.

Chapter 6

Obituaries

Nigel Starck

Capturing life, not death

There is nothing inherently gloomy about the newspaper obituary page: done well, it should capture life rather than wallow in death. The idea is to show, by character study and anecdote, what its subjects were like. These accounts of lives interrupted are often delivered with a serving of irreverent humour too:

> *Malcolm Hardee* (comedian) – *Daily Telegraph*
> He did an impression of Charles de Gaulle, his penis playing the part of the General's nose. ... Fans would greet his arrival on stage with cries of 'Get yer knob out.' He was said to be huge in Germany and Sweden.
> (*Daily Telegraph* 2005)

> *Sir Colin Cole* (Garter Principal King of Arms[1]) – *Independent*
> Something of a ladies' man, he nevertheless enjoyed a long and successful marriage, his wife Valerie being admirably tolerant of his many outside commitments.
> (Dickinson 2001)

The best obituaries, therefore, avoid the voice of mourning. But they do have their serious side as well: they serve as biographies in miniature, as important instruments of historical record, and they deliver society's first verdict on a life lived. They differ from the standard news story about death in this respect: obituary writers offer an appraisal of their subjects in much the same way that newspaper critics evaluate films, plays, books and restaurants for their readers. That critical approach is apparent in these classic *Times* character studies:

> *Dame Barbara Cartland* (author of romantic novels)
> There was a dashing vulgarity, careless of the censure of the literati, in a performance which shamelessly and repeatedly broke the world record for annual production of novels and gave her, quite absurdly, the longest entry in *Who's Who*... Cartland grew old in a unique style that she thought graceful

and many others found grotesque. She simply refused to compromise with age, and though the focus grew softer and softer, she continued to dress like a dazzling starlet of the 1940s. Diamantes remained the old girl's best friend.

(*The Times* 2000b)

Sir John Gielgud (actor)
He approached a character by exploring different aspects of himself, and one fascination of his work was to witness the extremes to which he could bend an always recognizable personality. Some things were outside his range. He never played in dialect. He was incapable of coarseness. ... If marble could speak, it would have sounded like Gielgud.

(*The Times* 2000c)

These life appraisals have enjoyed an extraordinary surge in popularity and influence during the past 20 years. They owe this state of health to the 1980s transformation of British newspapers through computerised typesetting: that latter-day industrial revolution in print imposed an urgent demand to fill an increased amount of column space with literate composition. Obituaries suited this cause, for they require some considerable research, a generous narrative, and an eloquence of expression. The quartet of 'quality' British dailies – *The Times*, *Telegraph*, *Guardian* and *Independent* – satisfy those expectations, and have nurtured the obituary into a refined and vigorous art form. Both *The Times* and *Guardian* now devote two pages a day to it; the *Telegraph* has published 13 collections of its obituaries, with each volume pursuing a defined theme; and the *Independent*, right from its birth in 1986, has given the British obituary an emphatic presence by using bold, graphic photography.

Obituary: its origins in word and practice

In essence, all this action represents a rebirth of an ancient craft. Taking its name from *obituarius* (Latin for 'pertaining to death'), the obituary is among the oldest expressions of journalism, first manifesting itself in the newsbooks (the forerunners of newspapers) in the seventeenth century. The earliest known example is found in a newsbook published on 2 July 1622 by Nathaniel Newbery and William Sheffard to tell readers about a sea battle between the British East India Company's fleet and four Portuguese warships. This journal has an overcooked, and erratically capitalised, title: *The True Relation of That Worthy Sea Fight Which two of the East India Shipps had with 4 Portingals of great force, and burthen, in the Persian Gulph*. But in relating the life and death of Captain Andrew Shilling, master of the *London*, it contains an obituary of force and authority.

After recounting some episodes of Shilling's early career, the unknown author wrote that the master had been 'so liked and looked upon with the judicious eyes of the East India Company' that he was appointed Admiral of the Fleet. On the voyage to the Persian Gulf, he had led that fleet through 'boysterous Seas, and mounting billowes, [and] fearefull stormes'. Through his 'vallour and directions, his Company were victors, and brought their ships to take in their lading ... into England'. Then came the engagement with the Portuguese: 'In the midst of the conflict, while we were wrapped in smoake and sweating in blood, a crosse shot crost us all and slue our Captaine; yea he perished in the midst of our triumphs' (Newbery and Sheffard 1622). In offering that career summary and an assessment of Captain Shilling's seamanship, the *True Relation* account satisfies the tenets of obituary definition. It has greater substance, through those biographical properties, than a simple chronicling of the fact of death.

By the 1660s, when the monarchy was restored, the obituary had established itself in journalism practice. It was employed in particular by Roger L'Estrange, journalist and censor at the court of Charles II, who was licensed to publish two weekly newspapers: the *Intelligencer* (on Mondays) and the *Newes* (on Thursdays). There was no serious competition. As censor, L'Estrange had been empowered to eliminate any printers suspected of seditious activity; after he had hanged and disembowelled one such miscreant (accused of inciting civil unrest), the press of the day found caution attractive. L'Estrange's obituaries became the exclusive valedictories for those who had remained loyal to the exiled King throughout the years of Oliver Cromwell's republic. The front page of a 1664 edition of the *Newes*, for example, was dedicated to appraising the life of an eminent royalist:

> This week affords but little but the sad news of the death of that great Minister of State, William, Earle of Glencairn, Lord High Chancellour of Scotland, a Person most Eminent, and well known in all his Majestyes Dominions, both for the Gallantry of his Spirit in the Noble Attempts against the Usurpers, as also for his sufferings during those times of Usurpation, and the many signal Services he hath performed in that high Station, wherein his Majesty most deservedly placed him since his happy Restauration. He dyed the 30th of the Instant of a Feavour in the 49th year of his Age, Beloved of his Prince, and Bewayled of all Ranks of his Majestyes Subjects.
>
> (*Newes* 1664)

Lives both virtuous and misspent

The style of obituary adopted by the royalist journals, and by the earlier newsbooks, was hagiographic in tone. All this changed with the arrival of the *Gentleman's Magazine*, an elegantly illustrated miscellany launched in 1731 and surviving until 1907. Its obituaries are as vigorous and informative to read today as they were during this magazine's influential existence; indeed, the founding Obituaries Editor of the *Independent* has acknowledged the *Gentleman's Magazine* as the inspiration for his own industrious practice of the art.

What makes the obituaries published by the *Gentleman's Magazine* markedly different from those which until then had appeared in the press was that they included, where the magazine found appropriate, hostile elements of character assessment. Obituaries were no longer the exclusive preserve of lives that, in an editor's opinion, had adorned society; instead, column space was found for those that had undermined it. This conferred upon the art itself a richer, more complete, definition. Among these discredited individuals was Peter Defaile, described on the *Gentleman's Magazine* obituaries page of January 1783 as the 'most notorious villain as ever became the scourge of private life'. He was the second son 'of a good family' in the west of England, he qualified as an attorney, and then forged a will so that his elder brother was disinherited. After spending the spoils, of more than £40,000, in a prolonged chapter of dissipation, Defaile became a singularly effective, if sinister, eighteenth-century rake:

> He insinuated himself, as soon as he found poverty approaching, into the good graces of a beautiful young lady of great fortune, whom he married, and spent all her money; and in succession, in the space of eleven or twelve years, married five more wives, all fortunes [sic], all which money he also spent, and these ladies died so very opportunely to make way for their successors, that when Defaile's character was better known nobody made any doubt of his having poisoned them.
>
> (*Gentleman's Magazine* 1783)

The obituary then recounts his gambling, arson and insurance fraud, swindling 'of an old lady out of a great deal of money', and killing of an opponent in a duel. Eventually overtaken by 'gout and stone', he died in a debtors' prison in Flanders. Continuing this Catholic policy, obituary selection for the *Gentleman's Magazine* was driven by the quality of the narrative as much as by the stature of the subject. So, while it devoted nearly three pages of close-set type to the obituary of Charles Wesley, prolific composer of hymns, it also found room in its March 1791 edition for obituaries of James Heaton, 'one of the most formidable poachers in the kingdom', and Winifred Griffith, a baronet's daughter who died 'in distressed circumstances' following 'an imprudent marriage' and 'the villainy of an attorney' (*Gentleman's Magazine* 1791). This variety of life stories is precisely in tune with the approach adopted by enlightened editors of contemporary obituaries.

Ethics, outrage and intrusion

A villainous life, as has been established in the history of Peter Defaile the rake, can offer a certain posthumous fascination; accordingly, British newspapers in recent times have appraised some seriously flawed characters. An accompanying, and delicate, question of publication ethics occurs, however, and it occurred in particular at the death in November 2002 of Myra Hindley. She had been sentenced to life imprisonment in 1966 for her part in the 'Moors Murders'. As the *Independent* recalled in its posthumous reflections: 'The killings were pitiless.

Some of the [murdered] children were photographed in humiliating poses; one tape recorded Lesley Ann [Downey] as she pleaded with her tormentors. The effect upon the nation, quite apart from the courtroom, was traumatic' (Morris 2002). The ethical question here was one of news value flavoured by concerns of precedent and moral judgement. Were a national paper's obituary pages, with their reputation for recording lives of rank, repute and achievement, the appropriate repository for an instant biography of a woman branded by the *Independent*'s sub-heading (Morris 2002) as 'an icon of homicidal infamy'? In company with the *Independent*, the *Guardian* took the view that this placement was acceptable. A month before Hindley's death, the obituaries editor of the *Independent*, James Fergusson, had already gone on the record as declaring that it was simply a question of news values; moral judgements, he said, were irrelevant. He argued that an obituary was required because:

> She is a villainess of our times. ... Yes, she did terrible things, but how is it that people become so enthralled by Hindley, villainess, that no Home Secretary dare release her, even though by all the rights of justice she obviously should be released? She was sentenced to a more-or-less fixed term, which she has long overstayed.
>
> (Starck 2004, p.189)

Of the two, it was the *Guardian*'s obituary which caused the greater measure of debate, as a result of Peter Stanford's intermittently sympathetic appraisal, which some observers (notably the *Spectator*, a weekly magazine) interpreted as being a posthumous apology for Hindley. These lines from the *Guardian* piece created particular attention through offering a form of overt opinion more commonly found in a newspaper's leader column:

> The authorities' repeated refusal to grant Hindley parole came even though she more than met the criteria. In the end, it was public opinion that kept her in jail. Britain's longest-serving woman prisoner was, in effect, a political detainee, and prejudice her jailer.
>
> (Stanford 2002)

In similar vein, there was consternation at a decision by *The Times* to publish an obituary of a notorious terrorist, Mohammad Atef, branded by *The Times* obituarist as an architect of the World Trade Center and Pentagon attacks. Defending its publication, the Obituaries Editor explained in an article syndicated internationally that villainous lives qualified for the page 'if it is judged that they have helped to shape the world we live in or affected its political history' (*Australian* 2001).

A related point of ethical judgement comes into the forum when the victims of such acts of outrage are considered. Selection for the obituary pages of the world's great newspapers has traditionally been determined by a potential subject's fame, notoriety or (because the entertainment factor remains seductive) eccentricity.

This process changed after 11 September 2001. No longer is there the same level of concentration on the A-list dead; ordinary lives can now be appraised and recounted – a brand of equality provoked by acts of fanatical outrage. An unpretentious existence can today achieve a measure of fame, simply through a random assault on its very unpretentiousness.

The seminal shift in obituary selection was started by the *New York Times*. Until the World Trade Center attack, its obituaries had largely been the preserve of political leaders, chiefs of the armed services, prominent entertainers, jurists, scientists, scholars and eminent figures of America's churches and corporations. Four days later, on 15 September 2001, came evidence of the change. Casting for the *New York Times* obituary columns suddenly struck an engagement with extras from the theatre of life, not necessarily the leading players.

It began that day with 'Among the Missing', a section dedicated to obituaries in miniature of the victims. The following day, the tag for these vignettes (of 150 to 200 words) became 'Portraits of Grief'; it was perhaps an odd title, given the upbeat tenor of each word picture. Their individual headlines alone were scented with Middle American achievement and satisfaction: 'Always trying to get ahead'; 'Humming the day away'; 'The Giants' biggest booster'; 'The heart in the 3-piece suit' (*New York Times* 2001). By the end of the year, when the 'Portraits of Grief' total had reached 1,800 and it was wound down as a daily feature, this *New York Times* initiative had transformed the scope of obituary writing.

A year on, Australian and British editors encountered their opportunity to address this newfound order. In October 2002, when 88 Australians died in the Bali Bombings, three leading newspapers – the *Australian* (national circulation), the *Sydney Morning Herald* and the *Age* (Melbourne) – each published a series of character studies. All three dailies broadened the obituary agenda by displaying a willingness to select youthful subjects; one of them, Abbey Borgia, was only 13. *The Times*, in London, pursued that course too, publishing a three-page section on British victims of the Bali terrorism. The character of an 'establishment' obituaries section was changed dramatically: an interpreter, a hotel manager and motor mechanics all had their lives recognised in *Times* type.

This transition contained questions of operational and ethical judgement for the editors. Conventionally, their pages rely heavily on material from their own files (which often include complete obituaries just waiting to go), from specialist contributors, and from syndicated sources. In the wake of those acts of outrage, however, obituarists had to track down the bereaved, intrude upon private grief, follow leads, make calls, perform interviews. And there was more to come: a *Times* series entitled 'London Lives', acknowledging 52 of the 56 fatalities from London's suicide bombings of 7 July 2005. That exercise in comprehensive accounting was supplemented two weeks later with an obituary of Jean Charles de Menezes, the Brazilian shot and killed by police when he was erroneously identified as a suspect.

The 2005 series provoked its own set of delicate challenges for *The Times*' obituaries desk. Names could not be released until identity was assured, one bereaved family demanded (without success) that a political statement concerning British military involvement in Iraq should be included, and police media notices frequently carried 'family request privacy' codicils (generally as a result of mawkish practices by non-resident correspondents acting outside the UK Press Complaints Commission code of conduct). There was the question too of the four bombers. They, after all, were British citizens whose deaths were included in the casualty list. One reader even called *The Times* to say that they also warranted obituaries; they were victims of a sort, went this argument, fatally distracted by zealotry. Ultimately, it was decided that any dalliance with that measure of inclusiveness would have been unpalatable.

Amidst all this trauma and repositioning, one comparatively happy story did emerge. The 19 October 2002 first edition of *The Times*, carrying the Bali series, contained a photograph and obituary of a 'hippy and child of the road' as one of the 26 supposed victims. By the second edition, the hippy was gone. He had been in a remote part of the Indonesian archipelago, and had phoned his parents at their Buckinghamshire home to say he was safe just a few hours before *The Times* went to press. The page was remade, a large photograph of a genuine victim was substituted, and an adjusted total of 25 lives became the focus of remembrance instead.

Prematurity, legality, eccentricity and taste

There have been some celebrated instances of obituary publication while the subject was still alive. Rex Alston, in his youth a Cambridge University athlete and in maturity a BBC sports commentator, was in hospital with food poisoning one morning in 1985. Though unwell, he was far from dead. But *The Times* that day suggested otherwise, for an appreciation of his life, written as an update by cricket correspondent John Woodcock, 'unaccountably found its way' onto the obituaries page. The error seemed to inspire a rapid recovery; Alston appeared on national television, from the hospital, at 7.15 a.m. to prove the announcement premature (*The Times* 1994).

Another such mistake is described in an August 2001 edition of the *Daily Telegraph*. The moral to be drawn from this story is that of the need to confirm information with a second source, no matter how trusted the first might be. The *Telegraph*'s misfortune had its origins at California's Motion Picture and Television Hospital, a sanctuary for veterans of the entertainment industry, where Dorothy Fay Ritter, 'an actress best remembered for riding the range with Buck Jones in Westerns made during the 1930s', had long been a patient. A hospital staff member noticed that Dorothy Fay was not in her room and, on enquiry, was told 'She's gone'. The staff member immediately rang a local obituarist, an established contributor to the *Telegraph*, and the paper was soon publishing an exclusive account. But she had 'gone', the obituaries editor discovered by email from the United States three days later, to another wing of the Motion Picture and Television Hospital (McKie 2001).

The job of editing an obituaries page, therefore, is a demanding one. Apart from resolving that essential point as to whether the subject is indeed dead, the business of taste and accuracy has to be satisfied in appraising a life. While a simple interpretation of British-inspired statutes would suggest that writers of obituaries can say what they choose about the dead without the restraint of defamation law (except, quaintly, in the Australian state of Tasmania), some related complexities do exist. For a start, it is unwise – and potentially defamatory – to suggest that neglect or other actions of an unsavoury nature by surviving family members contributed to the death in question. Then there is the matter of taste: just how candid should the writer be, and what measure of censure or even ridicule can be imposed? As well as being the first verdict of society, an obituary offers in another sense a final judgement; those who write them must, axiomatically, confront a duty of care in the words that they select.

This subtle affair of posthumous character study is demonstrated in two obituaries which chose to concentrate on the dress sense of their subjects. David Treffry, 'an Arabist of distinction', was remembered by *The Times* as having cultivated an eccentric appearance in Fowey, his home town in Cornwall:

> Seeing him striding with his walking stick about the narrow streets of the historic port in his trademark flannel trousers (the bottoms flapping several inches above the ankle), a tweed jacket that looked as old as Fowey itself, a faded striped tie (probably of the Duke of Cornwall's Light Infantry) and a battered cloth cap, one was reminded more of a classics master in an Evelyn Waugh prep school than of the international diplomat he had actually been.
>
> (*The Times* 2000a)

That succeeds as an endearing description of a man untroubled by fashion, mainly because of the gentle prod in the 'Evelyn Waugh prep school' direction. But when Britain's Press Association tried a similar tactic in its syndicated obituary of Lord Jay, an erstwhile cabinet minister, a touch of malevolence blighted the mood. In a narrative notable for a sustained meanness of spirit, it described him as 'a shambling figure' whose 'oratory was as mediocre and uninspiring as his appearance'. Emboldened possibly by the legal maxim *mors omnia solvit* (death dissolves everything), the PA obituarist added: 'Stories about his reputed tightness with money abounded. ... His attire was such that at one overseas gathering he was mistaken for a tramp ... one of his suits was accidentally posted off to Oxfam' (Bale 1996). While Jay himself, in death, could not be considered a victim of defamation, his surviving family was well placed to express collective umbrage. One of Lord Jay's twin daughters, Catherine Boyd, was working as a producer at the BBC and saw the piece as it emerged on the wire service. She rang the Press Association to complain, as a result of which the agency sent a memorandum to its clients, advising them that the obituary had caused offence. The incident itself made the front page of *The Times* the following day, with Mrs Boyd quoted as saying her father had indeed been 'shabby' because 'clothes were not important to him ... to go on about it so much was stupid. There. was nothing about him [in the obituary] as a human being' (Bale 1996).

Humanity of spirit, perhaps, remains a desirable quality for those seeking to wear the obituarist's cloak.

Snapshot and portrait

To capture life instead of death, writers of obituaries have to assemble more than the curriculum vitae. The challenge is to produce a portrait, rich in substance and embodiment, rather than the snapshot supplied by trotting out a résumé. In the instance of celebrity subjects, when newspaper files and online sources are bountiful, the major task is one of information selection and management. When the subject's life has gone unrecorded, however, the art of interview is employed – and it is here that only a line of acute enquiry will result in the required act of portraiture.

Obituarists, therefore, should pursue with passion the quest for anecdotes and characteristics which bring the subject back to life on the page. It is the degree of detail which counts, as in this vignette of 1920s poverty from the *Guardian*'s obituary of the comedian Charlie Drake: 'His mother, Violet, pawned the sheets and pillowcases on a Monday and retrieved them on the Friday, ensuring bed linen for the weekend' (Dixon 2006). At the same time, there must be constant avoidance of euphemism and cliché. Such atrocities are apparent in many amateur attempts at the craft, with the deadly application of: 'sorely missed', 'loving husband/wife/ father/mother', 'long illness bravely borne', 'passed away', 'the passing of' and the truly egregious 'warm smile lit up a room' (from a midwest obituary of recent vintage). The discerning obituarist has to eschew the sentimental tendencies and intimacies of the eulogy, and tell the life story for an audience of strangers. The further challenge, arising from this necessary estrangement, is that those readers should be made to wish – after reading the obituary – that they had known the subject.

It is essential also to minimise any engagement with religious testimony; that belongs, if at all, at the funeral service rather than within the obituary. In addition, assertions of a supposed afterlife will serve only to cheapen the product. An Australian newspaper's obituary, of a prominent athlete, lost all credibility in this respect when it declared that at a future championship meeting he 'will be there somewhere with those Aussie teams, cheering on his buddies' (Fraser 2002).

To some practitioners, notably those writing for the major American papers, the portrait is incomplete without inclusion of the cause of death. Britain's leading quartet of obituary publishers is less concerned with the point. Both *The Times* and the *Guardian* will seek it if the subject was under 70 or if the manner of death is germane to the account (as in the case of a mountaineer dying in an avalanche). At the *Independent* and the *Daily Telegraph*, cause is recorded only when it assumes an intrinsic element of the narrative (again, the unfortunate climber serves to illustrate the point).

The fully textured picture, therefore, presents the intending obituarist with some complex undertakings. When those are satisfied, there are formidable rewards for reader, writer and the cause of historical record. At *The Times*, Peter

Davies, who has been writing obituaries for more than 30 years, still regards the job with a mix of reverence and pride:

> There is nothing else in journalism, to me, that has the total satisfaction of writing an obituary. You are writing a piece of contemporary history. It's got real life and permanence in it. A lot of news stories are, after all, only position papers on something that's breaking or is going on. They're not the last word. Of course, an obituary isn't the last word – but it's the first of the last words.
>
> (Starck 2006, pp.102–3)

This potent element of newspaper publishing is, in essence, journalism that matters – for the obituary supplies a wellspring of biographical information and an enduring reflection of society's mores.

Note

1   England's chief heraldic authority.

References

Australian (2001) 'Lives of the Late but Not Lamented' 29 November Media, p.15.

Bale, J. (1996) 'Jay Family Anger at "Shambling Tramp" Obituary of their Father' *The Times* 7 March, p.1.

Daily Telegraph (2005) 'Malcolm Hardee' 4 February, p.24.

Dickinson, P. L. (2001) 'Sir Colin Cole' *Independent* 28 February Review, p.6.

Dixon, S. (2006) 'Charlie Drake' *Guardian* 28 December, p.34.

Fraser, A. (2002) 'Zestful, Restful Athlete' *Australian* 15 January, p.12.

Gentleman's Magazine (1783) vol. 53 January, p.93.

Gentleman's Magazine (1791) vol. 61 March, pp.282–4.

McKie, A. (2001) 'The Day I Managed to "Kill Off" Tex Ritter's Wife', *Daily Telegraph* 30 August, p.16.

Morris, T. (2002) 'Myra Hindley' *Independent* 16 November, p.24.

New York Times (2001) Selection of Headlines from 'Portraits of Grief' 16 September, A9 and 18 September, B10.

Newbery, N. and Sheffard, W. (1622) *The True Relation of That Worthy Sea Fight* 2 July.

Newes (1664) 9 June.

Stanford, P. (2002) 'Myra Hindley' *Guardian* 16 November, p.22.

Starck, N. (2004) 'Writes of Passage: A Comparative Study of Newspaper Obituary Practice in Australia, Britain, and the United States' Ph.D. Thesis, Flinders University, p.189 http://catalogue.flinders.edu.au/local/adt/public/adt-SFU20051205.171130/index.html. Accessed 25 October 2007.

Starck, N. (2006) *Life After Death* Melbourne: Melbourne University Press.

The Times (1994) 'Rex Alston' 9 September, p.21.

The Times (2000a) 'David Treffry' 11 April, p.25.

The Times (2000b) 'Dame Barbara Cartland' 22 May, p.21.

The Times (2000c) 'Sir John Gielgud' 23 May, p.25.

Further reading

Brunskill, I. (Ed.) (2005) *Great Lives* London: HarperCollins.

Glover, S. (Ed.) (2000) *The Penguin Book of Journalism* London: Penguin.

Johnson, M. (2006) *The Dead Beat* New York: HarperCollins.

Osborne, P. (Ed.) (2003) *The Guardian Book of Obituaries* London: Guardian.

Massingberd, H. (Ed.) (2001) *The Very Best of The Daily Telegraph Books of Obituaries* London: Pan Macmillan.

Chapter 7

Advice columnists

Angela Phillips

Advice columns have rarely been the subject of serious scrutiny by media scholars. They are more usually the butt of jokes but this chapter will argue that they are worthy of serious consideration. They are certainly very popular. In a 1989 survey Marje Proops was the most widely read writer in the *Daily Mirror* (Patmore 1993, p.314) but it is the porousness of the columns that makes them such a fruitful area of study. The unique two-way relationship of the columnists with readers means that, rather than performing, as is usually argued (Beetham 1996, p.23), a narrowly normative role, newspaper agony aunts can be instrumental in challenging norms. Their ambivalent role in a private, or feminine, space within what has been a masculine institution places them at the edge of discursive formation. Their position as non-experts arguably gives them a very special significance in the recasting of discursive boundaries – they are the lightning conductors of social unease. They listen to what has been unsayable, and in listening and then reproducing these forbidden discourses, they bring them into the realm of the 'normal' and sayable.

In recognising advice columns as 'female spaces' I have made use of a number of studies of women's relationship with media. In particular scholars have looked at magazines (Winship 1987; Hermes 1995), soap opera (Brunsdon 1984; Modleski 1984) and talk shows (Shattuc 1997). Problem pages have much in common with talk shows and one question scholars have asked in relation to talk shows is whether they provide an alternative 'public sphere' which could be empowering to participants (Mclaughlin 1993; Shattuc 1997; Livingstone 1994). Most recognise that the inequality in the power relationship between participants and host militates against any real empowerment, and the same could be said of the advice columnist. However, and this is perhaps the more important question, does the exposure of the columnist to the 'agony' of the readers change the way in which she/he presents the material? I would argue that it does. Journalists both make, and are made by, culture, and advice columnists, assuming the letters they receive are genuine, are exposed, more than any other journalists, to the unmediated, unsolicited, thoughts and feelings of readers.

They are all made up

In popular accounts of the genre it is clear that these columns have always been the subject of sneers, innuendo and jokes. Samuel Johnson set the tone when he dismissed the very first advice columnists, published in the *Athenian Gazette* (later the *Athenian Mercury*) in the late seventeenth century, as: 'A knot of obscure men who answered … questions sent, or supposed to be sent' (Kent 1979, p.3). More recently Petra Boynton (2004a) has also questioned the legitimacy of advice columnists on the grounds that they lack theoretical expertise. However, feminists, including myself, have long argued that purely theoretical expertise is not always the most helpful. It can also be the source of rigid and narrowly normative advice (Ehrenreich and English 1978; Phillips and Rakusen 1978).

Newspaper advice columnists combine the traits both of 'experts' and lay people. They may have medical training or they may be journalists who have specialised in this field and acquired a list of expert contacts upon whom they can call (Rayner 2003; Patmore 1993). Writing in the mass media they are open to scrutiny and have to be as certain as they can be that the factual information they provide is in line with current knowledge in their field – however controversial their opinions may be. I would argue, however, that the real 'expertise' of the advice columnists, and the source of their potential for subverting cultural norms, is their function as a conduit for their letter writers. People who write letters, I would suggest, are not only interested in advice. These letters are also attempts to be heard and if they are read as such then the function of the columnist is partly to disseminate ideas about how social and emotional life are conducted.

The other insinuation in much of the popular (and not so popular) literature is that the letters are invented. In the absence of any existing empirical evidence I went to the advice columnists themselves, or to accounts of their work, for information on this subject. Deidre Sanders of the *Sun* says: 'They are all real' (email communication December 2006). Marje Proops, for many years the advice columnist on the *Daily Mirror*, was equally clear: 'I don't make mine up' (Patmore 1993, p.257). Proops said that she received 1,000 a week (Proops 1977, p.200). When Claire Rayner took over as advice columnist for the *Sun* in 1974, she estimated that she received between 700 and 1,500 a week and she established a team of people to reply to them all (Rayner 2003, p.328). Sanders and her team currently receive between 100 and 300 letters and emails a day (email communication 2006). Hera Cook writing about advice manuals (2003b, p.193) mentions the huge number of letters sent to anyone who seemed likely to give them advice.

Virginia Ironside is credited with bringing advice columns to serious newspapers when, after cutting her teeth on the tabloids, she started the 'Dilemmas' column in the *Independent* newspaper. She told me (telephone interview December 2006) that she gets far fewer letters than she received on tabloid newspapers and magazines: 'Broadsheet readers are really far more interested in giving than in receiving advice', she said. In the *Independent*, in a reversal of the 'expert' role, readers are invited to write in with answers to dilemmas. Ironside edits them and writes her own answer alongside. This form has now spread to the *Guardian* (which leaves out the advice columnist and only prints readers' responses) and also to the *Daily Mirror*, where advice columnist Dr Miriam Stoppard regularly prints readers' advice alongside her own. At the *Independent*, Ironside is not above canvassing around friends and acquaintances for dilemmas to which her readers can respond but she insists that she doesn't make them up. She is merely doing what any journalist does: finding a story and publishing it as a 'real life story', while maintaining the essential interactive element in the publication of responses.

Selection and editing are always an important part of an agony aunt's job. Marje Proops, a seasoned journalist who cut her teeth door-stepping for the *Daily Herald*, is unapologetic about this process: 'You have to select on the basis that it has to be readable and encourage other letter writers. ... If you don't do that you serve no purpose at all.' When faced with an Editor who wanted something a little spicier she admits that she would be prepared to 'have another look'. But, 'if any editor said to me, "Make up some sexy letters, Marje," I'd say "Ta-ta!"' (Patmore 1993, p.257). Claire Rayner, a nurse who turned to advice writing, regards the letter writers as 'patients' and was appalled when, having moved from the *Sun* to the *Sunday Mirror*, she was asked to provide 'sexier' letters. She says in her biography (Rayner 2003, p.397): 'In all the years I had done this work, I had never let anyone use letters addressed to me as titillating fillers for a sexy page.'

While this evidence is far from exhaustive it does raise a question. Why should the problems be made up any more than the stories in a real life magazine, or the quotes in a news story? What does this widespread suspicion, unsupported by any evidence, tell us about the place of these pages in newspapers? It could be argued that the disbelief is part of an almost reflex denial of the importance of private lives in the public realm. Advice columnists, in providing space for private and emotional expression, in newspapers that have always been quintessentially public, bring these two spheres into collision.

A feminised space

The very first advice columns were, in fact, written by men. John Dunton, who went on to become the Editor of the *Post-Angel*, the first newspaper (published in 1701) to include an advice column, is said to have got the original idea because he was himself conducting an affair and was sorely in need of advice (Kent 1979, p.1). However, as the idea spread they gradually became, if not the preserve of women, at least a space in which most letter writers and most (though not all) advisers were women. As such I would argue that they have provided a feminised space within newspapers in the same way in which Margaret Beetham (1996) argues that magazines provide a 'feminised' media space. This is not to suggest that women were not interested in the other pages, but rather that those other pages refused, or trivialised, matters of personal life. Beetham (1996, p.3) argues that magazines, like other 'women's spaces', have a radicalising potential because they are a place where femininity is 'unfixed' and can be made and then remade by and among women. The same could be said of the newspaper agony columns where, by all accounts, editors rarely trespass. Ironside, commenting on her experience of advice columns on a number of newspapers before arriving at the *Independent*, describes a world in which: 'The agony column was always on a different floor. It was seen as "women's stuff", "other". The whole thing embarrassed everyone as though it was all about periods ... weird creepy things that women do in the dark and a mad old bat to advise them' (telephone interview December 2006).

Within the magazines Beetham (1996, p.23) saw the agony aunts as 'normalising' voices in contrast to the more subversive letter writers. This ignores the role of editing and selection in the presenting of material. In selecting the letters, the columnist could use them to 'float' ideas that they would be unable to put their names to in such a public space. It might be more useful to see the readers and the advisers as poles around which discourses circulate. Both the adviser and the letter writers participate in the making and remaking of culture (McRobbie 1996, p.392). Advice columnists Marje Proops and Claire Rayner write of being moved and disturbed by the letters they received. Proops says of her first exposure to readers' letters: 'I spent half the night reading. And worrying. Many of the problems seemed to me to be insuperable. They were complicated and often heartbreaking and I was desperate' (Proops 1976, p.9). Rayner remarks (2003, p.365): 'I became deeply embroiled in the problems of my readers ... the job politicised me.'

Changing discourse

In considering the 'normalising' role of advice columnists it helps to see them, not in isolation, but in the context of the particular discourse of their time.[1] In attempting to see how advice columnists both fit into, and help shape, the discourses of sexuality and relationships, I am indebted to the work of Hera Cook (2003a and b) and Robin Kent (1979). Cook, in *The Long Sexual Revolution*, describes how sexual behaviour was shaped over the period 1800–1975 by the impact of the Industrial Revolution on class formations and the changes in economic relationships between men and women. Kent provides us with evidence of the way in which relationship advice (mainly in magazines) assisted, at times resisted and then helped to normalise social change.

In the earliest period of advice columns in the late seventeenth and into the early eighteenth century, letters often dealt with seduction, loss of virginity or the advisability (or otherwise) of taking a lover. In this early phase, according to Cook (2003a, p.64), men and women shared both the economic and social support for children and there was social and legal pressure on men to maintain their children whether or not they were born in wedlock. Cook found that community surveillance broke down in the second half of the eighteenth century, and for a period at the end of the century, there is evidence of early parenthood and more casual sexual relationships among women, suggesting more relaxed social mores (Cook 2003a, p.63).

Over the same period, Cook describes a hardening division between the public world of work and the private world of the home. For women of the emerging middle classes (the major readers of the problem pages at this time), a 'good' marriage to a man with financial prospects became an essential precursor of motherhood. Women became goods to be owned and as such their 'purity' and use value must be guaranteed. The pressure on men to be economically independent before marrying led to a gradual rise in the age of marriage, and long periods of sexual abstinence were necessarily enforced as a result. During the course of the next century working-class women (the vast majority of the population) also began to reject sexual freedom because of what they stood to lose. Men were more mobile, work was moving out of the domestic realm and men were following it. Women who became pregnant could no longer rely on social pressure to keep men at home supporting their children. Changes in the Poor Law (1832) freed unmarried men from supporting their children. That meant that women who gave birth outside marriage faced total ruin.

A change of this magnitude in the lives of women could not have been accomplished without what Foucault describes as a 'discursive shift' (Foucault 1979, p.31). Cook notes that discussion of sexual matters was banished. What a girl didn't know about (it was assumed) she would be less likely to show an interest in. Cook suggests that economic and social constraints meant that women had to learn from childhood how to 'resist their own bodies' (Cook 2003a, p.92); however, she sees these new constraints, not as an internalising of external controls, but as a response from among women to extreme circumstances – a kind of voluntary abandonment of sexuality in the face of danger. Indeed she suggests that anger against the male refusal to take part in this self-denying ordinance was the wellspring of nineteenth-century feminism.

Kent traces this shift through the advice columns. Towards the end of the eighteenth century the boundaries between the married and unmarried started to harden. Questions of etiquette became a matter of concern as more socially fluid relationships solidified and society became increasingly stratified. Kent notes the gradual disappearance of any discussion of sex from the problem pages. There became, quite literally, a limit to what it was possible to think and to 'know'. The feminist discourse of the previous century did not disappear completely but it became marginalised. Increasingly, advice pages were written by men, rather than women. By the middle of the nineteenth century, they were no longer places where readers and writers exchanged ideas. They had taken on an educational role policing female behaviour (1979, p.15). Kent puts this change down to the rise in Evangelicalism (ibid., p.14). However, it could equally be argued that the rise in Evangelicalism was a response to social change rather than a cause of it. The readers of magazines were seeking advice to deal with the lives they lived and the magazines, ever sensitive to changing social conditions, obliged.

In order to look more closely at the specific role of newspaper advice columns I took another period of social change, 1974–2003, and compared the editorial coverage and advice columnists in the *Sun* and the *Daily Mirror*, both popular daily newspapers with largely working-class readerships. I wanted to see whether the approach varied, and to ascertain whether the advice columnists were more or less likely than other writers to uphold or resist existing normative values. I started with a period in early 1974, looking at the entire content of the newspapers, and then took a second period in 2003, using the cuttings database LexisNexis, which allowed me to search for key words across the whole newspaper for a whole year. I also interviewed Deidre Sanders, currently the advice columnist for the *Sun* newspaper, and Virginia Ironside, advice columnist for the *Independent*, and I read a biography of Marje Proops, of the *Daily Mirror* (Patmore 1993) and an autobiography by Claire Rayner (2003), who has worked both at the *Sun* and the *Sunday Mirror*.

In 1974 the *Mirror* and the *Sun* had embraced the sexual revolution. It was reported (*Daily Mirror* 7 March 1974, p.7) that a woman had been granted a divorce on what appeared to be the grounds that she had never had an orgasm. The 'Dear Marje' column was set in this context. The *Mirror* woman in the 1970s, in the editorial as well as the advice columns, was working class, of indeterminate age and still the centre of a family rather than an individual, but she was a sexual being. Proops was already very well established at the *Mirror* before starting her advice column in 1971. She attended editorial conferences and continued to write trenchant opinion pieces (Patmore 1993, p.163). She campaigned openly for legal abortion, easier divorce, better sex education and equal pay and opportunity, and she used her position on the paper to stop developments she disapproved of. She said: 'I used to get quite a lot of angry letters complaining about the boobs, and I was responsible for stopping the *Daily Mirror* from following the line of the *Sun*' (Patmore 1993, p.191).

As such a powerful influence at the *Mirror* it is perhaps not surprising that there is less of a gap between her advice page and the editorial of the *Mirror* than with any other columnists whose work I looked at. Over at the *Sun*, the agony columnists had no similarly central position. The battles were carried out in the private space of the problem page. Claire Rayner remembers an early encounter in 1973 with the then Editor, Larry Lamb:

> He said, 'My *Sun* is a man's paper, a working man's paper I want none of that nerdy stuff about finding their inner selves, no rubbish like that.... Nor do I want any suggestion ever that the Great British Man has sex problems apart from not getting enough. Right? I want no suggestion that he can't get it up neither'.
>
> (2003, p.359)

Rayner, as a new columnist, was in no position to disagree, so she waited for him to go on holiday and then published a letter about premature ejaculation, offering a leaflet for sufferers. It attracted 18,000 responses in ten days (ibid., p.361).

At the *Sun* in 1974 all women were 'dolly birds' for the service of men. One news story (6 March 1974, p.7) described how: 'A top referee's son paid the penalty yesterday for his behaviour on a soccer special. A court heard that Mark Kirkpatrick knelt on a seat and clapped as a young girl was stripped to the waist in a railway carriage.' The young woman is not quoted at any point and her experience is not the focus of the story. Against this background Rayner found her time at the paper something of a struggle. She was far more careful and more likely than Marje to refer her readers to other sources of advice; nevertheless she did open up the paper to the problems readers were having with sex, rather than simply following the *Sun* line: that it was all a bit of a laugh.

In the later research period 2000 and 2003 I was able to search both the *Sun* and the *Mirror* using key words. The mood had changed. Now the news and editorial were far more censorious and often completely at odds with the story being told on the problem pages. I looked at references to the morning-after-pill because of the link with teenage pregnancy – which was a key issue at the time. The first mention in the *Daily Mirror*, in January 2000, was in the advice column. A 17-year-old girl had unprotected sex then went to her doctor for STD tests and the morning-after-pill. The responses from readers and agony aunt Miriam Stoppard focused on the relationship between mother and daughter, congratulating both for their open relationship (18 January 2000, p.27).

A few months later the *Mirror* news pages picked up the subject of allowing the morning-after-pill to be taken off prescription. The coverage is entirely negative and groups opposing the new plans are given considerably more space and more prominence than those in favour. One opinion piece speaks out in favour but grudgingly as: 'A bitter pill we must swallow' (13 December 2000, p.9). A leader does finally come out in favour of the plan, pointing out that it is not just teenagers who might want access to the drug.

In March the same year a *Sun* news story blamed lack of availability of the morning-after-pill for a rise in the abortion rate after the millennium New Year celebrations. The same month the problem page provided advice on how to access the morning-after-pill. In July, however, the language of news changes, and negative quotes take over and build up. In December, Sanders is allowed a column to speak in favour of taking the pill off prescription, but the leader on 11 December headed 'Bitter Pill' is worth quoting:

> There will be those who will welcome the morning-after-pill today. But less than a fortnight ago the Government legalised buggery at 16. This was crashed through Parliament despite huge opposition in this country. Now we are told the morning-after-pill is to go on sale from New Year's Day. Where was the debate on this hugely contentious moral issue?
>
> (*Sun* editorial 11 December 2000)

I went on to look in more detail at the coverage of homosexuality in both newspapers in 2003. Again there is a difference between the newspapers. The *Sun* in February and March ran two consecutive stories about the private lives of MPs. One is about a relationship with a 'rent boy', the other about a casual homosexual encounter. These take up considerable space over a number of days. On the news and comment pages homosexuality is either a joke or a threat. However, on the problem pages attitudes are very different. Deidre Sanders chose to print letters about homosexuality on the day the news coverage started (26 February) and the day it ended (7 March). In both cases the letters deal not with the sex act but with the relationship that surrounds it. On the final day of the newspaper's attack on Ron Davies headlined, 'Hilarious new lie after gay romp in woods', Deidre is saying to a young man afraid of telling his mother that he is gay: 'Be honest with your mum, I expect she just wants to know you are happy' (*Sun* 7 March 2003).

The *Mirror* ignored the first *Sun* story but responded to the second, more serious one, with a leader (7 March) which stated: 'We couldn't give a monkey's what Ron does in his private life.' Later that month (13 March) there was a story about a homophobic Tory MP being forced to resign. On 25 March, Stoppard, on the *Mirror*'s problem pages, counsels a reader whose daughter is unhappily confused about her sexuality. Both she, and the readers who respond, underline (again) how lucky she is to have a mum she can confide in. Clearly, in the *Mirror*, on both news and advice pages, and in the advice columns of the *Sun*, the discourse has moved on. The emphasis is not on sexual acts (which are considered in most respects 'normal'). It is the relationship that has now been problematised. Stoppard goes out of her way to encourage behaviour she considers positive – rather than censoring that which she might deem negative. At the *Sun*, individuals are called upon to take responsibility for themselves; at the *Mirror* responsibility is about community values as much as individual values, and even the usual hierarchy of authority is disturbed by the use of readers' letters to support socially responsible actions. After 27 years as the *Sun*'s advice columnist Sanders says that they do now listen to her advice: 'I am seen as a litmus test of readers' attitudes' (telephone interview December 26). Certainly the *Sun*'s attitude to homosexuality has started to shift. It is perhaps some evidence of this shift that in 2006 Sanders was nominated as 'journalist of the year' by the gay rights group Stonewall.

Conclusion

There is clearly room for further work in this field but the tentative conclusion is that advice columnists are affected by their close relationship with their readers and that this has influenced the discourses produced and circulated by columnists in the last 30 years. Marje Proops was seen as integral to the newspaper and was able to channel the feminine discourse of the letter writers and use it to influence editorial policy. Sanders claims to have a similar relationship with the current Editor of the *Sun*. Rayner, who was only at the *Sun* newspaper for seven years and had an antagonistic relationship with the Editor, had less influence on the editorial tone; however, she did still manage to maintain a feminine space within a very masculine institution – a space in which female readers felt able to solicit help over the kinds of personal problems that the newspaper denied. The *Mirror* seems, over time, to have continued to resist some of the increasingly punitive discourses which predominate in the *Sun* newspaper. However, in both newspapers, where there are punitive discourses in the news pages, the advice columnists consistently take a more positive line.

This small glimpse into the work of the agony aunt seems to suggest that these columns pose an internal challenge to the masculine discourses of the news pages and to the male dominance of the news institution. That challenge may occasionally be direct as in the case of Proops and Sanders, who have been regarded as a useful link with, and test of, readers' views and values. However, it may also be indirect in providing a public space, largely outside the scrutiny and therefore the regulatory weight, of news agenda setters. As a private space in a public institution the problem page is able to say the unsayable and make it normal. These pages are subversive in the sense that, in spite of their huge popularity with readers, the lack of attention paid to them by agenda setters allows them to communicate a different, and in the case of this research, far less punitive, message to readers about changing social norms.

Note

1   I am referring here to discourse in the sense that Foucault suggested: as a specific set of behaviours, utterances, texts and bodily behaviours which at any given time/place provide the parameters within which people decide who they are and how it is reasonable to behave (Mills 1979, p.56).

References

Beetham, M. (1996) *A Magazine of Her Own?* London: Routledge,

Boynton, P. M. (2004a) hrrp://society.guardian.co.uk/publichealth/story. Accessed November 2006.

Boynton, P. M. (2004b) 'The Problem with Agony Aunts' *Press Gazette* 7 October.

Brunsdon, C. (1984) 'Writing about Soap Opera' in Masterman, L. (Ed.) *Television Mythologies* London: Taylor and Francis.

Cook, H. (2003a) *The Long Sexual Revolution* Oxford: Oxford University Press.

Cook, H. (2003b) 'Sex and the Doctors: The Medicalization of Sexuality as a Two-way Process in Early to Mid-twentieth-century Britain' in de Blecourt, W. and Usborne, C. (Eds) *Cultural Approaches to the History of Medicine: Mediating Medicine in Early Modern and Modern Europe* London: Palgrave Macmillan, pp.192–211.

Ehrenreich, B. and English, D. (1978) *For Her Own Good: 150 Years of the Experts Advice to Women* London: Pluto Press.

Foucault, M. (1979) 'Truth and Power: An Interview with Alessandro Fontano and Pasquale Pasquino' in Morris, M. and Patton, P. (Eds) *Michel Foucault: Power/Truth/Strategy* Sydney: Feral Publications, pp.29–48.

Hermes, J. (1995) *Reading Women's Magazines: An Analysis of Everyday Media Use* Oxford: Polity Press.

Kent, R. (1979) *Aunt Agony Advises: Problem Pages through the Ages* London: W. H. Allen.

Livingstone, S. (1994) 'Watching Talk: Gender and Engagement in the Viewing of Audience Discussion Programmes' *Media Culture and Society* vol. 16 no. 3 July, pp.431–47.

McLaughlin, L. (1993) 'Chastity Criminals in the Age of Electronic Reproduction: Reviewing Talk Television and the Public Sphere' *Journal of Communication Enquiry* vol. 17 no. 1, winter, pp.41–55.

McRobbie, A. (1996) 'Postmodernism and Popular Culture' in Marris, P. and Thorton, S. (Eds) *Media Studies: A Reader* Edinburgh: Edinburgh University Press.

Mills, S. (1979) *Discourse: The New Critical Idiom* London: Routledge.

Modleski, T. (1984) *Loving with a Vengeance* London: Routledge.

Patmore, A. (1993) *Marge: The Authorised Biography* London: Warner.

Phillips, A. and Rakusen, J. (1978) *Our Bodies Ourselves* London: Penguin.

Proops, M. (1977) *Dear Marje* London: Coronet.

Rayner, C. (2003) *How Did I Get Here from There* London: Virago.

Shattuc, J. (1997) *The Talking Cure: TV Talk Shows and Women* London: Routledge.

Winship, J. (1987) *Inside Women's Magazines* London: Rivers Oram Press.

Chapter 8

I, Columnist

Brian McNair

In the beginning there was news: the journalism of reportage and correspondence about events going on in the world sent back in handwritten letters from far-off places to readers among the political, business and military elites of post-medieval Europe. The function of early journalism was primarily that of environmental surveillance, providing those in need of it with a window on what was going on in the world beyond their castle walls and city gates.

From an early stage in its evolution, however, journalism stopped being only about the reporting of events and started to be about *making sense* of them. To the work of reportage was added over time the work of *analysis, interpretation* and *commentary* on the events covered in news. Over time the proportion of this type of journalism contained within first print and then broadcast media increased, and by the end of the twentieth century it was an oft-observed, and oft-criticised feature of newspapers. In the early years of the twenty-first century the emergence of online media has seen a further burst of what some have characterised as the 'commentary explosion', as bloggers and personal websites proliferate. This chapter explores the reasons for the rise of journalistic commentary, its role in the contemporary newspaper package and how changes in the media environment are impacting on its demand and supply.

A brief history of the column: from correspondence to complexity

Journalism's shift from reportage to interpretation and commentary reflected the changing needs of social administration, commerce and democratic politics as the transition from feudalism to capitalism gathered pace in early modern Europe.

For journalists to begin to see their work as about *making sense* of the events which they report was a logical extension of their surveillance function in a social world growing ever more complex. As state apparatuses, markets, cities and empires grew in scale, complexity and interconnectedness, it was no longer enough to know merely what was happening in the world. It was also necessary, if one was operating in the world as a political leader, a trader or a military strategist, to know *why* things were happening; what was the context to the content of news, and what, given that context, was likely to happen in the future. In such a world the journalist necessarily became more than a reporter, but also a sifter and sorter of an accelerating, increasingly voluminous flow of information into news items of differential value (applying news values and structuring social reality into stories of greater or lesser importance). Journalism expanded its remit from the production of facts (though this remained central) to the construction of meanings.[1]

With the emergence of democratic polities in Europe from the seventeenth century, and the expansion of suffrage, which endowed more and more people with the status of citizens, the sense-making function of journalism also acquired political significance. Liberal democratic theory called for an informed citizenry capable of making rational choices between competing party platforms at the ballot box, and reasoned judgements on the performance of a government or a leader. Journalism formed the cultural space, or *public sphere*, where one could be guided through the arguments for and against a particular party or policy, and be exposed not just to the facts underpinning political debate, but also to critical commentary on the powerful and their performance in office.

Commentary journalism was not merely analytical and interpretative, but opinionated and often partisan. The contemporary opinion column has its roots in the committed advocacy journalism of the English Civil War, in which journalists for the first time participated as political actors and not merely reporters of political action (Conboy 2004). As press historian Joad Raymond puts it, the print media of the 1640s 'participated in constructing the world around them, by means of polemicised intervention and political propaganda' (Raymond 1993, p.20). Journalists presented a commentary on the progress of the war, advice on how particular events should be interpreted, and appeals for appropriate responses from their readers.

Trusting the commentators

Journalism of this type, then and since, has depended for its effectiveness (if measured by the extent to which readers accept and endorse its arguments) on the projection of discursive authority. The journalist has to be trusted not merely as a reliable source of accurate information (although this is important even in the context of opinionated commentary) but as an insightful analyst and interpreter. From the early newspapers of the seventeenth century to the bloggers of the present day, a relationship of trust between reader and journalist has been essential in determining the degree to which comment and opinion are successful in their persuasive functions. The construction of this kind of journalistic authority (as opposed to the authority of the reporter, which is based on the perceived reliability of his or her information gathering) is built on the journalist's reputation for knowing and understanding things we, the readers, do not, but should.

This reputation may in turn be based on privileged access to the key players associated with a political debate or event, such as 'insider' knowledge of the type traded in by political columnists in the Westminster lobby. A leading columnist such as Polly Toynbee of the *Guardian* is persuasive only to the extent that her readers accept that she has a privileged knowledge of the issues she is writing about, because she talks to the people who matter. Her analyses of public policy, and then her opinions about what is happening in the political sphere at any given time, are persuasive because she has, over time, established herself as someone in a position to know what is 'really' going on, as opposed to what party officials and spin doctors may say in public. The longer that she has been in this position, the more authoritative she seems (although all columnists of this type have their shelf lives limited by such factors as changes in government personnel and the loss of access to knowledgeable contacts).

Trust is also a by-product of authority established in other, non-journalistic spheres. Many commentary columns are written by non-journalists who make their livings and their reputations outside the media world. Academics are frequently enlisted as commentators on issues and debates related to their fields. Years of research and publication as a scholar, or 'don' as the media may often put it, signify authority in the public sphere, and lead to invitations to contribute columns and other forms of media commentary. Former generals are invited to comment on military matters (serving military officers rarely do, because of the political sensitivity of their positions). Public figures like Bob Geldof and Bono, who have built reputations as campaigners, may be invited to comment on world poverty or debt relief. Prominent politicians, usually retired from front-line party responsibilities, such as Michael Portillo and Roy Hattersley, are regularly invited to comment on current political controversies.

Trust is not merely a factor of structural position or status, however. It can also be based on rhetorical skill, the persuasion of the reader by elegant, erudite or witty prose. We are won over as readers by the effective use of language, the construction of arguments, the deployment of evidence and other communicative tools. Good writing is not a prerequisite of authoritative commentary, and it is rarely enough on its own to establish a journalist as a trusted commentator, but insofar as any communication can be persuasive, commentary which is aesthetically and rhetorically skilful has an advantage over that which is neither.

On whatever basis the authority of journalistic opinion is constructed, the aim is always to persuade readers that this particular commentator is someone whose views have weight and validity beyond those of the ordinary reader, someone whose views should be trusted. In this respect the journalist is a *pundit* (from the Sanskrit term for wise man or village elder), a sage, a secular priest, licensed to tell us, from the pulpit provided by the newspaper (and in broadcast journalism, from the radio or TV studio) what things mean, and, where appropriate, what should be done about them.

The commodification of comment

Accompanying (and fuelling) the increasing complexity of capitalism in early modern Europe was the invention of print. From the late 1400s print technology gradually supplanted oral and scribal culture with mass-reproduced books, pamphlets and news sheets. These were sold as commodities in an expanding media marketplace, and thus had to compete for customers.

At the same time as a market for journalism was developing, Jean Eisenstein argues, 'print allowed a cult of individuality and personality to flourish' (1983, p.140), and to be expressed in literature and journalism. The growth of print, and the need to sell print commodities, created the conditions for the emergence of the author as an increasingly important element in the cultural transaction.

In the sphere of journalism (or what would become journalism) one of the first such authors was Michel de Montaigne (1533–92). Many cultural historians today regard Montaigne as the first essayist of the modern type. Not a reporter but a commentator, Montaigne's essays anticipate the emergence of the columnist, in that they stand for, and were sold to the emerging print market on the basis of the qualities associated with his particular literary personality. Montaigne had fans, and celebrity. Irrespective of its subject matter, his name attached to an essay was a unique selling proposition in an increasingly competitive cultural marketplace. The contemporary columnist 'sells' him- or herself on precisely the same basis. As the print media expanded, and competition between an emerging market of news-papers intensified, the value of subjective commentary, as opposed to objective reportage, increased. The personality of particular writers, expressed in style and content, became a way of attracting readers to a publication.

During this period, too, the function of the newspaper editorial changed (see chapter 4). Originally used as the proprietor's identifiable, direct mouthpiece, the editorial transformed into the anonymous public voice of the newspaper. As the modern form of the editorial evolved, the column emerged as the place where individual, subjective opinions were most often articulated. Christopher Silvester's essay on the history of the column notes that it was:

> An outgrowth of the traditional essay and a refinement of the genre ... a performance more than an expression of intellectual argument, it tends to react to contemporary events and shared experiences ... [a performance] in which the personality of the writer is a self-referential text along with the subject matter.
>
> (1997, p.xi)

As opposed to the detached objectivity of the reporter or correspondent, the columnist stresses the 'I'. Where the reporter says 'this is what happened', the columnist says, 'here is the news, as reported elsewhere. This is what I think about it'. And insofar as 'we' want to know what he or she thinks, we are prepared to pay for the privilege. In this sense the column can be regarded as an early form of *info-tainment* in a journalistic marketplace. The inevitable consequence of a competitive journalistic market is the requirement to entertain readers, at least some of the time. The column entertains as it analyses and interprets.

The opinions of the columnist entertain not only when they make the reader laugh or smile, but also when they engage readers in reflection around the topic under discussion. Furthermore, one may agree or disagree with the column, without this detracting from its entertainment value. Indeed, knowing that we will disagree with a columnist whose opinions occupy the other end of the ideological spectrum from our own is often what compels us to read. We love some columnists, and hate others. Julie Burchill, for example, often outraged her liberal readers in the *Guardian* with politically incorrect comments on Irish republicanism, Islamic fundamentalism and many other subjects. While it lasted, however, her column was a 'must read' feature of the paper. Ken Livingstone's columns for the *Sun* in the 1980s had a similar relationship with readers of the then aggressively pro-Thatcher tabloid. Insofar as the competitive function of the column is to build and maintain reader loyalty, provocation and calculated controversy have been among the most potent devices available to columnists since the form emerged. Love or hate them, as long as we opt to read them, and to buy the newspaper in which they appear, columnists have done their job and earned their often high fees. The late Peter Jenkins, a leading political columnist in his day, described the column as 'a star turn with the emphasis on turn; the columnist's job was to take an ego trip, to entertain his readers, preferably by annoying them, with strong opinions on each and every subject' (quoted in Silvester 1997, p.xv).

A leading exponent of this type of commentary in the UK in recent times has been Peter Hitchens, whose columns have been described as 'molten Old Testament fury shot through with visceral wit'.[2] Many columnist-polemicists cultivate a reputation for conservative, even reactionary views, although they are often anti-establishment. One leading exponent of the form, Richard Littlejohn, has been quoted as believing that 'the true job of the columnist is to chuck beer bottles from the back of the room at those in authority'.[3] The columnist's words are wielded as weapons for or against a cause, often claiming to represent the views of every man and woman as they rail against 'political correctness gone mad', environmentalism, multiculturalism or some other perceived folly of the liberal elite.

A typology of the column

The functions of the commentary column as set out above have led to the development of three types (McNair 2000).

- The polemical column, which addresses the reader in tones ranging from the counter-intuitive and the sceptical (does man-made global warming really exist?) to the indignant and even the outraged (isn't the British motorist a persecuted species?).
- The analytical-advisory column, in which the authority of the journalist is applied to in-depth consideration of a topic in the news, typically concluding with advice for the actors involved in the story, or for the readers following it.
- The satirical column, which with more or less cruelty, mocks those in the news, or who are otherwise significant enough to be the target of satire. In

this category of comment – usually found in diaries such as Simon Hoggart's for the *Guardian*, or the parliamentary sketches which Matthew Parris used to write for *The Times* – the journalist becomes a court-jester, poking fun at the powerful.

Paralleling the broader category of news, commentary columns cover the editorial range, from the staples of politics and economics to sport, culture and lifestyle. In the case of lifestyle, the idea of the columnist as the journalist of the 'I' is most obvious, since these columns largely comprise whimsical accounts of what 'I' did, or wore, or felt on a particular occasion. The expansion of the lifestyle sub-genre represents for some critics one aspect of the commentary-led degeneration of the public sphere which, it is argued, has been an unwelcome feature of journalistic culture in recent decades.

The columnar explosion

In the 1950s, notes John Lloyd, there were 'no' political columnists in the UK (2004), and relatively few of any other kind. In the United States there had always been more, including powerful 'kingmakers' such as Walter Lippmann, on whom Burt Lancaster's loathsome screen character, J. J. Hunsecker, was based (*The Sweet Smell of Success*, Alexander Mackendrick, 1957). The development of the column in the USA was driven by the syndicated structure of the press there, and its localised nature, and the special premium this placed on nationally known brand names like Lippmann (Starr 2004). In Britain, however, the dominance of the national titles kept both the number and status of columnists in check.

The growth of journalistic commentary in the UK in the late twentieth century arose from increased media competition in general, and changes in newspaper presentation, such as Andrew Neil's pioneering (in the British context) use of supplements for the *Sunday Times* in the 1980s, an innovation which his broadsheet and mid-market rivals duly followed. Newspapers expanded in size, with much of the increase given over to lifestyle and consumer coverage, including columns. Where straight news reportage and investigative journalism were research-based and resource intensive, the commentary column or 'think piece' was relatively inexpensive, beyond investment in the writer him- or herself. Columns made good business sense, and served the needs of an increasingly affluent society interested in interior design, fashion, cuisine and leisure activities.

The columnar explosion was not seen in leisure and lifestyle alone, however. The number of political columns also expanded, from a handful in the 1970s to around 600 per month in the UK's national press alone by 1998 (McNair 2000). Part of this growth was attributable to the increasingly packaged, intensively managed nature of democratic politics, and the rise of something called spin (public relations, but much more scientific and professionalised than ever before), which seemed to require a journalistic response in the form of 'process' journalism – commentary on the presentation and meaning of political discourse, as opposed to the validity or otherwise of its substance. In broadcasting too, this was the era of the 'special correspondent', the elite, insider journalist returning from the hidden corridors of power in order to 'sort things out' for the rest of us.

Columnists remain a key ingredient of a newspaper's marketing pitch, as journalistic outlets proliferate and the importance of brand identity increases. Observing in 2006 that British Editors are 'buying up big-name columnists as if they were footballers', *Guardian* columnist Christina Odone argued that 'in an age when news no longer sells newspapers, columnists are the miracle ingredient that can win you readers'.[4] In 2000 the late Hugo Young, until his untimely death himself a leading exponent of the analytical-advisory column, estimated that there were more than 220 columnists writing for the national press. For some, this was about 200 too many. In 2005 one anxious observer complained (in a column) about 'an eruption, or a Babel, of columnists'.[5]

Criticism of columnists is nothing new. Mackendrick's *The Sweet Smell of Success* was a dark satire on the abuse of a columnist's power, aided and abetted by Tony Curtis' sleazy PR man. Modelled, as noted above, on the life and career of Walter Lippmann, the film displayed what was by then already a widespread cynicism about the dangers of a journalism where force of personality and discursive elegance counted for more than truth, and where the celebrity journalist could become a bully. By the end of the twentieth century, however, criticism of columns had intensified, focusing on two main themes: first, that the rise of opinion journalism was at the expense of fact-based investigation and reportage, and therefore represented a decline in journalistic quality overall. This criticism was often linked to the broader thesis of journalism's 'dumbing down' and the negative effects of competition on newspaper bottom lines. While even a successful title like the *Sunday Times* reduced its editorial resources devoted to original investigation, its pages were filled with commentary.

Secondly, it was argued that the distinction between fact and opinion in journalism was being routinely blurred by a plethora of pontificating pundits, whose claims to authority were not necessarily valid, and in whom the readers' trust was quite possibly misplaced. Political columnists in particular were implicated in the 'corrosive cynicism' argued by some observers to have overtaken political journalism in the UK, as columnists eager to be heard railed against this or that government minister, this or that policy pronouncement, without providing their readers with adequate factual background. Columnists were 'grandstanding', more interested in displaying their own cleverness than serving the needs of the public sphere.

Columns *are* relatively inexpensive to run, as already noted, and in a competitive newspaper environment there can indeed be pressure to use them as a cost-effective means of filling space. It is also true that some columnists' opinions will be less valuable than others', and that some will adopt 'controversialist' rhetoric merely because they know that this is what will get them noticed and bring professional rewards. Against that, we should remember that commentary exists in an increasingly crowded marketplace of ideas, and that the columnist must compete for the readers' trust with many others, as well as with normatively preferred 'straight' news. In this sector of the cultural marketplace, as in others, quality counts, and the reader exercises choice as to which columns, if any, he or she reads.

Opinion online: the new commentariat

As with so many aspects of journalism, the commentary form has been significantly affected by the emergence of the internet. Where the column was once restricted to the print medium, now it is online, in the form of blogs and personal websites. These are of massively variable quality, but the best of the 'new commentariat', as the *Guardian* described them in 2005, rival and even outstrip the print columnists in their reach and influence. For one observer, 'what has emerged is a fully fledged alternative wing of the opinion industry, challenging the primacy of newspaper commentators', a 'new wave of political bloggers' competing with Britain's 'old media pundits'.[6]

Insofar as the internet is bringing into being a globalised public sphere (McNair 2006) it is one in which commentary and opinion are central. Matt Drudge pioneered online commentary and demonstrated its potential to set the mainstream news agenda in the context of the Clinton–Lewinsky scandal of 1998/9. Thereafter, driven by the post-9/11 environment of intense debate around matters of war and peace, and the related search for understanding of a new ideological and geopolitical configuration, a blogosphere has evolved, comprising thousands, millions of potential commentators on every conceivable subject.

The majority of the bloggers are and will remain unknown beyond their immediate circle of friends and fellow enthusiasts. A few – numbering the hundreds, worldwide – achieve a substantial online audience, and become agenda setters and opinion formers for the traditional media, as well as 'must reads' for the online generation.

For online commentators the building of trust and authority is just as important as it has always been for print pundits, and even more difficult to achieve. If there are literally millions of bloggers out there, all looking for attention, how to make *your* blog stand out? Being in the right place at the right time, perhaps, as the Baghdad Blogger was in 2003 when Coalition forces entered Baghdad; or having a distinctive and unusual voice, such as marxist intellectual Norman Geras and his Norm.Blog, who achieved crossover in 2006 for his perspectives on the War on Terror. As has always been true for print commentary, success online means establishing a unique selling proposition for one's blog or website, and winning the trust of the internet audience over time.

The rise of the internet has sharpened debates about the mobilisation and measurement of trust and authority in journalistic discourse. It has also democratised the commentary form, enabling millions of people without access to the traditional print and broadcast media to have an online voice. Forward-looking newspapers such as the *Guardian* have responded to the demand for mass access to commentary by making space for it on their *Unlimited* website, while also encouraging professional writers with established reputations to contribute pieces online. The internet has encouraged a culture of debate and argumentation, global in its reach, and more accessible to ordinary people than the print platforms of the past. The content of this culture will not always be of high discursive quality, and the processes by which some online commentators and not others cross over to the media mainstream remain opaque. It will reflect extreme views as well as more considered and reasoned articulations. But the presence of millions of bloggers in the globalised public sphere, as producers of commentary and opinion as well as consumers of it, is an important new factor in the evolution of journalism in the years ahead.

Notes

1   Jo Bardoel's 1996 essay expressed it well when he wrote that journalism's function increasingly lies in 'filtering relevant issues from an increasing supply of information in a crowded domain. Journalism evolves from the provision of facts to the supply of meaning' (1996, p.297).
2   Silver, J., 'Look forward in anger', *Guardian* 2005.
3   Ibid.
4   Odone, C., 'Columnists suffer from writer's bloc', *Guardian* 24 April 2006.
5   Fraser, I., 'Journalism is in terrible trouble…', *Sunday Herald* 4 September 2005.
6   Burkeman, O., 'The new commentariat', *Guardian* 17 November 2005.

References

Bardoel, J. (1996) 'Beyond Journalism: A Profession Between Information Society and Civil Society' *European Journal of Communication* vol. 11, no. 3, pp.283–302.
Conboy, M. (2004) *Journalism: A Critical History* London: Sage.
Eisenstein, J. (1983) *The Printing Revolution in Early Modern Europe* Cambridge: Cambridge University Press.
Lloyd, J. (2004) *What the Media are Doing to our Politics* London: Constable.
McNair, B. (2000) *Journalism and Democracy: A Qualitative Evaluation of the Political Public Sphere* London: Routledge.
McNair, B. (2006) *Cultural Chaos: Journalism, News and Power in a Globalised World* London: Routledge.
Raymond, J. (1993) *Making the News* Moreton-in-Marsh: Windrush Press.
Silvester, C. (Ed.) (1997) *The Penguin Book of Columnists* London: Viking.
Starr, P. (2004) *The Creation of the Media* New York: Free Press.

Part 2

Editorial contents

Chapter 9

Post-ironic page3: porn for the plebs

Karen Ross

> We have become so inured to sexploitation that its capacity to offend is devalued and only a handful of hard-core hairies not in on the post-feminist joke dare risk ridicule by mentioning it.
>
> (Hjul 2003, p.14)

The current insistence that we are living in a post-feminist age, where all the battles between women and men have been fought and won, is often accompanied by a backwards nod to the 1970s when second wave feminism is credited with fomenting dissent, rabble-rousing and finally getting sex equality on to the political agenda. To be sure, it was a profoundly important decade for a number of reasons and 1970 in particular saw the Equal Pay Act get on to the statute book and witnessed the first national meeting of the women's liberation movement take place at Ruskin College. In that same year, the Miss World contest was disrupted by those self-same 'women's libbers' armed with flour bombs and water pistols, Annie Nightingale became the first ever woman DJ on Radio 1 and Lloyd's of London admitted its first woman underwriter. In the same year, and making an equally important statement but for rather different reasons, the *Sun* published its first naked pin-up, and page3 was born. Nearly four decades later, the controversy that page3 first created shows no sign of resolution and the battle lines are drawn in almost exactly the same formation now as they were in 1970. This chapter explores the ways in which the debate around page3 has always been about much more than just a bare breast in a tabloid newspaper. Rather, page3 became, and is still, the catalyst for broader arguments about the place of sex in popular culture, the impact that routinised representations of women's bodies as commodity have on intimate relations in the real world, and the link between the airbrushed pin-up woman and trends in self-harm, cosmetic surgery and eating disorders among real and especially young women.

Legislating against page3: a very short history

Despite the heady radicalism of the 1970s or perhaps because there were too many other important fights to have, challenges to page3 do not feature heavily in feminist or other critiques of the media during that important decade or much of the following one, until Clare Short, MP for Ladywood since 1983, decided to take on the *Sun*. The way she tells it, her page3 campaign did not start out as a *cause célèbre* but rather emerged as a consequence of debating a completely different Bill about obscene publications. During her speech against this other Bill, she said that if the House really wanted to respond to women's anger about sexual intimidation, it should introduce a Bill banning page3. This was the start of a battle between Short and the tabloids which was to endure for more than 20 years.[1]

On 12 March 1986, having slept on the floor in Parliament in order to be first in the queue to be given permission to bring in a 10-Minute Rule Bill, Clare Short introduced her Indecent Displays (Newspapers) Bill to the House. The vote on the Bill was 97 for and 56 against, so she was given leave to bring in the Bill. Although she was, unsurprisingly, reviled in the press for her intervention, the response from Joanne Public was very different and Short received hundreds of letters of support. However, the Bill ran out of time and although she reintroduced it in 1988 and saw an even higher vote of support, it again ran out of time. Short did not try a third time, although, as we will see, this was scarcely the end of the story.

Challenging Clare

Unsurprisingly, the *Sun*, and the other tabloids which regularly feature naked women, responded to Short's challenge in their customary style, criticising Short for being a killjoy and making any number of personalised comments about her. Of course, Short was well aware that the *Sun* would use her and her campaign to both assert its own position as champion of the new enlightened era of sexual freedom but also to denigrate her as out-of-touch frump. She also knew that her Bill had very little chance of becoming law but rather saw its introduction as an opportunity to open a wider public debate about the invasion of sexual imagery in everyday life. The tabloids were considerably aided in their efforts to ridicule Short by reporting the comments of her fellow (male) MPs who spoke against in both debates: Tory MP Robert Adley, for example, infamously said that she was trying to spoil one of the few pleasures left in life (cited in Starkey 2006, p.8).

Years later, in 2004, Short made a throwaway remark on Radio 4's *Any Questions* that she still thought that page3 should be banned (Horrie 2004). This unrehearsed comment immediately sparked off yet another bout of vitriolic abuse by the *Sun*, including calling her fat and jealous, superimposing her face on a page3 model, headlining articles with 'Short on Looks, Short on Brains' and sending a gang of page3 models to camp outside Short's home (Bunting 2004). As with Short's previous page3 campaign efforts, there was never any danger that her Bill would actually pass into law, so this particular attack should more properly be seen as simply a serendipitous opportunity for the *Sun* to (re)animate a non-debate and resurrect its reputation as provocative, irreverent thorn in the side of the moralising nanny state. For Rebekah Wade, who took over as Editor at the

Sun in 2003, and who made her views on page3 clear from the first issue under her editorship by captioning the page as 'Rebekah from Wapping', falling sales represent a major challenge to the paper's survival, so any target is fair game. Resuscitating a phoney war is as good as it was probably going to get.

While it is to be expected that the *Sun* and the other tabloids will defend their right to print pictures of naked women, a much better tactic is to use women themselves to damn their critics. The following extract was the opener for the *Sun*'s lead story on 14 January 2004, and is typical of its ventriloquising tendencies and claims to speak for ordinary women and men:

> PAGE THREE girls say their arch-critic Clare Short is just 'jealous'. Nicola ... said: 'I think what she said is pathetic. Just because she's fat and ugly, doesn't mean to say we all have to cover up.' Nikkala ... said: 'They say, "If you've got it, flaunt it". Well, Clare Short obviously can't flaunt it.'

This kind of crowing bravado which denies debate is reductive in the extreme, attempting to silence dissent by naming it retrograde. The insistence on girl-power but defining it only in terms of the power to play with men's fantasies – the real fantasy being that women can actually exert control over men in this or any other way – may be progress, but not as most of us know it. Of course, name-calling is only one of the tools in the tabloids' box of tricks.

Reasons (not) to be cheerful # 4

reason 1 – jealousy
reason 2 – man-hater
reason 3 – spoilsport
reason 4 – cultural dinosaur
reason 5 – no sense of humour
reason 6 – snobbery

We have already seen the ways in which reasons 1 and 3 are routinely rehearsed to repel criticism, and reason number 2 is often inferred via rather more oblique turns of phrase, so in what follows I consider reasons 4, 5 and 6. The critical voices which continue to be raised against the casual sexualisation of popular culture are routinely dismissed as boringly old-fashioned, vestiges of values once held dear by Mary Whitehouse and her cronies, but so last century. What dinosaur feminists simply don't seem to realise is that we've been living in a postmodern, post-feminist era for the past decade, where women are having it all, are loud and proud and getting their bits out for the England squad because they *want* to.

The press now insists on reporting stories of in-your-face-girl-power, of successful women who are clever, articulate and proud of their curves. Phil Hilton, Editor of men's magazine *Nuts*, suggests that young women are queuing at his door to be photographed without their clothes for the magazine, and that those who criticise

Nuts for exploiting women are simply out of touch with young women's sexual liberalism (cited in Orr 2005). Hilton's comments, a year after *Nuts* launched in early 2004, convey a rather different sentiment to that which attended the pre-launch hype, when *Nuts* and *Zoo Weekly* (later truncated, aptly, to 'Zoo') were to be brought out within days of each other. Then, Mike Soutar, IPC's editorial director (publishers of *Nuts*), said that his market research showed that men were 'blocked' from buying men's magazines because of the volume of unsubtle female nudity and bad language: 'There's a boundary at which that becomes something which is a very solo pleasure rather than something that is socially acceptable to read on a bus or a train or leave lying around the house if you have kids' (Soutar cited in Burrell 2004, p.8). Soutar insisted that, in contrast with *Zoo*, which had an explicit agenda to feature sex, football and funnies, *Nuts* would contain 'simple' content, with extensive coverage of 'current affairs'. Phil Merrill (2004), Editor of *Zoo* on the other hand, had no such qualms about including acres of female flesh, insisting that in fact this was what 'real' men wanted. While one can read Merrill's limp justification for *Zoo* as self-conscious provocation or ad-man's hype or simply silly schoolboy stuff, he knows he's hitting a nerve with his bad-boy posturing. Given the apparent 'crisis of masculinity' which regularly features as a 'news' story in the opening years of this new millennium, most often blamed on the rise of the (castrating) career woman, it is perhaps unsurprising that one reaction is a crawl back to the Neanderthal. This return to the woods is exemplified by the success of magazines such as *Zoo* and *Nuts*, where men can exercise a hyper-masculinised sensibility by subordinating women, if only vicariously, through consuming their compliantly silent bodies. At the same time, they congratulate each other for their bravery in refusing to be cowed by political correctness, bearing their copy of *Zoo* or *Nuts* as a badge of honour (Jones 2006). The sneaky incursion of sexually explicit imagery into most aspects of mass culture has resulted, amongst other things, in the belief that it's actually rather cool for city types and carpenters alike to talk about 'hot' women: even Tony Blair wears naked lady cufflinks to demonstrate how über-now he is. What *is* rather clever, though, is packaging soft-core porn as simply 'a bit of a larf'. This means that absolutely no shame accrues to the reader because it's all good, clean, harmless fun and, more-over, handling these goods, in every sense, actually signifies an authentic masculinity. Jibes such as prude, frump and no-sense-of-humour can be routinely employed to keep girlfriends and partners onside and uncomplaining, fearful of sounding like their mothers or Mary Whitehouse. But can women really be pleased that their man is reading a magazine which features a 'tit-op' competition, which has the prize of a 'boob job' for their girlfriend? Or which asks men if they would still 'do' Britney, 'now that she's a slaphead' (*Zoo* 2 March 2007, p.10)?

Although I have to admit that I did not buy the launch issue of either *Nuts* or *Zoo Weekly*, I can say that three years later, they appear indistinguishable from each other. Good writing about current affairs is not the number one reason why men buy a weekly lad's mag like *Zoo* or *Nuts*. Although Mike Soutar argued that *Nuts* is a men's magazine and not a '*lads*' *mag*', he and I will have to disagree on that. During the course of researching this chapter, I bought one copy each of *Nuts* and *Zoo* (2 March 2007) to see how they actually do differ, if at all. Well, they are both exactly 106 pages long; they both featured an article on alternative comedy character Borat; they both covered sport (*Nuts* = 12 pages; *Zoo* = 18 pages); they both featured 'funnies' pages (two each); they both included film and TV reviews and programme guides (*Nuts* = 16; *Zoo* = 13); they both carried sex ads (five pages each). Importantly, the nipple count was almost identical, with *Zoo* dedicating 32 pages to pictures of women's (mostly) naked bodies, and *Nuts* slightly lagging behind with 30 pages. Whether Soutar was simply trying to pretend a difference or whether there *was* a difference in the early days, it is long gone now, as is any suggestion of covering news and current affairs. To the casual observer, they look exactly the same, inside and outside. After decades of equality campaigning and an insistence that we are living in a fair and equal society, lads' mags' continuing fascination with jugs, jism and Jackass presents a rather sad commentary on our contemporary life and times.

Interestingly, while lads' mags are still catering to the adolescent fantasies of their adult male readers, including keeping women soft and silent, part of the *Sun*'s response to the cultural phenomenon of girl power, or at least the version peddled by the Sugababes or Beyoncé, has been to give Danni her own voice and thoughts, allegedly. This tactic transforms 'Bouncing Beauty Becky' from slapper to sage, as she contributes her views on topical issues via a speech bubble. While the cynic in me sees this invention as an artful way of making literal the male denigration of topless models as 'bubble-heads', a kind of in-joke at women's expense (again), perhaps it could actually be seen as progressive? Blond but not necessarily dumb? During the writing of this chapter, I bought the *Sun* on a different day each week, over five consecutive weeks in early 2007, and noted what words of wisdom the page3 women offered their readers each day:

> Danni, 19, from Coventry: Danni is worried for Kate Moss after she tied the knot with junkie rocker Pete Doherty. She said, 'I think Kate is making a big mistake, but love can be blind. Pete is obviously the one for her – I just hope he packs in the drugs.'
>
> (Tues. 2 Jan.)
>
> Sam, 20, from Manchester: Sam was staggered to learn that Jade Goody secretly had liposuction. She said, 'It's really bad that Jade made such a big thing about losing weight naturally. This won't go down well with her fans.'
>
> (Wed. 10 Jan.)
>
> Zoe, 24, from London: Zoe is amazed that the events in Big Brother have sparked an international row. She said, 'I can't see any of the housemates becoming UN Goodwill Ambassadors.'
>
> (Thurs. 18 Jan.)

Bouncing beauties Mel and Becky plump up their pillows and indulge in the latest craze for girls. The page 3 lovers, both 24, went head to bed in a pillow-fighting duel.

(Fri. 26 Jan.)

Author's note: no homilies today, just the extra voyeuristic buzz in being told the two women are lovers.

Becky, 24 from London, Mel, 24 from Morecombe: Becky and Mel were shocked to hear schools can ditch French and Spanish lessons in favour of Urdu and Mandarin Chinese. Becky said, 'This is a silly idea. Kids should be taught languages to help them get jobs.' Mel added, 'It's all double Dutch to me.'

(Mon. 5 Feb.)

In each case, the page3 women are supposed to be commenting on an aspect of the lead story of the day while simultaneously providing a soft porn fix to the reader and, for a measly 50 pence extra, can also appear on his mobile phone, a new pair every day. But what are we to make of these pronouncements, these *bons mots* uttered under the catchy title of 'news in briefs'? Are these words their own, or are they simply regurgitating the crusty conservatism of the editor?

Sadly, whoever actually *writes* this copy doesn't seem to realise that billions more people speak an Asian language than French and Spanish put together, or that learning Mandarin is actually a very good career move, given the size of the Asian market and its attendant commercial opportunities. Are the page3 girlies' observations simply to be seen as a bit of fun and not to be taken seriously or are we supposed to really believe that *Sun* babes have never given a thought to cosmetic surgery, never taken drugs, aspire to become goodwill ambassadors in the footsteps of the sainted Diana?

It's just a bit of fun, get a life – reason # 5

But I'm probably just taking this a bit too seriously. The *Guardian*'s 'Soulmates' pages are full of ads where women ask for a GSOH (good sense of humour) as one of the primary attributes they look for in a man – Judy Finnegan (of Richard and Judy fame) said that what first attracted her to Richard was the fact that he was 'funny, intelligent and generally good company'. What attracted Richard to Judy was the fact that she was 'blonde ... lady of a certain age ... intelligent ... and great tits' (Vision 2006, p.19). Women's lack of a GSOH is often given as one of the reasons they can't see the playful side of other women's displays of nudity. In Attwood's analysis of the rather more explicitly pornographic *Fiesta* magazine, she suggests that there is something peculiarly British about the display of women's bodies in downmarket media which is as much about image as about a 'dirty' kind of style (2002). It could certainly be argued that giving 'Perky Pamela from Poole' her caption, and allowing her an extremely narrow repertoire of poses, combine to frame page3 as seaside postcard brought to life. The use of visual and textual codes associated with the 'saucy' postcard genre attempts to subvert the accusation of pornography and (un)dress it up as a bit of fun, nudge nudge, wink wink, know what I mean.

It's a class thang – reason # 6

Nuts editor Phil Hilton has more recently owned up to the reality of *Nuts* by saying that it was everything that men like, such as, 'cars, sport, random facts and lots of sexy girls … It's fun, trivial, racy and loved by thousands of men and a good number of women' (quoted in Cole 2006, p.15). He also offered another reason why lads' mags are unjustly criticised, which is 'snobbery'. For Hilton, this manifests as the middle classes trying to spoil the innocent fun of those 'real' (implicitly 'working-class') men who enjoy *Nuts*, notwithstanding that it has been suggested that the consumption of pornography was partially responsible for the atrocities perpetrated against prisoners at Abu Ghraib (Rich 2004). Hilton's class-based analysis attempts to simultaneously despise the *Guardian*-toting social worker while also claiming the moral high ground by his appeal to 'our' boys.

But seriously, what's your problem with page3?

As well as its contribution to normalising the routine consumption of women's bodies – the ultimate disposable meal – I would argue that the other serious problem with page3 is the impact these impossibly young and slender bodies, with mostly disproportionate sized breasts, have on 'ordinary' women's sense of self and own body image. Although it is easy to dismiss the influence of page3 by insisting that women (or men, for that matter) do not have to look, we cannot turn our heads away each time we are confronted with images of naked or semi-naked women. Even if we don't read the *Sun*, we know what page3 means and what it denotes. There *is* an impact. As with other investigations of social phenomena, determining the precise contours of impact and influence is an inexact science and this imprecision, coupled with methodological differences in study designs, means that research delivers contradictory findings about influence and effect (Jung and Lennon 2003). What is less contested, though, are the trends in eating disorders which show a steady increase throughout the western world in recent years, a trend which is regarded by many as a direct consequence of the valorisation of the young, thin and beautiful. The proliferation of diet plans and slimming aids, liposuction and stomach-stapling surgery, age-defying moisturisers and cellulite-busting body wraps perfectly demonstrates capital's double exploitation of women, damned as imperfect but then instantly redeemed if we buy our way out of fat, ugly hell.

Donna Armstrong, the Editor of the women's magazine, *More*, demonstrates perfectly the sly ways in which magazines actively collude with the *Sun*'s version of the ideal woman. Describing Keeley Hazell, who was voted readers' favourite page3 girl in 2006 and who posed for a feature article for the magazine, Armstrong described her thus: 'Keeley is a major influence to young women. She is entirely natural, not enhanced in any way. The anti-Jordan, if you like. She simply has an amazingly toned body, but with huge breasts – which is what all our readers ultimately crave' (Armstrong, cited in Duerden 2006, p.8). As much as some of us will reject everything that is denoted by Armstrong's glib but powerful remark, if the only women who are valorised by the media are glamour and catwalk models, film and pop stars and the girlfriends and wives of famous men, then it is scarcely surprising that young women have similar aspirations to be like these women. A recent survey of 1,000 British teenage girls aged 15 to 19 who are subscribers to the Lab, a mobile phone entertainment service, found that 63 per cent of those who responded considered 'glamour model' to be their ideal profession (cited in Cochrane 2005). While such a restricted sample cannot be said to represent all young women, this finding is worryingly plausible and reflects the reality of popular culture which gives Keeley and Jordan instant recognition simply on mention of their names.

However, it's important to acknowledge that not all women are forever victim to the media's dangerous predilection for showing them the skinny, digitally enhanced girl-woman as ideal type. For example, a number of studies, including several in the developing world, suggest that a strong sense of self-esteem is related to body-confidence, which in turn predisposes women to live happily with their bodies, regardless of their shape or (non-) conformity to the so-called western ideal (Jackson *et al.* 1988; Lee and Lee 1996). This is not at all to argue that this morbid fascination with weight and youth is entirely a western preoccupation, but it is to say that there is some evidence to suggest that it is probably more nurture than nature. But, the power of the media to subvert even the strongest will is considerable. As much as I might criticise the problematic impact on real women's self-esteem by the setting up of Gorgeous Gail from Gateshead as the ideal woman, I still go to the gym three times a week, telling myself these workouts are to keep fit and healthy, but acknowledging that they are also exercises in self-control. If not quite accepting Foucault's insistence that such discipline and punishment is simply capital's way of keeping me enslaved, I do recognise that many of us regularly engage in an internal struggle between our politics and our practices. But this is what makes us human. The acknowledgement of our own susceptibility does not undermine the potency of our arguments but rather makes them more crucial.

Coming full circle – back to the top shelf

In June 2006, Claire Curtis-Thomas, MP for Crosby, resurrected Clare Short's long-standing campaign against page3, when she introduced a Bill to restrict lads' mags to the top shelf on the grounds that a number of titles now contained hard-core pornography which made *Playboy* look tame by comparison and should be out of reach of impressionable young minds (Brown 2006). Curtis-Thomas had previously criticised the tabloids for their use of naked women and is campaigning on the wider platform of pornography in magazines generally. Her primary concern is less about content but more about availability in terms of who can reach to buy, her anxiety being that magazines which run articles on necrophilia and how to wrap a girl's (sic) head in cellophane can be accessed by minors. My concern is with both content and access, about lads' mags and the *Sun*. Locating *Zoo* between *PCUser* and *Period Homes* says clearly that gawping at women's breasts is just another normal, regular mainstream hobby, like model railways and macramé. Although the Curtis-Thomas Bill has absolutely no chance of becoming law for the same reason Clare Short's Bill failed, it might produce a little kick-ass to make news vendors implement the existing 'voluntary' code on where explicit material should be displayed. Joining the discussion, Conservative MP Angela Watkinson suggested that one solution to the problem of adolescent boys' interest in 'unsuitable' publications was to launch a lifestyle magazine which would be attractive to young male readers and acceptable to their parents (Treneman 2006). Although I might not have much of a sense of humour, at least I'm not a fantasist.

Twenty years after she first introduced the Indecent Displays (Newspapers) Bill, Short is bemused by the contemporary media's persistent framing of her as 'killjoy Clare', as if nothing she has done since has meant anything. 'I made two 10-minute speeches. The reaction is extraordinary. People don't want to allow me to talk about anything else' (quoted in Tressider 2005, p.27). When asked if she would do it all again, given what she knows now, she says, 'Knowing me, probably. But I might not have. I hope I would have been brave enough.' If only a few more of us were still.

Notes

1   http://www.epolitix.com/EN/MPWebsites/Clare+Short/a989e96d-5c05-4043-99a9-d3f8a5b7cb9b.htm. Accessed 1 March 2007.
2   These letters were eventually published in book form (Short 1991).

References

Attwood, F. (2002) 'A Very British Carnival: Women, Sex and Transgression in *Fiesta* Magazine' *European Journal of Cultural Studies* vol. 5 no. 1, pp.91–105.

Brown, C. (2006) 'MP Campaigning Against Lads' Mags is Banned from Quoting Sex Tips' *Independent* 27 June, p.16.

Bunting, M. (2004) 'Where's My Sense of Humour? The *Sun*'s Thuggish Tactics Against Clare Short are an Attack on Us All' *Guardian* 16 January, p.26.

Burrell, I. (2004) 'Men Offered Nudes or Hard News in the Battle of the Weeklies' *Independent* 10 January, p.8.

Cochrane, K. (2005) 'Is this your idea of glamour?' *Guardian* 15 November, p.24.

Cole, P. (2006) 'Tacky, Seedy and Sad but Boy are they Profitable' *Independent on Sunday* 2 July, p.15.

Duerden, N. (2006) 'Angel is a Centrefold' *Sunday Review* 26 November, p.8.

Hill, A. (2006) 'If You Want to Find True Happiness, Fake It' *Observer* 3 September.

Hjul, J. (2003) 'Why I for One, Will Secretly Miss Clare' *Scotsman* 15 May, p.14.

Horrie, C. (2004) 'Rebekah's Warmer Sun' *Independent* 27 January, pp.8–9.

Jackson, L., Sullivan, L., and Rostker, R. (1988) 'Gender, Gender Role, and Body Image' *Sex Roles* vol. 19, pp.429–43.

Jones, C. (2006) 'Reading Between the Lines' *Western Mail* 4 July, p.2.

Jung, J. and Lennon, S. J. (2003) 'Body Image, Appearance Self-schema and Media Images' *Family and Consumer Sciences Research Journal* vol. 32 no. 1, pp.27–51.

Lee, A. M. and Lee, S. (1996) 'Disordered Eating and its Psychosocial Correlates among Chinese Adolescent Females in Hong Kong' *International Journal of Eating Disorders* vol. 20, pp.177–83.

Merrill, P. (2004) 'Diary' *Independent on Sunday* 11 January, p.25.

Orr, D. (2005) 'Floundering in the Macho Media' *British Journalism Review* vol. 16 no. 1, pp.61–7.

Rich, F. (2004) 'It was the Porn that Made Them Do It' *New York Times* 30 May, Section 2, pp.1–16.

Short, C. (1991) *Dear Clare...This is What Women Feel About Page 3* London: Radius.

Starkey, J. (2006) 'All the Breast, Clare' *Sun* 15 September, p.8.

Treneman, A. (2006) 'A Top-drawer Debate on a Top-shelf Issue' *The Times* 28 June, p.12.

Tressider, M. (1995) 'A Brave Crusader in the Sex War' *Guardian* 18 February, p.27.

Vision, S. (2006) 'Smooth-talking Devil of the Week' *Mirror* 18 July, p.19.

Chapter 10

The monarchy

Ros Coward

Introduction

It is a commonplace in media studies that the British press is 'patriotic' (Conboy 2006), with an attitude to royalty that is essentially conservative. But while it would be hard to dispute the British press has an ongoing fascination with royalty and rarely espouses overtly republican causes, assertions that the press has one consistent attitude towards monarchy – across time and across different outlets – are simplistic. Even a cursory glance at newspapers in the post-war period shows an evolving rather than a static relationship, one encompassing extremes of near reverence to something closely resembling outright hostility in the immediate aftermath of Princess Diana's death.

In the contemporary press, differences between newspapers are striking. The first months of 2007 demonstrated this wide spectrum of coverage. *The Times* and the *Daily Telegraph* still carried the antiquated court circular informing about royal engagements, while the *Sun* and *Mirror* jostled for the latest shot of Prince Harry falling drunkenly out of a nightclub. Royal doings were subject matter for comment – often critical comment – in all papers. Both tabloids and broadsheets speculated on Harry's call up to Iraq and Camilla's hysterectomy, even if tabloids gave these greater prominence. William's girlfriend, Kate Middleton, featured in all papers, with speculation about marriage, scrutiny of her wardrobe, comparisons with Diana and, in April, news of the breakup of their relationship. The *Daily Express* continued to have front page pictures of Diana and extensive coverage of Mohammed Al Fayed's allegations against the royal family.[1] All papers reported the decision to conduct the enquiry into Diana's death in front of a jury. Most reported and commented on Andy Coulson's resignation. As Editor of the *News of the World* he had been implicated in the fallout from the royal phone tapping scandal.

Clearly there is massive interest in the royals. Most papers have royal correspondents, and most papers cover royal goings on, often to excess. Excess also characterises tabloid interest in royal persons, especially young 'dateable' royals like Princess Beatrice, whose ex-boyfriend sold his story to the *Mail on Sunday* in this period. However, coverage is far from cosy. Andy Coulson's resignation was the legacy of outright conflict between royals and tabloids about their methods, and several broadsheets speculated on this as a watershed moment. During this period the *Daily Mail* carried several stories connected with Channel 4's documentary, *The Meddling Prince*,[2] about Prince Charles' attempts to influence public political debate. It also ran pictures of Camilla, comparing her with Diana, low-key reminders of the paper's ongoing scepticism about Prince Charles. The broadsheets mocked Murdoch's decision to shun paparazzi shots of Kate Middleton, while using those supplied by citizen journalists. Typically this period shows press fascination with royalty but reveals a relationship of mutual distrust and occasional hostility.

Background

Understanding how the press reached this point requires a backwards look. With some notable exceptions, press coverage of the monarchy in the pre-war period reflected the predominantly unquestioningly monarchist attitudes of that time. The monarchy was not a subject of political or social debate, or royal behaviour the subject of detailed scrutiny.[3] Peregrine Worsthorne, a right-wing journalist for *The Times*, and then the *Daily Telegraph*, described how, up until the end of the 1950s, the monarchy 'was something that you didn't need to write about, you didn't need to argue about. It was reported, of course, because it did things like opening Parliament but it wasn't an issue. It was just a bonus, a blessing that you took for granted.'[4]

This excessive reverence was demonstrated dramatically by the conspiracy of silence surrounding Edward's affair with divorcee Wallis Simpson. American papers gave full details but most British newspapers eschewed it, a self-censorship which did them no credit in the public's eyes or those of their foreign counterparts. 'The fact of the matter is' announced the *New York Daily News*, 'that the British press handled the Simpson story clumsily, mistakenly and cravenly, it sought to suppress one of the biggest news stories of modern times – because British publishers didn't think their public could be trusted to know the story.'[5]

Most commentators agree that the 'modern' attitude towards royalty began to emerge during the period from the coronation until the mid-1960s. Around the death of George V and Elizabeth's coronation the papers were still highly deferential. Roy Greenslade writes, 'the death of George V was treated with the kind of solemnity which in hindsight seems out of all proportion to its importance' (2003, p.84). But royal coverage was gradually affected by general changes within journalism. Many post-war Editors were like Hugh Cudlipp[6] returning from the front with democratic ideals and new attitudes towards popular journalism. As regards monarchy, they were aware the profession had disgraced itself during the abdication crisis.

In the preceding week every front page was dominated by the coronation. Greenslade describes it as 'the popular press's genuflection at the dawn of the new Elizabethan era', but adds that the press soon betrayed its real intentions towards the royal family. 'Hollywood stars were a staple diet of news stories, pictures and features, but the homegrown Windsors had yet more sales-winning potential' (Greenslade 2003, p.85). The 'scandal' of Princess Margaret's affair with Group Captain Townsend was critical in growing press interest. She was young, glamorous, mixed with a 'fast set' and had been spotted with Townsend by a *Mirror* journalist at the coronation, confirming reports in foreign papers that she was having an affair with a divorcee. In June 1953 the *People* published a story about the romance, which was already being covered in the European and American press. This time the popular press took up the issue. The *Mirror* even carried a poll asking readers' opinions. Typically the broadsheets distanced themselves, *The Times* protesting about 'the cruel business of prying into private lives'. Meanwhile the Press Council (the precursor of the Press Complaints Commission, PCC) criticised the poll at its inaugural meeting as 'contrary to the best traditions of British journalism', an adjudication which many thought was 'daft' and 'a poor start for the apparatus of self regulation' (Greenslade 2003, p.85).

Two trends emerged as the press dropped its timidity towards royal doings. One was a more critical attitude towards the monarchy. Cudlipp at the *Mirror* openly criticised the 'underemployment' of the royal family, writing in 1954, criticisms which the *Daily Telegraph* called boorish and stupid slander. When journalists Malcolm Muggeridge and John Grieg wrote republican pieces they provoked massive public hostility.[7]

The second trend was the growing interest in the personal lives of the royal family. Royal historian Ben Pimlott dated the press' intense competition for royal stories to the period when Margaret's marriage broke down. It was 'the highway to a new more raucous kind of press voyeurism' (Pimlott 1996, p.438) The same period saw growing interest in the young Prince Charles, which started with the famous cherry brandy incident in 1963.[8] Interest intensified as he reached marriageable age and 'fevered speculation' started about the 'world's most eligible bachelor' (Greenslade 2003, p.352). Charles, like his father Philip, has had a conflictual, distrustful relationship with the press since.

Although the press is often blamed for this obsessive interest in the royal family, in fact the Queen and her advisers played a role. Simon Jenkins claims there were significant changes in how royalty presented itself: moving from 'the monarchy' to 'the family'. There was a period, he says, when the appearances on the balcony started getting larger and larger, part of a decision to make all the members of the royal family part of the institution of monarchy. 'It was not done in the nineteenth century. It was not done by George V. It was not done by George VI. It was a very specific decision to make the family in some way the means by which the concept of Monarchy seemed relevant to the public.'[9]

Commentators also point to a behind-the-scenes TV documentary made in 1969 about the royal family, another instance of something still not widely recognised: royalty has never been above attempting to use and manipulate the media to their own advantage. The then press secretary William Heseltine believed the royal family should promote themselves by letting a little light in on the magic – a decision often highlighted as the watershed which 'whet the appetite for more gossip'. After this the royal family were increasingly promoted (and promoted themselves) as representing the national ethos in idealised form. Several commentators believe these attempts to promote the family as just like the rest of us backfired. 'I believe (this) was a mistake' says Simon Jenkins,

> Here was a family like ours ... and we were supposed to see that they were ordinary children ... And of course you then noticed that they were rather rich and they talked in a certain way, so there was a very firm distinction about this family. It was a very odd family, a very special family, but you were expected to identify with them.[10]

Many journalists noticed anachronistic behaviour but censored themselves. James Whitaker describes one occasion where Charles behaved in a very unchivalrous way towards his then girlfriend Anna Wallace. 'He hid and cowered and left the young woman unprotected. He shouldn't have done that – I was ashamed for him – but of course I didn't print the story. He is after all, my future king' (Kelley 1998, p.216). Whitaker's comment is revealing. Many stories in the period preceding Charles' marriage to Diana went unreported. Indeed some suggest that the press still exercises considerable self-censorship about certain rumours. So although there was a slide towards more voyeuristic interest, the British press was also still deferential. Press relations with royalty in the period before Charles' marriage could be summed up as a cocktail of heightened interest, deference and self-restraint. And then there was Di.

The Diana effect: shifting press boundaries

The arrival of Princess Diana on the royal scene has probably been the single most significant factor in determining the press' relations to monarchy in the last 30 years. It is impossible to separate Diana's life from her relationship with the press and equally impossible to look at the press' relationship with the monarchy without considering the Diana effect. Throughout the 1980s and 1990s she was a tabloid sensation: the human face of royalty, the first glamorous and media-friendly British royal.[11] She also became half of an unprecedented royal divorce which exposed hitherto hidden areas of royal behaviour.

In hindsight it is easier to see how obsessive press interest generated by Diana was overdetermined, a cocktail of different elements, some connected with Diana herself, some with her role, some with contemporary cultural trends. Her own contribution was her film star looks, her approachability and especially her rapport with journalists. All royal photographers and correspondents remark on her electrifying arrival on the scene. They were more used to trailing round after grumpy and hostile royals. Diana by contrast, says Jenni Bond, 'spoke to the journalists. She was very friendly' (Interview 2004). Suddenly royal correspondents and photographers were clambering to go on royal tours, knowing their pictures and stories, however anodyne, would make front pages and boost sales. Not for nothing did media commentator Roy Greenslade dub her 'the princess of sales'. 'She was a phenomenon', said Alex Hamilton (2006).

Some factors which forced Diana into the spotlight were cultural. Alex Hamilton also remarked that Diana was the 'origin of the modern cult of celebrity', and, while exaggerated, it is certainly true the attention to Diana coincided with a new focus on fashion, glamour (particularly together in the form of the supermodel) and on celebrity in a much wider sense than its precursor the film star. The emergence of *Hello* magazine exclusively devoted to the lives of the famous and glamorous gives a flavour of the times and it is no coincidence it was Diana's favourite reading. She had an instinctive interest in fashion, a natural glamour and an intuitive understanding of the importance of cultivating the media, something which baffled and antagonised the older members of the royal family including her husband.

The interest in Diana was also part of the newfound interest in the wider royal family as mentioned earlier. During the 1980s when the Di phenomenon was new, I wrote about this in *Female Desire*, linking fascination with the royals to the emergent and increasingly popular soap opera format.

> In the 1950's the television soap found its feet. Using the fact of the permanent domestic presence of the television, a form of narrative developed which could, like life, go on almost indefinitely ... and in that very period, the press began to treat 'the royals' differently. Playing down statesmanship and aristocracy, the public were treated to more and more intimate revelations and points of speculation about the young family of Queen Elizabeth. Is it just a co-incidence that in this post war period when anachronistic institutions might have been cleared away, the press produced a new style monarchy – familial, more accessible and almost ordinary? Or was it that an infallible format had been discovered? Was it that the royals, like a soap opera, offered a rich vein of revelations based 'roughly on reality' which never has to end, which never has to be the subject of political debate?
>
> (Coward 1984, p.163)

In this analysis I argued the press shared narrative structures with soap opera, attributing different narrative functions (usually oppositions based around approval and disapproval) to different protagonists. At that point the pairs were good and bad princesses: Diana versus fat Fergie, or frigid Anne; dutiful Elizabeth versus flighty Margaret. Polarisations between Prince William's and Prince Harry's girlfriends reproduce this. Kate Middleton the good girl versus Chelsy Davy the party girl. Blain and O'Donnell (2003, p.32), developing this point, claim that splitting of negative and positive attributes between members of the royal family restricts critical views of the monarchy to limited personal judgements. 'In a culture in which serious republicanism is still not really a discoverable strand, the only measure ... to appear critical of the royal family [is] by expressing limited negative judgement'. They claim that this interpersonal judgement of individuals constructs a 'a simulacrum of a political space', while 'remaining monarchist'.

Often the polarisation of characteristics around elevated public figures (celebrities) or within an idealised or typical family is about articulating contemporary dilemmas. Fascination with Diana in the 1980s was partly a society reflecting on what it meant to be a modern woman. The 1980s was when feminism's values rippled out across society, and were being lived out in individual dilemmas: should mothers work; should women demand equality; how should they raise their children in democratic ways? Diana was cast as the modern girl: she worked (albeit in a rarified, upper-class way); she refused to promise 'obedience' at her marriage; she insisted on taking William on tour. She came to carry the connotations of challenger to stuffy, antiquated monarchy.

When I wrote about this narrative function, Diana's divorce and struggle to become her own person lay in the future, yet those events only heightened her role as the anti-traditionalist in popular imagination. As Diana and her marriage began to crumble, press interest became hysterical and many taboos were broken. This interest has to be contextualised within the press' own history. The *Sun* under Murdoch's ownership lacked any deference to the establishment, and where Murdoch went the others followed, desperate to emulate the *Sun*'s phenomenal success. Greenslade describes the 1980s as a sort of 'wild west' period for the tabloids: 'shoot first and ask questions afterwards' (2003). Even so, most Editors agonised over the sensational evidence of marital disintegration which royal correspondents and photographers were putting on their desks.

Simon Jenkins has described how the Palace Press Officer pleaded with Editors to lay off the Princess of Wales on the grounds that if the interest continued she would crack.

> At the time we kept saying, 'Hold on a minute. You've sold us this great love story. You really can't have it both ways. You invited a massive blanket, intrusive publicity into this relationship and now ... you're telling us to lay off.' Well as a human being I'd say 'yes' but I have to say on behalf of the Press 'pull the other one'. So you had ... a real tussle between the insiders, who were genuinely worried about a relationship going wrong, and a Press who let's face it had the biggest story they'd ever got. It was the love story gone wrong and as we all know, the only thing that's a better story than a love story is a love story gone wrong.[12]

The breakdown of Charles and Diana's relationship had a dramatic effect on the press' relationship with monarchy. Lord Deedes (2004) former Editor of the *Telegraph* has described how when Charles and Diana were first married the Queen summoned the royal correspondents to a meeting appealing to gentlemanly instincts to go gently on Diana. By the time the divorce was finalised such gentility was a thing of the past. Unthinkable taboos had been broken: first a long-lens shot of Diana pregnant in a bikini, then numerous photos of Diana in tears or

Charles and Diana cold-shouldering one another, through to the utterly shocking publication of transcripts of Charles' conversations with Camilla ('the tampon tapes') and Diana's conversation with James Gilbey ('the Squidgey tapes'). Charles even confessed to adultery on a TV documentary.[13] Each time the old boundaries which previously kept royalty's misdemeanours out of sight and beyond reproach were crossed.

The press, says Simon Jenkins, was in turmoil about the whole question of privacy intrusion at that period:

> When I was on the Calcutt Committee we would discuss these stories and my colleagues, who were not journalists, would show these stories at the table and they'd say 'How can you possibly defend that?' To which the answer was 'You can't possibly defend it … But do not draw conclusions from stories about the Royal Family for the rest of the Press, or for other stories about other families because this story is *sui generis*. This story's unlike any other story … This is just too big a story for the normal rules of ethics to apply.[14]

The old boundaries between press and royalty had also been breached. Andrew Morton's book, *Diana: Her True Story* (1992) caused an unprecedented scandal because it detailed Diana's deep unhappiness in the royal marriage. Andrew Neil's job as Editor of the *Sunday Times*, which serialised the book, was temporarily in jeopardy for publishing such sensationalist claims, until the ultimately shocking revelation came that Diana had collaborated herself. She repeated this with the memorable interview with Martin Bashir (*Panorama*, BBC, November 1996), recently voted the most memorable television interview ever.

The purpose of recalling this history is to demonstrate both how much contemporary press-royal relations have been affected by Diana's history and also, interestingly, how so many events connected with Diana were intimately linked with the whole process of what academics have called tabloidisation. The press pushed the boundaries of acceptable behaviour because of the sheer scale of interest in her. Consequently many key case studies about press legislation and ethics involve occasions in Diana's life, such as the 'snatched' pictures of Diana exercising or the persecutory behaviour towards her in her last year and as she lay dying. There was a small *crise de conscience* after her death from which her sons have greatly benefited.[15] But the goal posts had changed irreversibly. It is hard to imagine the press ever pulling back to pre-Diana levels of deference.

Diana was unique but there is also something symptomatic here about the press' relationship with royalty. In the UK, royalty elicits almost hysterical tabloid interest, but also occasional crises for the (self-) regulatory bodies. Cynics might call this plain hypocrisy where tabloids behave badly to get their material and then ineffectually criticise themselves. But it might be more accurate to see this as press operating in a space somewhere between what interests the public and what is of genuine public interest, often overstepping those unclear boundaries and being forced to retreat (usually having got their stories).

Press and media reaction to Diana's death has become the subject of much academic writing, some asserting that the media, especially television companies, 'orchestrated' the public mourning using it to engender a sense of shared national values in a royal figure. James Thomas (2002, p.7) asserts that Diana's mourning constructed a 'homogeneous myth ... of a nation united in tearful, adulatory grief for the People's Princess.' This assertion of a constructed media myth flies in the face of evidence. Journalists and broadcasters were taken aback by the level of grief but are emphatic that they followed, rather than created, the public mood. As for the press, there is little doubt that Diana's death provoked an unprecedented level of hostility to the monarchy embodied in the famous headline 'Show us you care, Ma'am'.[16] The 2006 film, *The Queen*[17] accurately conveys the volatility of the moment. This was no nation united in manufactured grief but a moment of real tension in which tabloids articulated popular hostility to the establishment as embodied by the 'old guard' royals, who were blamed for the death of their most popular member ever.

The aftermath of Diana: tabloids versus the monarchy

Diana's life and death still influences press attitudes towards royalty. In certain respects the 'War of the Wales' has continued after her death. As Diana's marriage disintegrated and she struck out independently, the press took sides – often Diana's. Charles had never been popular with Editors. He was touchy, took himself too seriously and bombarded editors with letters. Typically, Max Hastings (2003) describes Charles' self-pitying stance with obvious distaste. Nor did this end with Diana's death. Indeed, in the ensuing period, many Editors became further disenchanted with Charles as a result of a very assertive campaign run by Mark Bolland, his Press Officer, to win acceptance for Charles and Camilla. Bolland has admitted to using dirty tricks to make Charles look good, by running down other royals, manipulation which antagonised the press. Many still felt some personal loyalty to Diana and some were resentful of the royals' use of New Labour-style spin-doctoring techniques. They also resented Mark Bolland's influence, especially the fact of his close relationship with Guy Black, then head of the PCC.[18]

These were some of the elements behind the explosion of press interest in the wake of the Paul Burrell trial, which became as big a press story as Diana's death. Elsewhere (Coward 2007) I have examined the coverage of this case in detail. Suffice it to say here that assumptions that the British press is either straightforwardly or covertly monarchist did not stand up to scrutiny in relation to this story. When the Burrell trial collapsed the tabloid press, frustrated by the secrecy with which the trial had been surrounded, resentful of Charles' staff's attempt to manipulate the press and convinced there was still sensational information to be had, set about unearthing the lot.

Much of the coverage, such as details about Diana's lovers, was of debatable public interest. And many details emerged as a result of some very dubious tabloid practices in a dirty tabloid war. Details of a missing tape making allegations that a senior member of Charles' staff had raped a valet and that there had been a cover-up were brought out by the leaking of court statements by the *News of the World*. The story of alleged victim George Smith, who was suffering from mental problems and alcoholism at the time, was bought by the *Mail on Sunday*. Burrell sold his story to the *Mirror*, which then behaved aggressively to other papers who responded in kind.

The case brought out the best and the worst of the British tabloids, as John Humphrys recognised at the time:

> It's hardly surprising that the tabloids have gone over the top. This story is made in tabloid heaven: sex, intrigue in high places, the disappearance of mysterious tapes, feuding between famous families, the sacred Diana and, above all, royalty. Lots and lots of royalty ... Of course, it's the more salacious material that has kept the tabloids at fever pitch. But they didn't make it all up. They reported what others said ... The days have gone when an elite group of editors could decide not to share with the common herd the secrets they held lest we became too excited. That does not mean the press is in a terrible state. It means it's doing its job.[19]

Central to this dirty tabloid war were serious questions about whether the monarchy had abused its position in law and whether Charles' court had become a law unto itself. Coverage was often so hostile it went far beyond individual character assassination. 'Let's get rid of royals not fit to run a chip shop', said the *Mirror*, while the *Guardian* described how Charles' court 'put Louis XIV in the shade'. These press criticisms were undoubtedly serious and could perhaps have become a political critique had Parliament taken up some of the issues and had the timing of the Peat report been less felicitous.[20] The fact that Parliament did not follow up these issues is complex, perhaps connected with the unclear role played by the government in dropping the Burrell trial, together with a distaste for the tabloid nature of the story. The timing of the Peat report appears to have been another instance of the royal family using advanced techniques of spinning. The report was delayed three times, finally published days before the invasion of Iraq when the country's attention was elsewhere. There's no doubt, however, that royal advisers recognised how serious press critiques were, as they issued a series of unprecedented rebuttals of press reports during the Burrell trial.[21] These have now become a feature of royal interaction with the press.[22]

Conclusion

The press coverage was never wholly hostile to the monarchy during the period of the Burrell trial and its aftermath. At the height of press outcry at royal interference, the newspapers all carried pictures of the Queen shedding tears at Remembrance Day ceremonies, with sympathetic commentaries. Such ambivalence has dominated subsequently. Shortly after furious attacks during the Burrell episode, the press waxed lyrical about the Queen's Golden Jubilee celebrations. It was the same when the Queen Mother died. Similarly the tabloids gloated over Charles' mistakes around his wedding ceremony but raved about the wedding itself, some even reinstating the hated Camilla as 'a style icon'.

Since this period the press has focused on William and Harry with attention reminiscent of the soap opera days of Diana and Fergie. Like many celebrities, the princes are a focus for commentary and judgement. Yet the residue of Diana's life remains. Both broadsheets and tabloids put the split of William and Kate Middleton on front pages, no longer in any doubt about legitimate public interest in royal doings. A tone of real overt criticism of royal behaviour in both tabloids and broadsheets remains. William and Kate's split provoked critical commentary about royal snobbery in both broadsheets and tabloids, while 'friends' of the royals blamed press intrusion. Relations between press and royalty take place now in a negotiated critical space in which the people – if not the monarchy – have learned that the future of the monarchy depends not on divine right but on popular consent.

Notes

1   The *Daily Express* under the ownership of Richard Desmond has run a continuous campaign supporting Mohammed Al Fayed's hostile agenda towards the royal family.
2   4 February 2007.
3   It appears that the monarchy may have watched the press more carefully than the press watched the monarchy. It is now known that George V's doctor administered him a lethal overdose so that his death would be announced by the more 'appropriate' *Times* rather than the less salubrious evening papers.
4   Sir Peregrine Worsthorne, interview for *The Princess and the Press*, PBS 1997.
5   Quoted in *Public Opinion Quarterly* October 1937.
6   Hugh Cudlipp became editorial director of the *Daily Mirror* in 1952 and chair of the Daily Mirror Newspapers and the International Publishing Corporation until 1973.
7   Muggeridge criticised the British monarchy in 1958 in a US magazine, in 'Does England Really Need a Queen?' Right-wing commentators like Worsthorne were outraged: 'we couldn't believe our eyes when we read these attacks and there was tremendous anger and outrage that two men should choose to attack the Queen in this kind of really impertinent way, commenting on her voice … and the corgis and that kind of thing' (interview op cit).
8   An under-age Prince Charles was witnessed going into a pub and ordering a cherry brandy, which provoked acres of news coverage.
9   Simon Jenkins, interview for *The Princess and the Press*, PBS 1997.
10 Ibid.
11 'The thing you have to remember', says Simon Jenkins, 'is that from the moment that Diana Spencer arrived on the scene you were going to get media attention devoted to her unlike anything you'd seen in the world. No film star, no Pope, no Queen was going to get the sort of attention that she was going to get. The only question was when would she crack?' Interview for *The Princess and the Press*, PBS 1997.
12 Interview for *The Princess and the Press*, PBS 1997.
13 BBC documentary with Jonathan Dimbleby 29 June 1994.
14 Simon Jenkins interview for *The Princess and the Press*, PBS 1997.

15 The agreement with the press was that William and Harry would be protected from press intrusion until the end of their education.
16 *Daily Express*, 4 September 1997.
17 Directed by Stephen Frears (2006).
18 Simon Heffer wrote several extremely critical pieces about this: e.g. 'Perverts and the Course of Justice' *Spectator* 6 November 2002.
19 John Humphrys.
20 www.princeofwales.gov.uk/media/02_press_releases/2003/030313_peat_ report.html. Accessed 6 November 2003.
21 This included a somewhat surreal appearance of Charles' Private Secretary on television to announce that Prince Charles is not gay (6 November 2003).
22 After the documentary *The Meddling Prince*, Michael Peat again issued a point-by-point rebuttal of the allegations (11 March 2007).

References

Blain, N. and O'Donnell, H. (2003) *Media, Monarchy and Power* Bristol: Intellect Books.
Conboy, M. (2006) *Tabloid Britain: Constructing A Community Through Language* London: Routledge.
Coward, R. (1984) *Female Desire* London: HarperCollins.
Coward, R. (2005) *Diana: The Authorised Portrait* London: HarperCollins.
Coward, R. (2007) 'What the Butler Started: Relations between British Tabloids and Monarchy in the Fall-out from the Paul Burrell Trial' *Journalism Practice* vol. 1 no. 2, pp.245–60.
Greenslade, R. (2003) *Press Gang* London: Macmillan.
Hastings, M. (2003) *Editor, A Memoir* London: Pan.
Kelley, K. (1998) *The Royals* London: Warner Books.
Morton, A. (1992) *Diana: Her True Story* London: Simon & Schuster.
Pimlott, B. (1996) *The Queen: A Biography of Elizabeth II*, London and New York: HarperCollins.
Riddell, M. (2004) 'Interview with Mark Bolland' *British Journalism Review* vol. 15 no. 2, pp.7–14.
Thomas, J. (2002) *Diana's Mourning* Cardiff: The University of Wales Press.

Public Talks

Hamilton, A. (2006) *Royalty and the Press* (The Front Page, British Library September).

Interviews with the author

Bond, J. (2004) for *Diana, The Portrait*.
Deedes, W. (2004) for *Diana, The Portrait*.

Chapter 11

Crime reporting

Claire Wardle

Introduction

Crime news encompasses a wide range of topics including the reporting of specific crimes, investigations, when suspects are charged, trials, sentences and the eventual punishment. It is important to remember the wide spectrum of stories which can be included under the crime reporting banner, as an assumption remains that newspapers focus solely on the crimes themselves and the resulting 'whodunit?' stories. Perhaps surprisingly, a significant proportion of news stories actually concentrate on general criminal justice policies, including sentencing and prisoner rights.

Many scholars have considered this question of crime reporting from both criminological and media studies perspectives (Chibnall 1977; Ericson *et al.* 1987, 1989, 1991; Reiner *et al.* 2003; Schlesinger and Tumber 1994) and confirm the difficulty of assessing with any degree of confidence the relative 'amount' of crime news in the press. A meta-analysis of 36 studies concluded that between 1.6 per cent and 33.5 per cent of newspaper reporting included the coverage of crime news (Marsh 1991, p.73). This vast difference in percentages is understandable, although frustrating, given the bewildering array of methodologies, sampling techniques, definitions of crime, types of newspaper, and geographical locations. Despite these difficulties, a consensus remains that in western nations (where the vast majority of this research has been undertaken) significant proportions of daily newspapers carry stories related to crime (Reiner 2002).

One myth that endures is that prison is all but invisible in the newspapers. As Ericson *et al.* conclude, '[p]rison sentences are overrepresented although the nature of prison itself and other practices of criminal punishment receive very little attention' (1987, p.46). This has always been explained by the lack of consistent reporter–source relationships, unlike the professional media relations units located in police organisations today. Ongoing research being conducted by Mason (2006) monitors prison stories in the national British press and demonstrates that prison stories do exist, and although individual cases often remain invisible, there are on average 90–100 articles a month (in all daily and Sunday newspapers), with the majority focusing on prison policy and prisoners' rights (typically suggesting that prisoners have too many rights).

In this chapter, I argue that crime news has changed considerably over the past 20 years. Research into newspaper coverage has shown how norms relating to deviancy and control have shifted subtly. While it is impossible to disentangle the mutually reinforcing relationship between public opinion, newspaper coverage and legislation, it is difficult not to be increasingly troubled by the way newspapers attempt to shape public understanding of crime, and consequently public discussion. As coverage has become increasingly individualistic, emotive and focused on the rarest of crimes, newspapers are failing to provide a rational space for important discussions about crime and justice. But perhaps most unnerving is the way that newspapers, particularly tabloid newspapers, purport to encourage such debate. In reality, any debate is ultimately limited. Editors proudly advertise their role as 'voice of the people', appearing to facilitate discussion through online petitions and phone votes, while simultaneously limiting and shaping opinion through their polemical comment pieces and editorials.

Characteristics of contemporary news coverage

While the majority of studies of crime reporting focus on the narrative structure of the text, it is also important to consider the visual and linguistic choices made by journalists and editors, particularly in different types of newspapers. Tabloid newspapers are far more likely to use visuals, larger headlines, photographic spreads, and the language is more likely to be moralistic and emotional (Lumby 2000). However, the assumption that tabloids are the exclusive home for crime reporting remains unfounded. As Deutschmann (1959) found in his comparison of crime coverage in the *New York Times* and the *New York Daily News*, the latter tended to be more sensational in that it included a higher proportion of crime news; however, there was little difference in reported facts as both papers drew on the same police sources and records. This similarity has been confirmed in more recent research (Bird 1992; Sparks and Tulloch 2000) which has also demonstrated that tabloid newspapers typically included as much information as broadsheet newspapers when similar stories are compared.

One focus of the crime reporting literature is how effectively newspapers cover the reality of crime, with the general acknowledgement of Surette's (1998) 'law of opposites', which argues that the representation of crime and offenders is the polar opposite to the information available in official crime statistics and victim surveys. Research has also demonstrated that the news media focus predominantly on crimes which have been, or are likely to be solved, and the stories focus predominantly on the process of capture, arrest and charging the accused. Newspapers are significantly more likely to cover murder and other serious violent, especially sexually motivated crimes, despite the fact that they are the least frequent type of crime (Greer 2003).

In terms of how offenders and victims are portrayed Jewkes also discusses the power of binary oppositions on newspaper storytelling: '[s]tories involving crime and criminals are frequently presented within a context that emphasizes good versus evil, folk heroes and folk devils, black against white, guilty or innocent, "normal" as opposed to "sick", "deviant" or "dangerous" and so on' (2004, p.45). The concern with the infusion of moral undertones is that morality is founded on 'them and us' poles and 'such a consensus makes other views difficult to sustain because of the rigidity, comprehensiveness and power of these beliefs' (Howitt 1998, p.166). A reliance on moral tones reduces complex and important questions to a simplistic dichotomy which unconsciously can lead to more fervent support for punitive responses (see chapter 13 by Critcher).

Victims and offenders are the lynchpin of the coverage, with the 'innocence' of the former juxtaposed with the 'evil' of the latter. The offender will be discussed in one-dimensional tones, with little contextualisation, partly a consequence of prejudicial coverage laws, but also part of a trend to present offenders as isolated actors, infused with an inherent wickedness. Their images will be published almost entirely in black and white, with images specifically chosen, then cropped and refocused to emphasise their 'monstrous' features, their staring eyes and preferably a flash of their teeth. In comparison, victims are seen happy and smiling, underlying the tragic nature of the crime. Reiner *et al.* have demonstrated the 'profound change in the characterization of victims and their role within crime stories' (2003, p.26). Up until the 1980s, there were significantly more attempts to contextualise the offender in order to try to understand their motive, 'increasingly the victim–perpetrator relationship is presented as a zero-sum game: compassion for the offender is represented as callous and unjust to victims' (ibid.). Through the narrative structure, images and language, readers are asked to identify with the victims, capitalising on the fear that it 'could happen to you'.

Newspapers as moral guardians

Many scholars have considered the function of newspapers as moral guardians in the ways in which they report crime (Chibnall 1977; Katz 1987). As Ericson *et al.* state in the introduction to their crime reporting trilogy, '[t]he perpetual public conversation about morality, deviance and control in [the] media draws the contours of the moral boundaries of society ... Journalists provide a daily "common sense" articulation of deviance and control processes and their implications for boundary-maintaining and boundary-changing functions' (1987, pp.6–7).

A 'modern morality play in which the good met evil' was how Cohen describes the community reaction to the phenomenon of Mods and Rockers in Britain in the 1960s (1972, p.159). Describing how a society responds to the threat of illegal behaviour as a morality play has particular resonance as a way of understanding the role of newspapers and their coverage of crime and punishment. Krajicek, who offers a very critical analysis of the news media's behaviour in terms of covering crime, writes, 'stories are presented as morality plays, which allows the media to occupy the choir loft of moral sanctimony from which it can cheer the good guy and hiss the bad guy' (1998, p.14). Wilkie agrees when he also uses a religious metaphor to explain reporters' moral positioning, 'when likely victims present themselves, the journalists, our modern "priests" transform them into symbolically fitting victims whose characters and transgressions represent the ills of present in the hierarchy' (1981, pp.102–3).

An example from an editorial in *The Times*, taken from the coverage of the murder of 7-year-old Sarah Payne in the summer of 2000, demonstrates how this can play out:

> The requirement that those who murder in cold blood serve life imprison-ment is much more than just the instinctive cry of all our injured hearts. It is a moral necessity. If we fail to imprison those who murder so callously for the duration of their own existences we demean the value we place on innocent life. And if we fail to uphold that value then we lessen the respect society had for the rule of law, widening the distance between the values of the ruled and the rulers, encouraging the offended to vigilantism.
>
> ('Why it Matters Who Murders Your Child', 25 July 2000, p.16)

Katz (1987), who undertook a content analysis of crime coverage in New York newspapers in the late 1970s, also considers daily crime news reading as a 'ritual moral exercise'. He attempts to understand why readers were so interested in reading about crime and concludes that the audience had an active need to consider these moral questions, as a way of helping them navigate the moral dilemmas they faced every day.

Newspapers as storytellers

Golding and Elliott in their discussion of news values list 'drama' first, writing that 'news stories are, as the term suggests, stories as well as news. Good ones exhibit a narrative structure akin to the root elements in human drama' (1979, p.115). Dramatisation is certainly a key trait of western newsgathering (Darnton 1975; Tuchman 1976). The inherent drama of crime means it is unsurprising that crime coverage makes up a large proportion of the daily news.

It is not just the crimes. Court cases are themselves a drama with a theatrical setting, recognisable lead characters and often surprising plot twists and turns. As Fox and Sickel explain, it is 'the relatively slow moving nature of the criminal justice system [which] allows these cases to become national melodramas embed-ded in the social fabric' (2001, p.62). The daily turn of events which characterises trials fits closely with newspaper schedules, underlining Galtung and Ruge's (1965) observation that timeliness is one of the most important influences of story choices in news.

In a commentary about the Soham murder case, *Guardian* media commentator Peter Preston describes how there was '[a] cast of characters – including two photogenic victims, the heartbroken families, the detectives and, most oddly, the killer and his accomplice [...] introduced as they are in every Miss Marple. [...V]iewers were able to follow every twist and turn of the inquiry over a fortnight and even hear from the killer himself – and yes it did turn out to be the sinister-looking caretaker who told that odd story of how he was washing his dog as the girls passed' (Preston 2003, p.6).

Crime news is inherently dramatic but it is also the case that there are numerous tools used by journalists to create the sense of drama and concern. Crime stories often include powerful visuals, making them resonate in the culture because certain pictures have shared significance and invoke certain emotional responses. Whether it is family photos of lost victims or mugshots of dangerous criminals, most infamous crimes can be remembered by a visual, whether it is the grainy CCTV camera of Jamie Bulger being led away by his two abductors (Kember 1995) or the smiling schoolgirl photos after abductions (Wardle 2007). The personification of crime news results in the presentation of events through a focus on the emotional, personal and human aspects of the story, resulting in the context, background and analysis of the story being ignored.

News that is memorable is that which arouses readers' emotions. Crime coverage can be emotional; whether it is focusing on the individual emotions that occur when a crime has been committed or the collective emotions connected with irrational fears about crime. Crime stories fit perfectly within the age-old use of narrative in print. As Krajicek's description demonstrates, 'too many of these stories begin and end with who did what to whom, embellished with the moans of a murder victim's mother or the sneer of an unrepentant killer in handcuffs' (1998, p.7).

In many ways these two roles of moral guardian and institutionalised storyteller work in tandem. The news value which dictates an article should be dramatic and sensational to ensure the continued interest of the reader, also encourages reporters to rely on the traditional dramatic technique of situating right against wrong, good against evil. 'By defining social issues as straightforward struggles between good and evil, melodrama compels our attention and enlists our emotions' (Best 1999, p.159). As a result, newspaper coverage has an underlying tone of moral authority.

Crime news values

The two major roles played by newspapers – that of institutionalised storyteller and moral guardian – mean crime will always be a major staple of news reporting. There are, however, a number of crime news values that determine *which* crimes are included within the pages of our daily newspapers. As Reiner *et al.* assert 'deviance is the quintessential element of newsworthiness' (2003, p.13), and the specifics of newsworthiness and how it impacts on the way a particular story is told have been debated fully (Galtung and Ruge 1965). In Chibnall's classic consideration of the eight News Imperatives he writes, 'you can put six reporters in a court and they can sit through six hours of court verbiage and they'll come out with the same story' (1977, p.86), emphasising the influence of these news values. Chibnall's text remains a crucial explanation of news values, but an updated version appears in Jewkes' *Media and Crime* which discusses 12 news structures and values that shape crime news, and ensures almost identical crimes are covered across newspaper types (2004, pp.41–59).

Table 11.1 *Jewkes' (2004) 12 crime news values*

News Values	Stories are more likely to be covered if the crime:
Threshold	has a certain level of perceived importance or drama
Predictability	has a novelty value
Simplification	can be reducible to a minimum number of parts or themes
Individualism	can be explained through individual responsibilities for a crime rather than complex cultural and political explanations
Risk	has no motive – 'it could happen to you'
Sex	has a sexual element
Celebrity	involves celebrities or high-status people
Proximity	has geographical or cultural proximity (e.g. crimes including white middle-class victims are more likely to be covered)
Violence	involves violence
Spectacle or graphic imagery	involves the potential for graphic or emotive visuals
Children	involves children
Conservative ideology	supports a conservative agenda in terms of policing and the criminal justice system

Why does the coverage look like this?

There are two common assumptions about why crime coverage looks as it does. First, reporters and their editors hold assumptions about the types of stories readers expect to see in their daily newspapers. These are summed up by the news values described above. Secondly, there are institutional forces which shape newsrooms and news copy, namely the reporter–source relationships, in particular the relationships between journalists and police organisations. Early research on this (for example, Graber 1980) described a simplistic, unidirectional relationship between reporter and police officer that could be described as 'straight from the police blotter', with reporters relying 100 per cent on police organisations to provide descriptions of crimes which were noted almost verbatim in the news pages. As Hall *et al.* stated, police sources were the 'primary definers' of any crime (1978, p.19).

It is now accepted that the relationship between journalists and official sources is far more complex. As Ericson *et al.* (1989) successfully demonstrated, the relationship between the two parties is symbiotic. The media need the police in order to sell newspapers, which produces a supply and demand relationship, but the police need the media too. During high-profile cases, the media are needed for police appeals for information, family appeals, victim portraits, reconstructions and publicising awards (Innes 2003, p.57). But at the everyday level, there has also been a realisation that the police have to be proactive in terms of their image, by demonstrating public accountability, giving the boring everyday police work a ceremonial force, and reassuring the community that the police are doing their job (Mawby 2002). As a result police forces now have professional media relations units. Ultimately the relationship between the two cannot be separated. As Fishman (1981) argues in his case study of how the press 'constructed' a crime wave,

> crime news is mutually determined by journalists whose image of crime is shaped by police concerns and by police, whose concerns with crime are influenced by media practices … news organisations may choose what crimes to report but the pool of occurrences from which they draw is pre-selected and pre-formed with police departments.
>
> (cited in Krajicek 1998, p.104)

Conclusion

The impact of crime news stories remains unconfirmed. In the past it has been shown that crime news is absorbed and remembered (Sherizen 1978, p.209) and the question of whether such blanket coverage of crime encourages readers to become 'irrationally' fearful of crime, remains a popular one. Much has been written about how the public's measured fear of crime is increasing while crime levels (as measured by official surveys) appear to be decreasing (Hale 1996). Furthermore, a recent review of the literature by Ditton et al. (2004) states that a total of 73 studies had been carried out to explore the relationship between media consumption (including 14 studies concentrating solely on newspaper readership) and fear of crime and concludes only 27 per cent found a positive relationship, challenging a widespread assumption that news media coverage is the cause of rising fears about crime despite overall decreases in crime.

But more recently scholars have argued that theories about public fear of crime are seriously flawed because they are 'premised on rational, calculating individuals who routinely miscalculate their true risk of crime' (Hollway and Jefferson 1997, p.255). People's fears of crime should not be considered as rational impulses, rather as responses to the 'symbolic representation, discourse and the micro- and macro-contexts in which fear of crime is experienced and given meaning' (Lupton and Tulloch 1999, p.507). If someone is fearful of crime, it is inappropriate and actually unhelpful to suggest their fears should be dismissed because they are irrational. Ultimately, our crime coverage is patterned and structured, providing a one-dimensional analysis of the crime which takes place, those who commit those crimes, and how the criminal justice system treats these offenders:

> Cautioned against any signs of critical thinking, crime reporters hug the shoreline relying heavily on perfunctory findings by police and treating each crime in splendid isolation … the omission of broader discussions rarely startles readers, who have been conditioned not to expect them.
>
> (Lotz 1995, p.69)

While newspaper coverage continues to include such characteristics, with isolated, unrepresentative crimes repeatedly reported, with explanations which suggest individual wickedness is to blame rather than structural weaknesses, readers are much more likely to remain fearful, believing that next time, 'it could happen to them'.

References

Best, J. (1999) *Random Violence: How We Talk about New Crimes and New Victims* Berkeley, CA: University of California Press.

Bird, E. (1992) *For Enquiring Minds: A Cultural Study of Supermarket Tabloids* Knoxville: University of Tennessee.

Campbell, R. (1990) *60 Minutes and the News: A Mythology for Middle America* Urbana: University of Illinois Press.

Chibnall, S. (1977) *Law and Order News: An Analysis of Crime Reporting in the British Press* London: Tavistock Press.

Cohen, S. (1972) *Folk Devils and Moral Panics* London: MacGibbon and Kee.

Dahlgren, P. (1988) 'Crime News: Fascination with the Mundane' *European Journal of Communication* vol. 3 no. 2, pp.189–206.

Darnton, R. (1975) 'Writing News and Telling Stories' *Daedalus* spring, pp.175–94.

Deutschmann, P. J. (1959) *News-page Content of Twelve Metropolitan Dailies* Cincinnati: Scripps Howard Research.

Ditton, J., Chadee, D., Farrall, S., Gilchrist, E. and Bannister, J. (2004) 'From Imitation to Intimidation: A Note on the Curious and Changing Relationship between Media, Crime and Fear of Crime' *British Journal of Criminology* vol. 44 no. 4, pp.595–610.

Ericson, R., Baranek, P. and Chan, J. (1987) *Visualizing Deviance: A Study of News Organization* Toronto: University of Toronto Press.

Ericson, R., Baranek, P. and Chan, J. (1989) *Negotiating Control: A Study of News Sources* Toronto: University of Toronto Press.

Ericson, R., Baranek, P. and Chan, J. (1991) *Representing Order: Crime, Law and Justice* Toronto: University of Toronto Press.

Fishman, M. (1981) 'Police News: Constructing an Image of Crime' *Urban Life* vol. 9 no. 4, pp.371–94.

Fox, R. L. and van Sickel, R. (2001) *Tabloid Frenzy: Criminal Justice in an Age of Media Frenzy* Boulder, CO: Lynne Rienner Publishers.

Galtung, J. and Ruge, M. (1965) 'The Structure of Foreign News' *Journal of International Peace Research* vol. 1, pp.64–90.

Golding, P. and Elliott, P. (1979) *Making the News* London: Longman.

Graber, D. (1980) *Crime News and the Public* New York: Praeger.

Greer, C. (2003) *Sex Crime and the Media: Sex Offending and the Press in a Divided Society* Collumpton: Willan.

Hale, C. (1996) 'Fear of Crime: A Review of the Literature' *International Review of Victimology* vol. 4, pp.79–150.

Hall, S., Critcher, C., Jefferson, L., Clarke, J. and Roberts, B. (1978) *Policing the Crisis: Mugging, the State and Law and Order* London: Macmillan Press.

Hollway, W. and Jefferson, T. (1997) 'The Risk Society in an Age of Anxiety: Situating Fear of Crime' *British Journal of Sociology* vol. 48 no. 2, pp.255–66.

Howitt, D. (1998) *Crime, Media and the Law* Chichester: John Wiley & Sons.

Innes, M. (2003) '"Signal Crimes": Detective Work, Mass Media and Constructing Collective Memory' in Mason, P. (Ed.) *Criminal Visions: Media Representations of Crime and Justice* Collumpton: Willan, pp.51–72.

Jewkes, Y. (2004) *Media and Crime* London: Sage Publications.

Katz, J. (1987) 'What Makes Crime News?' *Media, Culture and Society* vol. 9, pp.47–75.

Kember, S. (1995) 'Surveillance, Technology and Crime: The Case of James Bulger' in Lister, M. (Ed.) *The Photographic Image in Digital Culture* London: Routledge.

Krajicek, D. J. (1998) *Scooped! Media Miss Real Story on Crime While Chasing Sex, Sleaze and Celebrities* New York: Columbia University Press.

Lotz, R. E. (1995) *Crime and the American Press* New York: Praeger.

Lumby, C. (2000) 'Gotcha: Life in a Tabloid World' *Journalism: Theory, Practice and Criticism* vol. 1 no. 3, pp.371–2.

Lupton, D. and Tulloch, J. (1999) 'Theorizing Fear of Crime: Beyond Rational/Irrational Opposition' *British Journal of Sociology* vol. 50 no. 3, pp.507–23.

Marsh, H. (1991) 'A Comparative Analysis of Crime Coverage in Newspapers in the United States and Other Countries from 1960–1989: A Review of the Literature' *Journal of Criminal Justice* vol. 19, pp.67–79.

Mason, P. (2006) February and March 2006 Bulletins, Prison Media Monitoring Unit, http://www.jc2m.co.uk/MarchBulletin.pdf. Accessed 9 February 2007.

Mawby, R. C. (2002) *Policing Images: Policing, Communication and Legitimacy* Collumpton: Willan.

Preston, P. (2003) 'How the Police Fed the Media Beast' *Guardian* 22 December, p.6.

Reiner, R. (2002) 'Media Made Criminality' in Reiner, R., Maguire, M. and Morgan, R. (Eds) *The Oxford Handbook of Criminology* (3rd edn) Oxford: Oxford University Press, pp.376–416.

Reiner, R., Livingstone, S. and Allen, J. (2003) 'From Law and Order to Lynch Mobs: Crime News since the Second World War' in Mason, P. (Ed.) *Criminal Visions: Media Representations of Crime and Justice* Collumpton: Willan, pp.13–32.

Schlesinger, P. and Tumber, H. (1994) *Reporting Crime: The Media Politics of Criminal Justice* Oxford: Clarendon Press.

Sherizen, S. (1978) 'Social Creation of Crime News' in Winick, C. (Ed.) *Deviance and Mass Media* Thousand Oaks, CA: Sage, pp.203–24.

Sparks, C. and Tulloch, J. (Eds) (2000) *Tabloid Tales: Global Debates over Media Standards* Lanham, MD: Rowman and Littlefield.

Surette, R. (1998) *Media, Crime and Criminal Justice: Image and Realities* Belmont, CA: Wadsworth.

Tuchman, G. (1976) 'Telling Stories' *Journal of Communication* vol. 26 no. 4, pp.93–7.

Wardle, C. (2007) 'Monsters and Angels: Visual Press Coverage of Child Murders in the US and UK, 1930–1990' *Journalism: Theory, Practice and Criticism* vol. 8 no. 4.

Wilkie, C. (1981) 'The Scapegoating of Bruno Richard Hauptmann' *Central States Speech Journal* vol. 32, pp.100–10.

Chapter 12

Sport journalism: persistent themes and changing times

Alan Tomlinson and John Sugden

Introduction

In 1955, journalist Archie Ledbrooke and his collaborator Edgar Turner noted that 'there are two ways of writing about a football match' (Ledbrooke and Turner 1955, p.161): as a form of self-contained entertainment; or as part of a wider cultural and historical context. They favoured the latter approach, what they called 'the larger framework' (ibid.). Ledbrooke was the football correspondent of the *Manchester Evening News*, and three years later was one of the journalists to die in the Munich air disaster that decimated the outstanding Manchester United crop of Busby Babes. Ledbrooke wrote with excitement of the new internationalism in football. His book *Soccer from the Pressbox* was first published in 1950, the year of England's disastrous World Cup debut in Brazil, where a journeyman USA team and then a Franco-inspired Spanish team both beat England 1–0, knocking the overconfident English out of the tournament. His book is spiced with insights from his international experience but also from his Manchester beat, based upon the close working relationship with his sources that allowed him and his peers on board the Manchester United charter to Belgrade and back, via the fatal refuelling stop in the snow at Munich.

Half a century later, the Manchester United manager Sir Alex Ferguson no longer spoke to the BBC, and the flow of information in the sports news was more a case of information management and controlled press briefings, alongside a surfeit of repeddled chit-chat and gossip, than of the earlier age of mutual trust and close working relationships. While the space dedicated to sport in the print media had expanded beyond anticipation from Ledbrooke's day, the nature of the coverage could be seen as less concerned with Ledbrooke's 'larger framework' than with the regurgitation of industry gossip and the flattery of celebrity. This chapter considers some of the key characteristics of contemporary sports coverage in UK newspapers in the light of these cultural and historical changes. First, the historical context is reviewed; then, in the heart of the chapter, we overview the institutions and practices of contemporary print-based sport journalism.

The media, journalism and sport: social contexts and historical reminders

Sport's contribution to the intensifying media profile of a globalising world is well established (Miller *et al.* 2001), as is the internationalisation of the ownership of production outlets for sport and related products (Law *et al.* 2002), and the all-embracing reach of the golden triangle of sport, sponsorship and the media (Sugden and Tomlinson 1998, chapter 4). Sport has stimulated as well as reflected the growth of media forms. Historically, newspapers have been central to the growth of modern sport forms, in Britain and the United States alike (Goldlust 1987, p.71). In Britain the press was essential to the wider dissemination of the new sporting values, forms and culture established in the public schools. As Mason puts it: 'The press was crucial in the process: advertising and publicizing, promoting, even sponsoring and emphasizing, a sporting world with its own seasons, festive and holy days ... By the mid-1880s the British public was supporting three sporting daily newspapers' (1988, p.46). Each of these – the *Sporting Life* (1859–1990s), *Sportsman* (1865), both London-based, and the Manchester-based *Sporting Chronicle* (1871–1983) – had been almost wholly dedicated to sport from their inception, and devoted extensive attention to horse racing and 'promoted and sponsored sport ... holding stakes, and providing judges, referees and trophies, sporting annuals and guides' (ibid., p.47). A weekly sporting press also thrived. One title, the *Field*, established in 1853, catered for hunting, shooting and fishing, although it began to decline in profitability in the 1890s. More geared to the broader sports agenda and the mass market was the *Athletic News*, established in Manchester in 1875, which preached the gospel of amateur sport to a northern public. It soon expanded its coverage to report on professional football and rugby in the winter, and cricket and athletics in the summer seasons. *Athletic News* became a penny paper in 1887–8, and sold 180,000 in the football season. It merged with *Sporting Chronicle* in 1931 (Hill 2002, p.58).

This buoyant specialist sporting press was challenged and undermined by recognition of the popular interest in sport, by the daily (morning and evening) and Sunday newspapers. By the turn of the century a sports page, or pages in some cases, featured in almost all newspapers, with up to 10 per cent of content devoted to sport (although *The Times* did not appoint a sports editor until after 1914). The Sunday papers expanded coverage, as a combination of a results service and commentary on the expanding Saturday schedules. In 1895 the *News of the World* gave 14 per cent of its content to sport, 'with cricket, football and athletics usually being given more prominence than horse-racing' (Mason 1988, p.49).

Hill (2002, pp.45–6) summarises the legacy of the emergence of this tabloid-based form of coverage (for example, in the *Daily Mail* in 1896 and the *Daily Mirror* in 1903, although the latter was initially aimed at middle-class women). First, it pitched at popular sports including football, cricket, boxing and horse racing, as well as at popular national events such as the Boat Race or Wimbledon. Second, it all but ignored women's sport and perpetuated 'a conventional wisdom that sport was a male preserve'. Finally, its coverage was 'markedly insular' and 'readers viewed the sporting world from a British perspective'. Such insularity was confirmed in a persisting sense of locality in the regional press, best exemplified in the football special that would be rushed out on a Saturday evening, often printed on coloured paper – the *Pink* in Burnley, the *Green 'Un* in Sheffield (for an overview of sport reporting in local and regional newspapers see Walker 2006). The sporting press was a kind of debating chamber, generating dialogue and debate on players, teams and results. It also began to create celebrities, including the sporting journalists themselves. By the 1930s, factual style, or the anonymity of those writing on sport for *The Times*, was forsaken for a sensationalist emphasis on features, drama and behind-the-scenes stories (Hill 2002, p.45). The specialist sporting press, including the short-lived 25-issue initiative *Sportsweek* in 1986–7 (Horne 1992) never again challenged the dominance of the national press' coverage of sport. It is hardly surprising that when radio began to broadcast sports events and results to live audiences, newspapers soon sought alternative angles and emphases. In the multimedia climate of the first decade of the twenty-first century (Boyle and Haynes 2004) the print media in their traditional newspaper forms were challenged like never before.

The print media today

In March 2007, Ian Wooldridge, considered by many of his peers to be the doyen of sport journalism, died aged 75. In his main column on 18 March, which was half feature and half obituary, the *Observer*'s Chief Sports Writer, Kevin Mitchell, chose the moment to reflect upon the seismic changes that are shaking the foundations of the sports desk. Mitchell drew upon his experience of giving the fourth annual 'Sport Journalism Lecture' at the University of Brighton earlier that week and noted his surprise when, 'I asked the students how many of them got their first sport news from the web? Nearly all put their hands up. It was a jolting response' (Mitchell 2007b, p.22). In his lecture and his column, he recounted a meeting that had been presided over by the Editors of sister newspapers, the *Observer* and the *Guardian*:

> It was daunting, but there was no avoiding the truth, which is, after all, what we deal in. We are irretrievably global now, an across-the-ether, around the clock, 24/7 brand, not just newspapers. And in that context, for better or worse, (sometimes both) we are married to the web. These are confusing and exciting times.
>
> (ibid.)

For the remainder of this chapter we will chart the main features of the changes that are radically transforming the occupational subculture of the sport journalist. In doing so we will argue that this is not just a question of quantity and accelerated technological sophistication; rather, the fundamental nature of sport journalism is changing and, contrary to Mitchell's tempered optimism, almost certainly not for the better.

Imagine an avid fan and reader of the sports pages who accompanies a time traveller from 1970 to the present day (2007). When she had perused a selection of broadsheet and tabloid newspapers, she would be struck by the massive expansion in the coverage that is given to sport in today's newspapers. In the mid-week press in 1970, only three or four of the back pages were devoted to sport whereas today sport colonises 12 or more in broadsheets and up to 20 pages in the tabloids. On Saturdays and Sundays this expansion is even more pronounced, with almost all papers producing multi-page special sport supplements for both days of the weekend.

Undoubtedly our time traveller would see straight away that the Goliath driving this expansion is football. Significantly more than half of broadsheet coverage is devoted to football, while for the tabloids it is closer to three-quarters. Not satisfied with saturation coverage of football in their weekend editions, many newspapers now offer special supplements on Monday devoted to rehashing, reanalysing and dissecting the thrills and spills of the previous 48 hours. On the basis of the expansion in column inches devoted to the sport, it is tempting to think that the amount of football being played has dramatically increased in the last 40 years and that press coverage has grown accordingly, but you would be wrong. If anything, the amount of people playing football at both professional and amateur levels has declined and as a whole so has football spectatorship.

So where does the increased coverage come from and what is it about? The vast majority of contemporary football journalism is concentrated on the affairs of a small professional elite. We choose the word 'affairs' deliberately, because sport journalism is no longer simply about sport reporting – there are too many columns to be fed solely by news of who crossed and who scored, or which unforced error or stupendous volley turned the match around. There has been an expansion in the numbers of feature-type stories, many constructed around interviews with leading sporting figures, but usually managers and administrators rather than players/performers and still not enough to fill the sport pages. 'Where are all the players?' former footballer Paul Gascoigne asked journalist Hunter Davies, having noted the preoccupation of the back pages with managers (Davies 2007, p.49). So, in addition to a traditional brand of sport reporting, led by 24/7 satellite television, the sport media industries, following showbiz precedents, have turned our leading sport practitioners, especially our most gifted footballers and those who manage and consort with them (the England players' wives and girlfriends labelled WaGs in Germany at World Cup 2006), into celebrities. Once this has been achieved there is little or nothing about their lives and lifestyles that cannot be considered worth writing about, both on the back and front pages. This is no longer journalism of the sort that Wooldridge and his generation would recognise or sanction. Mitchell agrees, pointing out that too much of what passes as sport journalism today is in fact views and opinion and not news, *pace* the *Independent* Editor Simon Kelner's claim that newspapers are now 'viewspapers'

(Mitchell 2007a). Journalist turned journalism professor and broadcaster, Ian Hargreaves, might have had the state of contemporary sport journalism in mind when he said, 'obsessed with a world of celebrity and trivia, the news media are rotting our brains and undermining our civic life' (2003, p.104). Mike Collett, Chief Football Reporter for Reuters International, likewise believes that his profession has been trivialised and is in no doubt about the identity of the main culprit:

> The amount of airtime they have to fill with analyzing stuff, that 15 years ago you wouldn't have even thought about. This has led to a change in what defines news, what is newsworthy and where hype begins and real news judgement ends. This is an enormous problem that creates an artificial agenda newspapers feel obliged to write about, and agency people like me feel obliged to tell the world about. Sky is setting an agenda that is not particularly newsworthy, and through which trivia becomes headlines. This is never-ending.
>
> (quoted in Sugden and Tomlinson 2007, p.51)

Once she had settled down to read her way through a proliferated sports press, our time traveller would be disappointed to discover that the vast majority of sport stories in all the different papers are in fact finessed versions of the same thing. There are several reasons for this. First, the vast majority of sport journalists draw upon the same sources, freely from the web or by subscription to the wire services, and most of these are secondary and non-exclusive. One consequence of turning sportsmen and sportswomen into celebrities is that access to the people who make the sport news is now more restricted than ever before. The level of trust that once existed between sport journalists and the performers they were charged to write about has long since gone, blown away by a liturgy of exposé-style headlines in the wake of the hunt for celebrity tittle-tattle. That it usually was not the sports desk that brokered such stories, being more likely a smash-and-grab raid from the news desk, did little or nothing to prevent the world of sport building fences with strictly managed gates between itself and the sport media.

In such a climate, sport journalists live in fear of losing their access, scant though it may be, to the people, places and spaces, where the sport news is being made. Often sport journalists are too much in love with the sports they cover, living in fear of losing their memberships of the cosy and collusive club that characterises their beat (see Boyle 2006, pp. 113 and 115 on the issue of access). This fear is a powerful medium of control which shapes contemporary sport news. As Mike Collett reflected:

> Sometimes I can't believe how lucky I am. Going around the world following the sports I love, getting the best seats in the house, meeting all of the top stars. Sometimes I wake up in a sweat thinking that I've done something, written something, to blow it and I'll be thrown out of this world.
>
> (quoted in Sugden and Tomlinson 2007, p.50)

Related to this, the growth of a major PR industry around sport is another crucial difference in the workaday world of the sport journalist. There are now legions of people, many of them qualified journalists, employed by major sport organisations and individual sport stars to manage the news about them. The mainstays of their job descriptions are threefold: to prevent potentially critical journalists from obtaining insider information about their charges; to manage and set limits around access given to the rest of the sport media; and to generate and distribute freely positive news stories. In this regard, given the amount of information churned out and spoon-fed to the media by the sport PR industry – press releases, official websites, media conferences, photocalls, carefully choreographed 'mixed zones' – it has never been easier to be a sport journalist. We would argue that it has never been harder to be a good one; that is to say that it has never been harder to go after and get hard news.

Our time traveller from 1970 also might have been surprised to be given a few free newspapers. Many of these will be unfamiliar titles, but if she happens to live in Manchester she might raise an eyebrow when a copy of the *Manchester Evening News*, a paper she used to pay for, is thrust into her hands without charge. She will find little or nothing new in its sport pages, however, as almost everything will have been culled from the collusive sources already alluded to. She could always walk into a local internet café and this will open up a whole new world of sports news in the form of websites, blogs and a host of other online sources. Alas, not much new here either, at least nothing she can trust. As Hargreaves points out, it is a startling paradox of modern media that at a time when, in the west at least, the press has never been freer, both in terms of cost and forms of political control, it has never been more self-censoring. In part he accounts for this by the informal influence of owners and editors who place corporate commercial concerns over more old-fashioned, public service or 'Fourth Estate' values. But he also points to the effect of the information age on the quality of journalism:

> Because there is so much of it (news) we find it hard to sort the good from the bad. The fact that it is mostly obtainable without direct payment means that we value it less. As a generation grows up unaccustomed to the idea that news costs money, the economics of certain kinds of resource-intensive journalism are undermined.
>
> (Hargreaves 2003, p.3)

Today global media are dominated by a small number of self-interested and self-censoring conglomerates (Said 1993). According to John Pilger investigative journalists are a threatened species. They are being crowded out, to be replaced by 'a new kind of "multi-skilled" journalist, who is not multi-skilled at all, but a sad Protean figure required to work for a range of very different publications in the group but be loyal to none. There is no time to investigate' (1999, p.535). The freedom of the press is likewise under threat, as ideology and spin replace factual news and critical analysis.

Nowhere is this more evident than in the mainstream sports press where investigative journalism is all but extinct and the province of a handful of marginalised 'mavericks'. Although there are honourable exceptions – David Conn (1999, 2004), on football; Andrew Jennings (2006), in institutional corruption in sport governance – they simply prove the proverbial rule. Together, for instance, the Stevens Inquiry, Lord Burns' review of the FA and the *Independent European Sport Review*[1] suggest a weighty agenda for a press that is serious about its Fourth Estate role, but they barely get a mention in the back pages of our newspapers. Yes, a Sunday tabloid might pull an ethically dubious 'fake sheik' stunt to wrong-foot and expose a feeble and vain England football manager, but where has been the serious investigative journalism into the abuses of power and corruption that sit at the heart of the organisation that employed Eriksson and made such a mess of replacing him? And don't be fooled by the diet of 'kiss and tell' stories about the often sorry and sordid private lives of B-list sports stars. These may interest certain sections of the public, but they are not in the public interest and they are definitely not hard-won, hard news.

A free and critical press is a fundamental prerequisite of democracy and a vital weapon in the fight against institutionalised corruption in society, including sport. In the 1970s all a journalist needed to ply his or her trade was a pencil and pad, knowledge of shorthand, access to a phone and typewriter, and the nose and appetite for a good story. Today, digital journalists are equipped with wireless laptops, iPods, micro recorders, sophisticated mobile phones and various other bits of 'e-tackle'. The kit of the sport journalist may have changed since the 1970s and so might the nature and variety of the outlets that he or she writes for, but this should not mean the nature of the job has fundamentally changed. Of all the things listed above the nose and appetite are the most important and we need a sporting press that behaves as a watchdog not like a lapdog. For this to happen the power of sport to restrict access to critical journalism must be removed and sport journalists themselves, backed by owners and editors, need to rediscover the quest for hard-won, hard news. As Hugh McIlvanney (2006) has stated: 'There have always been celebrities and deservedly so', but 'there are of course plenty of liars in sport'. A little more journalistic concern with the latter rather than mere celebration of the former would be a challenging direction for the sport journalist in the multimedia age.

Conclusion

Archie Ledbrooke saw the 'actual reporting' of a football match as a relatively simple affair (Ledbrooke and Turner 1955, p.163), identifying 'four kinds of report covering a normal Saturday afternoon match' (ibid.): the evening paper report; the Sunday paper story, written at most an hour and a half after the game is over; the Monday morning story, a more reflective opportunity thought through before the journalist goes to his office on the Sunday afternoon; and the broadcast 'running commentary'. This was a simple world of standard match schedules, shared cultural experience in spectating, daylight watching and writing, and based in the hegemony of the print media. It was a different cultural world to that of the multimedia age of instant information access and media-led live schedules described in the previous section.

Yet in terms of general content there is a degree of continuity in print-based sport journalism. Apart from special events, as we have said men's football dominates the extraordinary expansion of the sport sections of the national newspapers. Coverage remains insular. And there is a relentless search for a kind of feature-based novelty. Even as the scale of the sporting event and its concomitant coverage has increased, these elements, as identified by Hill (2002), have persisted, discouraging innovative or challenging or creative, let alone investigative, forms of sports writing or commentary. Research, analyses and commentaries (Whannel 2002; Rowe 1999, chapter 3; Boyle and Haynes 2000, p.29; Brookes 2002, p.39; IRSS 2002) bear out this point. Sports may well feature in newspapers beyond the sports pages, as scandal, policy or business stories (Brookes 2002, pp.34–6), but within the sports pages themselves readers are offered a remarkably consistent diet of gossip, statistics and opinionated preview. Pulling the sport sections of newspapers apart requires both a recognition of these thematic continuities as a prelude to a broadening of journalistic agenda and ambition; and a realistic appraisal of the changing technologies and conventions of (sport) reportage that are so woven into the fabric of the contemporary information industry.

Note

1   Lord Stevens of Kirkwhelpington led an inquiry into the football business, commissioned by the (English) Premier League. He and his company, the corporate intelligence agency Quest, scrutinised 326 player transfers from January 2004. David Bond (2006) wrote that it is 'a damning indictment of the way football conducts its business that a man of Stevens' standing has struggled to find a smoking gun'. Lord Burns led the Football Association's structural review, reporting in August 2005 that 'the present structure of the FA' is 'progressively less suitable' to administer the modern game, and is 'in need of reform' (Football Association 2005, paragraph 5). The *Independent European Sport Review* (Arnaut 2006) was launched by UK sports minister Richard Caburn during the UK's presidency of the European Union in 2005, and with particularly strong support from Europe's governing body of football, UEFA. Its recommendations included pan-European cooperation 'to detect and fight against criminal activities around football and in particular to deter match-fixing, fraud, money-laundering or any other form of corrupt or criminal activity' (ibid., p.136).

References

Arnaut, J. Luis (2006) *Independent European Sport Review 2006, Final Version October 2006* Unspecified place or house of publication: www.independentsportreview.com Accessed 7 November 2007.

Bond, D. (2006) 'Stevens Left with Sense of Anti-climax' *Telegraph.co.uk*, 12.47am 20 December http://www.telegraph.co.uk/sport/ main.jhtml?xml=sport/2006/12/20/sfnbun20.xml. Accessed 19 March 2007.

Boyle, R. (2006) *Sports Journalism: Contexts and Issues* London: Sage.

Boyle, R. and Haynes, R. (2000) *Power Play: Sport, the Media and Popular Culture* London: Longman.

Boyle, R. and Haynes, R. (2004) *Football in the New Media Age* London: Routledge.

Brookes, R. (2002) *Representing Sport* London: Arnold.

Conn, D. (1999) *The Football Business: Fair Game in the 90s* Edinburgh: Mainstream.

Conn, D. (2004) *The Beautiful Game: Searching for the Soul of Football* London: Yellow Jersey Press.

Davies, H. (2007) 'A Chat with Gazza: The Only Story in Town is the Managers, He Says. He's Correct, writes Hunter Davies' *New Statesman* 12 March, p.49.

Football Association (2005) 'Burns Structural Review' http://www.thefa.com/NR/rdonlyres/065021BA-7091-4204-9534-99F13FE44A43/63711/Details of Proposals.pdf. Accessed 19 March 2007.

Goldlust, John (1987) *Playing for Keeps: Sport, the Media and Society* Melbourne: Longman Cheshire.

Hargreaves, I. (2003) *Journalism: Truth or Dare* Oxford: Oxford University Press.

Hill, J. (2002) *Sport, Leisure and Culture in Twentieth-century Britain* Basingstoke: Palgrave.

Horne, J. (1992) 'General Sports Magazines and "Cap'nBob": the rise and fall of *Sportsweek*' *Sociology of Sport Journal* vol. 9 no. 2, pp.179–206.

IRSS (*International Review For The Sociology Of Sport*) (2002) *Special Issue: Sport in the Media and Cultural Industries.*

Jennings, A. (2006) *Foul! The Secret World of FIFA: Bribes, Vote Rigging and Ticket Scandals* London: HarperSport.

Law, A., Harvey, J. and Kemp, S. (2002) 'The Global Sport Mass Media Oligopoly – The Three Usual Suspects and More' *International Review for the Sociology of Sport* vol. 37 nos. 3–4, pp.279–302.

Ledbrooke, A. and Turner, E. (1955) *Soccer from the Pressbox* London: Sportsman's Book Club.

McIlvanney, H. (2006) 'Sporting Heroism', 10th Anniversary Lecture, International Centre for Sports History and Culture, de Montfort University, 26 October.

Mason, T. (1988) *Sport in Britain* London: Faber and Faber.

Miller, T,. Lawrence, G., McKay, J. and Rowe, D. (2001) *Globalization and Sport: Playing the World* London: Sage.

Mitchell, K. (2007a) 'All Change at the Sports Desk: The Future of Print Journalism', 4th Annual Sport Journalism Lecture University of Brighton, Eastbourne, March 7.

Mitchell, K. (2007b) 'Wooldridge Passes On, Taking an Era with Him', *Observer Sport* 11 March, p.22.

Pilger, J. (1999) *Hidden Agendas* London: Vintage.

Rowe, D. (1999) *Sport, Culture and the Media: An Unruly Trinity* Buckingham: Open University Press.

Said, E. (1993) *Culture and Imperialism* London: Chatto and Windus.

Sugden, J. and Tomlinson, A. (1998) *FIFA and the Contest for World Football: Who Rules the Peoples' Game?* Cambridge: Polity Press.

Sugden, J. and Tomlinson, A. (2007) 'Stories from Planet Football and Sportsworld: Source Relations and Collusion in Sport Journalism' *Journalism Practice* vol. 1 no. 1, pp.44–61.

Walker, A. (2006) 'Reporting Play: The Local Newspaper and Sports Journalism, c. 1870–1914' *Journalism Studies* vol. 7 no. 3, pp.452–62.

Whannel, G. (2002) *Media Sport Stars: Masculinities and Moralities* London: Routledge.

Chapter 13

Moral panics and newspaper coverage of binge drinking

Chas Critcher

Introduction: opening time

In an early collection of readings on the mass media and deviance, Cohen and Young (1973) included an appendix called 'Do-it-yourself-media sociology'. They briefly explained how to investigate the representation of deviance in the media. Nowadays, despite the many recent textbooks on methods in media studies, there is still room for efforts to explain in detail how to research a news issue. This chapter does that for a (possible) moral panic.

Moral panic is now a quite common term, even used by the upmarket press. Its most famous formulation is the opening paragraph of Stan Cohen's study of Mods and Rockers, *Folk Devils and Moral Panics*, first published in 1973:

> Societies appear to be subject, every now and then, to periods of moral panic. [1] A condition, episode, person or group of persons emerges to become defined as a threat to societal values and interests; [2] its nature is presented in a stylized and stereotypical fashion by the mass media; [3] the moral barricades are manned by editors, bishops, politicians and other right-thinking people; [4] socially accredited experts pronounce their diagnoses and solutions; [5] ways of coping are evolved or (more often) resorted to; [6] the condition then disappears, submerges or deteriorates and becomes more visible. Sometimes the object of the panic is quite novel and at other times it is something which has been in existence long enough, but suddenly appears in the limelight. Sometimes the panic passes over and is forgotten, except in folk-lore and collective memory; at other times it has more serious and long-lasting repercussions and might produce such changes as those in legal and social policy or even in the way the society conceives itself.
>
> (Cohen 2002, p.1)

Subsequent studies of moral panics have suggested revising the model to become more comprehensive and up-to-date. But this original paragraph remains a model of clarity so we shall use it here. All I have done is to insert the numbers which are not in the original. In my own work on moral panics (Critcher 2003) I suggest that Cohen's six stages of a moral panic – which I term a processual model – could be broken down into a series of discrete questions. These totalled 23. We cannot aspire to answer all those in one small project, so we will simply here gather some preliminary information about how Cohen's six stages apply to a recent issue which might resemble a moral panic.

As the example, I have chosen 'binge drinking', for three reasons. First, it is topical and likely to remain so, as the behaviour is unlikely to diminish (especially among students). Second, it is not a very serious issue, unlike AIDS or paedophilia or gun crime, where it would be necessary to undertake extensive background reading. Third, it is unlikely to have generated too large an amount of press coverage to handle.

We need first to select our news source. On this occasion I have chosen the *Daily Express*, like its arch-competitor the *Daily Mail*, a mid-market paper. These tend to be especially susceptible to moral panics, partly because their general worldview is that society is in a permanent state of moral decline. There are three elements to the analysis of the *Express* coverage. First, we will establish the extent of the coverage, when it occurred and what editorial formats it assumed (news, features, etc.). Second, we are going to construct the narrative or story of binge drinking. Third, we are going to analyse the news sources: who is allowed to talk at all and who sets the agenda. The first and third elements involve primitive forms of content analysis. There are now some reliable guides on how to do this (Deacon *et al.* 1999). The second involves simply summarising the main stories over the years.

A small measure: dimensions of coverage

First, we investigate the extent of *Daily Express* coverage. This is now easy to do, as there are search engines for this purpose. LexisNexis is one such. Using this programme it is possible to determine:

- which words you want to appear near or next to each other – in our case 'binge' and 'drinking';
- how often this has to happen in the same article for it to be selected – in our case I have arbitrarily decided on three or more;
- which paper(s) we want to look in – in our case the *Daily Express*.

We then have to specify a range of dates. We may not be sure where to start or end. Binge drinking seems to still be around (at the time of writing, early 2007) so the period could go through to about then. How far back to go will be indicated by when coverage begins. A quick preliminary search suggests that the start is 2003, with only two relevant stories in the first six months. So we ask LexisNexis to find all stories in the *Express* which feature the words 'binge' and 'drinking' next or near to each other, three times or more. We do this for the four quarters of each year from 2003 to 2006 inclusive, which provides preliminary totals for each quarter, but we need to clean up this data. A cursory read of stories reveals two problems. First, some of the stories appear in the Scottish but not the English edition. Second, because the English version has more than one edition, the same story sometimes appears on the list twice. Taking out the Scottish stories and the duplicates produces the revised totals as in Table 13.1; the original sample of 114 stories is reduced by almost 20 per cent to 92 stories (see Table 13.1).

Table 13.1 reveals the rise and fall of editorial attention to the story, which is quite typical of moral panics. Initially there is little or no interest throughout 2003 and most of 2004; then an increase in 2005, peaking in the last six months; finally a sudden loss of interest in 2006. The year 2005 accounts for almost half the total articles over the four years (44 out of 92). That is clearly the height of the 'panic' (if that is what it is).

Table 13.1 also identifies the distinctive editorial formats (news stories, features, opinion columns, editorials or letters) in which a discussion of binge drinking assumed the dominant subject focus.

Table 13.1 *Published items on binge drinking in the* Daily Express *by editorial format*

	News stories	Features	Opinion columns	Editorials	Letters	Totals
2003						
January–March						0
April–June	2					2
July–September	6	1	1			8
October–December	2	2				4
Annual total						**14**
2004						
January–March	2			1	1	4
April–June	2					2
July–September	4	1			2	7
October–December	6	1			1	8
Annual total						**21**
2005						
January–March	6	2	2			10
April–June	4		1		2	7
July–September	12	1	1		1	15
October–December	8	1	2	1		12
Annual total						**44**
2006						
January–March	1	1				2
April–June	1					1
July–September	6					6
October–December	3				1	4
Annual total						**13**
4-year totals	65	10	7	2	8	92
4-year totals (%)	(71)	(11)	(8)	(2)	(9)	(101)

The percentage figures reveal little, since there is no 'normal distribution' of editorial formats for comparison. Two features of coverage are notable. First, when coverage increases, it does so across the board. So in 2005 there are not only more news stories but also more feature articles and opinion columns. Second, there are only two editorials on the subject in four years. Perhaps for the *Express* this is not a pressing problem.

Distilling the essence: the binge drinking narrative

In 2003 the *Express* offers little coverage of binge drinking. The one important story comes in September. A report 'from the No.10 Strategy Unit' estimates the financial cost of binge drinking to employers, the NHS and the criminal justice system. Home Office minister Hazel Blears provides a commentary; campaigning organisations react. The final two articles of the year appear on the women's pages offering advice about the health implications of heavy drinking.

In 2004 interest builds slowly. A letter from then Home Secretary David Blunkett to Tony Blair emphasising the need to act on drunken behaviour is leaked in March. In May the Prime Minister is briefly reported to have made a speech to his own group developing a National Alcohol Strategy. He says, 'As a society we have to make sure binge drinking doesn't become a new sort of British disease'. In July the *Express* notes ITV News to be carrying nightly filmed reports on the problem. The women's and health pages continue to emphasise the negative effects of heavy drinking. The Department of Health publishes statistical data on drinking levels and the Home Office reports the results of its summer blitz on drink-related behaviour (5,674 arrests; 650 licensed premises caught selling to children). A story early in November notes that 'Ministers blame drunken yobs for half the violent attacks in Britain and have demanded a crackdown from police councils and pubs'. An academic survey of European students shows the British to be one of the worst at binge drinking. Ministers warn that on-the-spot fines will be issued for drunken behaviour over Christmas.

In early 2005 two opinion columns bemoan binge drinking. One opposes 24-hour licences. Another blames 'the over inflated welfare state' and unmarried parenting. Several strands are now being interwoven. A judge sentencing three men for burglary and affray calls them 'urban savages', so the *Express* sends out a reporter to Chelmsford in Essex to meet some. There are claims that plans for liberalising licensing laws are 'in chaos'; the government releases figures from its Christmas crackdown (300 licensed premises discovered selling to children, 400 on-the-spot fines, 6,000 drunks arrested and alcohol confiscated from 1,500 children and 1,300 adults). An inquest on an 18-year-old boy who died of alcohol poisoning is reported in early February, with yet another piece on health and alcohol on the women's pages. There is virtually no coverage in March and April. The pace quickens again in May: research on drinking levels from the *Journal of Public Health*; another inquest on a drink-related death, this time of a 19-year-old girl; a voluntary ban on 'happy hours' is mooted by the brewery trade. The head-line 'Drink laws in chaos' (20 May 2005) refers to the imminent (September 2005) liberalisation of drinking hours.

In July a Home Office study is published revealing young men between 18 and 25 as most likely to binge drink and become violent. Groups of senior police offi-cers and judges express severe reservations about the effects of longer drinking hours. In his speech to the Labour Party conference in Brighton, Tony Blair prom-ises extended powers of on-the-spot fines to deal with binge drinking. Some arti-cles claim the new licensing laws will not work. By the end of the year an ITV documentary reveals shocking facts about under age drinking, while a BUPA survey confirms the extent of the problem.

In 2006 coverage is routine, mainly of research reports, presented as isolated stories without follow-up.

Six observations about this narrative seem evident.

1) This issue is being defined and driven by the government. This establishes a pattern for articles: a government announcement followed by reactions from charities, medical experts and opposition politicians.
2) There are two different and gendered thrusts to the attack on binge drinking. Drunken males are represented as potentially violent and criminal. Drunken women are represented as potentially damaging their health or risking their safety.
3) The binge drinking issue is complicated by the fact that, at precisely the same time that the government was waging a campaign against binge drinking, it was also introducing longer opening hours. For some this was a contradiction.
4) Very large parts of the *Express* coverage are politically motivated by its invet-erate hatred of all things New Labour. It tries to portray a government blun-dering about in the area of drink policy.
5) This is not a big issue for the *Express*. Editorials are thin on the ground. There is little sense of engagement with the issue, more that it is an opportunity for a bit of New Labour bashing.
6) For binge drinking there are no big stories – tragic deaths or violent crimes – which often trigger or sustain moral panics. This is not an event-driven issue. The materials from which articles are composed are much more fragmented: statistical estimates, stories of binge drinkers and arguments about opening hours.

Especially because of 4 and 5, we would ideally compare the coverage in the *Express* with one or more other newspapers of a different type, such as one upmar-ket (*Telegraph, Independent, The Times* or *Guardian*) and one downmarket (*Sun, Mirror* or *Star*). This might give us a different perspective. That will have to await another day. For the moment we need to ask who in the *Express* is called on to comment on binge drinking and whether some contributions are valued more than others.

First to the bar: news sources

Most news stories involve people being asked to describe, explain or express an opinion on some event or issue. This is the role of news sources. In a famous formulation Hall *et al.* (1978) argue that the media act as 'secondary definers'. They follow the definitions laid down by 'primary definers', usually members of powerful elites. The media then require others to respond in those terms. We need to know who is defining the issue of binge drinking and who is responding.

Let us look at 2005, when coverage is at its highest. For each story we can note the first person quoted in the article and then which others follow. Of 44 published items in 2005, only 26 use sources. Most letters, opinion columns and shorter news stories do not. For the other articles we make a list of each news source quoted (directly or indirectly). Later we can group them: one of doctors and health personnel, another of the police and so on. Eventually we can devise a coherent list, like this:

- politicians: New Labour/government, Conservatives, Liberals
- control culture: judiciary and police
- medical authorities: hospitals, consultants, Royal College of Physicians
- brewery trade: associations and individual firms
- campaigners: Alcohol Concern and the Institute of Alcohol Studies
- academics: based in universities
- others: all other sources.

These are aggregated to produce Table 13.2.

Looking at the totals, politicians are the most prominent group, more (nearly twice) as likely to be from the opposition as from government. This seems to contradict our deduction from the narrative, that the government was driving the issue. The explanation lies in the right-wing politics of the *Express*. It wants to put a New Labour government on the defensive. So its news stories often amount to claims about the incompetence of the government made by others, to which the government is made to appear to respond.

Table 13.2 *News sources in* Daily Express *articles 2005*

News sources by groupings	1st source	Subsequent source	Totals
Politicians	6	13	19
Control culture	4	8	12
Medical authorities	5	4	9
Brewery trade	5	4	9
Campaigners	0	6	6
Academics	1	4	5
Others	5	1	6
Totals	**26**	**40**	**66**

After the politicians comes 'the control culture', a phrase used by Cohen. These are police officers and organisations, together with the judiciary. Some oppose relaxation of opening hours but mostly they stress the criminal aspects of binge drinking: its effects on public order and policing. Joint third comes the brewery trade, which appears mainly in business stories about the industry's reaction to adverse publicity. Also joint third is a group we have called 'medical authorities', recognised as providing accurate information about the health impacts of binge drinking.

Fifth out of six come groups campaigning for more awareness and control of alcohol-related problems. Never the first source, they do not define the problem but react to what others have said or done. Who are these people? They are called in alphabetical order Alcohol Concern, the Institute of Alcohol Studies and the Portman Group. Their websites tell us more about them.

Alcohol Concern (www.alcoholconcern.org.uk) is a federation of 500 local agencies tackling problems of alcohol abuse. It aims to 'reduce the incidence and costs of alcohol-related harm' and 'increase the range and the quality of the services available to people with alcohol-related problems'. It raises money through membership fees but also receives a hefty grant from the Department of Health.

The Institute of Alcohol Studies (www.ias.org.uk) is sponsored by the United Kingdom Temperance Alliance. The Institute claims that it 'does not have a view on whether individuals should drink or not drink' but merely seeks to 'serve the public interest on public policy issues linked to alcohol', through 'advocating for the use of scientific evidence in policy-making to reduce alcohol-related harm'.

The Portman Group (www.portman-group.co.uk) was 'set up in 1989 by the UK's leading drinks producers, which together supply the majority of the alcohol sold in the UK'. Its role is to act as a 'principal provider of responsible drinking advice in the UK' and to 'encourage responsible marketing practices through our Code of Practice'.

So of three organisations, one is an alliance of charities working with alcoholics underwritten by a government grant, one is a temperance group and the third represents brewery interests. None of this would be obvious from how these groups are presented in the media, as if who they are and their right to pronounce on the issue is self-evident.

The perhaps genuinely disinterested experts are the final group, of academics. They do appear occasionally but rarely to define the issue. Judging from the news sources used in the *Express*, the primary definers of binge drinking are politicians and the police or judiciary. Campaigning organisations respond most frequently to their definitions. Binge drinkers themselves are conspicuous by their absence.

Last orders: conclusion

Our conclusions can only be tentative. We can indicate what this limited evidence might say about how far Cohen's model of a moral panic applies to binge drinking. This can be done for each of the six stages.

1) A condition, episode, person or group of persons emerges to become defined as a threat to societal values and interests

Binge drinking was initially defined publicly as a serious problem by the New Labour government during 2003, though it must have caused concern beforehand. The problem needed a new name. Older dictionaries give a definition of 'binge' as: 'have a bout of heavy drinking etc; go on a spree' (*Shorter Oxford English Dictionary* 1993). In this received definition 'binge' already means to drink excessively. The problem might have been defined as that of 'bingeing'. Instead the phrase 'binge drinking' was coined even though the 'drinking' part is linguistically redundant. So somewhere along the line – and we do not yet know where, when or by whom – this new label was coined.

2) Its nature is presented in a stylised and stereotypical fashion by the mass media

If the *Express* and its sources are to be believed, all young men who binge drink are potentially violent and/or criminal; all young women who binge drink are potentially risking their health and/or sexual integrity. Such stereotyping peaked in the *Express* with the 'urban savages' label. In his paragraph Cohen does not stipulate that there should be a recognisable folk devil, though it is implicit in his argument. The binge drinker does not make an impressive folk devil. Binge drinking does not define the essence of those involved; it is an activity, not a state of being. It is a nuisance and can cause disorder on the street but is unlikely to make everyone feel as if they or their families are potentially victims, as in the way they feel about more obvious folk devils, such as muggers or paedophiles.

3) The moral barricades are manned by editors, bishops, politicians and other right-thinking people

Politicians are exercised by the issue. So are some of the *Express*'s opinion columnists and letter writers but not its leader writers. There is little sign of other moralising. Churches are silent on the issue. There are no petitions, demonstrations, commissioned opinion polls or similar expressions of public disquiet.

4) Socially accredited experts pronounce their diagnoses and solutions

The medical profession is legitimated as authoritative about the financial and resource costs of the problem, as well as its long-term effects on the health of adherents. Crucially, there is no opposition to the opinion of moralists and experts. Nobody disputes the existence of binge drinking or its serious consequences (as some do for cannabis or ecstasy). Even the Portman Group admits there is a problem and that the industry has some responsibility for it.

5) Ways of coping are evolved or (more often) resorted to

These are apparently extensive: heavier on-the-spot fines, increased arrests for drunkenness and more extensive investigation of under age selling. These involved the extension of powers already in existence, notably under the 2003 Anti-Social Behaviour Act. Other possible measures publicly – longer prison sentences, stricter licensing conditions – are not mooted.

6) The condition then disappears, submerges or deteriorates and becomes more visible

This we shall only be able to tell in the future. Binge drinking is actually a reworking of long-standing panics about drink, previously focused on alcopops in 1995–7 (Forsyth et al. 1997). It remains to be seen whether binge drinking continues to be a problem, persists and is ignored, or declines, with the campaign against it apparently vindicated.

Cohen's is the best-known but not the only version of moral panics. There is an American version which would ask rather different questions (Goode and Ben-Yehuda 1994). There are also recent British versions with a very different take on the nature and value of moral-panic analysis (Jewkes 2004). Using Cohen's model or 'ideal type', binge drinking is a fairly mild moral panic. It has a new name but lacks a folk devil. Some important people are worried about it but the public express less concern. No new measures are proposed because existing ones will do. Equally important is what using moral-panic analysis as a tool (a heuristic device) tells us about the construction of the issue. Campaigning on binge drinking is one of the many ways in which New Labour seeks to impose its version of order on the general populus, using increasingly authoritarian powers. It does not for a moment compare with the threat of terrorism and yet there are similarities, above all the idea that the solution is always to crack down.

This brings us to two important aspects of moral-panic analysis which can only be flagged up here. First, otherwise very similar issues may share a similar kind of rhetoric, what social scientists call discourse (Fowler 1991). Though political opponents, the *Express* and the New Labour government inhabit very similar discourses. Second, contemporary moral panics are argued to have increased in intensity because society is now generally much more conscious of risk (Lupton 1999). Many of the advice columns in our sample aimed at young women were pleas to consider the risks of binge drinking.

The perceived problem of 'binge drinking' may eventually be a historical foot-note but a brief study of it has been revealing. It told us a good deal about moral panics and the mid-market press. It may yet tell us more about the power of discourse and the ubiquity of risk.

References

Cohen, S. (2002/1973) *Folk Devils and Moral Panics* London: Routledge.

Cohen, S. and Young, J. (Eds) (1973) *The Manufacture of News* (1ˢᵗ edition) London: Constable.

Critcher, C. (2003) *Moral Panics and the Media* Maidenhead: Open University Press.

Deacon, D., Pickering, M., Golding, P. and Murdock, G. (1999) *Researching Communications* London: Arnold.

Forsyth, J. M., Barnard, M. and McKeganey, N. P. (1997) 'Alcopops Supernova: Are Alcoholic Lemonades (Alcopops) Responsible for Under-age Drunkenness?' *International Journal of Health Education* vol. 35 no. 2, pp.53–8.

Fowler, R. (1991) *Language in the News: Discourse and Ideology in the Press* London: Routledge.

Goode, E. and Ben-Yehuda, N. (1994) *Moral Panics: The Social Construction of Deviance* Oxford: Blackwell.

Hall, S., Critcher, C., Jefferson, T., Clarke, J. and Roberts, B. (1978) *Policing The Crisis: Mugging, The State and Law and Order* Basingstoke: Macmillan.

Jewkes, Y. (2004) *Media and Crime* London and New York: Sage.

Lupton, D. (1999) *Risk* London: Routledge.

Chapter 14

Politics and the press

Nicholas Jones

Unravelling the many interlocking relationships between politics and the press requires an understanding of the early struggle to publish reports of proceedings in the two Houses of Parliament. Establishing a right of entry for reporters was no mean achievement given the hostility which the printers of newspapers and magazines faced in the early 1700s. A long war of attrition between journalists and parliamentarians has continued to this day. In many respects Britain's democratic traditions have been strengthened by the development of a news media which has become well versed in challenging the political establishment of the day. Nevertheless Parliament retains the upper hand: within the Palace of Westminster journalists continue to be regarded as 'strangers' and their presence is only tolerated under sufferance (Sparrow 2005). Access to the press galleries is denied to photographers and television crews; the only images which are available to the press have to be taken from the output of the remotely controlled cameras which offer a continuous television feed of carefully selected pictures from the two chambers and committee rooms (Franklin 1992). While long-held animosities resurface quite regularly, politicians and journalists have usually managed to coexist at a practical and personal level without too much difficulty. Indeed the two sides could be said to have become locked together in a classic 'love–hate' relationship: reporters depend on the politicians for an unending supply of news, just as the elected representatives have to rely on journalists to publicise their policies and help them communicate with potential voters (Jones 2006).

What often makes these day-to-day cross-currents difficult to disentangle is that they are not always as straightforward as they might seem. Press versus politics is presented as a 'them and us' contest, with a fearless editor and a diligent reporter taking on the might of the state. However, once journalists spend any time at Westminster they soon discover that the reality is rather different: national newspapers invariably take their own individual approach to the politics of the day and much of their coverage tends to be slanted, however blatantly or imperceptibly, towards the beliefs and goals of one or other of the political parties. Over the decades newspapers have built up mass circulations on the back of political campaigning and the most successful publishers became formidable players on the political stage, be it the Lords Northcliffe and Beaverbrook of earlier years or more latterly Rupert Murdoch; they have all been feared and also courted by the Prime Ministers of their day. When the tone and direction of the day's coverage can be determined at the owner's whim, press reporters realise that however significant the events at Westminster might be, they cannot be entirely oblivious to the political leanings of their own paper when writing up their stories and features (Barnett and Gaber 2001).

Other powerful forces exert considerable influence over the way political news is presented. Not only are editors and proprietors angling perhaps for a knighthood or a peerage but politicians and journalists are themselves sometimes interchangeable; there has always been a cross-over between the two professions. Just as a fair few MPs have abandoned a career at Westminster when offered the chance to work as highly paid columnists and commentators, so some correspondents have become so enamoured of political life that they have decided to stand for Parliament, confident of winning the support not just of their readers but also the voters. Another trend which cannot be ignored is the marked increase in recent years in the number of political correspondents leaving journalism for public relations, public affairs and the darker, manipulative world of the political spin doctor (Blick 2005). Francis Williams, a former editor of the *Daily Herald*, became Winston Churchill's Head of Information in 1940, taking on responsibility for the wartime direction of news and censorship, a path which would be followed by an illustrious cast of journalists turned propagandists. Joe Haines (ex *Daily Mirror*) became Harold Wilson's Press Secretary in 1969; Bernard Ingham (ex *Guardian*) joined Margaret Thatcher in Downing Street shortly after she won the 1979 general election; and Alastair Campbell (ex *Daily Mirror*), who was first appointed Tony Blair's Press Secretary in 1994, went on to work with him for a further six and a half years as the Prime Minister's Director of Communications. Given the expertise of such powerful individuals, the breadth of the government's publicity machine and the combined effect of all the promotional efforts of the parties and their supporters, it is perhaps hardly surprising that political news commands such a dominant position in the daily output of broadcasting and the press.

When it comes to setting the agenda about the affairs of Westminster and Whitehall and attacking the government of the day, newspapers still retain the edge, despite the rapid and continuing expansion of news services on radio, television and now the internet. Britain is proud of a free press which by and large takes politics seriously and which is not afraid to adopt a highly partisan position on even the most sensitive issues. Late night programmes eagerly await the national newspapers' take on the day's events; the front pages of the first editions are sometimes considered news items in themselves; next morning a review of the national and regional press is a key ingredient in radio and television output; and later, once the phone-in programmes start taking calls, it is often the tone and direction of newspaper coverage which has influenced the selection of topics under discussion. By any objective test the impact of press reporting and comment is far greater on the political processes of the United Kingdom than in the United States or most members of the European Union, not least because despite the falls of recent years our daily sale of newspapers is still far in excess of that in America or our immediate neighbours. Unlike France, for example, where the leading daily titles struggle to sell several hundred thousand copies a day, we have seven national newspapers each with circulations of well in excess of a million (three dailies, four Sundays). With up to three readers per copy and a rapid acceleration in the online readership of newspaper websites, politicians have every reason to remain fearful of the British press and determined, if possible, to turn its exceptional reach to their personal or party advantage.

Across the political divide there is a recognition that newspapers continue to provide a unique platform for launching policy initiatives and provoking discussion. For journalists, the lobbies of Westminster and the corridors of Whitehall constitute an unrivalled marketplace for collecting information. Once acquired, the thrill and fascination of observing and then reporting political debate and intrigue can last a lifetime. Nothing can beat the buzz of being on duty in Downing Street during a time of national crisis or political turmoil, witnessing at first hand the impact of a change of government after a dramatic general election defeat or perhaps the highs and lows of a cabinet reshuffle. I have remained hooked for the last four decades, since I first stepped into the House of Commons press gallery in the autumn of 1968 on joining *The Times*.

The 1960s were the heyday of parliamentary reporting when the leading quality newspapers provided verbatim reports of the main debates, a service to readers which became redundant once the proceedings started being broadcast regularly on radio and television and then became available online (Straw 1993). I was one of a team of 12 reporters who filled up two pages a day with column after column of who had said what in the House of Commons and the House of Lords. We had a fast shorthand note; I could manage to get down up to 120 words per minute but I worked alongside more experienced hands who could easily reach 140 to 150 words per minute and whose shorthand was so accurate they often did extra shifts working for Hansard, the official report of parliamentary proceedings. We took it in turns, sitting in the gallery for 10 to 20 minutes taking notes. Once we had typed out our copy it was sub-edited inside *The Times* room and then taken immediately by messenger to a compositor who was housed on an upper corridor for direct input to the composing department at the printers. Ours was a critical but rather mundane role and like most of my colleagues in the press gallery we longed for the chance to become correspondents so that we could start writing for the news pages instead of just transcribing what had been said.

Journalistic demarcation lines were strictly enforced at Westminster in the 1960s: parliamentary reporters and sketch writers were confined to the press gallery; only correspondents with a lobby ticket could approach MPs to gather information, seek out quotes or attend lobby briefings in Downing Street. *The Times*, like the other broadsheets, offered readers comprehensive daily coverage: up to two pages of verbatim parliamentary reports; a separate parliamentary sketch; news stories from the political editor and correspondents; plus comment, analysis and opinion from some celebrated columnists. These separate roles, then clearly defined, have since been subtly merged and there has been a profound change in both the style and content of political journalism. Straight reporting of parliamentary debates has all but disappeared and most stories as well as features are written from a perspective which reflects the political agenda of each paper. Whether it is the hard news of the day, speculation about a forthcoming announcement, perhaps an exclusive on the latest leak or a profile of an up-and-coming politician, there is usually a clear political slant both in the storyline and the way the material is presented. Readers can pick and choose: whereas the *Sun* tends to back the authority of the state and is especially supportive of the police and armed forces, the *Daily Mirror* occupies political ground to the left of centre; while the *Daily Telegraph* rarely departs from its traditional stance as the in-house newspaper for the Conservative Party, the *Guardian* is equally comfortable in its role as a standard-bearer for readers of a left-wing or liberal-minded persuasion. Sunday newspapers stake out their own territory with equal clarity and conviction (Barnett and Gaber 2001).

Using news stories for agenda-setting purposes and expressing opinions, rather than restricting such activity to editorial and comment columns, has encouraged another significant shift in the mechanics of political reporting. Of all the changes which have taken place in my career, by far the most profound has been the phenomenal growth in unsourced quotes and unsubstantiated stories. I fear the widespread failure to attribute facts and quotations has undermined the probity of political reporting in the national press. It is not uncommon for the main stories leading the front pages of both popular and serious newspapers to be based entirely on anonymous sources yet I can say with some certainty that in the late 1960s and early 1970s it was rare indeed to find a lead story in *The Times* which offered the reader no direct attribution whatsoever. Evidence of this change leaps out from story after story: 'a Downing Street insider said ...'; 'a cabinet source disclosed...'; 'a ministerial aide revealed...'; 'a top civil servant confirmed...' and so it goes on, every 'source' imaginable is quoted except the source of the quote.

Ethical standards of press reporting have been undermined by factors both within and without the newspaper industry. So fierce is the competition for circulation among the national dailies and Sundays that political journalists are no longer judged solely on their reputation for fairness and reliability but more often than not on their hit rate when it comes to delivering exclusives. As a result of the switch in emphasis from factual stories to a style of reporting which tends to be personality-led and speculative, there have been some telling adjustments in the nature of the relationship between newsgatherers and information providers, probably no more so than in Westminster and Whitehall.

Researching and delivering a headline-grabbing story gets harder and harder when newsroom resources are being squeezed, deadlines get ever tighter and where even at the House of Commons reporters tend to be tied to the telephone, keyboard and computer screen and find it tempting to watch parliamentary proceedings on the nearest television monitor. What far outweighs the impact of this day-to-day hassle are the repercussions of the fundamental shift which has taken place in the balance of power between journalism and a much enlarged public relations industry which claims to be the originating source of anything from 60 to 70 per cent of the material printed by the national press (Davis, chapter 25. See also Lewis, Williams and Franklin 2008).

Information traders are in the ascendancy, be they government press officers, commercial publicists or political spin doctors (Jones 2006). They understand why journalists are at a disadvantage due to heightened competition within the news media and pressurised working conditions, an environment which has presented their profession with opportunities which have been exploited with ruthless efficiency. Key to the success of public relations practitioners is their realisation that the information which they control is like a currency that can be traded for favourable coverage with clients whose vulnerability renders them ever more dependent on potential suppliers. Although they know they are in danger of being manipulated, political correspondents hungry for exclusive stories have little alternative but to comply when told that a condition of any deal is that the anonymity of the source must be protected. Instead of the clearly defined roles and well-ordered structures of the 1960s there is a growing free-for-all which allows spin doctors to exercise their ultimate authority in deciding where and with whom to place an exclusive story. The twice-daily lobby briefings given by the Prime Minister's official spokesman, once considered of critical importance, have increasingly been bypassed as a channel for distributing information to political correspondents. Collective gatherings are shunned unless they are considered essential to attend and much of the trade in leaks and tip-offs is conducted on a one-to-one basis, either at lunch or on the telephone (Jones 2006).

To begin with, Tony Blair's spokesman, Alastair Campbell, followed the path of previous Downing Street press secretaries, such as Sir Bernard Ingham and Sir Christopher Meyer, in trying to use his briefings to explain and promote government policy. However, his desire to have an engaging and professional relationship with the lobby was short-lived because his adversarial approach encouraged a level of confrontation which proved damaging to both the government and the Labour Party. Repeated demands for the briefings to be televised were rejected both by Campbell and the massed ranks of newspaper correspondents who were determined to stop broadcasters dominating the proceedings. Nevertheless there were two significant innovations which exposed the Prime Minister and his government to greater scrutiny while at the same time wrong-footing the press. To his credit, and in an attempt to prevent himself from being misquoted, Campbell arranged in July 2000 for official transcripts of the Downing Street briefings to be posted on the No.10 website; in June 2002 Blair started holding monthly televised news conferences open to all journalists. An inevitable consequence of going over the heads of reporters direct to the public was a further downgrading in the relevance of lobby briefings. They tended to become little more than a notice-board for the day's events and any concerted attempt to probe government thinking was usually stonewalled by the official spokesman. By answering journalists' questions himself, live on television and radio, Blair upstaged his detractors in the newspapers and left their political correspondents facing an even greater challenge when it came to finding new angles on the day's events.

As with other newly elected Prime Ministers, Blair's arrival in Downing Street had been greeted with approval by most journalists and he enjoyed a honeymoon with the press which lasted longer than for some of his predecessors. During the long run-up to the 1997 general election, the Labour hierarchy succeeded in establishing a close working relationship with many editors, columnists and correspondents and once Campbell took command of the government's media strategy he initiated moves to tighten control over the flow of news from Downing Street and the Whitehall departments. Most members of the cabinet were allowed to recruit at least two special advisers who formed a new and highly effective cadre of ministerial spin doctors. Initially they worked under Campbell's guidance and like him they continued to owe their allegiance to the Labour Party despite having been granted the status of temporary civil servants. Such was their influence that it was they rather than the departmental heads of information who increasingly called the shots when it came to deciding how each ministry should seek to publicise the parliamentary statements and policy launches set out in Downing Street's weekly timetable of events. Simultaneously, in another move to seize the initiative, civil service information officers were freed from the constraints under which they had previously worked. They were told they had to raise their game in order to meet the challenge of a 24/7 media environment; one significant edict was an instruction to 'grab the agenda' by ringing round journalists to trail the contents of forthcoming announcements and policy proposals.

During the heady days of Labour's first parliamentary term Campbell became in effect an all-powerful information trader and he liked to regard himself as something akin to the editor-in-chief of an alternative news service. Once Labour's relationship with the press began to cool, Campbell's notoriety made him a target for criticism and he resigned in August 2003 after giving evidence to the Hutton Inquiry following the suicide of Dr David Kelly and the row with the BBC over the accuracy of the government's dossier on Iraq's weapons of mass destruction. Even before Campbell's ignominious departure, Downing Street had begun to lose its grip over the network of ministerial spin doctors whose activities had been causing mounting concern among the wider party membership. In a memorable attack on those close to the Labour leadership, the former International Development Secretary, Clare Short, warned of the divisive influence of aides who lived 'in the dark' and who were prepared to make derogatory comments about colleagues when briefing journalists. By more than doubling to over 80 the number of special advisers, Blair had inadvertently created a vast pool of 'anonymous sources' who inhabited a shadowy world in Downing Street and the political offices of cabinet ministers. They had grown accustomed to offering political correspondents guidance, tips-offs and leaks on an off-the-record basis but while there had been a fair degree of discipline under the tight regime enforced by Campbell this was soon dissipated once he resigned (Jones 2002).

Interminable infighting over the future leadership of the party fuelled a marked upsurge in unofficial briefings, and national newspapers became an invaluable conduit for the tit-for-tat point scoring between the rival supporters of Blair and the then Chancellor of the Exchequer, Gordon Brown. Appeals to aides and allies to cool it had little or no effect and just as political journalists were kept busy by the Conservatives' mounting disarray during John Major's final years as Prime Minister, so the press became the principal beneficiary of Labour's failure to police the activities of its burgeoning band of spin doctors. Of all Campbell's complaints about the failings of the media the one with which I had some sympathy was his criticism of journalists, columnists and commentators who blithely reused anonymous quotes without making any attempt to either verify their accuracy or establish whether there was any likelihood of the source being authentic. But from its inception New Labour was rooted in a political culture which relied on the art of presentation and which encouraged the manipulation of the news media, a phenomenon which required the anonymity of sources and the complicity of journalists. Campbell was the architect of a regime in the No.10 Press Office which relied on briefing political correspondents on a selective and partial basis. As he was subsequently forced to admit in his evidence to the Hutton Inquiry, he preferred to talk off-the-record to his chosen elite of 'editors and senior correspondents'. Yet in the six and a half years he spent in Downing Street, he had an unparalleled opportunity to drive up the levels of accuracy and fairness in political journalism; he could have tried to counter the growth in unsourced and exaggerated stories by insisting that he and the rest of the party spin doctors under his control always spoke on the record whenever possible and tried to ensure their own quotes were properly attributed. Instead he took advantage of the commercial pressures fuelling the demand for exclusives by facilitating deliberate leaks and off-the-record tip-offs from within the government.

The press can hardly be blamed for having taken advantage of the thriving trade in confidential documents and data when MPs themselves put so little effort into the task of defending parliamentary accountability. Surprisingly there is no parliamentary offence for ministers caught leaking their own decisions before making a statement to the House of Commons and the absence of any sanctions explains the ease with which the Blair government was able to trail its own announcements in a concerted bid to capture the headlines and influence the news agenda. Half the cabinet and their spin doctors might well have ended up in the dock if the non-attributable release of sensitive information about policy decisions was subjected to the same kinds of rules which the Financial Services Authority endeavours to enforce in the City of London in an attempt to prevent leaks to financial journalists of market-sensitive data about forthcoming acquisitions and mergers. Both Gordon Brown and the Conservative Party leader David Cameron have suggested a government they lead will turn its back on spin and try to reinforce traditional civil service standards of integrity. Cameron has gone further, promising to halve the number of political advisers, but I think an incoming Prime Minister will face precisely the same pressures which made life so difficult for Blair, and a new administration will become equally dependent on a network of ministerial aides to handle relations with newspaper publishers, editors and journalists.

As competition within an ever expanding media marketplace continues to intensify so the government of the day will find it harder to be heard, not least because the British press will be determined to go on reinventing itself. If there is one characteristic which marks out our newspapers from their counterparts around the world it is their prowess in setting the agenda. Indeed they remain among the most inventive and perhaps the most sensational when it comes to the art of manufacturing exclusive stories which are so effective in grabbing the head-lines that they cannot be ignored either by the rest of the news media or by politicians. Being assigned to work on a discreet investigation is always a welcome challenge and political correspondents cherish the sense of satisfaction which flows from delivering a story that has caught Whitehall and Westminster by surprise and has more than likely angered the powers that be. That elation is all the greater if the storyline was so strong that it had to be followed up by reporters from rival news organisations. Newspaper campaigns which force a swift policy U-turn or the hurried resignation of a beleaguered minister are a constant reminder of the sheer inventiveness and bravura of the British press. The first parliamentary reporters defied the threat of imprisonment to continue publishing their accounts of what was being said, and their dogged determination has not been forgotten by the political correspondents of today.

The House of Commons press gallery is unlike any other workplace for journalists. In a jumble of rooms behind the Speaker's chair there are rows of small offices which accommodate correspondents from national and regional newspapers, television and radio, and reporters from the Press Association news agency and other organisations. Friendships flourish amidst the hustle and bustle of the parliamentary day, and newcomers often find that once bitten by the political reporting bug they have taken the first step on a career that can last a lifetime.

References

Barnett, S. and Gaber, I. (2001) *Westminster Tales: The 21st Century Crisis in Political Journalism* London: Continuum.

Blick, A. (2005) *The People Who Live in the Dark: A History of the Special Adviser In British Politics* London: Politicos.

Franklin, B. (1992) *Televising Democracies* London: Routledge.

Jones, N. (2002) *The Control Freaks: How New Labour Gets its Own Way* London: Politicos.

Jones, N. (2006) *Trading Information: Leaks, Lies and Tipp-offs* London: Politicos.

Lewis, J., Williams, A. and Franklin, B. (2008) 'A Compromised Fourth Estate? The Quality and Independence of British Journalism' *Journalism Studies* vol. 9 no. 1.

Sparrow, A. (2005) *Obscure Scribblers: A History of Parliamentary Journalism* London: Politicos.

Straw, J. (1993) 'Parliament on the Spike' *British Journalism Review* vol. 4 no. 4, pp.45–54.

Part 3

Newspaper design

Chapter 15
Compacts

Peter Cole

As with so many revolutions, the 'compact revolution' within Britain's broadsheet press was born of adversity. The *Independent*, itself born of another kind of revolution, that of ownership, had failed to sustain its dream of independence from traditional baronial or corporate ownership. Under the slogan 'It is. Are you?' – independent, that is – it was, paradoxically, a product of Thatcherism, particularly of her routing of the trades unions. This had coincided with the advent of new publishing technologies allowing the 'direct input' of their words and pictures by journalists. No longer did they have to pass through the 'hot metal' stage, for so long under the unbending control of the print unions.

The *Independent*: compact pioneer

In 1986 the new age dawned with the launch of *Today*, Eddy Shah's non-union, mid-market national newspaper (MacArthur 1988), and much more significantly with the move of Rupert Murdoch's News International titles to Wapping. In October of that year the *Independent*, brainchild of Andreas Whittam Smith, the austere former *Telegraph* business journalist, published for the first time. Its ownership structure was that of relatively small parcels of investment, mostly from venture capitalists. Such were the economic conditions, the availability of venture capital, and the potential for profitable newspaper publishing rid of the costs of old technologies, that the new paper enjoyed a spectacular launch. It was fashionable; it caught the yuppie mood; and it was not owned by a traditional publishing conglomerate. Before long it was selling an average of 400,000 copies a day, taking them, in order of quantity, from its rival in the quality sector of the market, the *Guardian*, *The Times* and the *Telegraph*.

It was not to last. The economic climate changed for the worse, Thatcher was deposed, Wapping settled down and the cost of launching the *Independent on Sunday* stretched the *Independent* too far. It gained investment from *La Repubblica* in Italy and *El Pais* in Spain; but it was the beginning of the end of the dream. Rupert Murdoch had instituted his price-cutting war, dropping the price of *The Times* by one-third in September 1993 and inflicting considerable damage on his rivals in the quality sector. Whittam Smith responded with *Independent* price cuts.

But within months 'It is' wasn't, and the Mirror Group and its chief executive David Montgomery were in control. The relationship did not work, and sales decline continued. Although the *Independent* was now in corporate ownership, the minority shareholder Tony O'Reilly, with substantial newspaper holdings in Ireland, South Africa and other countries was of more benign attitude to the *Independent* and eventually gained full control in 1998.

The compact revolution was the product of O'Reilly's ownership, and two other men. He brought in as editor-in-chief Simon Kelner, a talented sports production journalist who had been on the *Independent* at the start before moving to executive positions on the *Sunday Correspondent*, *Observer* and, moving out of sport, as Editor of the *Daily Mail* supplement *Night and Day*. And O'Reilly appointed as Chief Executive Ivan Fallon, who had run his lucrative South African operation. Earlier Fallon was Business Editor and Deputy Editor at the *Sunday Times*.

At the end of 1998, as these three men contemplated the state of the *Independent* at the start of an era of stable and secure ownership, they saw a circulation as low as it had ever been, around 220,000 (it had sold over 400,000 during 1989 and 1990). It improved little over the next few years. The one consistent feature was that both Independent titles were the lowest selling in their market sectors, which meant the lowest selling national daily and Sunday newspapers in Britain. That was not really the problem – they always had been. Critical mass is more important. One title has to be the lowest seller. But to have presence, to have influence, to be relevant, not least to advertisers, you have to sell a significant, and preferably increasing, number of copies. Quality newspapers all punch above their circulation weight, because they are part of the political landscape. They are where the issues debates take place. They are read by the intelligent AB audience, the political classes, those who make the decisions.

The Independent titles had such a presence, a legacy of the unlikeliness and success of their launches – and of their survival. Launching new national newspapers is a most rare occurrence. To be there 20 years later is a triumph. But hanging on was not enough for O'Reilly, Fallon and Kelner, or for the morale and commitment of their staffs. Kelner had steadied the ship. The sixth editor in seven years, he too was still there. In 2006 he became the *Independent*'s longest-serving editor. He had presided over various relaunches, a common occurrence at the *Independent*, but had seen little change in the paper's fortunes. He began to think about the ultimate relaunch: turning the *Indy* tabloid.

The pros and cons were familiar. On the plus side, surveys conducted by broadsheet titles had repeatedly drawn a pro-tabloid response, particularly among commuters on crowded trains, younger readers and women readers, categories of great interest to advertisers. There was a long tradition of smaller format quality papers in mainland Europe. There would be tremendous publicity (albeit for a finite period) in changing format; the paper would be the centre of attention. And it was likely that sampling, even a gain in sale that stuck, would follow the relaunch.

On the negative side there was the peculiarly British association of the word tabloid (simply a measure of size, half a broadsheet) with downmarket, the *Sun*, *Mirror* and *Star* always referred to as 'the tabloids'. Would an upmarket audience regard downsizing as dumbing down? Would the format push the paper in that direction, with fewer stories on a page, pictures seeming to take up more space? There were problems, too, about advertising revenue. Would advertisers pay the same for a full page in a tabloid as a full page in a broadsheet?

It was clearly less risky for the *Independent* than for papers with more conservative audiences like *The Times* and *Telegraph*. *Indy* readers were younger, less resistant to change. And sitting at the bottom of the circulation league, the *Independent* had more to gain and less to lose by the change in size.

All these arguments were addressed by Kelner and Fallon. Kelner's rule was always to refer to his planned smaller paper as a 'compact'. It was not in fact a new idea, although everybody thought it was. As Roy Greenslade notes in *Press Gang* (2003, p.258) the mid-market *Daily Mail*, then broadsheet and losing sales, went tabloid in May 1971 to coincide with the closure of its sister (tabloid) title the *Daily Sketch*. At the time a report by McKinseys, the management consultants, had suggested a tabloid *Mail* might work better, and the circulation manager favoured the *Mail* becoming 'the first serious, really upmarket tabloid'. Lord Harmsworth, the Chairman of Associated Newspapers, publishers of the *Mail*, referred to his relaunched title as a 'compact', but the word never caught on. It did for Kelner. The *Mail* was selling 1.8 million before its 1971 relaunch. Today it sells 2.4 million.

The *Independent* decided to hedge its bets, first printing the compact version alongside the broadsheet (a costly exercise, but one minimised by the small sale of the paper). The compact *Indy* was launched inside the M25 on Tuesday 30 September 2003, Monday to Friday only. It performed very well; the audited circulation for October 2003 was up 17,000 on the previous month. Better figures were to come as the compact was rolled out across the country. By November it was up another 5,000, by the following April a further 20,000. A Saturday compact was introduced on 31 January 2004, and the final step, to stop printing any broadsheets, came on Friday 17 May 2004. A sale of 261,000 was recorded for that month, an increase of 40,000 year on year.

The *Independent* had had no real idea how the compact would fare, if it would prove popular, if it would draw readers from the broadsheet in substitute sales making little difference to total sale, or if it would lead to new sales and an increase in total circulation. It had become clear right away that a sizeable number of people already buying the *Independent* preferred to buy the compact. It was also clear that the small version was attracting new readers, and the indication was that they were coming from the *Guardian*. A triumphant Kelner told *Media Guardian* in July 2004:

> For the first five years of my editorship, on those afternoons when the monthly sales figures arrived, I used to look at them at a distance. Now I embrace them. They're phenomenal. We're 50,000 copies ahead year on year.

We've gone up almost 40% in some places. No one shows an increase in June; we did. We've got more women readers, more ABC1 readers, more young readers.

(Interview by Roy Greenslade 26 July 2004)

The rivals follow suit

The rivals went into overdrive discussing how to react. The public pronouncements, competitive sniping, were all about the desperation of the *Independent*, the smallest selling daily in the country, and a long way from relinquishing that title, about the high cost to a loss-making newspaper of producing broadsheets and compacts every night, and having greater returns (unsold copies) because this was a deliberate sampling exercise. And the rivals claimed to be unimpressed by the high figures for the percentage increase in sale. If you have a very low sale to start with, then any increase will give you a decent percentage figure. These statements were not entirely convincing, because it was clear that the rivals were worried. They too had done their market research and produced dummies of tabloid versions of their own newspapers. The *Independent* had stolen a lead, and whatever the rivals did now, however they explained it, they would be following.

Murdoch never worries about such niceties. He told his *Times* Editor, Robert Thomson, to prepare for a tabloid launch. After just a few weeks it came, on Monday 24 November 2003, while the *Independent* was still selling in both formats, still concentrating on areas where its core readership lived. Same size. Same approach: the compact on sale alongside the broadsheet version.

Thomson was forced to drop his attacks on the *Independent*. 'It is an undoubted success for which they deserve credit', he told *UK Press Gazette* (16 July 2004). 'We are grateful to them for having done the market research on how the audience would receive a compact quality newspaper.' *The Times*' own compact research was reported (in *The Times* 9 July 2004) by Brian MacArthur. It showed that 'nearly half of compact readers are aged between 25 and 44, 60% are in full time work, that 78% are ABC1s and that about 40% work in the business sector.'

But *The Times* was very different from the *Independent*. For a start there was the traditional image of the paper. *The Times* is probably the most famous British newspaper, known as the paper of the establishment, even, years ago, advertising itself as the 'top people's paper'. It was read by the political and professional classes. It carried the law reports. It was close to government, particularly Conservative government. It had its famous letters page. This was the heartland of the view that broadsheet represented upmarket quality – size was a badge of the influence and authority of the newspaper.

True, *The Times* had changed under Murdoch's ownership. It had joined the marketplace with a vengeance, with an aggressive price-cutting strategy designed to increase sale and intimidate the opposition. It had brought *The Times* to a clear second place in the quality sector, 200,000 copies ahead of the *Guardian*, 300,000 copies behind the *Telegraph*, which was Murdoch's target. Along the way *The*

Times had become less establishment, more mainstream, following the quality sector trend to carry news of broad interest, no longer ignoring popular culture or the tittle-tattle of celebrity gossip. Murdoch had invested heavily in his flagship title. Going tabloid was higher risk for that paper than for the *Independent*. The traditional *Times* reader, already buffeted by what he or she saw as a popularising of the paper in the interests of increasing sales – which had happened – could well be resistant to a change in shape.

But Murdoch went ahead, and there were two compacts on the market. *The Times* result, 5 per cent gain in sale over the first year, was not as dramatic as that of the *Independent*, but it was starting from a much higher base, with percentage increases in sale smaller. But the sale increased, in a declining market, although the move from broadsheet to tabloid by established readers was much less marked. Selling the compact alongside the broadsheet might need to continue for a long time. There were *Times* readers who would not willingly make the change. The risks, and costs, were considerable. But Murdoch had always pumped money into *The Times*, and could afford to. He dropped the broadsheet after a year of dual publication.

The two other broadsheet titles had different problems. The *Daily Telegraph*, the most conservative of the four, is the quality paper of middle England, selling many copies outside the London area. It is the paper of traditional values, defending hunting with hounds, private education, what it described as freedom of choice.

It too had investigated the tabloid option. But throughout the year of the compact *Independent* launch it had other things on its mind. It was for sale, following the financial scandal surrounding its proprietor Conrad Black. The sale was protracted before the Barclay brothers bought the papers for £670 million. They were new to national paper ownership, and decisions as fundamental as going tabloid were not going to be taken quickly.

The *Telegraph* circulation has declined from a consistent million plus to below 900,000 today. Now the marketplace had changed it was in a position where doing nothing was a decisive step. But the risks of going compact were probably greater for the *Telegraph* than for any other title, its readers most likely to be resistant.

Martin Newland, the then Editor, was appointed shortly before the paper was put up for sale, so he had a difficult time. Throughout the early period of compact *Times* and *Indy* he toyed with the idea of doing the same, but finally decided against. He was soon removed; the *Telegraph* was under the caretaker editorship of John Bryant for a long period, until a new Editor, Will Lewis, was appointed in 2006. He ignored the compact revolution, instead putting all his energy into converged, multi-platform publication concentrating on developing the website.

The situation was very different for the *Guardian*, which had circulation problems. The lead in sale over the *Independent* had shrunk from 177,000 when both newspapers were broadsheet to 112,000 a year after the *Independent*'s compact launch. It would continue to fall to 86,000. The *Guardian* is a direct competitor of the *Independent*. It has an international reputation as a radical, left of centre newspaper. Owned by a trust, it has no shareholders and has been sustained over the years by the *Manchester Evening News* and by some car sales publications. It bought the *Observer* in 1993, which remains a loss maker.

The *Guardian* has a reputation for innovation, which is why it 'felt' the *Independent*'s compact success badly. It introduced a range of tabloid sections, containing profitable classified advertising, in the 1980s. Its Editor from 1975 to 1995, Peter Preston, made no secret of his enthusiasm for continental tabloid quality papers, and it was widely thought that he would take the *Guardian* tabloid. He did not, and in 1995 was replaced by Alan Rusbridger.

They had tabloid dummies, and everybody was waiting for the *Guardian* to follow the *Independent* and *The Times* and join 'compact wars'. It did not happen. Rusbridger had profound reservations about the tabloid, and probably more reservations about having his paper playing catch-up to its minnow rival. He was concerned about the effect on content and the nature of the paper tabloidisation would bring. He watched the *Independent* and *The Times* carefully, measuring stories, comparing the content and presentation of the two versions of each paper ('Hugo Young Memorial Lecture', Sheffield, March 2005). But more than anything he wanted to do something different. Thus was born the Berliner concept, adopting for the *Guardian* not the well-known, in Britain, tabloid format, but the bigger, halfway house of the famous European papers like *Le Monde*.

Rusbridger commissioned designs, and set a team on producing internally a daily Berliner-sized version of the *Guardian*. He said:

> We started thinking about the Berliner size because it works so well. Tabloid forces change in terms of layout, one main story a page, one picture. It changes editorial and pushes you to an *Independent* style front page. With the Berliner you don't fall into that trap. You have calmer typography, and it is less intrusive. You can linger on a spread. It has a calming effect.
>
> (interview 2005)

The problems he faced were twofold. There were no presses in Britain configured to print a Berliner. The *Guardian* made a huge investment, more than £50 million, in new presses to print the new format. And the time taken building the presses would be time spent as a broadsheet competing with a compact *Independent* and *Times*.

The Berliner *Guardian* launched on Monday 12 September 2005, two years after the compact *Independent*, gaining 9.0 per cent in the first year. The *Independent on Sunday* went compact a month later, increasing sales by 15 per cent in its first year (ABC); the Berliner *Observer* launched in January 2006, putting on an initial 9 per cent. Apart from the *IoS* the increase was nothing like as dramatic as that of the first compacts. By now *The Times* and *Independent*, familiar as compacts, had passed through the early surge, although they were still enjoying circulation much increased over their previous broadsheets. Table 15.1 shows the effect of compact relaunch on all titles in the quality sector, showing compact gain in circulation over last broadsheet month.

Table 15.1 *Sales increases following transition to compact or Berliner format*

Title – compact launch date	Last true[a] broadsheet sale – month	One year later – increase over broadsheet (%)	Two years later – increase over broadsheet (%)	Three years later – increase over broadsheet (%)
Independent 30 Sept. 2003	219,000 Sept. 2003	265,000 21 Sept. 2004	263,000 20 Sept. 2005	265,000 21 Sept. 2006
The Times 24 Nov. 2003	656,000 Oct. 2003	691,000 5 Nov. 2004	691,000 5 Nov. 2005	654,000 0 Nov. 2006
Guardian 12 Sept. 2005	358,000 July 2005	389,000 9 Sept. 2006	n/a	n/a
Independent on Sunday 16 Oct. 2005	203,000 Sept. 2005	234,000 15 Sept. 2006	n/a	n/a
Observer 8 Jan. 2006	437,000 Nov. 2005	444,000 2 Jan. 2007	n/a	n/a

Source: ABC.

Note: Month of 'true' last broadsheet sale is last full month of broadsheet and excludes 'untypical' months like December and August.

Downsizing or dumbing down?

One of the fears, particularly among media commentators and academics, was that reducing the size of broadsheet newspapers might mean reducing the quality, by which they meant seriousness. That it might mean dumbing down. That debate had started long before Kelner first thought of a compact *Independent*. Perhaps it had elements of truth, perhaps not (Franklin 1997; Cole 1997, 2001). Certainly, editorial agendas change over time, but so does society. The embracing of popular culture, from rock and roll and soaps to celebrity, was a reflection of society, not led by newspapers. It is easier to criticise newspapers for not keeping up with social change than for leading change.

The broadsheet quality sector of the newspaper market had long embraced pictorial journalism, magazine-style features, dealing with issues through people, and featuring celebrities, fashion and trends. But they had done it in their own way, while still dealing with thoughtful criticism, comment and opinion, with political issues as well as squabbles, with mass culture as well as high culture. But the question remained: would the smaller 'tabloid' format lead to more tabloid content and presentation? Would the *Guardian* and *The Times* seem more like the *Mail*?

The editors know their audiences better than that. Of course the smaller format poses new challenges to the designers. In a visual age greater display is required by readers, greater effort to draw the reader into a story. The gulf between the brash, heavily pictorial, popular papers and the text-dominated broadsheet quality papers has closed. Computerised production technology allowing for the use of informative graphics and improved printing techniques vastly improving the quality of picture reproduction meant the 'serious' press took display as seriously as the tabloids. They did this not to trivialise but to aid comprehension. Clearly, producing serious newspapers which were the same size as the popular tabloids opened them to accusations of taking on a more tabloid agenda. The editors were well aware of this and developed designs that still sent out a message of seriousness, within a tabloid format. Dumbing down is about content and subject matter, not size. This did not stop Alan Rusbridger, the *Guardian* Editor, arguing that the *Independent* and *The Times* compacts looked more like the *Mail*, but he said it at a time when the *Guardian* was still a broadsheet.

The compacts have to be treated one by one. The *Independent*, which started it all, has adopted the 'poster', single-story front page, often containing simply a picture or elaborate graphic and few words. This has become the articulation of what Kelner describes, unashamedly, as his 'viewspaper'. The *Independent*'s front page usually takes a line, forcefully. It has consistently taken an anti-Iraq War stance. It campaigns on the environment, global warming and excessive packaging. The more conventional, and detached, news appears inside.

All three daily compacts now run daily pull-out second sections – *Extra*, *T2* and *G2* – in which longer features are run. These are targeted at a younger readership. And all have additional once-a-week sections, on subjects such as media and education. These are designed to attract classified advertising, at which only the *Guardian* is really successful. *The Times* is most susceptible to the dumbing down charge, not so much in losing its serious coverage but in diluting it with more popular (*Daily Mail?*) content, particularly in *T2*. It is, however, the best-selling compact. The *Guardian* has the most sober news section. It takes advantage of its larger Berliner format to feature more stories on its front page, most of them cross-references to more extensive coverage inside. Rusbridger has achieved his declared ambition to produce a 'calm' paper, and it 'feels' more serious than the other compacts. One product of its new printing presses is the ability to run colour on every page, and this is exploited with a new feature, running a picture across a double-page spread.

All three compacts run several pages of comment, opinion and letters, with their broadsheet columnists continuing to write in the smaller format. News page items are often shorter than they would have been in the old format, many gaining from that. Overall, the compacts have not dumbed down in any way that could be attributed to their smaller size. Is the still broadsheet *Telegraph* more serious or upmarket than the compacts?

It remains to be seen whether the compact era has halted the steady decline of newspaper sales in the serious sector of a market that is declining more rapidly overall, and bringing premature discussion of the death of newspapers. Certainly it has bought time, with the new compacts increasing their aggregate sale over the period since they were broadsheets.

The three compacts discussed in this chapter, all loss makers, have increased aggregate sale by 25,239 copies, or 2.02 per cent since the *Independent* started the downsizing. The one title to remain broadsheet, the *Telegraph*, has lost 37,865, or 4.05 per cent over the same period. If that seems a meagre result for all that has gone into format change, consider what might have happened without it. In the red top tabloid sector, sales have declined by 1.07 million over the same period – 15.56 per cent. Standing still is success in today's newspaper market. The compacts have achieved more than that.

Throughout the world broadsheet newspapers have turned compact since the *Independent*'s move. The World Association of Newspapers estimated in its 2006 World Press Trends report that the figure was around 80, but it also warned that circulation increases tended to disappear over time (World Association of Newspapers 2006).

Last word to Simon Kelner, who started it all in the UK. In an interview in *Media Guardian* (26 July 2004) he told Roy Greenslade:

> We've certainly made people think seriously about how their newspapers are packaged and delivered, and we've challenged the prejudices and preconceptions about whether it's possible to do an upmarket quality tabloid. Whether we've revolutionised the entire newspaper market we'll only know when the revolution is over. It's just the beginning.

References

Audit Bureau of Circulations (ABC) (n.d.) abc.org.uk. Accessed 7 November 2007.

Cole, P. (1997) 'Quality Journalism: An Oxymoron?' Professorial Lecture, University of Central Lancashire, 16 April.

Cole, P. (2001) 'What Chance Serious Debate in the Modern Media?' Inaugural Lecture, University of Sheffield, 7 February.

Franklin, B. (1997) *Newszak and News Media* London: Arnold.

Greenslade, R. (2003) *Press Gang* London: Macmillan.

Greenslade, R. (2004) 'It's the Most Effective Promotion in the History of Newspapers' *Media Guardian* 26 July, p.2.

MacArthur, B. (1988) *Eddy Shah Today and the Newspaper Revolution* London: David and Charles.

MacArthur, B. (2004) 'The Times, et al, They are A-changin' *The Times* 9 July, p.53.

Ponsford, D. (2004) 'Changing Times' *Press Gazette* 16 July, p.21.

Rusbridger A. (2005) 'What Are Newspapers For?' Hugo Young Lecture, University of Sheffield, 9 March.

World Association of Newspapers (2006) *World Press Trends* wan-press.org. Accessed 2 April 2007.

Chapter 16

Photography in newspapers

Eamonn McCabe

On the evening of 11 September 2001 Alan Rusbridger, the Editor of the *Guardian*, made a decision to clear 15 pages and let the photographs tell the story of one of the biggest tragedies ever to be reported in a national newspaper. The horror of the planes ploughing into the Twin Towers in New York had been witnessed by many on television around the world. Everybody knew what had happened, but nobody knew who was behind it. With so many dead and with so little real information Rusbridger's judgement was that letting the photographs tell the story would reveal the real power of photojournalism.

Double-page spreads were used to great effect and the biggest problem the sub-editors had was whether any text was needed on the page at all. Early editions had three or four words on a page; later editions carried no words at all. The photographs told the whole story, or as much as was known. Has there been a better use of news photography in any newspaper anywhere in the world? I doubt it.

Having said that, the recent downsizing of some of our broadsheet papers has led to the death of the traditional front page picture; something that was always seen as the best way to sell the paper on the news-stand. Now with papers on the web maybe this is not the concern it once was. The *Independent*, which launched itself on the power of its photography in 1987, now often has a single-themed text-led front page, with no photograph at all! It is an irony that the *Independent* recently launched a photography competition for its readers when it seems to have given up entirely on its own photography – including laying off many of the photographers that created the look so many readers responded to in the late 1980s.

Whenever I gave a lecture around those times somebody always put up their hand and said how great the *Independent* was for photography. I used to rage inside, and we at the *Guardian* made a concerted effort to take them on. I like to feel that on many a night we equalled or bettered them.

But the *Guardian* now sees its own front page in a very different light from those heady days of photojournalism when every other week seemed to provide a huge news event. As picture editors on all the quality broadsheets, we pushed the size of the front page picture, sometimes to cover the whole page; much to the annoyance of the writers. There was Lockerbie, the Armenian earthquake, the pleasure boat tragedy on the Thames, the M1 crash and numerous train crashes. What constituted a full front page picture: 20 dead, 30 dead or 50 dead?

The popular press also uses photography to sell papers. The *Mail* and the *Mirror* although tabloid in size often use pictures boldly on the front page and still continue to do so to great effect when there is a big news story. But the newly tabloid-sized *Times* and *Independent*, and the now slightly bigger, Berliner, *Guardian* have far fewer screaming front pages than in the 1990s. The *Guardian* these days has a policy of a very calm front page with a restrained photograph, often a portrait of a politician or celebrity.

Publishing shocking pictures

The *Guardian* would argue that it has its centre pages to promote the best in photojournalism, something that has become a real hit with readers and advertisers alike. Interestingly, if not ironically, it is the centre of the paper rather than the front page that is now the main worry every day. If another picture came over the wires like Kenneth Jarecke's staggering photograph of the dead soldier in the burned out jeep on the Basra road, would the *Guardian* put it on the front page or use it more dramatically on the centre spread? Or would they use it at all? This picture which expressed the futility of war and represented the death of thousands through the portrayal of one burned out skeleton of an Iraqi soldier strafed by American 'friendly ???' fire. The unfortunate soldier seemed so real it looked like he might move any minute.

When the picture came over in 1991 the *Observer*, then picture edited by Tony McGrath, was the only paper in the UK to publish the photograph. It transpires that not every paper in Britain got the picture: the censors stopped it running as soon as they realised its power. Even when the Associated Press in Dharam transmitted the picture to the US, some editor in New York took it off the wire, so the Americans never saw it in their papers. The American government does not like its citizens seeing their troops losing. It was never seen in newspapers or magazines in America until an agency called Contact Press Images got hold of the picture and even then it took a bold editor on *American Photo*, a photography magazine, to publish it.

In Britain readers were outraged, even professional photographers were not sure it should be used, was this too much? The *Observer* actually buried it on page 8. I argued at the time: why not the front page? As Harry Evans in his excellent book, and the only bible of picture editing, *Pictures on a Page*, wondered: 'Why did such a simple grainy black and white photograph arouse such a reaction?' I wrote a piece on the Monday in the media pages of the *Guardian* saying it should have been used in every newspaper, not just the *Observer*, but there was some confusion as to how many papers actually received the photograph here in Britain. On the Monday a reader rang in to complain bitterly that she had spent the whole of Sunday hiding the picture from her children, and there I go and use it again on the media pages of the *Guardian*. Surely the media papers were the right place for the debate? And I had showed the picture again, in context! I feel you cannot edit papers for children. There are times when you have to show disturbing photographs in order to make the readers realise what is happening in the world and hopefully get something done about it.

Every time there is a big domestic tragedy or a war, an outcry always follows about why newspapers choose to publish photographs of dead bodies. In my time as picture editor I had furious letters about Armenia, Lockerbie, Kosovo and the Gulf War and many more. The arguments always made the same three points. Would you publish the picture if he or she were white? How could you do that to the dead person's family? How would you like it if it were your son or daughter? And yet tragedies need bodies. Two disasters that had no pictures at all of the dead involved were the Marchioness pleasure-boat incident on the Thames in August 1989, where the police denied newspapers any access – they later admitted it was a mistake—and the 9/11 tragedy in New York. We all know that thousands died in the latter case but the photographers had only pictures of buildings and panic in the streets. Somehow the photographs of dead bodies prove something had happened, it brings closure to an event and helps people grieve.

Every time one of these pictures comes over the wires a small team of executives on every newspaper debates long and hard whether or not to use it. You cannot sanitise the news, but you can choose when and where to publish. Photographers at breaking stories cannot be editors. They often shoot pictures without knowing the real story. When I was working at Heysel Stadium on 29 May 1985 and 38 people died I was accused of being a ghoul … but you now know the full story. When I was taking pictures it was just a wall breaking and some football fans running amok. Later I shot pictures of dead bodies (which we at the *Observer* never used) and people injured on the pitch, but when I was working I didn't know what it all meant. You can blame the picture editors for showing you the wrong pictures but not the photographer for taking them.

The editor, the senior news editor of the day, the picture editor and the front page designer all discuss whether or not to show a horrific picture. It is often a question of taste: how much do you show and do you have enough information to give you the confidence that what you are showing is truthful?

The biggest debate I got involved in during 13 years of picture editing was the use of a photograph of a woman hanging from a tree outside a refugee camp in Bosnia. The picture was very disturbing, but I remember being really shocked by how ordinary she looked; it was as if she has just stepped out of a Marks and Spencer store in England. Luckily, Maggie O'Kane, the great war correspondent, was in the office. She felt passionately that we should use it. We took the picture into the newly appointed Alan Rusbridger to get a decision. He was worried: was it genuine? We had to find out. We didn't use it the night it came in because of this concern. Then we had a stroke of luck. Julian Borger our correspondent in Bosnia had actually witnessed the grim scene. We had our eyewitness, our proof. We knew it had actually happened. We published it on the front with Borger's report. The next day was Saturday and editors like their paper to have a lighter feel to the front page, for a day of leisure, not to see a dead woman hanging from a tree to look at over the toast and eggs. We ran the picture and the next morning at about six o'clock the phone rang and it was Rusbridger. I was nervous. I never had an editor ring me at home, let alone so early in the morning. But he was ringing to say thanks for pushing him to use it.

The *Mirror* was the only other paper to run it, small and inside, but I was still a bit nervous. The readers were split roughly down the middle in favour of our using it and many strongly against. For days I had letters (this was before email, remember) from university professors saying that there was no way that the woman had hung herself: they argued the rope was too short, and that she was facing the wrong way. How do people know these things? Without Borger's eyewitness we would never have run it.

The veracity of photographs

Newspapers run contentious pictures only after they have checked the facts on the ground. Sometimes these circumstances change even between editions of the same paper on the same night. Nowadays with over 6,000 photographs coming over the wires on a busy day, all appearing as small thumbnails on screens all around the office, the worry is that a rogue picture will get through the system. With Photoshop being so easy to use, anybody can alter a picture's meaning. Picture editors have to trust the bona fide agencies like Associated Press, Reuters and The Press Association here in Britain to have established the authenticity of a photograph before they send it.

There was a case in which a photographer altered a photograph being sent from Beirut. It was a picture of a war scene but the sky was a bit insipid. With Photoshop the photographer added some more smoke to make the picture look more authentic and dangerous. The picture was published around the world and when the alterations to the original were discovered, the photographer was fired. The reputation of Reuters was preserved and picture editors globally still trust their output.

On a lighter note there was a case of a monk who was photographed with a 17-year-old girl. The *Sun* had the photograph, except that the monk was in civvies (and it didn't look right). The picture editor got the biggest photographer out of the rest room and photographed him in a hired monk's habit. They then stuck the face of the real monk on the photographer's body, complete with habit, and published the picture. The moral of this story is that the readers of the *Sun* saw a picture of the monk and a girlfriend and believed it to be true, because it looked right!

Piers Morgan, the flamboyant former Editor of the *Daily Mirror*, lost his job because he published something he thought looked right, but which to this photographer's eye and those of many others so obviously wasn't. The set of pictures supposedly came out of Iraq and showed a group of beaten-up Iraqis in the back of a British Army truck. The camera apparently belonged to a soldier's wife. But the pictures looked too good and they were in black and white! Where would you get black-and-white film in the desert?

These days readers know picture editors can manipulate photographs as easily as they themselves can on their computers at home. Long gone are the days when you could squeeze a three-column football picture into two columns by moving the ball. The readers now know you can do it; so why not alter a picture from Israel or Iraq? In the early days of photojournalism readers were not so knowledgeable about technique and could be fooled or should we say persuaded by a bit of manipulation. Malcolm Brady, who photographed the American Civil War, was not adverse to a bit of reconstruction to help the readers understand what was really going on. He would photograph dead bodies in trenches, but often they were too far apart and he felt the pictures were not showing the real horror of war. So he dragged the bodies together so that it looked like hundreds were dying. The use of his photographs on the front pages of American papers helped stop the war.

The rise of the picture agency

Most photographs in newspapers are now supplied by agencies. It is hard for an individual to make a name now. Bill Gates and Paul Getty Junior are going around furiously buying up image libraries by the day. They believe that if they own all the rights then the web will be their oyster. The downside of all this is, will there ever be another Jane Bown, Chris Smith, Monte Fresco or Denis Thorpe, whose names readers came to know well and for whom readers even bought papers just to look at their work?

Look at the side of most photographs in your morning paper, if you bought one. (I have just done a lecture at Nottingham Trent University to a bright group of kids on a photography course and not one of them read, let alone bought, a newspaper on that day.) Many photographs only have the name 'Getty' or that of Bill Gates' outfit Corbis beside the picture. The individual who took the photograph no longer gets any obvious credit. An even more worrying trend is of agency photographers setting things up to illustrate subjects that are difficult to photograph. Up and down the country models are being photographed as if they are in the workplace, children taking cough medicine, doctors pretending to be talking to patients. This is all because managing editors fear that if they use pictures of real people they may be sued. The model release form that these 'actors' sign protects newspapers and agencies from being chased by lawyers; they also help managing editors sleep at night.

Now this fear is understandable if you show pictures of former prisoners who have later gone on to hold down decent jobs or pictures of hospital patients who may have later died, but this glib, boring, set-up photography is so uninspiring. Can real life really be portrayed through the photography of over-made-up models pretending in a barn in Northampton? Soon we will have all photographs in newspapers either supplied by Getty and Gates (sounds like a music hall double act!) or by agencies with more models on their book than photographers.

Citizen photographers?

The other major source of photographs for newspapers will be the readers themselves. Now everybody has a camera albeit in a mobile phone. This new form of photography has been labelled 'citizen journalism'. The most memorable photographs of the London Bombings of 7 July 2005 were taken by an amazingly composed traveller on one of the stricken underground trains.

This was the day that 'user-generated content' (UGC) or 'citizen journalism' came into its own in Britain. The BBC alone was sent over 300 photos – 50 within an hour of the first bomb going off – and several video sequences, ideal for use on the web. It didn't matter that the quality was awful and that it was hard to make anything out in the gloom of the pictures. It was raw news and readers do not question the quality if it is from the right place at the right time. The next day, better-quality pictures are often used but the ones readers remember are those that were the first to be published. Who will forget the picture of the double-decker bus with its roof blown off, taken from a bedsit high in a block of flats in Bloomsbury, and not taken by a news photographer: many of whom were held back around a corner by a police barrier for hours before they were let anywhere near the scene.

Even the royals are now getting nervous of mobile phone cameras or citizen journalists. What were once thought of as innocent snaps that hardly anybody would see, are now seen as potential earners of thousands of pounds, as newspapers and magazines seek to outdo each other. The royals relax when they are not being chased by the paparazzi, but now everyone armed only with a mobile phone could easily join these photo hunters.

A growing number of picture agencies increasingly rely on members of the public for the pictures they sell to newspapers and magazines, and the photographer receives 50 per cent of the sale. Photographs of members of the royal family are the big sellers, followed by show business stars and sporting celebrities such as David Beckham and Wayne Rooney. A photograph of one of the young princes kissing his girlfriend on a ski slope could be worth £20,000, industry sources claim.

Further reading

Evans, H. (1979) *Pictures on a Page: Photojournalism, Graphics and Picture Editing* London: Heinemann.

Taylor, J. (2000) 'Problems in Photojournalism: Realism, the Nature of News and the Humanitarian Narrative' *Journalism Studies* vol. 1 no. 1 February, pp.119–44.

Taylor, J. (2005) 'Iraqi Torture Photographs and Documentary Realism in the Press' *Journalism Studies* vol. 6 no. 1 February, pp.39–50.

Chapter 17

Supplements

Nicholas Brett and Tim Holmes

When a newspaper proprietor appears to give something away, there must be a catch. The current manifestation of this largesse is DVDs, posters and books (the last being a very old form of giveaway – the *Express* was doing it in the inter-war years of the last century), but before this upsurge in blatantly promotional gifts there was the supplement. Newspaper supplements range from the traditional but now almost defunct sports extra produced at breakneck speed and smudgily printed on green or pink newsprint, right through to beautifully designed colour supplements printed by photogravure on art paper (or a close relative).

The *Sunday Times* is widely credited with inventing the truly magazine-like colour supplement, although when it was launched under Mark Boxer's editorship on 4 February 1962 it was actually called the *Colour Section*. There was, however, no real invention since colour magazines were already in existence and colour supplements to newspapers were relatively commonplace in North America; what the *Sunday Times*, or rather its proprietor Roy Thomson, did was to persist with the idea in the face of scepticism from his fellow proprietors and indifference from the advertising industry. Nevertheless, once the colour ads – and the concomitant revenue – started to flow in, the supplementary magazine became an accepted part of a newspaper's make-up and the colour section turned out to be another of Lord Thomson's licences to print money. First it was the Sunday papers which followed his lead, starting with the *Sunday Telegraph* and the *Observer*, but then the Saturday issues of daily papers jumped on the bandwagon and now it seems that everyone has joined in.

Supplements, moreover, are not just a European or American phenomenon. India's new financial daily *Mint*, a joint venture between the *Hindustan Times* and the *Wall Street Journal*, wraps the newsprint element of its Saturday edition inside a magazine – although it has to be said that this is an idea from the fertile brain of newspaper design expert Mario Garcia, whose work can be found in papers around the globe.

However, 'supplement' is not a synonym for 'magazine' and the revival of the Saturday editions of newspapers shows why. Less than 20 years ago, Saturday used to be the softest sales day for national dailies, certainly the broadsheets; some were rumoured to be considering abandoning Saturday altogether and scaling back to weekday publishing only. Today, Saturday on the quality papers has become so strong that Sunday papers are suffering.

The earliest adopter of the magazine way, at least on Saturdays, was the *Financial Times*. It was almost as if the pinstriped one felt it needed to dress 'smart casual' on a Saturday. The mid-1980s saw the *FT* introduce a clutch of soft features – a gardening column by Oxford don Robin Lane Fox; Lucia Van Der Post's 'How To Spend It' shopping page; and a food and recipe page – followed by a full-blown Saturday section.

Ian Hargreaves, former Deputy Editor of the paper, is very clear about the development of, and rationale for, this section.

> 'How To Spend It' began as a broadsheet newsprint set of pages, became a broadsheet supplement, and now has an identity as a magazine. It's much more analogous to the other style mags in the quality papers than anything else, though it was something of a pioneer. Its job was to boost sales and loyalty to the Saturday *FT*, which in the UK has always had a higher sale than the Monday to Friday paper because it appeals both to the small investor, counting their money once a week, and the business executive 'in his sweater', therefore up for stuff about golf, as well as shopping.[1]

The *FT* has been restrained in comparison with some other papers, although Ian Hargreaves recalls that it would publish supplement-like surveys 'when specific advertising volumes were secured to justify them as a business proposition. The *FT* was always very keen, however, to prevent the surveys being seen as "advertorial" and it's true they were treated very seriously editorially.' The survey or special report is still a feature of the paper.

It can be seen, then, that supplements generally have both an editorial and a commercial function, and the commercial function may be on a macro or micro level, where macro implies general sales promotion and reader loyalty, and micro involves specific advertising revenue and niche reader appeal. The latter has become increasingly important as newspapers, which once dominated the media landscape, have had to work harder to attract particular audiences. It could be argued that the cornucopia of supplements shows that newspapers have learned from other media; it is certainly true that in appearance, intention and content newspapers have gone through a dramatic transformation, abandoning to a certain degree their hard news rationale and adopting the ways of magazines and in particular the magazine creed, the greatest of which is 'give the readers what they want'. One way to achieve this is to create niches of specialised interest within the paper in order to attract quantifiably specific groups of readers – and the advertisers who follow them. Travel, finance and particular types of employment are all strong candidates for supplementary treatment, classic examples of the third being the *Guardian*'s Monday and Wednesday supplements – *Media* and *Society* respectively – that both mop up the job ads in those sectors and subsidise other parts of the paper that do not attract so much revenue (see chapter 21 on advertising).

The corollary of this is that reliance on such lucrative supplements makes the newspaper concerned extraordinarily vulnerable to changes in the media landscape. Listen to Alan Rusbridger, Editor of the *Guardian*, talking about the future of newspapers[2] and it is not long before he turns to craigslist, the immensely successful classified advert site which is seen to have sucked the lifeblood from many newspapers in the United States. In the *Guardian*'s case, it is not so much craig as national and local government that is increasingly putting public sector vacancies – such as those found in the *Society* supplement – online.

Supplements thus ebb and flow with changes in the economy and society. During the first dotcom boom in the late 1990s the *Daily Telegraph* published a consistently interesting and well-written new media supplement, but when the ad revenue dried up along with boo.com's[3] capital and customers, so did the section. The coming and going of these sections may also give students of cultural development an indication of how the world is changing: *La Repubblica*, for example, now has a weekly insert called *Metropoli* which targets the relatively new, and growing, immigrant communities in Italy.

If this sensitivity to change is a comparatively new characteristic for newspapers, it is also a major source of neologisms for media commentators. It is a commonplace to say that newspapers have been 'magazine-ified' but now the 'ifieds' are becoming much more specific. Writing about Saturday newspaper magazines, Janice Turner notes a general 'girlification' (Turner 2006), while Jayne Thynne narrowed it down even further when she called the same phenomenon the 'Grazia-fication of Fleet Street' (Thynne 2005), after the trendsetting weekly fashion-and-celebrity magazine. Even Andrew Neil, under whose editorship the *Sunday Times* expanded its supplement count enormously, has joined in the chorus. He was slightly less specific but far more damning when he stated in August 2006 that the future of print was in magazines, not newspapers. Of course, he had just transformed his newspaper the *Business* into a magazine, so it is possible he may have had an ulterior motive for this statement.

Recent apostates aside, this general trend is not new as we have seen above. Newspaper supplements have abounded, with special sections and even specialised magazines, such as the *Observer*'s sport, music and food monthlies, now an expected part of the package. Nor is it confined to the national press: regional newspapers have been just as assiduous in developing offshoots, with 'county' magazines fuelled by full-colour property advertising being a favourite. In August 2005 the Newspaper Society released a survey that showed that the number of supplemental magazines and spin-off niche publications, ranging from bridal titles to walking guides, had risen by 48.5 per cent in 2004. As media commentator Roy Greenslade noted, 'all newspaper owners are finally understanding why niche-marketed magazines have been so successful' (*Media Guardian* 5 September 2005, p.10). There have, then, been a number of drivers leading newspapers to borrow magazines' clothes, some historic, some continuous and current. Among the foremost agents are commercial, technological and social changes.

The 1980s saw the birth of a new social category, the young urban professional or yuppie, many of whom were women. This group was experiencing considerable wealth, stereotypically through their City bonuses, and a great optimism about life; the social and political mores of that period also meant that many people who did not have the economic clout of the genuine yuppie aspired to a similar lifestyle. Complementing this social development was a global advertising boom. The problem for newspapers at this time was that they didn't have the space, literally, to suck up all the ad revenue that was available to them, nor did they have an appropriate editorial environment in which to comfortably and engagingly show off this aspirational advertising to their new audience of yuppies and would-be yuppies.

Hand in hand with this came new patterns of leisure and consumption. Whereas Saturday was once if not a day of work then certainly one for chores and Sunday the only true day of rest (the 'snooze/snews' day as the *Sunday Times*' ad campaign called it), this was changing in the 1980s. Retailing laws were relaxed and Sunday became a shopping day too. So, after a week of long 'burn-out' days, the yuppies were more than ready for a cappuccino and croissant in bed with the Saturday papers.

The 1980s also witnessed a revolution in newspaper production from the archaic, costly and inefficient unionised hot metal to the photo-composition of Eddy Shah's Warrington and Rupert Murdoch's Wapping. With the means of production both transformed and back under the control of publishers and journalists, it was now possible to make big papers quickly and efficiently with sections and *colour* that would both appeal to the new yuppie audience and soak up the glut of advertising.

And there was a new demographic to which to direct advertising – yuppie women worked hard and felt they deserved to play hard, using their City bonuses to lavish money on themselves without guilt. This was the decade that saw the surge of designer labels and luxury brands. Newspapers recognised they needed to feminise their products if they were to compete with the glossy, high-end magazines for this increasingly important advertising revenue. Women, too, radicalised and politicised, were demanding that newspapers like those other male bastions, the City and gentlemen's clubs, should open their doors to them. It was probably David English's *Daily Mail* that took the initiative with *Femail*, Angela Levin's big interviews and Lynda Lee Potter's opinion pieces.

> At *The Times*, Charlie [editor Charles Douglas Home] and I realised that the paper wasn't speaking to half the population and that we needed to broaden our appeal. We realised, too, that you couldn't do this by adding a women's page or some token features – you had *to edit* the paper throughout with women in mind.
>
> (personal interview, Charles Wilson, 10 February 2007)[4]

More women began to be promoted into senior editorial roles on national newspapers, though admittedly this still tended to be predominantly in softer roles such as diary editor, columnist or feature writer. But one genuine change seemed to be an increase in the traffic of women editorial executives from magazines to newspapers. For instance, Jo Foley,[5] doyenne of women's magazines, became Features Editor of *The Times*.

Women readers have become increasingly important to newspapers and supplements, and specifically magazines have been a key element in attracting their attention and loyalty. The first paper to move wholeheartedly in this direction was the *Mail on Sunday*, which transformed *You* into a weekly women's magazine. Not that everyone in the Daily Mail and General Trust seems to be able to summon quite the right tone when discussing it. 'Now, under the editorship of Sue Peart, it is designed to appeal mainly to our women readers, with horoscopes by Sally Brompton, problem page from Zelda West-Meads, Barbara Toner's Home Life column, plus regular fashion, food, health, shopping and beauty features as well as general articles', writes John Wellington on the DMGT's website (Wellington n.d.). Nevertheless, the *Mail on Sunday*'s promotional pages claim over 3 million women readers every week. Doubtless this figure was prominent in the decision to expand *You* into a stand-alone news-stand title in the first week of March 2006. The solus *You* used better paper, added a fifth colour to make the cover brighter, and sold for just £1 every Tuesday. It was withdrawn from sale in August 2006, having failed to reach its sales target of 50,000 per week.

Naturally the post-mortems speculated widely on this failure but two common themes emerged. First, the experiment seemed to bear out research reported by the Periodical Publisher's Association (PPA) that the relationship between reader and newspaper colour supplements in magazine format was weak, a 'rare case' where 'the reader/magazine personal relationship ... is not a strong factor' (Consterdine 2002, p.20). Secondly, the supplement's huge print run and consequent long lead times meant that it could never be as up-to-date with celebrity news and gossip as the *echt*-magazine weeklies like *Grazia*. This has a secondary implication that we will examine later, but primarily it touches on something that has affected the absolute core proposition of newspapers: the provision of news.

It was not the arrival per se of new media, such as radio and then television, that forced daily newspapers to concede some of their hard news high ground and look to magazines – but more the moment that television was acknowledged by consumers as the unbeatable and always available medium for immediacy, a moment which came some time between the Falklands War and the first Gulf campaign. During the Falklands, for instance, when a major incident such as the sinking of the Argentine battleship the *Belgrano* was reported in a television or radio broadcast, it would prompt the average person to think, 'I must go and buy a newspaper'. Indeed, the *Mail on Sunday* was launched at this very moment (2 May 1982), leading with news of an RAF bombing raid on Port Stanley airport.

Something changed dramatically with the arrival of Sky's 24-hour news channel. Suddenly, everyone could watch news actually happening – witness watching live from a Sky News crew's hotel bedroom the cruise missiles travelling along the streets of Baghdad at lamp-post height or, of course, more recently, witnessing that second plane flying into the Twin Towers. Newspapers were suddenly enfeebled and exposed for what they were – a rather arrogant and dated vehicle that had always decided what news and when to provide its readers, safe in the knowledge they had nowhere else to go. Increasingly, magazine staples such as views, reflection and colour, seemed the sensible and inevitable way to go. The newspaper became increasingly the 'viewspaper' (as the *Independent*'s Simon Kelner has it), a tendency that seems likely only to increase under the onslaught of the internet and mobile telephony.

Acknowledgement of this new reality seems to lie behind Richard Wallace's statement that 'today's newspapers aren't necessarily about "news"'. Wallace, Editor of the *Daily Mirror*, added, 'It's no secret that I have taken the *Mirror* down a more magazine-style road, and skew a degree of content to the 35-plus working woman' (Brook 2007). Such an approach may or may not work for newspapers, but it strongly implies a need for clear understanding of the ways in which magazines work, and this understanding is not always evident in practice.

When Sarah Sands relaunched the *Sunday Telegraph*, one of the key planks in her vision for the title's makeover was a brace of new magazine supplements – *Seven* covered the arts and listings, while *Stella* was characterised as an upmarket women's glossy. Sands described the latter as 'just the loveliest thing on the market' and added, 'Nothing can be in there that doesn't make you gasp "it's so lovely"' (Ponsford 2005). Could this be the same publication which Janice Turner described five months later – at around the same time as Sands lost her job – as 'intelligence-insulting froth' (Turner 2006)? It was. A magazine does not survive because 'it's so lovely': loveliness may well be one of the things that readers appreciate or even expect but it is not a driving principle of magazine success.

Nevertheless, despite some specific failures in apprehension of the basic rules, there appears to have been a gradual realisation by national newspaper journalists and publishers of something that magazines have known since their emergence as a distinct media form – the reader must come first.

Up until the 1980s when the sorts of changes discussed above kicked in, a daily newspaper's editorial floor was definitely a divided place. 'It was a bit like a rugby team where the forwards would say, and probably still do, "give it to the girls", meaning the backs. That was definitely the way the news people thought about features', says Charles Wilson (personal interview).

> When I was married to Sally [legendary women's magazine editor, Sally O'Sullivan] she used to always be saying to me 'Who are your readers?' Her people were obsessed with readers. When they were researching a new magazine idea they'd start with the likely reader and spend months debating and refining where she'd shop, what she thought, the colour of her eyes. I used to think it was a bit marketing speak.
>
> But we increasingly began to see its value. Instead of deciding what we'd give readers and when we'd give it to them, we began to think that we should give them what they wanted. I guess what I used to call my 'news sense' was just some other words for 'marketing sense'.

It was thoughts like these that drove direct marketing initiatives on newspapers, such as the tabloids' bingo promotions; *The Times*' adoption of its posh bingo, Portfolio, in the 1980s; reader events, offers and holidays; and the *Daily Telegraph*'s introduction of a form of subscription with pre-paid coupons you could redeem at news outlets. These were all the tried-and-tested means of magazines to get closer to their readers. 'We looked enviously at magazines and the direct relationship they have with their readers – subscriptions', Wilson continues. 'With newspapers it was the retailer who had the relationship with our readers.'

None of this is secret knowledge. The magazine industry, both individual publishing companies and the PPA, produces a constant flow of research that contains such findings as: 'The magazine medium's essential strength lies in the active way in which readers choose and use their magazines. Magazines are an active medium, with the reader in control' (Consterdine 2002, p.6). There are signs, as we have seen, that some newspaper editors and proprietors have begun to realise this, and there is evidence that magazine journalists have skills of value to newspapers and vice versa: when Jane Johnston launched *Closer* in September 2002, she recruited her deputy editor from the *News of the World* and her news editor from the *Sun*, preferring journalists with newspaper experience for their scoop-finding abilities.

Nevertheless, despite increasing convergence between the media, there are still platform-specific practices and mores, and those producing newspaper supplements often fall between two stools. It seems likely to remain true for some time to come that, 'Newspaper journalists see supplement staff as lightweights and divas, shielded from the rigours of the edition. Magazine folk regard them as half-baked dabblers with zero style and crap paper' (Turner 2006).

Notes

1   Personal interview 15 March 2007. In an 11-year spell on the *FT*, Ian Hargreaves held a variety of positions, including Transport Correspondent, Labour Correspondent, New York Correspondent, Social Policy Editor, Resources Editor and Features Editor. He left the *FT* in 1987 to be Managing Editor, then Director, of BBC News and Current Affairs. Returned to the *FT* as Deputy Editor in 1990, before becoming Editor of the *Independent* in 1994. Editor of the New Statesman, 1996–8.

2   Lecture at Cardiff University, 22 February 2007.

3   Boo.com was a website which sold fashion items. It has become shorthand for the kind of online business that burned through a large amount of start-up capital without ever achieving its targets. After the original business went bust the name was bought and boo.com relaunched in May 2007 as a travel site.

4   Personal interview. Charles Wilson was Managing Director of Mirror Group plc from 1992 to 1998, having been Editorial Director of Mirror Group Newspapers from 1991 to 1992. He was Editor of *The Times* from 1985 to 1990, having joined as Deputy Editor in August 1982, and Editor of the *Glasgow Evening Times*, *Glasgow Herald* and the *Scottish Sunday Standard* from 1976 to 1982.

5   Jo Foley was an IPC legend as editor of *Woman*, *Options*, etc.

References

Brook, R. (2007) 'Wallace Aims for "Magazine-style" Mirror' *Media Guardian* 1 February.

Consterdine, G. (2002) *How Magazine Advertising Works* London: Periodical Publishers Association.

Newspaper Society (2005) 'Analysis of the Annual Regional Press Survey Findings for 2004' www.newspapersoc.org.uk/pdf/RP-analysis_04.pdf. Accessed 7 November 2007.

Ponsford, D. (2005) 'Sands Hopes to Inspire Love and Devotion in New Female Readers' *Press Gazette* 3 November.

Thynne, J. (2005) 'Beauty, Fashion, Food, Health and Love: Is that All Women Really Want?' *Independent* 6 November.

Turner, J. (2006) 'The Subtle Distinction of the New Monthly Weekly' *Press Gazette* 23 March.

Wellington, J. (n.d.) www.dmgt.co.uk/aboutdmgt/dmgthistory/themailonsundaystory/. Accessed 4 February 2007.

Chapter 18

Page layout and design

Mark Tattersall

Introduction

Why does page layout and design matter in a newspaper? After all, we buy news-papers to read articles, check sports results or do the crossword. If we want to admire fine design, we'll go to a museum. Not many of us will turn to our friend or colleague on the bus or train, or to our partner on the sofa, and ask: 'Have you seen the way this page is designed?' Rather, the question will be 'How did United manage to lose that?' or 'Have you worked out the anagram in 16 down?'

There are precious few who will admire the typographic quirkiness of the descender in a Trebuchet typeface lower-case 'g', the subtle use of a 0.2pt border to frame a picture, or the carefully calculated use of white space between a head-line and its accompanying text. And why should they? Any journalist worth their salt would surely insist the message is more important than the medium. And they would be right. Any newspaper designer worth their salt would – or, at least, should – tell you the same. Readers read stories, look at pictures, study scorecards or puzzle over crosswords. It's what we're here for.

The successful page designer, layout artist or sub-editor will have anticipated the reader's needs, chosen their typefaces and type sizes, cropped and placed their pictures, and presented their work on a carefully and thoughtfully designed page. Readers notice these things only when they don't work. They will remark on a great exclusive story, they will rave about a stunning photograph, but they will only notice the layout artist's originality, or how assiduous or otherwise a sub-editor has been, when it has gone wrong.

But how does the reader navigate that long article about American foreign policy without getting lost? Why do they pause to linger over a photograph? How can they read that tiny text in a cricket scorecard? How do we ensure they can glance comfortably back and forth between crossword clue and grid (and are the squares big enough for the cruciverbalist to insert their hard-won solution)?

These are the considerations a good page designer or sub-editor should have at the forefront of their minds as they go about their unheralded task of putting a newspaper page together. Some will have a 'templated', or pre-designed, page in which to place the articles, headlines and pictures they are given; others will have the luxury of a blank canvas on which to work from scratch. But all should have the end-user – the reader, the *customer* – and their needs constantly informing their decisions.

Sadly there are too many designers out to impress other designers with a too-clever visual gimmick, too many sub-editors looking for cheers (or groans?) from colleagues for an unwieldy headline pun, without a thought in their heads for how this will play on the page for the person that really matters – again, the reader, the *customer*.

'The customer' – for that is what the reader who buys the newspaper ultimately is – is a term heard all too infrequently, if ever, in a newspaper newsroom. The customer is, or should be, the focus of any successful business, yet somehow the concept seems to get lip-service – at best – in the journalistic process. 'How will the reader read this?' is a question the good reporter will constantly ask as they write an article. They will then tailor their writing for impact, explanation and, above all, clarity. And the good layout artist or page designer will do exactly the same.

So those are the basic principles to which a page designer should work, and we will look at how they are brought into play in different parts of a newspaper, and different types of newspaper – and how those principles have changed in the modern newspaper era.

But first the page designer must understand the sometimes arcane world of typefaces and type sizes, column widths and colours, sub-heads and skylines – the tools and terminology of the trade.

Tools of the trade

There is probably no area of the journalist's craft that has changed as radically as page design with the introduction of computers. A reporter progressed from writing a story on a typewriter to writing it on a rather quieter keyboard with the words appearing on screen rather than a piece of paper – hardly a quantum leap in working practice. For the page designer, the technological revolution which began in the 1980s was just that – a revolution.

Time was, the designer would draw a page design on a piece of paper and this would be prepared for the printing press via a whole raft of crafts, from typesetter to 'pasting-up' a page, to plate-making. Now, the designer will complete all these operations on their own computer screen. But while the methods may have changed, the principles discussed in the introduction are the same, and much of the weird and wonderful terminology of newspaper page make-up has survived.

Typography

Anybody with even the most rudimentary home computer these days will have become familiar with the vast range of typefaces available to the designer. Thousands of styles are available, and all can be modified for boldness or lightness, condensed or expanded, underscored or capitalised or italicised, but all still fall into two broad groups – serif and sans-serif. The simple dictionary definition of a serif is 'a decorative cross line at the end of a stroke' (of a letter), while those with even a bare pass at GCSE French will know that 'sans' means 'without' such a decorative flourish. And in the typographical world, sans-serif is almost always abbreviated to simply 'sans'.

Depending on their tone, newspapers use a mixture of both sorts of typeface or 'fonts' (so-called because in earlier printing days the individual letters used to make up lines of text were stored in bowls similar in shape to the vessel in which baptisms take place). Serif faces are seen as more traditional, and tend to be used for headlines in more staid newspapers. Sans faces are considered 'cleaner' and more modern, and are more commonly used for headlines in the bolder, brasher, usually tabloid 'newspapers' (see chapter 20).

Despite the perceived 'cleanliness' of sans faces, though, they are rarely used as the typeface for standard body text – in other words, that used for the bulk of the actual articles in a newspaper. That is because the decorative flourish of a serif typeface makes each letter more distinctive from its neighbour, an important consideration given the relatively small size of the type in that context. Sans-serif letters are, almost imperceptibly, more difficult to distinguish from each other at small size and therefore take longer to read.

As noted, there are a host of ways in which a typeface can be manipulated. Bold and light and italic are effects that require no explanation, but there are a couple of terms frequently heard on art desks which the newcomer might not be familiar with. 'Kerning' refers to the manipulation – either condensing or expanding – of the space between each individual letter, while changing the 'leading' refers to the space above and below adjacent lines of text. Both can be useful techniques, often to increase impact, but both should be used carefully – overdone, either can reduce legibility, thus making things more difficult for the reader and defeating the object of the exercise.

Other common devices will involve the colour of the headline and the background on which it sits. Although coloured text is still largely the preserve of magazines, rather than newspapers, it is common to see headlines printed in white on a black background (white on black, or 'WOB' in printing terminology), or black on grey (BOG), or any other combination of black, white and shades of grey. These can clearly increase impact, and can also be used to avoid a clash between two adjacent headlines, but should always be used thoughtfully. Overuse will give a page a dense, cluttered and therefore daunting appearance.

Type size

The size of printed type is measured in points, of which there are – as near as makes no difference – 72 to an inch. So, for example, the lettering in a 144pt headline will be two inches, or five centimetres, high. The 'anorak' reader will now place their ruler on a newspaper headline and complain that the lettering is actually slightly smaller than that. This is because, in the days of hot metal printing, the point size referred to the height of the metal 'slug' on which the letter stood, allowing space for the ascenders and descenders on, for instance, a 't' or a 'g'. Nevertheless, the system is more than 200 years old and has happily survived computerisation.

The biggest difference in headline type sizes is clearly between different sorts of newspaper – generally speaking, larger on more popular or tabloid newspapers, smaller on serious or broadsheet newspapers, although, of course, those distinctions become blurred during the recent transition of the more serious British newspapers from broadsheet to compact (see chapter 15).

Where there is less difference is between the point size of 'body type', that used for the text of the actual articles rather than headlines. Depending on the typeface used, this will usually be somewhere between 7½pt and 9pt in most newspapers. Furthermore, and again depending on which typeface is used, body type is an area where 'leading' is an important consideration in the search for a balance between legibility and economy of the designer's most precious commodity – space. An extra half a point of leading is most commonly used so, for instance, 8pt text with an extra half a point of leading would be expressed as '8pt on 8½pt'.

Variations to these sizes come in a variety of areas. The intro – first paragraph of a story – will often be a point or two larger, and often in a bolder typeface, and the second paragraph will sometimes be halfway between the two. So the setting for a page-lead story might be 10pt bold for the intro, 9pt light (or 'roman') for the second paragraph, 8pt light for the body of the article. Results and league tables on a sports page, or listings on a television page, for instance, will often be smaller, but anything below 6pt – 5½pt at the very least – will become almost illegible to the average reader.

As with all areas of the craft, impact on the reader should be the overarching consideration in choosing the size of text: a larger, bolder intro to draw in the reader's eye to the start of the article; smaller text for the body type to optimise the available space; smaller still for detailed results or listings – but always with legibility in mind. And it is always worth bearing in mind that the average age of many newspapers' readerships is increasing – and as that increases, eyesight decreases.

Rules

The narrow lines between different stories on a newspaper page, or the border around the edge of pictures, are always referred to as 'rules' rather than 'lines'. These are rarely more than 1pt in width – very often they are ½pt or even less – although they can sometimes be thicker or in different shades or colours depending on either house style or a special effect being sought, and have two principal uses. On a simple level, they are a visual device to alert the reader – almost subconsciously – that two neighbouring stories are actually separate and distinct from each other; this helps to divide the page into easily digestible pieces. The reverse is also true – the absence of a rule between two articles will suggest the two are in some way connected. But there can be a more important use for rules between two adjacent articles: to make it *explicitly* clear the two are unrelated. Inadvertently omit a rule between an article about a murder suspect and an adjacent but unrelated picture of a well-known celebrity, and the page designer might quickly discover that they, too, are subject to the laws of libel.

Column widths

All newspaper pages are presented in a series of vertical columns. These can vary from page to page and even from story to story within a single page, but all newspaper pages will have a basic, underlying grid of columns. On a broadsheet, this will normally be between eight and ten columns, on a tabloid between six and eight columns. When the *Guardian* adopted their 'Berliner' or mid-size format, they opted for five slightly wider than average columns.

Whatever the number of columns, and therefore the width of those columns, they will have a definite effect on the way the reader reads an article. Fewer columns will obviously mean the text in any given column is wider; more columns will mean narrower text. And even if a newspaper's basic grid has, say, six columns, a designer might set text in four wider columns across that whole width. Any deviation from the standard column grid is known as 'bastard measure'. This is also often employed to accommodate material alongside advertisements, which are often based on a different column grid to editorial.

Column depth or length is almost always measured in centimetres these days, but column width – which, apart from type size, will have the most significant effect on reading – will still be measured in some newspaper offices in a variation on the point system. You might hear a designer refer to a column as being ten 'ems' wide. Technically speaking, an 'em' is the width of a letter 'm' in any point size, so an 8pt 'em' is obviously larger than a 6pt 'em'. Historically, different point sizes had different names, and a 'pica em' referred to the width of a 12pt letter 'm', and it is this that has now become known as simply one 'em'. So some basic maths tells us six 'ems' make an inch or 2.5cm.

If that all sounds a bit complicated, you'll be pleased to know most designers nowadays measure their column widths, as well as depths, in simple centimetres! An average newspaper column will be around ten 'ems', or about 4.2cm, wide, and this is deemed the most comfortable width at which to read newspaper text. There are upper and lower limits, but the important thing to understand is that the narrower a column, the quicker it will be read; the wider it is, the slower it is to read.

So news stories will generally be set across a fairly narrow measure, for a quick and urgent read, while feature material will normally be printed slightly wider – up to about 15 'ems' or 6.3cm – for a more leisurely read, appropriate to the subject matter. But there are those limits: set text too narrow and words will begin to break up and hyphenate too often and become difficult to read; too wide and it becomes difficult to navigate from the end of one line back to the start of the next. As ever, think how easy it is for the reader.

House style

As we have seen, there are an almost infinite number of typefaces, effects and sizes that can be applied to text in a newspaper. And every page designer or layout artist will have their own favourites. That can be a recipe for disaster.

Newspapers will have a strict house style guide, limiting the typefaces, and sizes of typefaces, used on their pages. Often, these will be physically limited by the style-sheet attached to the computerised page template – and with good reason. A newspaper's limited 'basket' of allowable typefaces is what defines its physical appearance and even its tone or 'feel'.

The reader might not realise it consciously, but this consistency helps them identify with 'their' paper. Try it for yourself – cut the masthead off a selection of newspapers and it will still be surprisingly easy to determine which is which.

Designers will sometimes feel constrained or limited by this approach, but the good newspaper designer is one that can design imaginative, original and attractive pages *within* a house style, rather than by breaking that style.

The page designer's quick glossary

Bastard measure: non-standard column width.

Body type: main text of the article.

Byline: reporter's name.

Caption: explanatory text accompanying a picture.

Cross-ref: line of text referring the reader to an associated item elsewhere in the newspaper.

Deck: a line of headline text. A four-deck headline would be printed on four separate lines.

Folio: a line at the top of a page featuring the dateline, page number, the name of the newspaper and often a simple title indicating content, such as 'news', 'comment' or 'sport'.

Headline: large text highlighting the content of an article.

Indent: a small inset for the first line of a paragraph (an intro will normally not be indented, but subsequent paragraphs will).

Intro: the first paragraph of an article.

Leg: term for a column of text.

Masthead: the title of the newspaper at the top of the front page.

Plug: promotional material, usually at the top of the front page. Also known as puff, boost or skyline.

Rule: narrow line separating one story from another.

Sidebar: secondary or explanatory article separate from the main text. Also known as a box-out or panel.

Splash: front page lead story.

Sub-head: secondary and smaller headline.

Wing: column on extreme edge of page.

The page

So now armed with a basic understanding of the aims of the page designer, and the terminology and tools, where does the designer with the blank canvas begin?

They will have one or more stories to be displayed in an orderly and logical way, some more important than others, some with pictures or sidebars, some without. From this jumble, the designer must create a page which is easy for the reader to navigate – understanding what goes with what, and where to go next – and be balanced and visually attractive.

The key to this is understanding the principle of 'entry points'. These are literally the points at which a reader enters a page, and the two main ones will almost always be the headline on the page lead article, and the main picture on the page. For that reason, the lead headline should be markedly larger than any other – if another headline is of similar size the reader will not know where to go first, and will be immediately confused. Similarly, two pictures of similar weight will compete for attention and reduce the impact of both.

It is good to have several entry points into a page – the designer's aim should be to retain the interest of the reader for as long as possible – but the entry points should be graded in size and impact, and – equally importantly – be well spaced out. If all the main impact elements of a page are packed together in one area, the remainder of the page will inevitably be grey, uninviting and daunting by comparison.

One annoying habit of newspaper readers should always be kept in mind by the page designer or sub-editor: as soon as they happen upon something that doesn't interest them – a dull or poorly written headline, a boring picture or a confusing layout – they have a nasty habit of turning the page immediately, thus missing a whole host of other items on the page they leave behind. It is therefore the designer's duty to keep the reader engaged by giving each article the care it deserves, an appropriate weight of headline and size of picture, and to ensure each element of the page is balanced in relation to its neighbours. That is particularly important on inside pages, where there are almost always more elements to balance. The mindset on the front page has to be slightly different. When designing an inside page, or spread of pages, the designer is attempting to present material in a way that retains the reader's interest. On the front page, you have to grab that attention in the first place.

In the days when many more readers had the newspaper delivered through their letterboxes, this was less of an imperative – the newspaper had, after all, already been sold. Now, the vast majority of newspapers are sold off the newsagent or supermarket shelf, where the front page must fight for attention alongside myriad rivals.

That means front page design, while still needing to follow all the above guidelines, also becomes an exercise in selling. You want your newspaper to shout 'buy me' at the potential reader; otherwise all the care lavished on the rest of the paper is for nought. The traditional way of doing this would be with an eye-catching headline on an exclusive front page splash, accompanied by an attractive or startling picture. But the proliferation and availability of news from other media means newspapers nowadays must work harder to sell their wares. Rarely in the modern world does the news consumer learn of a news-break first from their newspaper. More likely they will have been alerted by radio, 24-hour news television, internet sites or mobile phone alerts.

Changes in content and tone to handle this dilemma are dealt with elsewhere in this book, but there is an impact on the designer too: the front page promotional panel – or plug or puff or boost or skyline – has become critical to selling newspapers. In the British national morning newspaper market, this is most obvious, and perhaps most extreme, at weekends, when these panels will dominate front pages. Tabloids, particularly, will devote the bulk of their front pages to promotional material.

Whether promoting a free magazine, book or CD giveaways, or advertising exclusive content within the paper, they will frequently dwarf the space and atten‍tion given to the splash, let alone the masthead. For the designer on the dwindling number of broadsheet newspapers, it is important to constantly keep in mind where the paper is folded – little point in having promotional matter 'below the fold' when it will be hidden from view on the news-stand.

All this means new skills, and a new mindset, for the designer. In many ways it means adopting the methods of the magazine designer, where cover-lines (the text on a magazine cover which promotes content) and cover-mounts (the free gifts such as CDs or books fixed to the front of a magazine) have long been employed to shift copies off shelves. As with many other areas of newspaper activity, it isn't about news at all any more. It's about selling, and the page designer has a central role to play.

Conclusion

The student journalist with their heart set on a career as a writer or reporter may now be wondering why they have been told all of that. Surely, they will think, it has little to do with the business of reporting and writing. They would be wrong.

Teaching production skills to a trainee journalist not only gives them an extra skill – another string to their bow in a world that increasingly demands multi-skilling – it also gives them an understanding of the processes, which in turn should inform the way they construct their articles. Understanding the page design and sub-editing process should, for example, make clear why a sidebar might be desirable, why an intro shouldn't be much longer than 25 words, or why the key facts in their article should be right up front, and not buried somewhere near the end.

Nothing will infuriate an editor more than a reporter who does not read their own paper or, worse, sees that their copy has been altered and does not learn from that change. It will imply a reporter who does not care about their work, who does not want to improve. So if you really want to know, ask a sub.

References

Evans, H. (1974) *Handling Newspaper Text* London: Heinemann.

Evans, H. (1984) *Newspaper Design* London: Heinemann.

Frost, C. (2003) *Designing For Newspapers and Magazines* London: Routledge.

Frost, C. (2005) 'Design For Print Media' in Keeble, R. (Ed.) *Print Journalism: A Critical Introduction* London: Routledge, pp.189–224.

Garcia, M. (1993) *Contemporary Newspaper Design: A Structural Approach* London: Prentice-Hall.

Garcia, M. and Stark, P. (1991) *Eye on the News* St Petersburg: Poynter Institute.

Giles, V. and Hodgson, F. W. (1996) *Creative Newspaper Design* (2nd edition) London: Focal Press.

Hutt, A. and James, B. (1989) *Newspaper Design Today: A Manual for Professionals* London: Lund Humphries.

Chapter 19

Online editions: newspapers and the 'new' news

Jim Hall

Media convergence and the shift online have radically changed the way we read our news and where we get it from. In the time it once took to browse our favourite daily paper and watch the nine o'clock news we can now skim an encyclopaedic range of complementary news sources. A rapid survey of the day's news online, any day of the week, produces a dizzying diversity of style, form, content and perspective. As I write in 2007, the front pages both of the *Guardian Unlimited* and CNN.com offer a report (augmented by CNN with an extended video report) on huge increases in Chinese military spending. English.Al-Jazeera.net makes no mention of that but leads with a report on the opening of the 'National People's Conference' in Beijing and an article on the new generation of American nuclear warheads. Reports from Iraq and Afghanistan absorb the front pages of the national press in the west and the English-language pages of Al-Jazeera, yet, for today, those wars have left the front pages of Tehran's newspapers' websites and those of other Islamic countries. They seem more interested in relations with Eastern Europe and the Arab world. On the other hand, the present global slide in stock-market prices is interesting editors everywhere, even in Cornwall, where the *Western Morning News*, the most established newspaper in Britain's south-west (1860), leads with a highly competent video round-up of the local news and a live-to-screen report on the region's sporting prospects for the week.

Many of these stories include a link enabling me to contribute my own thoughts and one more click allows me to read other readers' responses. I can also click to audio-visual material including video reports and galleries of photographs as well as significant archives of related material. Twenty years ago none of this would have been possible; however, even then, media commentators were discussing media and technological convergence and how they would affect the future of news journalism.

One factor that few of them foresaw was that news journalism would no longer be the exclusive domain of the media companies. My brief trawl for the day's news might also include material that even a decade ago would not have been considered news at all: blogs, written by journalists and non-journalists alike, giving me context and the 'news behind the news', and the citizen journalism that is available through sites like english.ohmynews.com but which also appears in the mainstream news media, expanding and contextualising it. Finally, drawing on all the above sources, there are the news aggregators such as Google News which index the day's news for me according to how many other readers have clicked to it. As search engines become more sophisticated consumers are increasingly able to put together their own aggregations of sources. Online editions operate in very different circumstances to their print antecedents.

The 'new' news

In 2006 many of Britain's most established newspaper titles, including the *Financial Times*, the *Daily Telegraph* and *The Times*, announced plans for the imminent integration of their print and online newsrooms. At the same moment newspaper management around the world was introducing general reskilling programmes that would enable journalists to produce multimedia news. Lead stories would henceforth be presented with embedded video and audio reports, and print news itself would become a second-line product, repurposed from the online, multimedia journalism that appears to arrive at no cost to its consumers on screens of every size. The news cycle itself had already become a historical curiosity in a 24/7 information world with rolling deadlines. Newspapers are no longer 'put to bed'. The move resonated through every aspect of the newspaper business: its traditional financial models, its relationship with its sources, the manner in which its markets work, and its journalistic forms; the way in which news stories are told. Fundamental shifts have occurred in news production and consumption. The age of newsroom convergence has finally arrived.

News on the internet, while it had preceded the World Wide Web by more than a decade through text services offered on subscription by partnerships between internet service providers and news organisations, really took off with the arrival of web and graphical interfaces such as Mosaic which allowed the seamless dissemination of integrated text and image. In 1994, as Tim Berners-Lee's innovation rapidly found applications beyond the world's scientific community, newspapers such as *Kommunal Rapport* in Norway, the *Palo Alto Weekly* and the *Raleigh News & Observer* in North America and the *Daily Telegraph* in Britain were offering free news online. A year before that, AOL had offered a subscription edition of the *San Jose Mercury News* on the web; however, the rise of free news made such ventures anachronistic practically before they were launched. By the late 1990s most newspapers around the world, with the exception of some belonging to corporate sceptics such as Rupert Murdoch's News Corporation, offered a free online edition.

For print journalists the new medium necessitated a complete rethink of the values and processes through which they understood their work. The publication or news cycle, for instance, became redundant. As with television news services, breaking stories were disseminated as they broke but with a depth of contextual material that television couldn't muster. In 1999, when two students of Columbine School in Littleton, Colorado attacked the school with guns and explosives the event had been reported around the world even as the attackers were establishing themselves in the school. For the next few weeks the world's press was able to offer developments as they happened by quoting from or directly linking to the websites of local newspapers and broadcasters around Denver. Print news, even in Colorado, could not begin to keep up, and, in terms of the development of the story, was reduced to providing digests of events, context and background. Even so, news production systems geared to print meant that online editions, no matter how urgently they were updated, still comprised material that had been repurposed from copy prepared for print or transcribed directly from broadcast media. That process was dismissively referred to, even in 1999, as 'content shovelling'. Denver's newspapers' websites did, however, expand their coverage to include views and comments, photographs, messages of consolation and eyewitness accounts of the event, in innovations that were partly intended to support and comfort the local community. Some of these elements signalled what was shortly to become known as citizen journalism. The online press found that it was able to deliver initiatives and information which directly affected the aftermath of the tragedy. International readerships, on the other hand, were able to comprehend the story through its local contexts. Online editions were beginning to give indications of a potential that would be realised repeatedly in the reporting of the important stories of the succeeding decade.

The failure to realise fully the potential of online journalism during the 1990s was overdetermined. First very few newspapers had the web-server capacity to meet the peak demand that the important stories of the time imposed. When the Twin Towers were attacked in 2001 news servers were simply not able to meet the demands placed on them. More importantly, as newspaper editors became more imaginative about their online editions, as the emerging conventions for online news came to be understood and accepted by journalists and consumers alike, and as more and more readers, especially younger ones, transferred their custom to the web as their main, now free, news source, print circulations, already on the decline due to a range of cultural and economic reasons, plummeted. That decline affected the confidence of advertisers. This raised very real questions among journalists, editors and proprietors about the economic viability of the new news. Were they debasing their primary asset? Even in the new millennium, there were those who simply avoided the crisis by shutting their eyes to the new medium. Rupert Murdoch admitted in 2005, 'In the face of this revolution, … we've been slow to react. We've sat by and watched while our newspapers have gradually lost circulation.' But even the most visionary newspaper proprietors were right to be wary of the web.

The problems around advertising on the web were several. Its effects were very difficult to quantify and in its first decade there was some uncertainty even about how it worked. Various forms were tried, most of which were based on the principle of drawing consumers to the advertisers' information pages, thereby potentially losing them to the newspapers' own pages. The advertisers rapidly realised that newspapers were perhaps not the best vehicles to encourage consumers to link to their adverts. If there is a true mass-media form in the new century it isn't necessarily newspapers. Other online vehicles, such as search engines, portals and peer-to-peer media-sharing applications, auction sites, even, on occasion, blogs, seem able to draw as much traffic as the newspapers' websites and more consistently. The problems around declining income from advertising and reduced circulations coincided precisely with the effect of disintermediation, the removal of intermediaries in the journalistic supply chain: the realisation that journalism had lost exclusive access to its primary sources of news and that its own readers were frequently beating it to the important stories. Not only had journalism lost first-call on its primary backers, it also seemed to have lost its *raison d'être*.

Multimedia technologies and media convergence have changed the expectations of news consumers. Once the carrier technology had evolved the bandwidth to carry video and audio along with the images and text which had brought newspaper readers their news for the past century, and once that technology was available in most homes, certainly in the more affluent parts of the world, consumers changed the ways in which they read their news. The important global news providers of the early twenty-first century looked set to become organisations such as www.news.bbc.co.uk and www.CNN.com: the broadcasters of the previous century. If the newspaper titles were to survive in this new world they realised that they would have to completely embrace multi-platform and multimedia storytelling. Would they be able to compete with the established broadcasters who were also rapidly putting their own news operations online? Perhaps as importantly, would there be any difference between the way in which broadcasters used the moving image and the way newspapers used it? In the case of some cross-media corporations there was an abrupt reversion to the shovelling of their own broadcast video material, created for completely different contexts, into their newspaper pages. Those companies with backgrounds in newspapers, however, while they could simply use agency feeds, also tended to experiment with new approaches to video and audio. Newspaper journalists, who tend to use video to expand and contextualise their stories rather than lead them, are able to work 'on a different level from broadcast TV. The new dimension is intimacy. ... The model of the TV interview with its list of questions is forgotten. This is a print journalist at work, gently prompting and listening' (Grant-Adamson 2006).

In 2006 Gannett (with the possible exception of Tokyo-based Yomiuri Shimbun, the world's largest newspaper company) instructed its newsrooms in the UK, the 300 Newsquest titles, that with immediate effect their titles would lead with their web editions and that henceforth print would effectively be repurposed from web, inverting the relationship through which we have come to understand newspapers. This turnabout seemed to follow the newspapers' readers. When the Buncefield oil depot was destroyed by fire early one Sunday in December 2005 the *Hemel Hempstead Gazette* (Johnston Press), which is not published until the middle of the week, implemented a web first strategy which trebled its website traffic immediately and 'by Monday morning five of the 10 principal links on the first page of Google News search were to hemeltoday.co.uk' (Grant-Adamson 2005).

In addition to this immediacy the new approach to news journalism means, as Roy Greenslade (2006) has said, that:

> For the journalists, ... there will be no split of functions between print and web. And, in addition to providing text, they will also transmit audio and video for podcasts and vodcasts. And many staff are already building their new skills, appearing on camera to read their own scripts – downloaded on to a self-operated auto-cue – and cutting their own footage after barely an hour's training.

Journalism commentators have been forecasting the changes that will emerge from these practices since the 1980s. By 1997 John Pavlik was able to articulate the development of news online in three stages, beginning with shovelware:

> News content on the Internet has been evolving through three stages. In stage one ... online journalists mostly repurpose content from their mother ship. In stage two ... journalists create original content and augment it with such additives as hyperlinks ... interactive features such as search engines ... and a degree of customization – the ability to choose what categories of news and information you receive.
>
> Stage three ... is characterized by original news content designed specifically for the Web as a new medium of communication. Stage three will be characterized by a willingness to rethink the nature of a 'community' online and, most important, a willingness to experiment with new forms of storytelling. Often this is 'immersive' storytelling, which allows you to enter and navigate through a news report in ways different from just reading it.

We are only now getting the first indications of just what those emergent forms will look and sound like. Those of us wishing to document the changes in contemporary news journalism must accept that, at best, our accounts are provisional. The first generation of the technologies that deliver the new news are now firmly in place and the so-called web-natural forms that can fully exploit those technologies are beginning to emerge. What has become clear is that any discussion of 'online news' or 'online editions' is an anachronism. When we talk about news journalism we are referring to a set of technologically and, increasingly, formally, converged media and forms.

Emergent forms

The web is rapidly changing the basic forms of news writing in terms of how it is read, how it looks and how it works. Stories have become shorter and are constructed to conform to the demands of search engines. They routinely employ graphics (sometimes animated), video and audio, frequently embedded into stories, and, of course, with the replacement of the indented first line to signify a new paragraph by explicit white space, the screen looks completely different from the printed newspaper page. Some home pages continue to use the first paragraph of the story as the teaser that will encourage readers to click through to the body text. Others, in the knowledge that most readers will skim the home page, only clicking into one or two stories, use a summary instead.

Consumers employ a range of devices or platforms from which to read their news. Stories are produced to be accessible to all of them. For the moment most consumers read from computer screens, although news is also downloadable as podcasts (for phones and MP3 players), in combinations of text, audio and image for phone browsers, and for the ultra-light reading tablets known as electronic paper, usually used in association with phones. And of course those wood-pulp devices which many of us grew up with, so effective for carrying print and image, are likely to be around for at least another 40 years. The point of departure for the multi-platform revolution was the development of the World Wide Web, conceived in 1990 and in general use in the developed world by 1994.

The enabling innovation of the web and its outgrowths such as online news was the hypertext link: the combination of anchor and target attributes which, in principle, allow any piece of information on the web – text, images, audio, video – to click to any other piece of information. To describe the resulting text, as many researchers of the web have done, as non-linear is not strictly true. However, any linearity of information is determined here by the reader in a way that might seem less constrained than with print, or such unequivocally linear media as audio or video. What is certain is that hyperlinks can enable the reader to share the organisation of information with the writer and extend narratives beyond their original intent.

In the mid-1990s, as journalism began its transition to the web, it employed hyperlinks in a variety of ways. Designers and journalists could provide depth by suffixing stories with related material, providing readers with their history and development. It rapidly became clear, especially for the newspapers of record such as the *Telegraph* in the UK and the *New York Times* in the US, that, while the news of the day seemed to have little or no face value in the new economy, the archives which gave news its context and which were coincidentally 'the first draft of history' (the phrase is attributed to Philip Graham, publisher of the *Washington Post, 1946–63*), now carried a significant market value. Titles extended that archival record to include material from the time before the web. In 2006 the *New York Times* completed its online archive: 13 million searchable articles, back to 1851, available at $4.95 each. More importantly, every article now published by the title is appended with links to a set of recent articles and further searches of related material back to 1996.

In the early days of online journalism key words and phrases in the text itself would be linked to ancillary material to explain and expand them. It was rapidly realised that readers did not tend to use these embedded links and in some cases merely found them irritating. News, unlike history, does not require footnotes.

Journalists could also provide their work with additional depth by linking to sources and other related material beyond their own websites. In 1998, linked directly from news commentary on the federal grand jury report on aspects of President Clinton's second presidency, consumers could read every word of the 445 pages of the Starr Report, placed on the web by Judge Kenneth Starr's own office. Starr had bypassed the news media to take what he saw as the problematic issues around the Clinton administration directly to the American electorate. Disintermediation gave news journalism pause for thought. If the actors in news stories were themselves going to place their stories, raw and unmediated, before the public, what was now the role of the journalist? Henceforth, apart from advertising, links that took readers away from the newspaper's own website were treated with circumspection and appeared much less commonly. In a few instances the only aspect of interactivity left on the screen is the email link allowing readers to contact the editor or writer. The economic factors which partly determine the conventions emerging around online news, increasingly help to limit its potential.

Those conventions are, perhaps, most elegantly exemplified in the *Guardian*'s website, www.guardian.co.uk. It uses a left-justified three-column layout centred on the screen for its home page and section headings. The central column (usually comprising either two- or three-fifths of the space available to the design) carries a list of headlines and sub-headings which will click to individual articles and features laid out in screens of two columns. The left-hand column of the home page carries links to other sections of the site and picks of the day, while the right-hand one links to other news services offered by the title, display ads, subscription services, sponsored features, events and offers, and information about the title. In terms of clarity and legibility the design, which in its *Guardian* articulation is defined by the white space on the sides of the screen, has become the dominant form. The precise disposition of the columns will be associated with individual house styles – the difference between news.bbc.co.uk and edition.cnn.com – but the basic structure, usually referred to as the 'Brody Blocks' after Neville Brody, the graphic designer who relaunched the *Guardian Unlimited* website in 1998, remains more or less constant. Research Studios, Brody's company, describes the design as:

> a modular system based around 'blocks' placed together on a strict grid. These blocks could be used as 'containers' for pure colour, image or type. They become flexible anchor points to which the rest of the page was composed. The [*Guardian*] site consisted of many subsections, known as the [*Guardian*] Unlimited network, some of which were often complete websites in themselves. These 'micro' sites needed to retain their own separate identity, whilst simultaneously appearing to belong to the 'whole' that was the *Guardian Unlimited* brand.
>
> (Research Studios 2007)

Developments of the layout, such as the Swedish *Svenska Dagbladet* (www.svd.se) extend it to four columns, reserving the far right column for advertisements.

Other models certainly exist; however, in online news design, less does seem to amount to more. Any comparison between designs based on the Brody Blocks and others such as the the *New York Times* must favour the former in terms of readability. By trying to pack as many links as possible on to the front page, including advertisements and repetition, www.nytimes.com can also be rather confusing. It frequently carries around 100 more links than the *Guardian Unlimited*'s front page.

Revenues and readers

The newspaper is now in the process of transforming itself from a print-web artefact to a web-print one, a hybrid in which the print component can be expected to diminish fast. The relationship of this mutating form with its advertisers forces questions about the viability of newspapers. Even when we have factored out those increasingly attractive entertainment media, the web brings newspapers into direct competition with the news broadcasters as well as the bloggers and citizen journalists who Robert Kuttner has described as the 'army of amateurs' (2007). At a time when proprietors are still seeking a 20 per cent plus return from newspapers in the UK and North America, questions around advertising become paramount. The migration of the classifieds to specialist niche providers seems to have been stemmed by the diversification of newspaper companies into initiatives such as Fish4, created by a consortium of the UK's regional newspaper proprietors, and the *Guardian*'s Workthing Limited (now sold to a specialist recruitment company). Even allowing for the uncertainties about just how much of advertising's spend will go to newspapers in the future, Fish4 allowed a large group of regional titles to remain in the highly lucrative classified jobs, cars and houses markets and proved that it was possible for the newspaper industry to retain its foothold in advertising on the web. But advertisers require verifiable circulations and those will only hold up if newspaper titles are able to forge a sustainable role in the new information economy.

The online edition is an established fact. Whether their inclination was to embrace interactivity or not, managers and editors now find themselves forced to consider the impact of the reciprocal relationships that have always been implied between news journalism and its consumers. News is no longer a one-way process nor can news workers determine the news agenda as print and the broadcast media once allowed. Interventionist public or community journalisms, which before the web were regarded by the larger news organisations as marginal and unprofitable, and citizen journalism, have helped to show journalism how to make news a fully interactive process. If our present titles are to survive it must also be a profitable one.

Journalism's dual role in the information age is to act as an informed moderator for that interaction and the cartographer of the information that feeds it. Information by itself, no matter how new it is, is not news. For it to become news it must be integrated into a discourse, contextualised and organised – mapped. Google News has shown us how far even the best aggregators and news portals are from being able to do that. As long as citizens continue to invest in their communities there will be a role for journalism. Unfortunately, as advertising appears to be discovering, while that role will certainly outlast print and paper, its long-term future, as we currently recognise it, is by no means guaranteed.

References

Allan, S. (2006) *Online News: Journalism and the Internet* Maidenhead and New York: Open University Press.

Boczkowski, P. J. (2005) *Digitizing the News: Innovation in Online Newspapers (Inside Technology)* Cambridge, MA: The MIT Press.

Grant-Adamson, A. (2005) 'Slick Operators' *Guardian Unlimited* December 14 www.guardian.co.uk/uk_news/story/0,,1666991,00.html. Accessed 10 February 2007.

Grant-Adamson, A. (2006) 'Guardian hits the Road to Multimedia Storytelling' www.wordblog.co.uk/2006/11/11/guardian-hits-the-road-to-multimedia-storytelling/. Accessed 15 February 2007.

Greenslade, R. (2006) 'Leaping into the Future at the *Telegraph's* Camelot' blogs.guardian.co.uk/greenslade/2006/09/post_2.html. Accessed 20 January 2007.

Hall, J. (2001) *Online Journalism: A Critical Primer* London and Sterling: Pluto Press.

Kuttner, R. (2007) 'The Race' *Columbia Journalism Review* February www.cjr.org/issues/2007/2/Kuttner.asp. Accessed 24 February 2007.

Li, X. (Ed.) (2006) *Internet Newspapers: The Making of a Mainstream Medium* New Jersey: Lawrence Erlbaum Associates.

Murdoch, R. (2005) Speech to the American Society of Newspaper Editors (ASNE), 13 April, www.newscorp.com/news/news_247.html Accessed 12 January 2007.

Pavlik, J. (1997) 'The Future of Online Journalism: A Guide to Who's Doing What' *Columbia Journalism Review* archives.cjr.org/year/97/4/online.asp. Accessed 10 December 2006.

Research Studios (2007) www.researchstudios.com/home/003-projects/theguardian/theguardian.php. Accessed 8 January 2007.

Chapter 20

Headlines

Eamonn Rafferty

Mentioning the term 'headlines' is invariably a cue for those infamous examples from the tabloids, usually the *Sun*: 'Gotcha', 'Freddie Starr Ate My Hamster'... 'Paddy Pantsdown'. Here, the headline is remembered long after the details of the original story (in Starr's case, a concoction) are forgotten. Or occasionally the unintentional: 'Drunk gets nine months in violin case', where the headline's construction is at fault.

But it should be the other way round: readers should recall the story rather than the headline because the latter is there to 'tempt' people to read the full report – a sort of shop window. And, in keeping with the analogy, if it says in the shop window that shirts are, say, £15.99, then that is the price you expect to pay in the shop. So, should we apply the same criteria to headlines? Should they be a faithful, literal interpretation of the story? Most people have long abandoned the idea (even if they held it) that tabloid headlines serve that function. We don't really expect the *Sun*'s headlines to match up in the £15.99 stakes; instead, we look to them to offer a little light relief through puns and alliteration. They tend to be an 'end' in themselves, a 'take' on the story, rather than a signpost or precis of the report. The story tends to serve the headline, not the other way round.

Tabloid 'splash' headlines are often 'arted' into the page. That is, the headline is thought up first, usually by the 'backbench' (the senior editorial executives: chief sub, night editor, etc.), designed to fit the page and then the copy moulded to suit. Even then, great skill and verbal dexterity is required to make them 'work': 'Orf with their heads' (a headline about how Prince Charles' staff boil seven eggs, cut the tops off and allow him to choose which one he wants). Often, these headlines are brilliant in their ingenuity and composition; the only problem is that the story is usually contrived, or chosen because its tenuous subject matter lends itself to a clever headline. Tabloid headline writing exists in a different world from that of the 'qualities' (*Guardian*, *Telegraph*, *The Times*, etc). Quality papers do not usually have the luxury of 'back-written heads' – certainly not on the run-of-the-mill news pages, where type size and column widths, and decks (the number of lines) all determine the types of words that can be used. They tend to be more literal, and in that sense, conform to the £15.99 principle. And what's more, they are *expected* to. They are also more utilitarian – few remember a *Guardian* headline) – and tend to form a backdrop to the story.

Qualities

At the risk of imitating Hamlet without the Prince, I intend to focus on the qualities, rather than the tabloids. The tabloids and the qualities do not just inhabit differing physical spaces in terms of subject, neologisms, typography and layout (the 'compacts' notwithstanding), but a different cultural space as well. The function and, therefore, the status of the sub-editors on both differ. On the tabloids, the subs are 'king' (rarely queen) and don't they know it? Here, the 'copy' serves them. The story is there to be moulded into a desirable shape, from which a headline can be fashioned. Reporters play second fiddle in this process, often treated as glorified gatherers of facts that are then finely honed by subs. As a result, tabloids are often known as a 'sub's paper', in effect run by a bunch of superb technicians with barely concealed distain for writers.

On the qualities, life is very different. Here, the writer is king (and, yes, queen). The senior editorial executives are usually from a writing background and they are keen to allow that side of the paper to flourish. Here, the sub-editor serves the copy. Reporters dislike any 'tampering' with 'their' story and also seem to think they can write a better headline. Whether consciously or not, this attitude seeps into the forlorn melodrama that often characterises subs' working lives. That said, subs are much better and more experienced than their writing colleagues usually think. Partly, that is because much sub-editing is done *sotto voce*; many reporters are unaware that their copy has been 'subbed' – their tenses changed, their misrelated participles corrected and the possessive gerund used where it should be. This 'nip-and-tuck' approach is often the way of subbing; there is always much fussing over 'style' and the finer points of grammar, even if subs *d'une certain age* are always moaning of a drop in standards (the virtual elimination of 'that' in the use of transitive verbs, for example. Or the lack of distinction between 'that' and 'which').

I remember, as if it were yesterday, my first night subbing, about 25 years ago. In the middle of my 'shift', a rather taciturn sub-editor became suddenly animated and jumped up, ran downstairs to the composing room (where the compositors typeset sheets of 'copy'). Later, I found out that his urgency was prompted by the realisation that he had omitted an apostrophe from the name of a football field (it was St Paul's, not St Pauls). I was astonished at this attention to detail and realised there and then that this 'subbing' business was a serious one and I had better shape up, or ship out. From that day till now, I have devoured books on journalism, grammar, layout – you name it. I watched how my headlines were changed by the dreaded 'Revise sub', looking for ways to improve my efforts. Along the way, many people have helped me; some, as was their way, a little more bluntly than others ('what sort of f****** headline do you call that?').

Signposts

Headlines are a necessary part of any story – can you imagine a newspaper without them? They serve, first, as a signpost for readers, telling them what the most important stories are; those with the bigger headline size. Second, they act as a precis of the story, or at least they should, typically summarising the 'gist' of the report. Often, these nine or ten words are all a reader will see, given that surveys suggest that few people spend more than 40 minutes on a paper. Therefore, the headlines will have certain 'trigger' or 'key' words to signify 'who' or 'what' the story is about. Words such as 'PM', 'No. 10', 'Brown', etc. easily denote a political story. 'Iraq' and 'Iran' invariably signify a 'bad-news' report of some sort. Though this wasn't always the case. Headline words tend to 'evolve' with the story, and at a certain point, trigger some sort of expectation in the reader as to what the report is about.

But this 'evolution' takes time and it is always a matter of debate within newspapers as to when a certain headline word has reached this 'recognition' point. For example, Tony Blair wasn't always 'Blair' in headlines – it took time for that. Fifteen years ago, he was only a shadow minister trying to emerge into the limelight and his policy initiatives would have been more likely to have been headlined 'Labour's answer to crime…' or 'Labour would…'.

The first time I subbed a story about Aids, probably about 1984–5, it was about a deadly virus that was hitting the gay community in San Francisco. Then the headlines tended to be about 'Deadly virus', but over time – I don't know how long – Aids came to mean 'deadly virus' in headline terms.

The same has happened with Bird Flu today. Now 'HN51' is more likely to appear in headlines than Bird Flu as, somewhere along the way, there has been a 'tipping point'. Again, I don't know precisely when, but it is now 'safe' for headline writers to use 'HN51' without ambiguity. That means the rest of the headline can easily move to the 'action', such as 'Fears over HN51 spread', because this triggers the assumption of something serious. Also, companies such as Google, eBay and YouTube are all common names in headlines, but they too started out life as 'Online search engine' or 'Online auction site' in headlines. At some point, they metamorphosed into just plain Google and eBay. The skill is knowing *when* that transition has occurred.

Headlines are still denominated in 'points' – a throwback from the older printing days. Basically, 72 points equal an inch; 36pt = half an inch, and so on. At one time (long ago), headlines were rarely above 72pt, even on the tabloids. But current tabloid headlines are regularly twice that size with page leads well over 100pt. Even quality papers' headlines have been growing, often in inverse proportion to the importance of the story. One of the biggest headlines I remember from working on the *Daily Telegraph* was 'Hanging offence', right across page 3. It was an artful concoction about some Bufton Tufton-types at war with their parish council over the size of hanging baskets. It only 'worked' (if at all) because of the headline – the story served no other function because it was so contrived.

Comment

With the recent arrival of the 'compact' – *The Times, Independent, Guardian* – headlines have also become larger and more commenty: 'How I cheated death' – that sort of thing. These headlines have to be big to work:

How I cheated death (24pt) is not as effective as:

How I cheated death

(48pt). And that's relatively small in headline terms and would certainly not be a 'lead' headline in any of the papers. For subs, the obvious thing about headline size is, the bigger it is, the fewer words you can say. The next big variable is column width. A headline across six or seven columns will be able to muster a stronger, visual presence. For example, 'Blair defiant over Iraq' fits neatly across five or six columns in 60pt to 74pt (horizontal style). If that story were a two-column lead, it would cause problems both visually and with the count.

**Blair
defiant
over
Iraq**

This is called a 'four-deck' vertical headline and one can see that its impact is less than that of the horizontal version. Also, the headline leaves a lot of 'white space' on each line (or 'is shy'), which subs try to avoid. The problem is that **Blair** and **defiant** are unlikely to fit across most two columns in 60pt or 64pt. The only way to 'fill' out the line is to add an '**is**' or a '**still**' (**Blair is…** or, **Blair still…**) on the 'top deck' – the first line. But headline writers try to avoid these auxiliaries and their use is often a sign that the headline is shy. In headline terms, **is, still, again, will**, etc. rarely add to the meaning and are signs that the subs had difficulty filling out the headline.

One solution is to use horizontal headlines all the time, but that would lead to the pages being 'stacked' – and impinge on the layout, which should use a variety of shapes and photographs to 'tempt' readers into the story. Layout is a subtly evolving landscape, where the objective is constantly to freshen a paper's look without being too radical.

Designers

All sorts of page 'furniture' are constantly tweaked – straplines, tint boxes, typefaces – to that end, and most newspapers employ 'designers' to oversee that work. Subs often complain that these people dream up various changes that are impractical or do not suit the live newspaper environment. Back at the coalface, subs say, the real job is still trying to summarise often complex stories in a dozen words. Anything that complicates that process (especially designers) is to be avoided. (Of course, not you Chris.)

Over the years, words such as, **hits, slams, tot, perv, cop, chopper, PM, No. 10, probes**, have become part of the subs' canon because they are 'small' words, in terms of 'count' – the number of letters you can get into each column. But these neologisms have also tended to become words of choice, even when a larger word would fit (inquiry, instead of probe). So, **Cash for honours probe** is normally preferred to **Cash for honours inquiry** because 'probe' has been colonised as a 'subs' word', along with other phrases, initially because of space, but later they become part of the landscape.

Take, for example, a story about a police force that did not fully investigate the activities of a sex offender and as a result he was allowed to slip through the net and carried out further crimes. This resulted in a headline in one tabloid newspaper of **Perv bungle cops blamed**. Inexplicably, this headline manages to do two things. One is that it somehow succeeds, to me anyway, in telling the reader that somebody somewhere who had been labelled a pervert has done something that the police should have stopped. But uncoupled from the page and the story, it also serves as an example of how headline language has become so mangled that it becomes a parody of itself.

The 'count'

Before computers, subs had a headline sheet that 'counted' off each headline style and size per column. Each letter was given a numerical denomination, in relation to 'E' – the base letter. Therefore, 'i', 'l' and 't' had a half-character count (because they were smaller than an 'e') and the likes of 'w' and 'm' about one-and-a-half or two. Count sheets showed how many characters one could get in a typical column (single columns in the old eight-column pages tended to be about 4.1cm wide; 8.4cm for a double column; 13cm for a triple, depending on the gutters). Counts also differed from serif typefaces (Times Roman and Bold) and sans faces (Arial, Helvetica). Few headlines are less than 14pt, so the old 'count sheet' might have the following:

Times Roman 14pt (serif)

Times Roman (Bold) 14pt

Arial (14pt) (sans)

Arial Bold (14pt)

It is easy to see the different widths these particular fonts make in serif and sans typefaces, light and bold in 14pt; obviously the bigger the headline type, the fewer letters one could get in each column.

Also, most headlines follow a particular construction, which avoids the use of verb auxiliaries (is, are, etc.) and possessive pronouns (his, her). These are *inferred* in the headline but they also save valuable space, such as: **Man takes dog to vet** in everyday-speak is really **A man takes his dog to the vet**. Notice, too, how headlines all tend to have present tense verbs: **Blair slams critics**, even though the report is about something that *has* happened, not something that is *currently* happening. This convention is widely followed, the few exceptions being when the report concerns a forthcoming court case, when it is common to say **Man killed wife in drunken rage** to denote that this incident happened some time in the past.

Approval

Headlines are the most obvious sign of sub-editors at work. These nine or ten words are supposed to tell readers the essence of the story. In truth, however, no one *really* knows for certain what encourages readers to read a story. It is most likely a combination of things but sub-editors are always told that the headline is a key component. Headlines, however, are written by sub-editors *for* other sub-editors' approval and though the reader is often invoked, few subs ever write a headline with them in mind. Only the very good and the very bad headlines seem to attract readers' attention, judging by the editor's postbag.

That said, certain conventions are rigidly enforced in most papers with this mythical reader in mind. One that always puzzled me was 'doubles'. This means that a headline word can only be used once on a page. If you have two stories about a bank, then the word 'bank' can only appear once on the page. A suitable synonym has to be found (lender). It is surprising how ardently this 'rule' is policed on most subs' desks. No one has a genuinely credible reason for it, other than it is done not to confuse the reader. Yes, think for a moment. How many readers would be *really* confused to find the word 'bank' used twice on the same page? Again, this article of faith points to what I term the 'culture of subbing'. This is a set of values, carefully insinuated into new recruits, whose initial incredulity at these strictures gives way over time to upholding them with an almost Jesuitical fervour.

That is why subs will pull back a page because they have spotted a 'double', or a comma where the 'house style' is to use a colon. This 'style-over-substance' approach (or as I term it, 'living too close to the Pyramids') often means subs pay too much attention to the 'grout' and not enough to the 'building blocks'. As a result, subs become technicians and lose their influence in shaping the overall sense of an article because they focus on the literal construction of a report to the detriment of making an editorial judgement on it.

Skills

Headline writing is only one part of the sub-editor's work. Other skills are the ability to lay out pages on the screen, crop photographs, write the copy and 'standfirst' (mini-headlines), teaser boxes and all sorts of different little bits including captions to photographs. And of course all of this is done against the clock. Say we have a story about pilots and other airline staff going on strike. So the headlines will obviously reflect the nature of the story, and because so many people are flying these days, it is important to look at the possible implications for airline travellers. A business newspaper, such as the *Financial Times*, is likely to stress the industrial relations and company angle – how much revenue is likely to be lost, etc. A tabloid newspaper may more likely want to focus on the misery ahead for travellers. So they may write something like **Airport chaos looms**. Same story different approach.

Gender

Another thing that has changed over the past 20 years is the gender profile of sub-editors. When I joined it was the last bastion of the male-dominated profession and in fact I worked on many desks where there were no female sub-editors. This then resulted in a tendency on the part of male sub-editors to write headlines that reflected a chauvinistic sort of attitude. One classic example of this was when the Conservative government introduced a Tessa (Tax Exempt Special Savings Account) in the 1990s. This was an encouragement, as if one were needed, for sub-editors to write barely concealed headlines full of sexual innuendo: **Get on intimate terms with Tessa**. I do not think the same headlines would have been written if John Major's government had set up a Tax Exempt Rollover Rate Yield. The same pernicious attitude applied to Aids, when, for a long time, it was referred to as a 'Gay plague' in headlines. It took some effort on the part of health professionals and the National Union of Journalists to consign this particular construction to history.

Perhaps the biggest imponderable of headline writing and, by extension, for subs is, can readers 'read between the lines' on headlines? By that, I mean, are readers able to know that when a headline like '**Electronic eye to end goal disputes**' is used, it is far from 'a done deal'? In this case, it depends on the technology's being fully tested before being implemented into soccer matches and is a couple of seasons away, if at all. So a more literally correct headline should read, **Electronic eye might end goal disputes by about 2010**. We know how much subs loathe such constructions, given their dislike of equivocation. But the question still remains, do readers expect the literal truth in headlines, or have they factored subs' predilections into their reading? The short answer is I don't know, because (and I stand corrected) little research has been conducted on what readers think about headlines. Some research has focused on how people read pages (start at the left, move down and then up again – a bit like a 'W'). Without those answers, subs' predilections about headlines will continue to rule the roost.

And...

No discussion about headlines would be complete without reference to puns. If anything is the leitmotif of sub-editing, then surely it is the pun. Subs (even on the qualities) will do almost anything to get a pun into a headline. It is as if no headline is complete without one. As a result, tired, contrived puns are recycled year after year without any sense of their being outmoded. Airline profits invariably *soar*; there are always **Jams today and jams tomorrow**; **Champagne sales sparkle over Christmas**.

These words add little to headlines and in some cases the desire to force a pun into the construction can render them inaccurate. Take, for example, a story over Christmas 2006 about the computer company, Apple, which had become mired in controversy over the granting of stock options to its head, Steve Jobs. The controversy had started to affect the company's share price but a key internal report did not uncover any deeper problems and as a result the shares *actually* rose. However, some headlines in papers went along the lines of **Stock option storm fails to bite into Apple share price**. In fact, the shares rose nearly 6 per cent, which is definitely not the same as '...**fails to bite into**...'. Here, the subs were blinded by their need to inject a pun at the expense of the headlines' accuracy.

A casual reading of the headline could reasonably imply that the share price was *unmoved* (fails to bite into) when in fact it rose substantially. A fairer reflection of the story and keeping the pun in could have been, **Apple shares blossom despite**... .

Divergence

A trend of 'divergence' is a growing phenomenon in headlines. By divergence, I mean the tendency to 'move' the headline on to the next stage of the story. This has been common for political stories for some time. It is an arrangement that seems to suit both parties. I am unclear about the mechanics, but political spin doctors tell journalists that the Prime Minister or minister is going to announce something the following day about a change of policy, say on school exams. The reporter duly writes up the story along the lines of 'The education minister is set to announce today changes in the way exams are...'. However, the headline appears as **Minister changes exams**...', or something similar. So the headline says the change *has* happened, but the copy says it is about to be announced.

So what? Well, for a start, it breaks the headline writing rules, and is wrong. The problem, however, is that subs do not like equivocation of any sort, even 'qualification' is not liked. The headline should have read something like, **Minister set to announce change to exams**...'. But most subs shun these headline constructions because they think they are (a) boring and (b) put people off reading the story. By what authority these *ex cathedra* pronouncements are made has always baffled me. It is certainly not based on any survey of readers. Instead, I think, it has been a gradual insinuation into the subbing psyche that headlines must try to avoid any 'iffy' construction.

The net result of this has been a gradual 'divergence' of headlines from the stories that accompany them. When I first started subbing, this was frowned upon. But now, it is commonplace. All the major newspapers do it regularly with perhaps the exception of the *Financial Times* (where I work) whose devotion to 'set to', 'might' and 'likely' in headlines is a discipline no other paper shares. (It is also immensely frustrating at times.) True, the other papers' headlines *look* better but is that the point?

For the last time (honest) let me return to our old friend, the £15.99 shirt. If it says £15.99 on the headline then surely it must be the same price in the story and *now*, not in two months' time (when the changes the minister has announced come into effect) but there and then. Any retreat from that position – the require-ment that the headline be literally accurate – is wrong. Yet, this retreat has happened. The instances of 'divergence' are commonplace. Subs might call it 'cheering' up a piece of dull copy, but ultimately that's no excuse.

If (in that overblown aphorism) journalism is the first draft of history, then surely headlines are the first 'abstract' (for want of a better word); the story might turn out to be inaccurate (as if) but the headline *should* be correct.

Finally, an anecdote to drive home the point. Shortly after Labour came into power, I subbed the lead for a Sunday paper. It said that a certain bunch of Labour rebels faced expulsion from the party on the following Tuesday. I duly wrote some-thing along the lines of **Labour rebels face expulsion**. When the first edition proofs came up, I noticed that the headline had been changed to **Labour rebels are expelled**. When I pointed out to the chief sub that they had not *actually* been expelled, I was told that it was 'more or less done and dusted'. On the Monday, the so-called rebels got a high court injunction to stop the expulsion hearings. And as far as I know, they never took place.

Acknowledgement

My thanks to Mick Murphy and Peter Crompton of the *Financial Two* (two subs *d'une certain age*) for their help with this chapter.

Further reading

Evans, H. (1972) *Newsman's English* London: Heinemann.
Evans, H. (1974a) *Handling Newspaper Text* London Heinemann.
Evans, H. (1974b) *News Headlines* London: Heinemann.
Evans, H. (1973) *Newspaper Design* London: Heinemann.
Hicks, W. and Holmes, T. (2002) *Subediting For Journalists* London: Routledge.
Reah, D. (2002) *The Language of Headlines* London: Routledge, Taylor and Francis.

Part 4

Non-editorial contents

Chapter 21

Advertising

Peter Meech

Attitudes to advertising and newspapers can divide sharply. For some it was advertising that originally freed the UK press from state control almost three centuries ago (Koss 1984); others maintain that independence from political subsidies, far from establishing the much-vaunted Freedom of the Press, merely led to its early enthralment to commercial interests (Boyce 1978). In this chapter my focus is mostly on developments in the field over the past 50 years, although I begin with some historical background. Thereafter I consider the economic relationship of advertising and the press and the process by which ads come to be published, concluding with a discussion of newspapers and advertising in the digital age.

In their long history newspapers have always had a dual function: to inform and to advertise. From the seventeenth century they have provided readers with news and comment alongside promotional messages. But it was not until the 1730s that it became routine practice to make the non-editorial function explicit in their names, something that continues to this day in the regional press (*Ormskirk Advertiser*, *Perthshire Advertiser*, etc.). The typical 'small ads' of the period – for wigs, books, theatrical performances and, above all, for quack medicines – were set in the same single columns, typefaces and small point sizes as those used throughout the publication. For almost two centuries the front page of publications like *The Times* comprised such classified advertisements (the paper replaced them with news and photographs as recently as 1966, the last national title to do so).[1] Papers require the income from advertising to augment what they receive from cover sales. (In the case of free newspapers, such as the *Metro*, this is their sole source of revenue.) On the other hand, commercial advertisers have always needed a public platform to help sell their products and services. The relationship between the two parties is thus – and always has been – symbiotic and economic (Doyle 2002).

The economics of newspaper advertising

What is the economic impact of advertising on newspapers? At £19 billion, the UK had the highest annual overall advertising expenditure of any European country in 2005. Germany ran it a close second, with France, Italy and Spain in third, fourth and fifth place respectively, but following at some distance. The remaining countries in Europe lagged even further behind (Advertising Association 2006). Within the UK, what have been the long-term trends regarding adspend and newspapers? What kinds of advertising have increased or declined and what impacts have there been on different types of paper? Since 1970 the total expenditure on national newspapers has grown, but not continuously. There have been fluctuations – a dip in the 1970s, for example – typically corresponding to the general downturn in the economy at the time. The year 2000 marked the highest point in terms of revenue (£2.25 billion), since when there has been an almost constant decline (ibid.).

Total adspend provides an overall view, but it obscures an important fact: national newspapers' percentage slice of the UK cake has been worsening for half a century. In 1957, for example, they received a share of 19.4 per cent, whereas by 2005 that figure had been almost cut in two, to 10.1 per cent (regional newspapers experienced a similar rate of decline – from 26.6% to 15.8% – over the same period) (ibid). A further phenomenon masked by aggregate total data is the contribution made by advertising to the net revenues of the four broad categories of national title. A breakdown by these indicates that while for popular dailies the 2005 percentage was 47.4 (significantly up from the 1985 figure of 27.1%) and for popular Sundays 43.7 (1985: 48.7%), the corresponding figures for quality dailies were 56.2 per cent (1985: 61.9%) and quality Sundays 61.2 per cent (well down on 1985 at 75.1%) (ibid.). In other words, 'quality' papers still rely more heavily than 'popular' titles on advertising support, although the overall gap between them is narrowing.

There are also differences in the two main advertising streams: display and classified. Display advertisements, often large items comprising photographs and other graphic illustration to attract the casual reader's attention, typically appear on the same or adjacent page to editorial material. A decade ago, display advertising accounted for 60 per cent of total press advertising; it is now half. The smaller and simpler classified ads by contrast are usually to be found in dedicated sections, where they are actively sought out by readers looking, for instance, for a job, house or second-hand car. Display advertising has suffered over the years from competition with television, and, more recently, from the internet. Classified advertising, on the other hand, has long been the lifeblood of newspapers, national, regional and local, offering a service that television has been unable to provide. The *Guardian* is a prime example of a national title that has successfully built up its recruitment advertising in specialist supplements (media jobs and stories on a Monday, education on a Tuesday, etc.). That, however, is changing with the rapid rise of the internet, a topic we shall return to later. But first a look back in time.

Newspaper advertising: a brief history

As a conspicuous social and cultural phenomenon it is scarcely surprising that there have always been criticisms of press advertising. Already in the eighteenth century Dr Johnson was censuring advertisements on moral grounds (Turner 1965, pp.27–8). In more recent times advertising in general has been attacked for its contribution to the rise of consumerism. Another criticism is levelled at how the distribution of advertising money distorts the newspaper market, and yet another that advertisers exert direct pressure on the editorial content of papers by threatening to withdraw their custom unless certain material is either included or excluded. Limitations of space mean that only the last two, more specific issues can be dealt with here.

Writers such as Curran and Seaton (2003) argue that since the Second World War the UK national press has been over-represented by right-wing and centrist publications at the expense of more socially critical titles, the result of decisions taken by advertising executives rather than readers. This was particularly so during the 1970s and 1980s, when a preponderance of titles supported the Conservative Party. Although that situation has shifted in recent years, it remains the case that the political spectrum is not fully represented in the UK press, since there is no national newspaper that consistently reflects socialist views. Two Royal Commissions on the Press, Shawcross (1961–2) and McGregor (1977), considered, respectively, proposals to limit the amount of advertising per paper and to provide selective public subsidies for the press, which would have benefited alternative titles (Curran 1978). Both proposals were rejected as being inimical to a free-market society.

Tunstall (1996) attributes the characteristic distinction between 'quality' and 'popular' titles (or 'broadsheet' and 'tabloid', before the recent introduction of format changes) to the selective allocation of advertising money. There is no doubt that this has had an impact on the ecology of the national press, but focusing on it as the main causal factor is to underestimate the purchasing preferences of readers. UK national newspapers operate in a highly competitive marketplace. In order to survive, they, like other brands, need to distinguish themselves from their rivals by identifying a group of readers and providing them with journalism that corresponds to the latter's interests and prejudices. Advertisers consider the reader profiles of newspapers in deciding where to place their ads. But no amount of advertising revenue can guarantee the survival of a newspaper in the long run if it does not secure a loyal readership.

The criticism that advertising influences the editorial content of papers also has some validity. Although Anthony Sampson somewhat overstates the situation, he clearly has a point in maintaining: 'The advertisers determine the allocation of space – the pages devoted to consumers, travel, entertainment – which look more and more alike. And they're not interested in foreign news, books, investigation' (Sampson 1996, p.45).

This is most obvious in the growth of supplements such as those in the *Observer* as well as (non-news) sponsored pages and the barely disguised promotional stories carried by many local newspapers and national magazines known as 'advertorials'. Mostly promoting consumer products, these are typically written, reluctantly, by a publication's journalists to a sponsor's requirements and sometimes labelled 'advertising features' (Franklin 1997). The more serious accusation – that advertisers exercise the power of veto over the very selection and content of stories in the national press – is more difficult to substantiate.

Threats to withdraw advertising are certainly made from time to time. Two examples from the past illustrate different outcomes for newspapers from the actual, or threatened, withdrawal of advertising. The first, from the 1970s, concerned Distillers, manufacturers (through a subsidiary) of the drug thalidomide. They chose to withdraw all their advertising from the *Sunday Times* because of the campaign for compensation for victims of the drug started by Editor Harold Evans in 1972. At £600,000 per annum, Distillers were the paper's biggest advertiser, but both the editor-in-chief and proprietor backed the Editor to pursue the campaign despite the loss of income (Evans 1983, p.64). In 1987 the opposite fate befell the Editor of the *Star*, Mike Gabbert, who was sacked largely as a result of threats from Tesco and other retailers to withdraw their advertising. Under his direction the tabloid had gone further downmarket in a vain attempt to outrival the *Sun*, prompting the resignations of several journalists. Concern for the reactions of housewives/shoppers as well as their female workforce prompted the supermarkets into taking the action they did (Chippindale and Horrie 1990, pp.226–7).

Overt outcomes of the Gabbert/*Star* variety are rare. But what of the consequences of the covert pressure on journalists and editors exerted by advertisers through newspapers' advertising departments? By its very nature this is an area where hard evidence is difficult to come by. Journalists themselves are understandably reluctant to admit to self-censorship; after all, pulling or slanting stories to conform to advertisers' wishes runs counter to basic journalistic values. On local papers that set out not to offend and whose journalists may well live near and socialise with business people in the area, this is a fact of life. By contrast, national titles, operating in a far more competitive environment, and less reliant on a restricted range of advertisers, are better placed to resist such pressures – and need to in order to maintain their credibility. Research by the Pew Center in the US indicates that most journalists 'did not perceive advertiser pressure as a major problem […] although varying degrees of self-censorship were admitted' (cited in Franklin *et al.* 2005, p.9). While there is a lack of hard evidence in relation to the UK national press, this kind of pressure appears to present less of a problem, at least for the time being (McNair, 2003, pp.58–9).

Buying and selling advertising

At a practical level, what is the process by which advertisements come to appear in newspapers? Before a new paper or a new supplement is launched, executives from the publication's advertising department will normally give presentations to ad agencies, media buying agencies and advertisers. Using dummy copies of the planned publication, they explain to these existing or potential clients why it should appeal to a particular readership and why they should therefore add the new title to their roster of media options.[2] A rate card for display advertisements will be devised, setting out the costs for everything from a full-page colour ad to a two-centimetre, single column, black-and-white ad. 'Run-of-paper' advertising (as compared with a specified location) is likely to attract a discount, as is repeat and bulk buying (Brierley 2002). On the other hand, non-standard shapes and positions designed to have extra impact, such as 'fireplace' ads in the middle of pages or across spreads, will command premium prices. Negotiations between seller and buyer of advertising space mean that the actual rates paid can be very different from the published rates. Papers with a high upmarket readership, such as the *Financial Times*, are generally able to charge more per copy than those, such as the *Sun*, whose readers are mainly working class or elderly. This stems from the fact that many advertisers are prepared to pay a premium to reach a relatively small number of readers who are likely to have high disposable incomes of their own and who may also be in charge of corporate budgets – and to do so in a conducive editorial environment.

The total amount of advertising on a given day will determine the number of pages of a newspaper, its pagination. At a later stage, when they are scheming and laying out individual pages, journalists then have to take into account the ads, which are already in their appointed position. If the advertising department is in any doubt about the suitability of an item, it will be referred to the editor for a judgement. Care is usually taken at this stage to avoid unfortunate clashes. For example, running a feature on barbecues on the same page as a charity ad for famine relief would be insensitive and might well result in the advertiser demanding a rebate or a free insertion. The same applies if an ad is poorly reproduced in some way or even fails to appear. The production of classified ads is more straightforward, most of which are set in-house from copy phoned or emailed in.

All complaints about advertising, whether from the public or from commercial rivals, are dealt with by the Advertising Standards Authority, a non-statutory body comprising both industry and lay members (www.asa.org.uk/asa). Since 1962 the ASA has acted as a watchdog, investigating and adjudicating on complaints to ensure that advertising complies with the British Code of Advertising, Sales Promotion and Direct Marketing (CAP). It also monitors and can take action without waiting for complaints to be made. That action involves requesting an advertiser to remove or amend an offending ad. If persuasion fails to work, the ASA can refer the case to the Office of Fair Trading, which has the statutory power to prosecute, which the ASA as a self-regulatory body lacks. Newspapers are expected to provide space free of charge for the ASA's own ads. From time to time a particularly newsworthy case will attract media attention (which may have been part of the advertiser's original strategy). But for the most part individual print ads prompt relatively little public concern. Of the 30 million that appear annually only 446 had to be withdrawn or amended as a result of an ASA investigation in 2005 (Advertising Association 2006, p.256).[3]

Newspaper advertising: television, the internet and other competitors

Complaints about individual ads may not be a source of great concern for newspapers, but competitive pressures certainly have been and remain so. The launch of UK commercial television in the mid-1950s posed a potentially serious threat to the press (Brierley 2002). The new medium, with its jingles, its speech and – above all – its black-and-white moving images, offered opportunities for display advertising denied to print. Revenue would, it was feared, be drawn away from the press, creating a financial crisis for the newspaper sector. ITV did indeed attract a lot of advertising and succeeded in making a great deal of money as a monopoly supplier of commercial airtime. While a number of national newspapers folded in this period, for many of the survivors the arrival of a competing medium provided new opportunities: TV listings as well as editorial coverage of programmes and personalities (Tunstall 1996). Over the course of time advertising-funded colour supplements became essential elements of Sunday newspapers, to be followed later by those in the Saturday broadsheets and by a proliferation of financial sections, all contributing to a major increase in pagination in a period of escalating newsprint costs (Franklin 1997). And total advertising expenditure grew all the while.

Fast-forward to the later 1990s, when a similar threat appeared in the form of the internet. Unlike television, the internet got off to a rather shaky start, in terms of attracting advertising, but after just a few years established itself as a serious rival not only to the press but also to television. Combining the ability to communicate messages using television's audio-visual features with print's advantage of offering 'long copy', if necessary, it also had something that neither of these older media possessed initially: interactivity. This was inevitably of interest to advertisers, especially for the classified ads that have increasingly migrated to non-newspaper websites. In particular the use of search engines like Google and, more recently, AdWords/AdSense, alongside the emergence of online classified sites like craigslist, have revolutionised over a very short period of time the way business is now conducted. The consequence was that total UK internet adspend for 2005 was estimated at £1.4 billion, a dramatic increase of 66 per cent on the previous year. However, despite this exceptionally high rate of growth, internet advertising still only accounts for just over 7 per cent of total UK advertising expenditure (Advertising Association 2006).

It took a while before newspaper executives came to realise that the new medium was not necessarily their nemesis as far as advertising was concerned but could be exploited commercially with sufficient imagination and investment. Initially newspapers tended to respond defensively with pared-down and frequently under-resourced online editions. In time, however, many metamorphosed into well-designed websites, no longer offering pale imitations of their print versions but exploiting the possibilities of the web, not least by making available archive material. One of the most successful, *Guardian Unlimited*, offers RSS/web feeds and podcasts (including by Ricky Gervais in 2006) as well as subscription-only digital editions that reproduce the hard copy originals. It now has nearly half as many readers in America as in the UK (*Economist* 2006a). However, for many publications the problem still remains of 'monetising' readers; that is, deriving revenue from people who have come to expect to access online news and comment free of charge.

Given that the UK national press is one of the most competitive in the world, it is perhaps not surprising that newspaper groups resisted for so long the idea of collectively promoting the medium to advertisers. Rather, in the spirit of 'dog eat dog' they saw a chance to pick up additional ad revenue in the event of the demise of a rival title. But, following the example of commercial radio operators, who had earlier set up the Radio Advertising Bureau, the various newspaper groups established the Newspaper Marketing Agency (NMA) in 2003. This initiative recognised, somewhat belatedly, that there was considerable merit in acting together to meet the new media challenge. Accordingly, full-page generic ads appear from time to time in the press citing case studies of effective campaigns that used newspapers, while a website acts as a portal for a range of information about the press as a successful advertising medium (www.nmauk.co.uk).

Newspaper advertising: prospects and pitfalls

There has been much discussion recently about whether newspapers as we have known them can survive in the digital age (e.g. *Economist* 2006b). Circulations have been declining for years, both in the UK and in many other developed countries, as growing numbers of people come to rely less on print and more on electronic sources for news and comment. Advertisers, wishing to communicate with them – and to do so with greater precision – are increasingly turning to the more targeted opportunities provided by online ads, which allow consumers to respond directly and for advertisers and ad agencies to monitor this response more accurately.[4] With reduced levels of advertising revenue traditional newspapers seem to be left with the sole option of raising cover prices, which in itself is likely to reduce circulation figures even further – a downwards spiral from which there seems to be no escape. So, do they have a future?

The sector itself, while not unconcerned about threats to its long-term survival, points cautiously to advantages that national print newspapers continue to enjoy over other media. The most obvious of these is that with the proliferation of niche media and the consequent fragmentation of audiences, they still reach a mass market of readers. The figures speak for themselves:

> Thirty-seven million people read a national newspaper every week, and 84 per cent of UK adults read a national newspaper on a monthly basis. In the age of rolling 24-hour news coverage, national newspapers are read by 76 per cent of adults in a week. This amounts to 26 million readers on weekdays and 31 million readers at weekends.
>
> (NMA 2007)

Nor to be underestimated is the fact that, in addition to their portability and low cost, they also offer a very different visual and tactile experience to that provided by the ubiquitous screens of desktop computers, laptops, mobile phones and BlackBerries. For many this results in a more concentrated read, something that the NMA has chosen to highlight in its slogan, 'Newspapers: The Attention Medium'. Lastly, recent research by the NMA (in association with Millward Brown) has demonstrated that brand advertising can be twice as effective if a campaign includes national titles than if it does not and that UK readers are more likely to trust newspapers than other sources (Myers 2006), possibly the most significant factor for their future survival. In the short to medium term it seems likely that online newspapers will provide a valued complement to print versions, offering additional opportunities for advertising in both display and classified forms and making an important contribution to integrated campaigns across different media. By once more reinventing themselves, newspapers hope in this way to earn the necessary revenue to ensure the survival of their journalism, however it is delivered.

Acknowledgement

Many thanks to Raymond Boyle and John McLennan for comments and suggestions.

Notes

1   Its forerunner, *The Daily Universal Register* (1785), used its own title piece to advertise a typesetting innovation the patent for which the paper's owner had acquired.
2   Readership profiles of newspapers are researched and published by the National Readership Survey (www.nrs.co.uk). Circulation figures are verified by the Audit Bureau of Circulations (www.abc.org.uk).
3   A total of 1,296 complaints were investigated in 2005.
4   The integrity of internet advertising recently suffered a setback as a result of so-called 'click fraud'.

References

Advertising Association (2006) *Advertising Statistics Yearbook 2006* Henley-on-Thames: World Advertising Research Center for the Advertising Association.
Boyce, G. (1978) 'The Fourth Estate: The Reappraisal of a Concept' in Boyce, G., Curran, J. and Wingate, P. (Eds) *Newspaper History: From the 17th Century to the Present Day* London: Constable, pp.19–40.
Brierley, S. (2002) *The Advertising Handbook* (2nd edition) London and New York: Routledge.
Chippindale, P. and Horrie, C. (1990) *Stick It Up Your Punter!: The Rise and Fall of the Sun* London: Heinemann.
Curran, J. (1978) *The British Press: A Manifesto* London and Basingstoke: Macmillan.
Curran, J. and Seaton, J. (2003) *Power Without Responsibility: The Press and Broadcasting in Britain* (6th edition) London and New York: Routledge.

Doyle, G. (2002) *Understanding Media Economics* London: Sage.

Economist (2006a) 'Who Killed the Newspaper' 26 August.

Economist (2006b) 'More Media, Less News' 26 August.

Evans, H. (1983) *Good Times, Bad Times* London: Weidenfeld and Nicolson.

Franklin, B. (1997) *Newszak & News Media* London: Arnold.

Franklin, B., Hamer, M., Hanna, M., Kinsey, M. and Richardson, J. E. (2005) *Key Concepts in Journalism Studies* London/Thousand Oaks/New Delhi: Sage.

Koss, S. (1984) *The Rise and Fall of the Political Press in Britain* London and Chapel Hill: University of North Carolina Press.

McNair, B. (2003) *News and Journalism in the UK*, (4th edition) London and New York: Routledge.

Myers, Chris (2006) *The Case for National Newspaper Advertising* London: Newspaper Marketing Agency/Millward Brown.

Newspaper Marketing Agency (2007) www.nmank.co.uk/nma/do/live/whyNewspapers? sectiononarticleTypeId=25. Accessed 7 November 2007.

Sampson, A. (1996) 'The Crisis at the Heart of our Media' *British Journalism Review* vol. 7 no. 3, pp.42–56.

Tunstall, J. (1996) *Newspaper Power: The New National Press in Britain* Oxford: Clarendon Press.

Turner, E. S. (1965) *The Shocking History of Advertising* Harmondsworth: Penguin.

Chapter 22

TV pages

John Ellis

The *Daily Mail*'s veteran TV critic Peter Paterson retired in September 2006 and was not replaced. His column had consisted of reviews of the previous night's TV. It was replaced by more previewing of programmes for the upcoming evening. The paper that had pioneered popular TV reviewing with writers like Peter Black had decided that the sub-genre was dead. The complex relationship between national daily newspapers and national daily TV had taken another lurch forwards. On both sides, it is a love–hate relationship, one of media that are similar and need each other, but are consequently often antagonistic.

The media of television and newspapers have much in common. They are both ephemeral, to be used and then discarded. They are both in wide circulation. They are dominated by a small number of providers. Both are in the business of information and entertainment. They are both sustained by a mixture of advertising and purchase. And they are usually interested in the same people and events. However, there are some significant differences. Newspapers can say what they want, or rather what they can get away with under the laws of libel. But television is still controlled, though in an increasingly relaxed way, by the special legislation of the BBC Charter and the successive Broadcasting Acts. These impose requirements of fairness and balance which newspapers would, to say the least, find onerous. A frequent complaint of several papers, especially the *Daily Mail*, is that the BBC is not fulfilling its public service duties, or that TV has been making up stories, a practice not unknown in the press (Ellis 2005). Such stories spill out of the TV pages and become news. At this point, the antagonistic side of the relationship becomes evident. When TV becomes news, the newspapers will use the opportunity to vent their spleen at TV, which is a medium that competes for both news exclusives and consumer advertising. This is especially the case for those groups, like the Associated Press group (*Mail, Standard, Metro* etc.), that have no significant television interests. However, the everyday relationship between press and television is played out on the television pages, which have a much more intimate relationship with television, and are significant for both media. The TV pages sell newspapers, and they also significantly enhance the television experience for viewers.

TV pages consist of listings, previews, feature articles, gossip columns and, in most papers, reviews. Some even incorporate significant reader/viewer feedback in letters columns. The overall impression of contemporary TV pages is of dense information. There are listings for multiple channels using the full range of colour and featuring postage-stamp stills of actors. Listings will usually provide ultra short capsule comments as well as programme titles. Squeezed into side columns are selections of highlights which can be given as much as 200 words. In the surrounding pages there are soap updates, picture-led features on personalities, display ads for new programme (or even channel) launches and a small area devoted to radio listings. The double-page listings spread forms the heart of the TV pages, and in some papers in the early 1990s occupied the centre spread. A typical 32-page paper will carry four pages of television information, and in a mid-market or tabloid this will be a greater amount than the City pages.

At the weekend, newspapers' television coverage burgeons. Every daily publishes a programme guide for the next week with its Saturday (or even Friday) edition, and the Sundays repeat this exercise. These are sometimes small magazines in their own right, like the Saturday *Guardian*'s A5-sized *Guide*, which combines television with cinema, music and arts listings, or the *Sunday Times TV Guide*. These contain seven-day television listings and more extensive preview and feature material that often becomes more discursive about trends in television, with writers like Jackie Stephen, Jim Shelley (aka Tapehead) or Victor Lewis-Smith indulging their considerable skills in perceptive invective. These are semi-magazines, designed to lie around waiting to be used for the next week, and so attract distinctive advertisers looking for a longer form of exposure, particularly for DVD releases, books and music and home improvement commodities.

Such a pattern of television coverage is relatively recent, coming into being in the early 1990s. It has been the product of a slow evolutionary process. Newspapers grafted TV listings on to the existing radio listings in the early years of television broadcasting in the late 1940s, but these newspapers were very different objects to modern papers. Pagination was smaller, and feature content was confined to the op-ed pages. Arts coverage in the broadsheets like *The Times*, *Telegraph*, *Manchester Guardian* and *News Chronicle* concentrated on the traditional 'high' arts, covering theatre and opera first nights but, initially, not television or radio. Television reviewing emerged in the mid-1950s when television ownership became common and as television developed in cultural ambition and confidence. Initially the daily or weekly television review formed part of general arts reviewing. The real growth of TV pages around listings and reviews took place in the 1960s with the increase in pagination, the growth of feature writing and the launch of successive waves of supplements. Even then, these TV pages were significantly held back in their development by restrictive practices on the part of the broadcasters, which were the subject of campaigning and legislation that led to substantial changes in 1991. The nature of the coverage has changed as well, with the rise of personality journalism around television actors, and the increasing availability of previewable material as the technologies of television developed towards easy recordability. The development of television coverage over the period since 1950 has shifted from reaction and review to anticipation and preview. The abolition in 2006 of the television critic post at the *Daily Mail* is one manifestation of this development.

The Times provides a vivid illustration of these developments, because it developed from a conservative newspaper of record to a component in a trans-media empire with significant television interests. In 1958, three years after two-channel television had arrived in the UK, it ran rudimentary listings at the bottom of a page, which started with radio and simply listed the times and titles of programmes in a continuous run of prose. There was no TV review, but television did at least get a mention on the arts page on 19 September because both of the major ITV companies in the north, Granada and ATV, had donated generously to the refurbishment of Manchester's repertory theatre. This news appeared alongside a review of an opera first night ... in Siena, Italy. These editorial choices dramatically demonstrate the then cultural priorities of the newspaper. No television critic was appointed until the summer of 1966, and, along with other *Times* critics of the period, they were anonymised as simply 'our television critic'. A typical review is that of 19 September 1966. It appeared on the arts pages and discussed in 250 words the repeat of a George Orwell adaptation and David Sylvester's interview with the artist Francis Bacon, both on the BBC, and the single drama in the *Armchair Theatre* slot on ITV. During this period, TV listings grew to a properly formatted column and a half. For selected programmes it carried brief details of episode title and cast or presenters' names. By this time, Britain had three TV channels (BBC1, BBC2, ITV), each broadcasting for at least eight hours a day.

During the 1970s, *The Times* began to give serious attention to TV, gradually expanding its listings and incorporating some previewing of programmes. The daily TV review still remained on the arts pages, however. In 1972, the listings were headed by a 75-word piece that picked out 'the plum programmes', signed 'LB'. Recognisably modern listings appear later in the decade, using a distinct typographic template and authored by Peter Davalle, who continued for many years to provide both a general preview column and capsule comments on many programmes. The established TV critic Stanley Reynolds was still anchored to the arts page and limited to 250 words. With the arrival of Channel 4 in 1982, *The Times* decided to give Peter Davalle most of a page to list and preview the day's programmes, but filled the rest of the page with small ads for the West End theatre rather than run Celia Brayfield's TV column to create a unified page. In fact, the creation of a unified coverage of television did not appear in *The Times* until the end of the 1980s, when the paper had been in the ownership of Rupert Murdoch's News International for several years. The broadsheet newspapers all show variations of this pattern, tending to classify listings and previews as one type of copy and reviews as another. This changed dramatically at the beginning of the 1990s, when Britain had four national terrestrial channels, two satellite providers (British Satellite Broadcasting (BSB) and Sky), and a developing cable network. The reason was the dramatic change in the availability of advance programme information from the broadcasters.

Two forms of advance details about television programmes were for many years denied to newspapers. Until 1991, newspapers were limited in their television coverage by the existence of a monopoly on advanced TV listings operated by the broadcasters. In addition, television's own technology meant that, until the beginning of the 1980s, it was difficult to preview many programmes in advance of their transmission. It was relatively difficult for newspapers to provide much coverage of television until these restrictions had been resolved. At that time, the conjunction of freely available advanced information combined with the growth of celebrity-based journalism (particularly centred on television performers) to produce a rapid growth in newspaper TV pages. The resolution of the listings issue and the technology question both took place in the same few years, but as they are very different in nature, they have to be examined separately.

The *Time Out* case

Both BBC and ITV owned seven-day listings magazines, *Radio Times* and *TV Times* respectively. Both broadcasters refused to allow newspapers to run anything more than listings for the day of publication. The result was that the two listings magazines were among the most lucrative weekly magazines in the UK, especially as neither listed the competing broadcaster's programmes. Keen television viewers had to buy both. The *Radio Times* peaked at an average weekly sale of over 8 million between 1954 and 1958, and settled at between 3 and 4 million between 1968 and 1990 (Currie 2007, p.242). The demographic spread of the readership was formidable, and the publications were used throughout the week in many homes. So they were key to the advertising buy of many marketers during the period. Christmas editions bulged with tour companies offering summer holidays. Weekly editions carried page after page of ads for furniture, clothing and domestic appliances; for new cleaning and food product launches; for mail order catalogue operations; and, infamously, products for the elderly like stairlifts and walk-in baths.

The existence of these publications had been tolerated by the daily newspapers since the beginning of television in the UK. While many mass-market weekly publications like *Picture Post* had disappeared partly because of the pressure from television, *Radio Times* and *TV Times* continued to grow. Newspapers regarded TV pages as a relatively low priority through the 1960s and 1970s. During this period, newspaper advertising by television companies themselves did not exist. Television's own promotion of future shows was left to on-air trailers and the *Radio Times* and *TV Times*. Television was a relatively scarce resource and promotion largely took care of itself (Ellis 2000, pp.39–73). So from the newspapers' point of view, the TV listings took up space with no major advertising revenue pay-off. Some editors and proprietors regarded it as providing free promotion for a competing medium, especially the Associated Newspaper group, which had few investments in television. Newspapers of the period were less oriented towards celebrity culture, a term which scarcely existed. The goings-on in the lives of television stars were newsworthy only when the latter appeared in court, charged with 'importuning' (especially before the legalisation of homosexuality), or when involved in an interesting divorce case. Their personal traumas, their struggles with weight or with cancer, their relations with their siblings and children, all remained personal issues, unless they were explored in the pages of magazines like *Woman* or in a biography (Rojek 2001).

The growth of celebrity and lifestyle-based newspaper coverage initially emerged in the Sunday titles with the launch of magazines and supplements, a development largely pioneered at the *Sunday Times* in the 1960s. This coverage was concentrated on leisure areas that could provide substantial advertising revenue, from motoring to travel to health, food, home improvement and gardening. In their wake came the development of celebrity features and the personalisation of social issues around celebrities. However, at the outset there was little coverage of television issues and personalities in these leisure supplements. The glossy supplements were advertising driven, but television at that time had no reason to advertise its programmes. Advertising for television programmes and services began to emerge as a significant part of advertising spend only in the 1990s with the growth of competing TV services. The challenge to the dominance of the *Radio Times* and *TV Times* began before the newspapers saw the coverage of TV as a potential money-spinner and magnet for display advertising. So the challenge to the *Radio Times* and *TV Times* was spearheaded by another type of publication: the events listing magazine *Time Out*.

Founded by Tony Elliott, *Time Out* had gone mainstream by the late 1970s into essentially the form it has retained ever since: a thick set of listings of all cultural events in London published on a weekly basis. Its supremacy in the London market was twice challenged, once by Richard Branson and once by the magazine's own striking staff, with the far more durable left-oriented *City Limits* (1981–90). But Elliott's juggernaut won through, and it tried to increase its TV listings, which, because of the *Radio Times*' and *TV Times*' monopolies, were restricted to selective listings and previews. Elliott wanted to carry complete weekly listings for television just like he carried for every other entertainment medium available to Londoners. In late 1982, this was exactly what he did, taking advantage of his midweek copy date to pirate listings from the *Radio Times* and *TV Times*. He received considerable support from the new breed of independent television producers working (at that time) exclusively for Channel 4, a channel whose own management chafed at the space given to its output by *TV Times* as well as its rather downmarket editorial restrictions. Channel 4 launched in November 1982, and this provided Elliott's justification for publishing complete weekly listings. *TV Times* took *Time Out* to court, however, for breaking their existing agreement, and they won, with costs awarded against *Time Out*. So with the support of many independent producers, Elliott mounted a rather raucous lobbying campaign for the derestriction of weekly TV listings. In 1988, the campaign gained significant momentum with a landmark European Union ruling on monopolies and the publication (in the format of the magazine of the prestigious Edinburgh International Television Festival) of the lobbying document

Restricted Vision. The 1990 Broadcasting Act legislated to derestrict TV listings from March 1991 as part of a larger raft of legislation that opened up broadcasting to a competitive market. This included requiring BBC and ITV to take a minimum quota of productions from independent companies. Section 176[1] of the act required broadcasters to make available to all publications requiring its schedule information up to 14 days in advance of the broadcast date. Broadcasters were disgruntled because it seemed to imply that their competitors would be able to rearrange their schedules to take advantage of particular gaps, but in practice schedules have continued to be adjusted right up to the day before broadcast for competitive reasons (Ellis 2000, pp.130–47; Ytreberg 2002, pp.283–304).

So the modern TV listings guides, supplements and TV pages were born in March 1991. During that year, the sales of the *Radio Times* dropped by 1 million year on year, demonstrating the level of readership that the new TV pages had gained. The real winners were not Tony Elliott and *Time Out.* They had performed a stalking horse role for the national newspapers and particularly their weekend editions, which rethought their television coverage completely. The other winners were the BBC, who adroitly set up the central clearing house for listings information, which they have since sold off.[2] With the 1990s' expansion of TV channels, ever more ingenious variations on the time-grid system of listings layout were developed, and the surrounding coverage of television celebrities increased as celebrity culture grew. Leading up to this point, as well, the ability of TV pages to preview programmes had vastly increased. This was due to changes in the way that television addressed the issue of publicity for its programmes, and the changes in technology that made previewing possible.

'No preview tapes were available at the time of going to press'

The technology of television had developed as a means of live transmission of moving image and sound. The ability to record those signals developed subsequently, and easy editing of those signals later still. The first professional video recorders were acquired by the BBC in 1959 (a BBC that had begun regular television broadcasts in 1936) and editing of those tapes required technology that did not develop until the 1970s. So until the mid-1960s programmes were either shot on film or broadcast live. Some programmes on film were shown to interested journalists but these were the exception.[3] For daily journalism, reviewing for the following morning was the only option until the 1970s. This is why the television reviews appeared on arts pages for so long: in copy terms they were essentially the same as theatre or concert reviews, which were phoned in between 11pm and midnight to catch the London edition.

During the 1970s, more producers and broadcasters of prestige television programmes wanted to secure publicity for them. So previews were organised for television critics, often in the same viewing theatres that were used by film reviewers. However, much television material was not shot exclusively on film (even some prestige drama) so it was not available for this selective previewing. Clive James at the *Observer* made much play of his reviewing practice during the period: he claimed he watched television rather than attended cosily arranged previews, and tales exist of him sitting doing so as removal men (and his wife) busied themselves in moving home around him (for Clive James' influential reviews see James 1981 and 1984). It was the rapid spread of domestic VHS tape recording at the very end of the 1970s that enabled a much greater spread of previewing. This was the first technology that provided cheap bulk copying of tapes. Instead of previewers having to move around between viewing theatres (which meant a theoretical maximum of 15 shows at three a day), they could preview 15 shows within a day's work with judicious use of the fast-forward button. VHS enabled the capsule previewing of substantial amounts of the day's television; VHS enabled it, but other developments made it happen. The stable broadcasting environment of three-channel television which lasted from 1964 to 1982 was changed by the arrival of Channel 4. A distinctly more aggressive promotional culture developed among both broadcasters and producers. This culture seized on the VHS preview as its primary means of promotion, and the streets of London became crowded with motorcycle couriers with their precious freight of last-minute preview tapes. By the end of the 1980s it became the sign of something seriously wrong with a new production if 'preview tapes were unavailable'.

This was still a relatively closed circuit of people: most television producers knew at least some of the previewers and reviewers, and press departments at the broadcasters were adept at making life difficult for writers whose copy they felt was hostile. It was also a time when publicity could be controlled by press departments. To inform one of the new breed of 'media correspondents' about a forthcoming controversial programme would often trigger coverage in the news pages and even moralistic editorials.[4] The launch of *EastEnders* by the BBC in 1993 was surrounded by a press blackout on stories about its actors, who were under considerable production pressure at the time. Indeed, it was notoriously difficult to get *EastEnders* stories for several months into the production when it had become a massive success. The proliferation of channels both on television and in print has made it more difficult to control publicity in this way, or to need to do so. Now writers like Jackie Stephen can speculate freely about events in soap operas as a service to readers whose PVRs may have malfunctioned, or who have simply not enough time to catch up any other way.

Current TV pages reveal much about the newspapers in which they appear. With the proliferation of channels, it is now impossible to list the schedules of even those that aspire to schedules (which channels like Bid-Up TV do not). So the choice of which to run and which should have prominence is a major indicator of the newspaper's view of its readership. In 2006, the *Daily Mail* alone began to give prominence to 'Freeview channels' as a category in its listings, clearly regarding its core readership as one that is taking the middle way towards digital television and is wary of BSkyB. News International's papers give much greater prominence to Sky's channels, but even here *The Times* will preview BBC4 programmes, while the *News of the World* ignores the channel almost entirely. TV pages now editorialise silently as well as explicitly about television, but are still framed within a culture of offering a service to their readers. When television becomes a matter of polemic and controversy, this still takes place within the news and editorial spaces of the dailies, with the possible exception of some of the more blatant promotion for BSkyB in the TV pages of the *Sun*, *The Times* and *Sunday Times*.

Notes

1   (2) The duty imposed by subsection (1) is to make available information as to the titles of the programmes which are to be, or may be, included in the service on any date, and the time of their inclusion, to any publisher who has asked the person providing the programme service to make such information available to him and reasonably requires it. (3) Information to be made available to a publisher under this section is to be made available as soon after it has been prepared as is reasonably practicable but, in any event – (a) not later than when it is made available to any other publisher, and (b) in the case of information in respect of all the programmes to be included in the service in any period of seven days, not later than the beginning of the preceding period of four-teen days, or such other number of days as may be prescribed by the Secretary of State by order. (http: //www.opsi.gov.uk/acts/acts1990/Ukpga_19900042_en_1.htm)
2   This information has, since 1997, formed the basis of the TRILT database of TV programmes provided by the British Universities Film and Video Council (BUFVC) at http://www.bufvc.ac.uk/databases/trilt.html. Accessed 13 November 2007.
3   At the BBC written archive in Caversham, there exists the following memo that vividly illustrates the slow development of the TV preview: July 1959. From Tel. Press O. Subject MOTHER COURAGE. To: H.D. Tel.
    You will have noticed from today's press that there were extensive reviews of Mother Courage in *The Times*, *Daily Mail* and *News Chronicle*. There was nothing in *The Telegraph*. The reason for this could, perhaps, be that at the request of certain papers, we were able through the co-operation of Frank Kaye, to lay on a preview. The three critics who came were able to write their reviews at leisure instead of scrambling a piece between eleven and midnight. All three critics expressed their appreciation of the special facility we had laid on. Tel. Pub. O. feels it would be a good thing to arrange previews for World Theatre plays on a similar basis in future, particularly when the play gets a late placing and runs over ninety minutes. Laying on a preview would, of course, depend upon the availability of resources and we should limit ourselves to having only the small number of critics who make a special request for the facility. Could we have your views please?Nest Bradney ((BBC WAC T5/2,253/1). My thanks to Billy Smart for bringing this to my attention.
4   http://www.rhul.ac.uk/media-arts/staff/ellis3.htm. Accessed 13 November 2007.

References

Currie, T. (2007) *The Radio Times Story* Tiverton: Kelly Publications.
Ellis, J. (2000) *Seeing Things: Television in the Age of Uncertainty* London: I. B. Tauris.
Ellis, J. (2005) 'Documentary and Truth on Television: The Crisis of 1999' in Corner, J. and Rosenthal, A. (Eds) *New Challenges in Documentary* Manchester: Manchester University Press, pp.342–60.

James, C. (1981) *The Crystal Bucket* London: Cape.
James, C. (1984) *Glued To The Box* London: Picador.
Rojek, C. (2001) *Celebrity* London: Reaktion.
Ytreberg, E. (2002) 'Continuity in Environments: The Evolution of Basic Practices and Dilemmas in Nordic Television Scheduling' *European Journal of Communication* vol. 17 no. 3, pp.283–304.

Chapter 23

Horoscopes and popular culture

Nicholas Campion

The horoscope column is a familiar part of most modern newspapers, and has been so for half a century. Its popularity is huge, if difficult to quantify: the best we can say is that somewhere between 25 per cent and 70 per cent of the adult population of most western countries read horoscope columns, although with varying frequencies (Campion 2004, chapter 11). According to the opinion pollsters, Gallup (1979, p.185), 'Attesting to the popularity of astrology in the United States today is the fact that astrology columns are carried by 1,200 of the nation's 1,750 daily newspapers'. The horoscope column is considered an essential feature of most modern media aimed at a mass audience and I have been told by a number of editors that the first freelance contributor to be hired for the launch of a new women's magazine is the astrologer. The journalist and religious commentator Anne Atkins stated in 1999 that, in her opinion, the horoscope column is the most popular piece in any newspaper, with the agony aunt coming a close second (Atkins 1999). Even if this latter claim is an exaggeration, every single magazine aimed at women and teenage girls in the UK carries a horoscope column. The 'tabloid' newspapers, the *Daily Mail*, *Daily Express*, *Daily Mirror*, *Daily Star* and *Sun* all carry daily horoscopes. The greatest space devoted to any astrologer is given to Jonathan Cainer currently with the *Daily Mail*; in the 1990s Cainer was allocated an unprecedented whole page in the *Daily Mirror* to publish his column and its associated features. On Sunday the publication of horoscopes extends from the tabloids to the upmarket 'broadsheets' including the *Sunday Times*, *Independent on Sunday*, *Sunday Telegraph* and *Observer*. The last three papers, though, have an uneasy relationship with astrology, either giving it minimal space and promotion (*Independent on Sunday*), running a spoof column to compete with the genuine one (*Telegraph*) or periodically cancelling their column (*Observer*). They also tend to publish sceptical pieces, contemptuous of popular interest in astrology (for example, Lawson 1996). At the level of mass popular culture represented by the tabloid newspapers and women's magazines, though, sun-sign astrology is considered an essential ingredient.

Most investigations of horoscope columns are concerned with astrology's truth claims, which are usually found, in narrow scientific terms, to be false (Kelly 1997). Attempts are then made to explain astrology's psychological appeal, usually accountable by the argument that its statements are so general that anyone can recognise them as 'true' (Fichten and Sunerton 1983). Only the Marxist-Freudian Theodor Adorno set out to establish an authoritative and comprehensive critique of horoscope columns in the 1950s. He decided that they appealed to what he termed the 'authoritarian personality' which he considered characteristic of individuals who surrender authority for their own lives to a higher power, bully those weaker than themselves and are likely to support fascist regimes (Adorno 1994). This aspect of Adorno's work, however, has been rigorously critiqued (Campion 2004), leaving us to consider the question from a more tolerant and realistic perspective.

Definitions

First, a few definitions. The horoscope column consists of 12 paragraphs, one for each of the 12 groups of people born at the times of year when the sun is in one of the 12 zodiac signs. These 'horoscopes' are based on brief readings for individuals born with the sun in the respective signs of the zodiac and they consist of a combination of generalised advice and prediction. Such columns are the main vehicle for the transmission of astrology into popular culture. Astrology itself is best defined in wide-ranging terms as 'the practice of relating the heavenly bodies to lives and events on earth, and the tradition that has thus been generated' (Curry 1999, p.55). The zodiac sign occupied by the sun at birth is known as the sun-sign by astrologers, or frequently as the 'birth-sign' or 'star-sign' in public discourse. Astrology's penetration into popular culture, aided by horoscope columns, was embodied in the classic 1960s chat-up line, 'what's your sign?' (Rudhyar 1970, p.viii). Such triviality is symptomatic of astrology's generally superficial reputation in the modern west. Astrology has a huge appeal and it is implausible to suggest, as its critics do, that it is, or should be regarded as, merely a matter of mass entertainment, even if horoscope columns tend to appear alongside jokes and cartoons. Until recently the *Daily Mail* horoscope column was located on the 'Coffee Break' page, the editorial theory being that the typically female reader would rest her weary feet, taking a break from her housework (or, if a young secretary, snatch a few minutes away from the boss's gaze) to drink a cup of coffee, read a cartoon, do a crossword, enter a quiz and generally relax. Astrology's appeal, though, seems to be deeper than editorial theory would suggest.

A brief history of astrology

There is a long history of the veneration of the sun for religious purposes and, in the last centuries BCE, the Greeks and Egyptians developed the concept of the 'central spiritual sun', which occupied the same space as the physical sun, but acted as a lens for transmitting the divine light of God into the visible universe. This idea was adopted by the influential English astrologer Alan Leo (1860–1917), who argued that the sun was therefore the heart of all astrological interpretation, and by his American successor, Dane Rudhyar (1895–1985). It is possible that it was Rudhyar who then suggested the now familiar 12-paragraph sun-sign format to his editor, Paul Clancy. Whatever the truth of that suggestion, Clancy's successful news-stand magazine, *American Astrology*, ran a horoscope column from its first issue in March 1933. Rudhyar's religious motivation was profound. In 1938 he proclaimed that:

> Today is a new birthday for the ancient gods. New men call for new symbols. Their cry rises, beyond their logical intellects ashamed of mystical longings, for new gods to worship and to use in order to integrate their harrowing mental confusion and to stabilize their uprooted souls. Young gods, fresh and radiant with the sunshine of a new dawn, glorified with the 'golden light' of a new Sun of Power, ecstatic with virgin potentialities after the banishment of ancient nightmares.
>
> (1938, p.xiii)

Mass popular newspaper astrology had begun a few years earlier when the *Sunday Express* on 24 August 1930 (Naylor 1930) published an analysis of the horoscope of the infant Princess Margaret, daughter of the future George VI. The feature was written by the popular astrological lecturer and author R. H. Naylor and he included, along with an analysis of the Princess's birth chart, general political predictions and about 50 words per day of birthday predictions for each day of the coming week. Reader response was instant and favourable and the newspaper was clearly delighted with the response to Naylor's column. Arthur Christiansen, the Entertainment Editor of the *Express*, who hired Naylor wrote that, 'Naylor and his horoscopes became a power in the land. If he said that Monday was a bad day for buying, then the buyers of more than one West End store waited for the stars to become more propitious' (Christiansen 1961, p.65).

While Naylor appears to have been the first of the high profile media astrologers, it was six years after his first *Sunday Express* feature that he composed his first 12-paragraph horoscope column on the American model. By then the *Express* had acquired imitators, including its rival, the *People*, which had launched its column, in late 1933. The *Daily Express* launched a daily column in 1934 but with a much lower profile than the Sunday version. It was anonymous and consisted of about 100 words for the birthday of the day and 20 words to sum up the day as a whole for all other readers. In spite of its brevity, the feature was regarded in some quarters as a major success. James Leigh (1936, p.98), the Editor of *Prediction*, reported that,

> The *Daily Express* will never again doubt the interest which its readers take in Astrology. Some days ago it published on its main page an article which told what happened behind the scenes when through pressure of other matter [sic], the Editor decided to leave out the daily horoscope. No sooner had the paper been dispatched for distribution than the editorial powers regretted

their rashness. From 1 a.m. the newspaper was besieged by 'phone and personal enquiries indignantly demanding to know what had happened to the horoscope! A special staff team was delegated to deal with these queries. It spent several working days reading the horoscope over the telephone and sending proofs to readers who lived in the provinces. If the city page, or the shopping notes or the features are curtailed (says the *Express*) no one raises any objection. But the day when the horoscope was omitted will always be remembered, for it caused endless inconvenience in the office, and disturbed the peace of thousands of readers.

The greatest boost to the power and popularity of horoscope columns in recent times was technology. In the 1970s some magazines, such as *She*, began selling computerised horoscopes composed of pre-prepared paragraphs based on the readers' individual date, time and place of birth. This technology was picked up by the national press in 1986, first by *Today*, which employed Jonathan Cainer and provided him with a whole colour page to promote his feature, at a time when other newspapers were still generally providing columns of a quarter page or less. *Today*'s tabloid competitors began to take notice, especially when, around 1988, it became possible to run pre-recorded voice tapes, usually for weekly or monthly horoscopes, sometimes daily. Such were the potential profits that all the newspapers which carried columns, along with the most prominent women's magazines began promoting their astrologers as celebrities. The last to join in this rush was the *Daily Mail*, in 1999.

Earnings could be huge. The *Daily Mail*, which was the last to launch phone lines and never achieved the income that other papers achieved (companies were already preventing their employees from calling horoscope lines by installing call-blocking technology), earned a gross of £1 million a year, of which 50 per cent went to British Telecom, 20 per cent to the line provider, or 'server', 20 per cent to the paper and 10 per cent to the astrologer. The *Mail* astrologer's earnings increased from £7,800 p.a. in 1986 to around £100,000 p.a. in 1991. When Jonathan Cainer was providing the *Mail* horoscopes in the late 1990s he was reputed to be earning £1 million a year. In 1999 Cainer was working for the *Daily Mail* where his lines were receiving around 17,000 calls a week, less than 1 per cent of the circulation of 2.5 million, bringing in a gross income of approximately £1 million p.a., partly because he owned the 'server' technology and took the *Mail*'s percentage in return for declining a salary. While the figure of a million-pound turnover can make for dramatic headlines, the actual percentage of readers calling was very small. This is typical; a high readership is not necessarily translated into the active decision to call a horoscope line.

Earnings from individual printed, computerised horoscopes tended to be lower. Sean Lovatt described the situation he found when he was engaged in producing computerised horoscopes for the *Daily Express*. In 1991 the newspaper offered readers a computerised horoscope which could be obtained by sending in a cut-out coupon. About 5,200 were sold at £9.99 each, earning a gross income of

£520,000 but representing a response of only 0.5 per cent of the total circulation of over a million. He recalled that,

> When the *Express* didn't put a coupon that was cutable out in the paper, just an advert saying please send these details off to this PO Box number, the response was much, much smaller. By the time that we had been doing it for a few years, this is for birth charts, for character analysis that I am talking about. By the time we had been doing it for a few years, it seemed to me that the pool of *Express* readers who were interested in this had dried up somewhat and we were getting about 2,200 to 2,500 each time they did a reader's special offer, which they did twice a year. Some of those people, I recognised from my database, were past purchasers of the reports who were buying them for other people. Their children, friends, husbands, family, and others were new people. So it seemed that there was only a percentage of *Express* readers who were prepared to part with their pounds to get an astrological printed report and once they had got that, they didn't necessarily want another one. We then introduced another product which was a 12-monthly forecast. That did better. People seemed to be more interested in their future than their character. Of course, the fact that the two are indivisible is another matter. We did better with that and more reorders and there would be people who would over a period of five to six years, every year order their 12-monthly forecast.
>
> (Lovatt interview 2001)

A more recent development was the spread of astrology to the internet, a medium which can expand the print formula of the standard 12-paragraph horoscope column to the supply of downloadable computerised readings based on the customer's exact birth data. In 2001 Jonathan Cainer, the *Daily Mirror* astrologer, reported that his website www.cainer.com received 100,000 'unique' visits per day; each page the visitor then looks at constitutes a 'hit', so if each visitor looked at between three and six pages, the site received between 300,000 and 600,000 hits per day, which made it Britain's fourth most popular website (Cainer interview 2001). Cainer also reported that when he worked on *Today* newspaper in the late 1980s, when the first horoscope phone lines, running pre-recorded tapes, were launched, the weekly call figures were 25,000 out of a circulation of half a million – 5 per cent of the circulation.

Astrology, cultural theory and popular culture

It is clear from Naylor's instant success in 1930 that there is a public appetite for astrology, that this preceded its launch in the *Sunday Express*, and that a pre-existing demand is being met. Cultural theorists tend to avoid astrology but may provide some clues to its appeal. Does astrology constitute an identity culture, in the sense that it reinforces 'a sociable, populist and traditional way of life, characterised by a quality that pervades everything and makes a person feel rooted or at home' (see Eagleton 2000, p.26)? Is it part of the culture industry, as defined by Adorno, in the sense that it plays its part in oppressing people by providing false solutions to real problems, encouraging an otherwise rebellious population to remain servile (Strinati 1995, p.64)? Or is it a part of popular culture, and hence in an automatic position of opposition to elite culture (Lynch 2005, p.3)? The last suggestion would certainly explain why astrology thrives in 'downmarket' publications and is regarded with suspicion in 'upmarket' ones.

Stuart Sutcliffe (2003, p.6), a sociologist of religion, considers astrology's ability to address personal concerns while providing a metaphysical framework, converting the 'vast occult cosmologies' of the nineteenth-century visionary, H. P. Blavatsky, the psychologist C. G. Jung and the mystic G. I. Gurdjieff, into a form which 'could travel socially and speak both to everyday concerns of love and happiness and grand theories of meaningful coincidence'. The most perceptive comments, though, come from 'insiders'. Carl Weschke considers that sun-sign astrology's mass appeal, 'was all part of the adventure of self-knowledge. That is what was really new in the twentieth century. Never before had there been any system that could be applied on a mass-market basis that "revealed" one's self to oneself' (Weschke interview 2002).

I asked Shelley von Strunckel, who writes for the *Sunday Times* and the London *Evening Standard*, how she accounted for astrology's popularity. She argued that astrology fulfils an unsatisfied public need for a contemplative, philosophical perspective:

> In our culture today, what we are pleased to call education doesn't go anywhere near anything about philosophy ... simple education doesn't teach people to observe how they think or to pause and be still. Therefore, part of the process in their ... reading a column, even something as short as an entry in the *Standard* ... is that an individual is introduced to this new way of being with their mind in which they step outside of themselves ... because most people don't know how to pause, so their appointment with their astrology column ... may be their only time in their life when they have stillness.
>
> (Von Strunckel interview 2002)

And, indeed, if we consider Cainer's writing, it is a mixture of discussion of issues concerning the individual's sign as a whole, advice, prediction and uplifting optimism. On 3 March 2007, for Pisces, the sign containing the sun at the time, he wrote

> When astrologers talk about Pisces, they become like painters trying to create a colourful picture with only one pot of purple paint. They twitter on about the 'dreamy', 'poetic', 'idealistic' nature of your sign. On the rare occasion they remember to credit you with common sense, they grudgingly describe it as 'intuitive'. They imply that your wisest choices are made more by luck than judgement. They forget that Einstein was a Piscean. He may well have had a creative side to his personality but he was a powerful, rational thinker too.

Neptune and Saturn, this month, suggest you've got a tough choice to make. And you're about to get it brilliantly right.

(Cainer 2007)

Cainer's optimism has influenced others in the field. For the same day Justin Toper in the *Daily Express* wrote, 'There's an eclipse in your chart that affects relationships. Something has to change but don't get radical – take your time', belying Adorno's thesis that horoscope columns involve the surrender of self-responsibility (Toper 2007). Debbie Frank in the *Daily Mirror* gave a similar reading indicating that both she and Toper, like Cainer, were following astrological rules: 'This week's eclipse puts the spotlight on relationships and you will discover there is a lot at stake. The important message is to think positively if you want the planets to work their magic' (Frank 2007). Mystic Meg in the *Sun* followed the same theme: 'The lunar eclipse visits your marriage chart and love that has been ticking over could start to plan a wedding. If you are free to meet someone new, this is a key day' (Mystic Meg 2007). All three regarded their readings as not a matter of absolute truth, but a matter of a certain future potential which needs to be matched with circumstances ('if you are free') and in which consciousness plays a role ('think positively'). We are approaching that sense of personal union with something greater that the French anthropologist Lucien Lévy-Bruhl termed 'participation-mystique' (1985, p.330).

The twentieth-century psychoanalyst Carl Gustav Jung, discussing the role of therapists in modern life, provided one answer to the question of why people visit astrologers. Some doctors, he said, deal with people as if they were mere machines, devoid of any need for meaning. Even though meaning is what most educated people are looking for, they would never think of consulting a priest (Jung 1969, pp.330, 336). The alternative, in Jung's opinion, is a therapist, or equivalent, including astrologers (as long as, he would have argued, they have suitable therapeutic training). Astrology's essential appeal is that it establishes an intimate connection between the heavens and earth.

The best way to evaluate horoscope columns is as a series of thoughts for the day (or week, or month). These brief thoughts may shed light on a reader's state of mind, and the reader is then able to project their feelings about life on to the ideas expressed in the column (Campion 2006, pp.90–1). The Chinese oracle, the *I Ching*, works in this way, by posing a riddle for the reader. Jung explained this when he wrote, 'Don't you see how useful the *I Ching* is in making you project your hitherto unrealised thoughts into its abstruse symbolism?' (Jung 1951, p.xxiii). The same process is at work in many newspaper and magazine columns. The horoscope column is written in such a way that the reader can find significance in it. It is not scientific and, if we want to understand its appeal and cultural context, then its claims are neither true nor false. They are either meaningful or not. In this sense we should consider horoscope columns as part of the informal, folk, 'common', 'hidden', vernacular religion of the modern west (Campion 2004, pp.282–3). It is part of what Bowman and Sutcliffe (2000, p.6) defined as 'the totality of all those views and practices of religion that exist among the people apart from, and alongside, the strictly theological and liturgical forms of the official religion'. And it conforms to what Bryan Wilson (1969) termed 'privatisation', the modern tendency for those of a religious persuasion to construct their own private spirituality in contrast to the public dogma on offer from established churches. True to the spirit of contemporary alternative spirituality, popular astrology, through the medium of the newspaper horoscope, is best seen as part of a typically modern religion of self-awareness rather than as the worship of a single divine truth.

References

Adorno, T. (1994/1953) *The Stars Down to Earth* London: Routledge.

Atkins, A. (1999) 'The Message' BBC Radio 4, 4 June.

Bowman, M. and Sutcliffe, S. (2000) *Beyond New Age: Exploring Alternative Spirituality* Edinburgh: Edinburgh University Press.

Cainer, J. (2007) 'Your Week Ahead: Pisces' *Daily Mail, Weekend* 3 March, p.86 (also see http://www.cainer.com/weeklyframe.htm).

Campion, N. (2004) 'Prophecy, Cosmology and the New Age Movement: The Extent and Nature of Contemporary Belief in Astrology' PhD Thesis, University of the West of England.

Campion, N. (2006) *What do Astrologers Believe?* Oxford: Granta.

Christiansen, A. (1961) *Headlines all My Life* London: Heinemann.

Curry, P. (1999) 'Astrology' in Boyd, Kelly (Ed.) *Encyclopedia of Historians and Historical Writing* London: Fitzroy Dearborn.

Eagleton, T. (2000) *The Idea of Culture* Oxford: Blackwell.

Farnell, K. (2007) *Flirting with the Zodiac* Bournemouth: The Wessex Astrologer.

Fichten, C. S. and Sunerton, B. (1983) 'Popular Horoscopes and the Barnum Effect' *The Journal of Psychology* vol. 114, pp.123–34.

Frank, D. (2007) 'Pisces' *Daily Mirror*, p.43.

Gallup, G. H. (1979) *The Gallup Poll: Public Opinion 1978* Wilmington, DE: Scholarly Resources Inc.

Harvey, C. (1973–4) 'Town v Gown' *The Astrological Journal* Winter vol. XVI no. 1, pp.28–40.

Jung, C. G. (1951) 'Foreword' in *I Ching or Book of Changes* trans. Richard Wilhelm London: Routledge and Kegan Paul, pp.xxi–xxxix.

Jung, C. G. (1969) 'Psychotherapists or the Clergy' in *Psychology and Religion: East and West* Collected Works vol. 11 trans. R. F. C. Hull London: Routledge and Kegan Paul, pp.327–47.

Kelly, I. (1997) 'Modern Astrology: A Critique' *Psychological Reports* vol. 81, pp. 1,035–66.

Lawson, N. (1996) 'Astrology and the Need to Believe: Why are We Going to New Age Cranks for Old-style Cures?' *The Times* 13 November, p.17.

Leigh, J. (1936) 'Editorial' *Prediction* April vol. 1 no. 3, p.98.

Lévy-Bruhl, L. (1985) *How Natives Think* Princeton: Princeton University Press.

Lynch, G. (2005) *Understanding Theology and Popular Culture* Oxford: Blackwell.

Mystic Meg (2007) 'Pisces' *Sun* 3 March.

Naylor, R. H. (1930) 'What the Stars Foretell For The New Princess And A Few Hints On The Happenings Of This Week', *Sunday Express* 24 August, p.11.

Rudhyar, D. (1938) *New Mansions for New Men* New York: Lucis Publishing Company.

Rudhyar, D. (1970/1936) *The Astrology of Personality* Garden City, NY: Doubleday.

Strinati, D. (1995) *An Introduction to Theories of Popular Culture* London: Routledge.

Sutcliffe, S. (2003) *Children of the New Age: A History of Spiritual Practices* London: Routledge.

Toper, J. (2007) 'Pisces' *Daily Express Saturday Magazine* 3 March, p.82.

Wilson, B. (1969/1966) *Religion in Secular Society: A Sociological Comment* Harmondsworth: Pelican.

Interviews

Cainer, J. 8 September 2001.

Lovatt, S. 16 March 2001.

Von Strunckel, S. 31 October 2002.

Weschke, C. L. 4 May 2002.

Chapter 24

The Press Association and news agency sources

Paul Manning

Introduction

News agencies are wholesalers of news; from the time of their earliest origins in the mid-nineteenth century they have existed because news retailers, newspapers and news broadcasters have found it cheaper and more efficient to purchase some of their copy from a relatively small group of wholesale suppliers. The logic of pooling resources via shared news agency operations has always made economic sense for newspapers.

This chapter briefly considers recent changes in the structure and development of the main news agencies, distinguishing those that have achieved a global presence from those that remain primarily rooted in particular national markets. It then turns to consider the impact of these changes upon the kind of news copy they supply to newspapers. These changes are associated with the growing intensity of pressures to maximise profitability and survive in competitive and globalised information markets. The chapter will focus, in part, upon the Press Association (PA) as a case study. The PA, one of the oldest established national news agencies, has recently responded to contemporary challenges by attempting to diversify its core activities beyond the wholesale supply of news. The implications of these changes pose important questions with regard to the kinds of news the PA, and by implication other similar agencies, supply to newspapers and in terms of the kinds of constraints that journalists have to negotiate as they construct and utilise agency copy.

News agencies and contemporary challenges

Historically news agencies began as telegraphic technology first afforded rapid communication across national boundaries, and markets for news grew in the mid- to late nineteenth century. Some, such as Reuters and AFP (Agence France Presse), operated as independent commercial companies but were, in practice, intimately associated with the communication needs of national government and empire, with independence or, in the case of AFP, relative independence from government only being achieved as commercial imperatives grew stronger through the decades of the twentieth century (Boyd-Barrett 1997; Read 1992).

For others, including the PA, their origins, also in the mid-nineteenth century, lay in the needs of regional newspapers for efficient and reliable supplies of wholesale copy (Scott 1968, pp.22–3). The PA, for example, was established in 1868 as a cooperative, by the leading provincial newspapers in the UK, who were dissatisfied with the 'cavalier, untrustworthy, inaccurate and often downright stroppy' commercial telegraph companies (Moncrief 2001, p.7).

For the newspaper industry, Reuters and Associated Press (AP) are often identified as the two big contemporary global agencies. Boyd-Barrett and Rantanen (2000) now describe Agence France Presse as the largest national, as opposed to international, agency, partly because it trails Reuters and AP in terms of profitability and partly because it remains more strongly rooted in national and European markets. In terms of Boyd-Barrett and Rantanen's distinction, most news agencies remain primarily *national* as opposed to global organisations, in part because they lack access to the resources and economic muscle required to compete with the larger global agencies. The most significant challenges threaten both national and global agencies alike. Indeed, Reuters and AP now enjoy their global presence as a result of the strategies adopted to manage these challenges, but not all agencies are in a position to successfully follow in their path.

The PA remains a national agency in terms of Boyd-Barrett and Rantanen's distinction, though recent developments within the organisation confirm that it seeks to emulate the Reuters model. But while Reuters began to both diversify and globalise its activities in the early 1980s, the PA has really only embarked upon such a strategy since the turn of the new century. What are the pressures compelling news agencies to adapt and change? They are, of course, much the same interlinked pressures, political economic and cultural, that have forced significant changes in so many retail news organisations since the 1980s. From the 1980s onwards, proprietors such as Conrad Black in Canada and the United Kingdom, Rupert Murdoch in most parts of the world (except mainland Europe), Berlusconi and Agnelli in Italy, Axel Springer in Germany, for example, all demonstrated that serious money could be made from newspapers, providing production structures were ruthlessly streamlined, costs driven down and commercial news values prioritised (Manning 2001 pp.92–9). The opening up of global markets and the rise of transnational media corporations in the last two decades has intensified the pressures to commodify news, to select and package news and to fashion copy in ways primarily intended to sell.

While in the past the strength of public service broadcasting (PSB) institutions in many European societies produced something of a 'halo effect' even within newspaper newsrooms which kept more aggressively commercial news values at bay, with the weakening of European PSB institutions through deregulation and marketisation, this is less the case and news agencies have responded in kind. The proliferation of news outlets around the world has intensified competition. The arrival of CNN and 24-hour television news services in the early 1990s signalled to Reuters and the other big agencies that they must adapt or decline (Read 2001, p.15). By 2000, 23 per cent of Americans reported that online news was their main source (Pew Research Center cited in Paterson 2006, p.2). A quick mouse click on the Akamai Net Usage Index for News underlines the point that the astonishing growth of the web as a major source of news poses a sharp issue of survival for the traditional news agencies. In North America daily use of the leading 100 news portals usually runs at around 2.5 million visitors per minute in any 24 hours; in Europe the figure is around 333,000 visitors per minute (Akamai 2007). With online news now being accessed not only from PCs but also wireless laptops, mobile phones and other PDA devices, these figures will inevitably grow. If traditional global news flows have been disrupted and diverted by these techno-logical developments, so the traditional news agencies have been compelled to change, too.

Online agencies

Significantly, both international agencies like Reuters and national agencies such as the PA have taken steps to move into online news and electronic data markets. For Reuters the provision of online financial data is now the core activity. However, the changes unleashed by the rise of online news may be even more profound. With the arrival of Web 2.0, consumers become producers and, accord-ing to web optimists, citizens become journalists, with a multitude of cyber citizens loading up their own eyewitness reports and commentaries relating to everything from war in Iraq to weather-related school closures in middle America. For some, the arrival of the news blog heralds a new era of journalism characterised by a postmodern genre of personalised and fragmentary reporting (Wall 2005), while for others, professional journalists will battle to preserve and maintain traditional conventions and professional norms even in cyber space (Singer 2005).

The two biggest global news agencies have developed strategies to accommo-date the threat posed by the proliferation of information flows across the web. Reuters and AP now occupy a dominant position in the supply of routine interna-tional online news. Paterson (2006) concludes that the apparent proliferation and diversity of online news sources and information flows is illusory: a combination of slick marketing and user conservatism has led to a situation where majorities of online news consumers routinely rely upon a very limited number of major conglomerates for most of their online news. In the US, industry surveys regularly report the dominance of online news sites owned by Microsoft, Google, Time Warner and Yahoo, with one recent survey reporting that 46 per cent of online users accessed their news via sites linked to mainstream television channels such as MSNBC or CNN, while 39 per cent of online users accessed portal websites such as Google or Yahoo (Paterson 2006, p.12). In the UK, the BBC continues to prove to be one of the most popular online sources but otherwise the same corpor-ate players dominate. But where do these major online news sources actually get their copy from? In his own content analysis of online news copy, Paterson is able to demonstrate that with the exception of the BBC, the two major news agencies, AP and Reuters, supply remarkably high proportions of routine, international reports to the main online news sites. For example, verbatim use of this agency copy was 94 per cent in the case of AOL routine international reports and 97 per cent in the case of Yahoo (Paterson 2006, p.17).

In other words, the cutbacks in staffing at some online news organisations, and complete abandonment of original newsgathering activities in the case of a few, following the bursting of the dotcom bubble in 2001, have provided Reuters and AP with an opportunity to position themselves as the dominant suppliers of online routine international news. To what extent can a more nationally based agency such as the Press Association employ similar strategies to meet the contemporary challenges?

Diversify or decline

By the mid-1990s the intersection of new pressures to reach global news markets, drive down costs in an ever more competitive industry and find new revenue streams resulted in the restructuring of the larger, international agencies in order to survive. Reuters increased its R&D investment from £6.2 million to £200 million between 1982 and 1996 (Boyd-Barrett and Rantanen 2000, p.98) in an effort to diversify towards new products and new markets. Reuters was well placed to do this because it already had a historic role in the supply of financial news. It is now estimated that more than 90 per cent of Reuters' revenues depend upon financial markets rather than traditional newsgathering functions (Citigroup 2006, p.4). Traditional newsgathering is a relatively small part of four divisions in the Reuters company structure providing research and asset management services, financial data, advertising, software, web design and graphics, together with video and online news services. Recent performance included annual revenues from all these activities of £2.4 billion (Reuters 2006), confirming the agency's success in fighting off competition from Bloomberg in the global financial data market. AP has stuck more closely to its traditional core function of news dissemination but through this model has diversified into online and digital news services, video and news-related activities including advertising, news editing software, graphic, photo and broadcast technologies.

The Press Association in the new century

To what extent can the PA emulate the same model of global diversification? It faces two significant handicaps in that its roots lie in domestic rather than international news and its strategic position does not immediately offer opportunities to build close relationships with global conglomerates, though News International is now a major shareholder. However, the recent history of the PA is clearly one of diversification in regional and national markets, allied to some significant overseas expansion. This section briefly describes diversification at the PA before turning to consider the implications of these processes for reporting and the production of news copy.

With the entry of Britain into the European Community in 1972, the PA established an office in Brussels that began to extend its coverage 'south of Dover' (Moncrief 2001, p.5). As Britain became more regularly engaged in military interventions, the PA sent reporters to the Falklands battle zone, both Gulf Wars, and Afghanistan. The PA opened an office in New York in 2001, a reflection of the growing importance of the US for the UK news agenda. At the same time, Reuters began to encroach more on traditional PA territory, particularly in the area of sports news. Recent restructuring of the PA reflects this intensified competition, the economic imperative to find new markets for PA 'products', the need to exploit opportunities opened up by new technologies but also a significant shift in news priorities among PA clients. The PA was jolted by a near-fatal threat in the mid-1990s when the Leicester-based UK News agency, formed in 1992, succeeded in poaching several regional contracts from the PA and very nearly secured agreements with major national newspapers, including the Mirror and Express groups. By 1996 both the Express and Mirror groups were ready to defect and were only persuaded to stay with the PA through the offer of a cut-price deal (Moncrief 2001, pp.264–5).

It cost the PA £5 million in potential tariff revenues to keep the Mirror and Express groups on board. The damage to revenues was addressed in two ways. First, even greater priority placed upon commercial news values (ibid., p.267). Secondly, the PA embarked upon a strategy of staff cost-cutting with an erosion of pay and conditions that continues to provoke staff discontent and complaints from the National Union of Journalists. The NUJ noted that while the Editor of the PA, Paul Potts, earned £418,000 in 2004, some trainee journalists at the PA enjoyed salaries of just £11,000 (*UK Press Gazette* 2005a).

The drive for greater efficiencies and profitability underpinned the move from Fleet Street to Victoria in 1995 (Fordham 1995) and a significant push into overseas markets with the acquisition of a 50 per cent stake in Canada Newswire in 2001, the purchase of a US sports news agency in 2006 and the expansion of offices in Northern Ireland, Scotland and Eire in 2004. A contract to supply copy for Teletext services was also secured. However, most significant was the change in name to the PA Group in September 2000, clearly intended to signal a determination to embrace diversification, with the creation of four divisions: PA Sport, PA Entertainment, and PA Business to sit alongside the PA news agency. The PA Group now sells a diverse range of 'products', all related to or spun-off from the original 'core' activity of wholesaling news copy. The acquisition of the Dutch Meteogroup allows the PA to 'sell weather'. In 2004 magazine publisher IPC cut staff and contracted in the PA to supply listings for titles such as *TV Times*, and *What's On TV*; in May 2004 the PA bought The Editorial Centre journalism training business; and also in May 2004 it bought Empics, a sports photo agency and digital sports image archive.

The PA group now also partly owns TNR, a corporate communications company specialising in the production of video news releases. TNR claims to bridge 'the worlds of journalism and PR – creating real news stories for our clients' (TNR 2007), though given the point that TNR is based in the Victoria headquarters of the PA newsroom in London, there are, at least potentially, significant tensions between corporate promotional and traditional news reporting functions. The PA Group also supplies information and news services to businesses and government through PA Business, but one of the strongest growing areas is in sports information. PA Sport, based in Leeds, supplies a results service for online and traditional news media, and has signed deals to supply copy to organisations including the England and Wales Cricket Board (ECB). In 2006, the PA bought iKnowledge, a sports media technology company to supply digital sports material and enhanced graphics packages (Thomas 2006). With Empics within the PA Group, the PA is in a position to exploit new demands for sports material generated by new media, delivering sports results, pictures and graphics via mobile phone.

In 2005, the PA established a multimedia department that allows it to sell video news as well as traditional newswire copy to organisations including the BBC, 'new media' organisations such as Tiscali, as well as 'old media' entering online markets, such as the *Sun* (*UK Press Gazette* 2005b and c).

News agency content: going digital, going down market?

What do these developments mean for the kind of news copy the PA now produces? The recent history of senior appointments to the PA reflects the more commercially driven news priorities of the new PA Group. There is the appointment of a Multi Media Editor in October 2004, with a specific brief to develop new digital products, and a Deputy Editor in 2005, but other appointments signal an important reprioritisation of generic news values. The PA appointed its first Entertainment Editor in September 2004 but this was followed by the appointment of a show business correspondent in Los Angeles, another in New York and a further 'celebrity correspondent', also based in New York. These appointments, made in early 2005, all point to the determination of the PA, following the jolt supplied by UK News in 1995, to fully cater for the appetite of the UK national papers for celebrity gossip and 'show biz stories'. There is, of course, a huge demand for celebrity and entertainment news among the digital news suppliers, as well as traditional print media. And the coexistence of new media and traditional news forms contributes to the gentle erosion of 'hard' news values because newspapers cannot compete with the speed of reporting and continuous updating afforded by online news sources; they seek instead to compensate for this by searching for 'softer', human interest angles behind the 'news events' (Ungerer 2000). In turn, the PA anticipates these changing copy priorities.

Content: agencies and the standardisation of news copy?

The drive to maximise profits, increase the 'return' on copy, and maintain competitiveness, has made the PA Group an aggressive player in the news wholesale market – with important potential consequences for traditional local newspaper journalism. Recently, the PA Group has struck deals to supply 'standardised' lifestyle and sport supplements as inserts for local papers (*UK Press Gazette* 2005d). While regional newspaper groups sometimes defend this practice on the grounds that such supplements include detailed feature articles that local newspapers rarely have the resources to produce, the fear is that this may signal a further erosion of genuinely local reporting. There is quite simply less space for local news. However, the PA Group clearly intends to extend the logic of standardisation. In October 2006, the Managing Editor of the PA Group contacted a number of regional newspaper groups suggesting that they bought in the PA's 'Lobby Extra' service as a cheaper alternative to employing their own reporters at Westminster. There are around 23 members of the Westminster Lobby working for the regional press and news of this PA attempt to replace them with 'Lobby Extra' was interpreted as a cost-cutting threat to 'the diversity of regional journalism' by the NUJ, while one former lobby correspondent argued that: 'PA reports what MPs say. But a good regional Lobby journalist builds up contacts with all the local MPs' (Lagan 2006). At one time, most regional newspaper groups employed at least one correspondent at Westminster with a brief to identify the stories that made national politics relevant to the local context. Now the interlinked pressures associated with cost-cutting and changing news values pose a question mark over their future and provide an opportunity for the PA Group to exploit. And given the 'efficiencies' that the PA Group has extracted from its staff this is a very real threat because they allow the PA Group to undercut in-house staff.

Here the PA provides a localised, national example of a global logic. The dangers of a growing concentration of ownership in global wholesale news supply are familiar (Boyd-Barrett 1997; Herman and McChesney 1997). It has been argued that an over-reliance upon agency copy, driven by strategies to reduce staffing and cut the numbers of expensive foreign correspondents, has led to a standardisation of overseas reporting with fewer foreign correspondents available to provide local contextual detail or an informed knowledge of local cultures and politics (Paterson 1997). Several studies point to the danger that the main global agencies interpret the world primarily through a western lens, thus threatening to limit the diversity of perspectives in global news and marginalise the voices of those beyond the global centres of economic and political power (Rauch 2003). Whether it is the reporting of war (Horvit 2006), development issues or human rights (Giffard 1999), or UN Summits (Giffard and Rivenburgh 2000), these case studies reveal that the news copy produced by the two main global news agencies, Reuters and AP, is characterised by a very limited selection of topics and news angles, driven by the preoccupation with western news agendas. To the extent that they depend upon these agencies, the main retail news outlets reproduce the same narrowness of perspective.

Conclusions

The drive to diversify, to offer new 'products', expand markets and to maximise the return on the commodification of information is a feature of the international news agencies but now also of national agencies such as the PA. The consequences of these patterns are likely to be mixed. There is evidence of a determination on the part of staff working within news agencies to preserve traditional norms and practices associated with professionalism and quality control (Palmer 2003; Read 2001). And the PA has certainly not moved towards exploiting the cheaper but more questionable sources of copy afforded by 'public' or 'citizen' e-journalism. Nevertheless, there are some clearly emerging tensions generated by the drive to diversify, and it is possible to anticipate, at the very least, potential conflicts of interest and, at worst, a compromising of professional values.

First, the ownership structures of news agencies may place constraints upon diversification if this is likely to impinge upon the other business interests of shareholders. The PA Group, for example, was only able to move into the increasingly lucrative betting and sports information market by keeping certain shareholders, including News International, Express Newspapers and the Daily Mail group, sweet with heavily discounted rates on news copy (Boyd-Barrett and Rantanen 2000, p.98). But, secondly, tensions may be more profound. For agencies that have moved significantly into markets for the provison of financial services and data, there are potential tensions between traditional newsgathering and journalism, on the one hand, and the interests of corporate clients, on the other. Newsgathering journalists may require the circulation of financial data, while clients may expect confidentiality. Similarly, there is a long-standing tradition of journalists committing PR company press releases instantly to the dustbin, but what happens when the PR company is part of the same group as the news agency that journalists work for? In the case of the PA Group, where staff of the PA Group public relations and video news release company TNR work in the same building as PA journalists, there is a potential tension and danger that the 'internal organisational walls' dividing traditional journalism from corporate PR functions are weakened in problematic ways.

And then there is the danger of standardisation. This is a gloomy picture of journalism as a professional enterprise. For Paterson, the main global news agencies provide 'a bland and predictable news product, devoid of colour and enterprise reporting and dependent upon official sources and definitions of news' (2006, p.6). As the recent history of the PA Group suggests, the logic of diversification and standardisation is likely to unfold at the national as well as the global level. It is a history that points to a long and protracted parallel struggle to preserve the better features of regional and national journalism within national news agencies.

References

Akamai (2007) http://www.akamai.com/html/technology/nui/news/index.html. Accessed 19 January 2007.

Boyd-Barrett, O. (1997) 'Global News Wholesalers as Agents of Globalization' in Sreberny-Mohammadi, A., Winseck, D, McKenna, J. and Boyd-Barrett, O. (Eds) *Media in Global Context: A Reader* London: Arnold.

Boyd-Barrett, O. and Rantanen, T. (2000) 'European National News Agencies: The End of an Era or a New Beginning?' *Journalism: Theory, Practice, Criticism* vol. 1 no. 1, April, pp.86–104.

Citigroup (2006) 'Reuters Group PLC Core Progress' Company Flash, Citigroup 26 July.

Fordham, E. (1995) 'How PA News Shapes Up the Office' *Business Equipment Digest* vol. 10, October, p.34.

Giffard, C. A. (1999) 'The Beijing Conference on Women as Seen by Three International News Agencies' *Gazette* vol. 61 nos. 3–4, pp.327–34.

Giffard, C. A. and Rivenburgh, N. K. (2000) 'News Agencies, National Images, and Global Media Events' *Journalism and Mass Communication* vol. 77 no. 1, pp.8–21.

Herman, E. S. and McChesney, R. (1997) *The Global Media: The New Missionaries of Global Capitalism* London: Cassell.

Horvit, B. (2006) 'International News Agencies and the War Debate of 2003' *International Communication Gazette* vol. 68 no. 516, pp.427–48.

Lagan, S. (2006) 'Jobs Snatch Row' *UK Online Press Gazette* 25 October http://www.pressgazette.co.uk/article/251006/pa_in_parliament_job_snatch_row. Accessed 10 January 2007.

Manning, P. (2001) *News and News Sources: A Critical Introduction* London: Sage.

Moncrief, C. (2001) *Living on a Deadline: A History of the Press Association* London: Virgin Books.

Palmer, M. (2003) 'News: Ephemera, Data, Artefacts and … Quality Control – Iraq Now and Then' *Journalism: Theory, Practice and Criticism*, vol. 4 no. 4, pp.459–76.

Paterson, C. (1997) 'Global Battlefields' in Boyd-Barrett, O. and Rantanen, T. (Eds) *The Globalization of News* London: Sage.

Paterson, C. (2006) 'News Agency Dominance in International News on the Internet' *Papers in International and Global Communication* 01/06 Centre for International Communication Research, University of Leeds.

Rauch, J. (2003) 'Rooted in Nations, Blossoming in Globalization? A Cultural Perspective on the Content of a "Northern" Mainstream and a "Southern" Alternative News Agency' *Journal of Communication Inquiry* vol. 27 no. 1, pp.87–103.

Read, D. (1992) *The Power of News: The History of Reuters* Oxford: Oxford University Press.

Read, D. (2001) 'Don't Blame the Messengers: News Agencies Past and Present' *The Historian* vol. 69, pp. 9–15.

Reuters (2006) 'Third Quarterly Revenue Statement' Reuters PLC 18 October.

Scott, G. (1968) *Reporter Anonymous: The Story of the Press Association* London: Hutchinson.

Singer, J. (2005) 'The Politics of the J-blogger: "Normalizing" a New Media Form to Fit Old Norms and Practices' *Journalism: Theory, Practice, Criticism* vol. 6 no.2, pp.173–98.

Thomas, L. (2006) 'PA Sport buy UK tech firm' *On Line Press Gazette* 2 June http://www.pressgazette.co.uk/article/020606/pa_ikowledge_buy_sport. Accessed 24 January 2007.

TNR (2007) http://www.tvnewsrelease.com/about.asp. Accessed 24 January 2007.

UK Press Gazette (2004) 'IPC Cuts 53 Jobs as TV Listings Move to PA goes Ahead' *On Line Press Gazette* Thursday 23 September 2004 http://www.pressgazette.co.uk/article/230904/IPC_cuts_53_jobs_as_TV_listings_move_to_PA_gets_the_goahead. Accessed 10 January 2007.

UK Press Gazette (2005a) 'Recognition Drive for PA Journalists' *On Line Press Gazette* Thursday 14 April http://www.pressgazette.co.uk/article/140405/recognition_drive%20_for. Accessed 25 January 2007.

UK Press Gazette (2005b) 'PA Zooms in on Multimedia News Service' *On Line Press Gazette* Thursday 21 April http://www.pressgazette.co.uk/article/210405/pa_zooms_in. Accessed 9 January 2007.

UK Press Gazette (2005c) 'PA Agrees Bulletins Deal with Tiscali' Thursday 11 August http://www.pressgazette.co.uk/article/110805/pa_agrees_bulletins. Accessed 24 January 2007.

UK Press Gazette (2005d) 'PA to Produce Lifestyle Titles for Johnston Newspapers' *On Line Press Gazette* 14 January http://www.pressgazette.co.uk/article/140105/pa_to_produce_lifestyle. Accessed 10 January 2007.

Ungerer, F. (2000) 'News Stories and News Events: A Changing Relationship' *Pragmatics and Beyond* vol. 80, pp.177–96.

Wall, M. (2005) 'Blogs of War: Weblogs as News' *Journalism: Theory, Practice, Criticism* vol. 6 no. 1, pp.153–72.

Chapter 25

Public relations in the news

Aeron Davis

Introduction

This chapter looks at the increasing encroachment of public relations in the news production process. Three perspectives on the topic are explained. The first compares the changing resources of the two industries – journalism and public relations. The second details the nature of the social relationships that form between journalists and public relations practitioners (PRPs). The third reveals some of the common public relations 'tricks of the trade'. While the chapter discusses the issues as they apply across news sectors the examples focus more specifically on political journalism. There is one general line of argument running through the piece. That is, that public relations and 'spin doctors' have always played a key role in news production; rather more than journalists and sources acknowledge. However, in recent decades, the roles and relationships of the two sectors have significantly shifted in directions detrimental to news journalism.

Resource shifts: a tale of two industries

The reason, above all others, that public relations has increased its part in news production is resources. Sigal (1973), Gandy (1982) and Fishman (1980) in earlier studies of news in the United States all observed that, as journalist resources became stretched, so dependency on external source supplies rose. Gandy refers to these as 'information subsidies'. Sigal's study of the *Wall Street Journal* and *New York Times*, for example, finds a direct correlation between staffing and resource levels and the number of stories based on source supply. In recent decades, many established news producers have been forced to cut editorial resources and, as in these earlier cases, have looked to external information subsidy providers. The public relations sector has, in turn, grown to fill that gap.

Looking at the UK case reveals a consistent decline in the editorial resources available to news producers. Since the early 1980s, the following trends can be observed with some consistency. There is more news but also greater competition and fragmentation with fewer consumers per outlet (Tunstall 1996; Franklin 1997, 2005; Barnett and Gaber 2001; Davis 2002; Curran and Seaton 2003). New technologies, with multiple news outlets and 24-hour news, deregulation and market liberalisation, price wars and global market pressures have all contributed. Market segmentation and entertainment alternatives have meant a steady decline of advertising revenues for most single, commercial news outlets. Consequently, most national newspaper and terrestrial broadcasters have presided over a long-term decline in audience figures since the 1970s.

In an effort to remain profitable, papers raised prices above inflation. They also increased output and news sections while simultaneously cutting back on staff. Journalist numbers per publication were cut or, in the best cases, increased minimally but not enough to match output demands. A comparison of Tunstall's (1971) and Franklin's (1997) journalist estimates of national journalist numbers suggests a drop of between 25 and 31 per cent over the period. Tunstall (1996) estimates that, between the 1960s and 1990s, individual output had at least doubled. Other changes included the introduction of 'multi-skilling', 'pooling' of journalists and sub-editors, merging of sister papers, and contracting out operations. In a 1996 survey, 62 per cent of journalists claimed to work 59 or more hours in the office each week and one-third claimed to have recently suffered from stress-related illnesses (*Press Gazette* 12/7/96). In 2006 a quick glance reveals the industry picture to be similarly bleak. In 2006 (NUJ 2006) 31 per cent of journalists are part-time or work 'flexible hours' and 41 per cent are 'freelance' (there is a large overlap between these groups). The average salary has gone up but a greater proportion (11.6%) than in 1994 (9.6%) earn less than £10,000 per year.

In contrast, the public relations sector has grown impressively in the UK since the early 1980s. According to Miller and Dinan (2000) the sector rose as a whole by a factor of 31 (or 11-fold in real terms) between 1979 and 1998. Indications are that, during the 1990s, professional PR also began to spread into many other sectors of British civil society. Deacon's (1996) survey of the voluntary sector found that 31 per cent of organisations (57% of large ones) had press/publicity officers and 43 per cent (81% of large ones) used external PR agencies. A survey of trades unions by Davis (2002) found that two-thirds of unions had at least one part-time press officer, 25 per cent used PR consultancies and 57 per cent used agencies to monitor the media and provide other services. Between 1979 and 2006 the numbers of PR staff employed in public institutions also increased considerably: the Commission for Racial Equality and the BBC both went up from 5 to 19 (280%), the Inland Revenue up from 5 to 49 (880%), and the Metropolitan Police up from 6 to 65 (983%) (all figures in IPO Directories, COI 1979–2006).

Estimates for 2005 claimed that there were 2,500 agencies and 47,800 people working in the public relations profession in the UK. This figure excludes the 125,000 people working in the associated advertising and marketing industries, those working in PR support industries (e.g. press cutting, media evaluation, news distribution services), and the many professionals who have had media training. The estimated total turnover of the industry in 2005, consultancy and in-house, was £6.6 billion (all figures in Key Note 2006). The increase in PRPs in a selection of government departments is recorded in Table 25.1.

Table 25.1 *Changes in numbers of information officers employed in government departments 1979–2006*

	MoD	FCO	Home Office	DTI	PM's Office	Treasury
1979	58	19	27	38	6	12
1997	47	30	50	67	12	16
2006	230	41	145	84	24	31
Percentage increase	297	116	437	121	300	158

Source: Figures compiled from COI 1979–2006

Clearly, as journalist numbers and resources, per publication, have been cut so, conversely, public relations numbers and resources, per source organisation, have increased. Virtually every journalist I have interviewed over the years, regardless of paper or news section, has offered a personal account that matches up with this larger picture. All spoke of daily pressures rising as a consequence of competition. Many also saw that such changes had opened up the opportunities available to the PR sector. For established political journalists:

> I think that our news desks are quite demanding that we shouldn't be running at seven o'clock the next morning a story that was on Sky at six o'clock at night ... the story is now often about what's going to happen tomorrow rather than what has happened during the day. Spin doctors, they played their part in that, because they have used the rise of, or the arrival of 24-hour news as a way of promoting their charges.
>
> (interview, Philip Webster)

> All of this, marketisation of society and technical transformation of communications are both pointed to the same direction: enormously more speed and the need to get your message across rapidly because if you don't ... somebody else's spin will be halfway around the world if yours isn't, which has also helped to create the problem with spin... Ministers have much larger communication apparatuses to deal with this, the demands of 24/7 news, having to feed the beast all the time.
>
> (interview, Michael White)

Journalist PR relations: negotiation, exchange, conflict and control

A key part of the debate about public relations' influence on journalism is to be located in work on news sources and journalist–source relations. This work underlines the fact that such interactions have always been fundamental to the production of news. Building on earlier studies (Sigal 1973; Gans 1979), media sociology has renewed its interest in the nature of such relationships (Schlesinger and Tumber 1994; Manning 2000; Davis 2002). In the case of political news sources and journalists a clear two-way exchange between the sides is regularly observed (see also Barnett and Gaber 2001; Hess 2003); Nicholas Jones describes such exchanges as 'trading information' (see chapter 14 above). Journalists needed political information and comment and politicians needed publicity and to promote their messages. Exchanges can be very good or rather strained dependent on the circumstances of this 'tug of war' relationship.

When interviewing either journalists or politicians these exchange relationships appear to be an accepted part of the professions involved. Clearly, it is also something that political journalists are aware of when writing news copy and it can become part of the calculation when deciding whether to pursue a story and on what terms:

> To be in the loop you have to be quite friendly with people before they're going to trust you enough to tell you anything much about what's going on. But once you have that relationship of trust, you are then bound to them, to some degree, personally, you're not likely to rubbish them, you might still be very rude about the party or the policy, but those become people that you feel instinctively embarrassed about being critical of.
>
> (interview, Polly Toynbee)

> At the same time you are thinking about the person you are writing about and his or her friends and enemies. And you never stop thinking about your contacts. It's always a concern in journalism, to think about your contacts, A, because you like them, and B, because you want to be able to come back to them again.
>
> (interview, Kevin Maguire)

However, as journalists have become more insecure and pressured, and public relations more resourced and sophisticated, so those relationships have been altered. One important issue is that the influx of PRPs means that an information barrier is created. This means greater control of the messages emanating from political parties and governments and, also, restricted access for journalists seeking to talk to politicians:

> This government is different. They are the most tight-fisted group when it comes to the dissemination of any information and they use all sorts of rules to control journalists' access to ministers and relations with journalists ... Now they [government] feed you a story and you have to be grateful that you have got your scoop from a press release – but that's not journalism.
>
> (interview, Trevor Kavanagh)

> Number 10 has a strong grip on the information coming out of departments. From their point of view it's very sensible but, from another point of view, they go to great lengths to limit debate and discussion and to stop journalists

from finding out what's going on ... during their time in opposition Labour developed a highly efficient machine.

(interview, Andrew Grice)

A significant part of the shift in relations also comes down to the fact that an increasing number now working in PR have prior experience of working in journalism. In fact, the proportion of NUJ members who work in PR has also risen. In 1994 (NUJ 1994) the 'press/PR' sector made up 7.3 per cent of NUJ membership. In 2006 (NUJ 2006) 28 per cent worked in 'press/PR'. In addition, many organisation leaders now have media training from former journalists. So, for example, over half the communications staff working in trades unions, corporations and consultancies have prior media/journalism experience (Davis 2002). Similarly, a considerable proportion of the top 'spin doctors' in the main political parties have senior press and/or broadcasting experience. In recent interviews with UK MPs (Davis 2007), just over four-fifths of those asked had had formal media training and/or previous experience in journalism.

The advantages of such inside knowledge mean the PRPs, working in the political sector, are better able to take advantage of news routines and reporter competition. So it is easier to influence newsgathering and news cycles as well as playing journalists off each other:

> When Labour came into power, Alistair Campbell, because he'd been a lobby journalist, told Ministers not to go through the Members' Lobby. And you find that unless somebody is in trouble and wants to be approached by journalists, ministers tend to avoid the Members' Lobby. They go out by the back way, which is technically behind the Speaker's Chair. We don't have access to behind the Speaker's Chair unless we're invited.
>
> (interview, Colin Brown)

> Some will try and put you off the scent and others will try and lay off your story with another paper to reduce the importance of it. In part it's gotten worse. Now all the parties operate a policy of restricted semi-exclusive briefings ... It's all become a bit Pavlovian – a bit of reward and sanction. Report the way they want and you get more briefings, report it another way and you get excluded.
>
> (interview, George Jones)

PR or journalism? Tricks of the trade

Working out what proportion of news content is public relations material, or initiated by PR, and what is journalism, is a complex task. Many PR ploys for getting organisations and messages into the media have become so commonplace that neither the public nor journalists themselves now seem aware of the differences. In many cases it is difficult to distinguish between a public relations practitioner and a media-trained (but otherwise newsworthy) source. Lastly, PR messages are considered most effective when working invisibly and/or through third parties from sources sympathetic to newswire services. This last section, however, attempts to present some of the more common 'tricks of the PR trade' observable in most forms of news coverage.

First, there are now a range of standard PR techniques used to gain attention and news coverage. As Nelson declares (1989, p.50): 'The press release, the press conference, the photo op, the pre-arranged interview, and press tour have all, over the years, become fully integrated into the fabric of what we perceive as "the news".' Many such information channels and 'pseudo events' (Boorstin 1962) do, of course, result in a story. In fact it is now rather easy to identify press release-instigated news stories. Many pieces report an event or speech that is happening the day of publication and could only have come from pre-event press releases, sending of speeches and personal discussions in advance.

These PR-led stories are now a standard part of newsgathering and production and are not considered to undermine journalist authority in particular. However, such routine means of story generation have also come to be abused by prominent sources. In the political sphere politicians and their PR staff employ a number of methods for influencing news agendas and frames. For example, PRPs may wait some time before 'burying bad news' on eventful news days or at the same time as they release other stories. 'Kite-flying' is a method used to take advantage of the anonymity of the lobby briefing system. Ministers may float policy ideas through journalists and then wait for responses to the coverage before acting more publicly. They may also leak information in advance of important meetings or votes in an effort to influence outcomes. For journalists it is news but, at the same time, it is part of a public relations–inspired action (see a range of examples in Jones 1995, 1999; Rawnsley 2001; Price 2005):

> It's useful to fly kites. A minister will introduce a bill for some exotic policy – say murder of the first child – and will float it over for the journalists and then wait and see what happens. If he gets 50 MPs signing an Early Day Motion opposing it then he will scrap it or save it up for later. So it's an opportunity to float ideas. It's also used to dominate one's enemies. Ministers get briefed against by other ministers all the time.
>
> (interview, Paul Routledge)

Taking advantage of daily news routines and news values is also a common ploy for experienced PR practitioners. Thus, 'the human interest story', 'the demonstration', the 'new research' or 'report', 'financial contribution', 'the award', 'the record breaker', the 'in-vogue theme' and the 'celebrity angle' are all PR devices for getting information into the media. Each of these issues appears to be a newsworthy story but each, also, can be created with the express purpose of getting the profile of an issue or organisation raised. Awards may be made to prominent individuals where the primary goal is to gain media publicity for the awarding organisation. New research or a political promise for 'more money' may not be new at all. Any big event, from the 2012 London Olympics to *Big Brother*, may be used to tag a story on to:

> Heseltine's theory was if you're an opposition spokesman you flick on Ceefax, you look at the top ten stories and see if you can muscle in on one of them during the day, and there's some truth in that.
>
> (interview, John Maples)

> I want to know what the topical stories of the day are ... I would want to see if there's any stories I think are maybe going to go on over the next day or two that I can get in on ... if I know what's topical, then they are going to be more interested in my opinions on that subject that's been up their agenda that day.
>
> (interview, Danny Alexander)

A commonly employed strategy in public relations is to use other individuals and organisations to present an organisation or make a case. It is quite clear that those working in public relations believe that it works most effectively when either invisible or presented through respected and newsworthy individuals. I refer to this as 'access by proxy'. In the profession it is usually referred to as 'third party endorsement'. This comes in many forms. In some cases organisations make use of celebrities or other 'primary definers' to gain coverage for their activities. In other cases a variety of scientists, 'experts' and other 'authorities' (the 'alliance with science') are used to put a case more 'objectively'. For many resource-poor campaigning groups, struggling to gain coverage or legitimacy, these methods are essential for publicising issues (see examples in Wilson 1984; Hansen 1993; Davis 2002; Cottle 2003). For political parties and individual politicians forms of third party endorsement are sought in all areas. Celebrities, think tanks, interest groups and, of course, the news media are all encouraged to promote a party, policy or campaign:

> In terms of opinion formers political parties will take anyone who will endorse them, from foreign dignitaries to financiers to the City, to anything.
>
> (interview, Tim Bell)

> Obviously you would target a particular group with a particular message and you target them through particular media outlets – the *FT* when it's the City ... Now we are the party that's strong on the economy rather than the Tories. So yes a lot of work went into trying to change that through the *FT* newspaper.
>
> (interview, Charlie Wheelan)

A concerning escalation of the third party approach has been the creation of fake or 'astro-turf' organisations to artificially promote a case. In these instances propaganda is organised through seemingly independent, public and scientific organisations but, actually, directed and funded by the same powerful corporate organisations and political parties (see Stauber and Rampton 1995, 2002; Ewen 1996; Miller 2004; Monbiot 2006; Centre for Media Democracy (CMD) and Spinwatch). News is now peppered with surveys, institutes and associations, with authoritative-sounding names, some of which are blatantly misleading. Surveys may instead be 'straw polls' and hastily put together. They may also contain leading questions that limit respondents' possible answers and/or encourage particular responses. Reports (and 'dodgy dossiers') by established research organisations and public bodies are often commissioned and directed with preconceived conclusions established in the remits. Unfavourable findings are not released. Political opponents are undermined by smear campaigns from seemingly independent associations.

Conclusion

As argued here, public relations output, whether emanating from PR professionals or publicity-seeking news sources, has always made a significant contribution to news production. The relationship between journalists and their sources has been core to the profession. However, the influence of PR has steadily grown in recent decades and those relations and routines have been transformed. This is because the resources used in PR supply have increased, as those of journalists have decreased, and promotional techniques have become more sophisticated.

There are three obvious consequences. First, the ability of journalism to fulfil its professional remit – to be authoritative, objective and independent – has been weakened. Second, those with greater PR resources are more likely to be shaping journalist agendas and reporting frames. Third, public trust in journalists and those organisations which use public relations extensively and cynically – political parties, corporations and some campaigning groups – continues to decline.

References

Barnett, S. and Gaber, I. (2001) *Westminster Tales: The 21st Century Crisis in Political Journalism* London: Continuum.

Boorstin, D. (1962) *The Image* London: Weidenfeld and Nicolson.

CMD (Centre for Media and Democracy) (n.d.) http://www.prwatch.org. Accessed February 2007.

COI (1979–2006) 'The IPO Directory: Information and Press Officers in Government Departments and Public Corporations' (formerly called 'Chief Public Relations, Information and Press Officers in Government Departments, Public Corporations, etc.') London: Central Office of Information.

Cottle, S. (Ed.) (2003) *News, Public Relations and Power* London: Sage.

Curran, J. and Seaton, J. (2003) *Power Without Responsibility* (6th edition) London: Routledge.

Davis, A. (2002) *Public Relations Democracy: Public Relations, Politics and the Mass Media in Britain* Manchester: Manchester University Press.

Davis, A. (2007) *The Mediation of Power: A Critical Introduction* London: Routledge.

Deacon, D. (1996) 'The Voluntary Sector in a Changing Communication Environment' *European Journal of Communication* vol. 11 no. 2, pp.173–99.

Ewen, S. (1996) *PR! A Social History of Spin* New York: Basic Books.

Fishman, M. (1980) *Manufacturing News* Austin: University of Texas Press.

Franklin, B (1997) *Newzak and News Media* London: Arnold.

Franklin, B. (2005) 'McJournalism: The Local Press and the McDonaldization Thesis' in Allan, S.E. (Ed.) *Journalism: Critical Issues* Maidenhead: Open University Press.

Gandy, O. (1982) *Beyond Agenda Setting: Information Subsidies and Public Policy* Norwood, NJ: Ablex Publishing Corporation.

Gans, H. J. (1979) *Deciding What's News: A Study of CBS Evening News, NBC Nightly News, Newsweek and Time* New York: Pantheon.

Hansen, A. (Ed.) (1993) *The Mass Media and Environmental Issues* Leicester: Leicester University Press.

Hess, S. (2003) *Organising the Presidency* (3rd edition) Washington, DC: Brookings Institute.

Jones, N. (1995) *Soundbites and Spin Doctors: How Politicians Manipulate the Media and Vice Versa* London: Cassell.

Jones, N. (1999) *Sultans of Spin: The Media and the New Labour Government* London: Orion.

Key Note (2006) *Public Relations Industry: Market Assessment 2006* Hampton, Middx: Key Note.

Manning, P. (2000) *News and News Sources* London: Sage.

Miller, D. (Ed.) (2004) *Tell Me Lies: Propaganda and Media Distortion in the Attack on Iraq* London: Pluto.

Miller, D. and Dinan, W. (2000) 'The Rise of the PR Industry in Britain, 1979–98' *European Journal of Communication* vol. 15 no. 1, pp.5–35.

Monbiot, G. (2006) *Heat: How to Stop the Planet Heating Up* London: Allen Lane/Penguin.

Nelson, J. (1989) *Sultans of Sleaze – Public Relations and the Media* Toronto: Between the Lines.

NUJ (1994, 2006) *National Union of Journalists Surveys of Members* London: National Union of Journalists.

Price, L. (2005) *The Spin Doctor's Diary: Inside Number 10 with New Labour* London: Hodder and Stoughton.

Rawnsley, A. (2001) *Servants of the People: The Inside Story of New Labour* London: Penguin.

Schlesinger, P. and Tumber, H. (1994) *Reporting Crime: The Media Politics of Criminal Justice* Oxford: Clarendon Press.

Sigal, L. V. (1973) *Reporters and Officials – The Organisation and Politics of Newsmaking* Lexington, MA: Lexington Books.

Spinwatch (n.d.) http: //www.spinwatch.org. Accessed February 2007.

Stauber, J. and Rampton, S. (1995) *Toxic Sludge is Good For You – Lies, Damn Lies and the Public Relations Industry* New York: Common Courage Press.

Stauber, J. and Rampton, S. (2002) *Trust Us We're Experts: How Industry Manipulates Science and Gambles with Your Future* New York: Tarcher/Penguin.

Tunstall, J. (1971) *Journalists at Work* London: Sage.

Tunstall, J. (1996) *Newspaper Power: The National Press in Britain* Oxford: Oxford University Press.

Wilson, D. (1984) *Pressure: The A to Z of Campaigning in Britain* London: Heinemann.

Interviewees cited

Danny Alexander, Liberal Democrat MP for Nairn, Badenoch and Strathspey, 28 February 2006.

Lord Tim Bell, Chairman of Bell Pottinger, former communications adviser to Conservative Party and Margaret Thatcher, 20 November 2001.

Colin Brown, Deputy Political Editor of the *Independent*, 1 August 2006.

Andrew Grice, Political Editor of the *Independent*, 5 September 2001.

George Jones, Political Correspondent at the *Daily Telegraph*, 7 August 2001.

Trevor Kavanagh, Political Editor of the *Sun*, 28 August 2001.

Kevin Maguire, Chief Reporter of the *Guardian*, 6 November 2001.

John Maples, Conservative MP for Stratford on Avon, Deputy Chairman 1994–5, former shadow cabinet minister 1997–2000, 28 March 2006.

Paul Routledge, Chief Political Commentator of the *Daily Mirror*, 19 September 2001.

Polly Toynbee, Political Columnist for the *Guardian*, 25 August 2006.

Philip Webster, Political Editor of *The Times*, 9 August 2006.

Charlie Wheelan, former Press Secretary at the Treasury, 9 August 2001.

Michael White, Political Editor of the *Guardian*, 1 August 2006.

Index